Leisure Systems:
Critical Concepts and Applications

James F. Murphy, Ph.D.

E. William Niepoth, Ed.D.

Lynn M. Jamieson, Re.D.

John G. Williams, M.S.

©1991 Sagamore Publishing Co. Inc., Champaign, IL 61824-0673

Book Design: Judith Saak
Cover Design: Michelle Dressen
Editors: Sheila Ryan and Mary Rose Cottingham

Printed in the United States of America

Library of Congress Catalog Card Number: 91-60386
ISBN: 0-915611-17-1

TABLE OF CONTENTS

Contents

PREFACE

An earlier text, written by three of the current authors, was titled, *Leisure Service Delivery System*. This book was based on the premise that there is an "ecological" relationship between the recreation and park field, the society within which the field operates, and the various constituents the field hopes to serve. Changes occurring in one of these dimensions influence each of the other aspects. A further premise was that the different elements of the field itself (philosophy and goals, personnel, and physical resources) stand in a dynamic relationship to each other. It was because of these premises that the text was titled *Leisure Service Delivery System*.

The need to be aware of the systems nature of our profession is even greater today than it was at the time we wrote the earlier book. There is greater diversity in society and among those served by the field. Continued population growth and mobility, technological advances, changing economic conditions, expansion and sophistication of communication processes, the broad human rights movement, and other factors have contributed to this diversification. Demands for leisure services have increased and become more complex. The essential interrelationships between demographic, social, economic, political, and environmental conditions and the leisure service delivery system may be more difficult to discern because of this complexity. However, the relative scarcity of resources for serving people's leisure needs and increasing public expectations for quality services and accountability make it imperative that these relationships be recognized.

The field itself has become much more specialized in the last fifteen years. Therapeutic recreation services have continued to mature; an expanded special terminology, based on medical and rehabilitative concepts, symbolizes this maturation. The private enterprise sector has emerged as one of the dominant emphases in our field. Such concerns as market analysis, promotion, and investment management have become common subjects for conversation and topics at professional conferences. Military recreation is now a very visible part of our profession. Expanded interest in sports, motivated in part by fitness and health goals, has encouraged the development of a recreational sports management specialization.

These events, and others, have been reflected in the dramatic increase of specializations (options, emphases) in college and university leisure service curricula. In addition to existing courses, such as philosophy, programming, leadership, and administration, faculties have developed new classes specifically related to new emphases. New texts have followed.

The preface to *Leisure Service Delivery System,* written in 1973, contained the following observation:

> Almost every text written for recreation and park curricula conceives of the various important aspects of leisure services as separate, distinguishable parts. A customary practice is the publication of texts on programming, leadership and administration to provide students and practitioners with an understanding of the particular phases of the overall delivery of leisure services. However, this disjointed approach does not provide any meaningful guidance to the reader since each of the various aspects of the delivery system are not seen as complementary and mutually supportive. They are typically viewed as requiring separate attention in different courses at various levels within the major curriculum.

We believe this situation continues to exist.

The 1973 text attempted to provide leisure service personnel and students with an understanding of the system characteristics of our field. This current book also has that goal. It differs from the earlier publication in its (1) attention to the expansions and diversifications of the field that have occurred since 1973, (2) fuller treatment of the implications of a systems approach to leisure service delivery, (3) presentation of an updated overview of critical concepts, and (4) application of a service-oriented structure for the management of leisure organizations. We have written with a different approach to textbook selection and use in mind. Contrary to the standard practice of using a different text for each different course, we developed this book as a "synthesizing" volume. Our aim is to provide a text that ties together all the various separate subject areas in the leisure services curriculum. It is well-suited for use in an administration course, but our hope is that it will serve instructors and students across a much broader course spectrum. We envision that it will be required in one of the first courses taken by recreation and park majors. The specific nature of that course will vary from curriculum to curriculum. In the typical course, taken at the beginning of the major, an overview of the field is presented. This text will serve that purpose extremely well. Then, in subsequent courses, the text will serve as a vehicle for showing the relevance of the specific course content to the overall leisure service delivery system. It is in this sense that the text would serve as a unifying volume. We know that people learn most readily when they see the meaning of concepts in terms of the larger whole, and so we believe that this book will facilitate classroom learning.

We developed the book with the hope that students will obtain it early in their academic careers and keep it. This departs from traditional textbook practices. However, we believe that the present nature of the field demands the presence of a unifying force in university curricula. We are convinced that this text contributes to that impetus. Further, we believe that the concept of a synthesizing volume is educationally sound. The publisher shares those beliefs.

We wish to extend our sincerest appreciation to H. Douglas Sessoms, Professor and Chair, Curriculum in Leisure Studies and Recreation Administration, University of North Carolina, who reviewed the manuscript and provided many cogent suggestions for improving the quality of the text. Additionally, we are in-debted to several colleagues who provided examples of state-of-the-art holistic management concepts and practices they use to enhance the delivery of leisure and nonleisure support services: Dr. Liz Stefanics, Executive Director, New Mexico AIDS Services, Inc.; Ms. Anne Idema, Recreation Director, Prusch Farm Park, Department of Parks and Recreation, San Jose, California; Ms. Lisa Holeman, Community Program Coordinator, Do-It Leisure, Chico, California; Mr. Andy Holdnak, Ph.D. Candidate, Pennsylvania State University and former Recreation Director, Sandestin Beach Resort, Florida; Mr. Jack Harper, Associate Professor, Recreation Studies Programme, University of Manitoba, Winnipeg, Manitoba, Canada; and Dr. John Crossley, Associate Professor, Department of Recreation and Leisure, University of Utah, Salt Lake City,

Utah. Support and encouragement that the authors received from Dr. Joseph J. Bannon to pursue the development of a second edition of this text was greatly appreciated.

The authors are deeply persuaded that a service-oriented, systems perspective is essential for understanding the interrelationships that exist within each aspect of the leisure service delivery system. With this understanding, service providers can effectuate the provision of individual and group opportunities for leisure expression and foster a sense of community. If we have not communicated that fully, it is a shortcoming of writing rather than belief. The authors worked closely together throughout the development and writing of the book. Each author assumed responsibility for one of the three parts of the manuscript: Jim Murphy (Part I), Bill Niepoth (Part II), and John Williams and Lynn Jamieson (Part III). While there was agreement on the content of each section of the book, differences in writing styles will be observed by the reader. We hope these differences will accentuate the many possible ways of characterizing leisure service delivery and maximizing academic and practitioner perspectives.

James F. Murphy, San Francisco, California
E. William Niepoth, Chico, California
Lynn M. Jamieson, San Luis Obispo, California
John G. Williams, Sunnyvale, California

INTRODUCTION

What is meant by the terms *leisure systems,* or *the leisure service delivery system*? Why leisure service? a delivery system? system? What has this book to do with the field of recreation and parks? or with my role in the field? What is this book all about?

These questions and others may come to mind as you look at this text. The authors think it very appropriate for readers to approach the book with such questions. We want to anticipate some of those and try to answer them in this introduction. We assume that you are going to read the book or are at least considering doing so. If you do, you will be committing time and energy, and for that reason, we would like to give you a preview of what the book is about. Moreover, the background in this introduction should make the rest of the book more understandable and useful.

What, then, is the leisure service delivery system? Let's briefly look at some of the concepts associated with it.

Society

By society, we mean the physical, social, economic, and political environments within which people live, work, and play. They are the settings where the processes of government, education, and worship take place. They are economic, political, and geographic entities. We conduct business in them, dispense information, enforce laws, make judgments involving justice, provide medical care, and raise children. We pass along different values in these from place to place and time to time. Societies differ in the degree to which they encourage or permit diversity in values. Some are more homogeneous in this respect; others permit or foster a range of values.

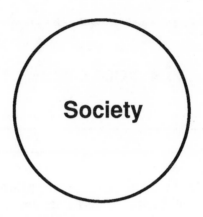

Recreation and Leisure

Leisure service agencies operate in society. They are a part of society and society enables recreation and leisure to occur. Let's examine these two concepts.

Recreation is an important part of the lives of the authors of this book; we assume it is an important part of your life, as it is a part of everyone's lives. We believe that people have engaged in what we now call recreation from the beginning of recorded history and we assume that this will continue to be true in the future. Some of the forms of recreation have changed through the years; we expect that more changes will occur in the future. We might say that recreation is a cultural universal; that it exists in all cultures, in all times. But what *is* recreation? For the moment, say that it is something you do, of your own choosing, for the satisfaction and enjoyment that comes from doing it. We will say more about that later, but that's sufficient for now. Since you have a choice in what you do, it follows that it is done in what we might call "free time." You are not required by someone else to do it.

Recreation takes many forms. It may be highly active or very quiet. It can be engaged in with others or by yourself. It can occur indoors or outdoors. It can be spontaneous or the result of long and detailed planning. It is a cross-country skier gliding through a snow-carpeted forest, a traveler watching a European landscape flash by the train window, an amateur painter highlighting a spot of color on a still-life, a couple dancing at a downtown nightclub, a reader moving through the ageless pages of a great book, a family watching and laughing at a situation comedy on television, old friends visiting over coffee after a long period of being apart. The list of activities is nearly endless.

What results from recreation participation is an emotional response. The response will vary from individual to individual and from activity to activity. But in all cases, you feel something — a sense of accomplishment, enjoyment of companionship, a feeling of relaxation, a condition of overall well-being, excitement—something. The experience at the time you feel something can be thought of as leisure. Some scholars focus more on the time aspects, believing that leisure is free time. Others emphasize the condition of life that is associated with free time. For them, leisure is a state of being. Some believe it is leisure only if that state is one of tranquility or deep satisfaction. For now, let us say that leisure is intricately associated with recreation. Leisure is the more encompassing phenomenon within which recreation occurs, or to which recreation leads.

Leisure Behavior

Leisure involves another concept—behavior. We experience the world, including leisure, through behavior. We see, we hear, we touch, we move, we communicate, we interact, we think, we feel, we behave. Leisure behavior, or recreation behavior, has the characteristics of all behavior. It is goal-oriented and influenced by a variety of social, psychological, and environmental factors. What we know about behavior in general applies to leisure behavior. But leisure behavior also has some unique characteristics. It is intrinsically motivated; that is, we engage in it because of the enjoyments that come directly from the experience rather than some other secondary motivation. We engage in it without external obligations, except for those we knowingly accept, and because we anticipate enjoyment and satisfaction.

Let's examine leisure behavior a little further. Remember, this is why the field exists: to provide opportunities for people to engage in leisure behavior. This behavior takes on many different forms; it produces a great variety of individual benefits and responses and is influenced by a wide assortment of social, psychological, and environmental factors. Two additional points need to be understood.

The first is that individuals live and function as total organisms. They do not have just leisure needs; they have needs for food, shelter, security, knowledge, and so on. People do not come to our leisure service opportunities with their recreation expectations isolated. They come as whole persons, with the wide array of feelings and states of being that describe the human condition. They might be tired or rested, worried or relaxed, angry or happy. They might have just learned that they were given a promotion at work; or they might have been told they were fired. They might come with a past history of failures or with a record of successes. They might be shy and timid, or highly extroverted. They will have some characteristics in common with other people, but in many ways they will be unique. These characteristics and uniquenesses influence their behavior. The senior citizen who worries about the safety of public transportation at night will respond differently to an invitation to a social evening at the recreation center than will another individual who does not fear being out after dark. The fourth grade child who has been successful in the past may be more willing to try a new recreation activity than one who has experienced considerable failure.

We need to recognize the holistic nature of human beings. To do so enables us to serve them better. At the least, it helps us to understand their behavior. It may also allow us to enhance their abilities to enjoy leisure more fully. We may not be able to provide transportation for the senior who is worried about the safety of public transportation, but we can help make transit authorities more aware of the problem. We may not be able to provide counseling for an insecure child with low self-esteem, but we can help the youngster experience successes in our programs. And we can suggest other sources of professional help if the parents are receptive.

The second point is that people often engage in leisure behavior in groups. Much recreation occurs with other people. True, there are many individual activities, and sometimes we seek solitude. However, the chance to interact with others in leisure settings frequently is a strong motivation. Therefore we often work with groups, and understanding group processes facilitates our efforts.

The Field of Recreation and Parks

The field is that complex of agencies and organizations that exists to provide opportunities for people to engage in leisure behavior. As we've said, that is the most basic purpose. There are others, of course, but each of the various types of agencies has as its main goal the provision of certain kinds of places and personnel to enable people to experience leisure. The places may be parks, swimming pools, hiking trails, art studios, libraries, concert halls, or gymnasia, and so on. The personnel may be leaders, instructors, interpreters, maintenance workers, supervisors, counselors, therapists, or administrators.

For example, the U.S. Forest Service manages wilderness areas and employs backcountry rangers who are available to help hikers experience the beauty, solitude, and challenge of undeveloped forests and areas above timberline. Residential care centers for the aged staff activity rooms with recreation coordinators who help older adults enjoy a variety of activities suited appropriately to their interests and needs. Commercial marinas provide berths, fuel docks, chandleries, and repair shops for boat owners; and they employ the various specialists who equip, service, and repair sail and power craft. Thousands of other examples could be given. In all, the primary end product is the provision of opportunities that enrich the lives of those served by the agency.

Agencies that comprise the field of recreation and parks have different characteristics. They serve different constituents, provide different kinds of services, manage different kinds of places, and employ different kinds of personnel. Yet they are similar in that all use the basic resources of places and personnel to provide a service. In addition they are all influenced in one way or another by laws or legislation and they all require funding of some sort to enable them to operate. Some are tax-supported, some operate through philanthropy or voluntary contributions or membership fees, and others are profit-seeking. Some serve a national clientele; others are statewide, regional or local. Together, they constitute the field of recreation and parks.

The Leisure Service Delivery System

We now get to the idea that is the basis for the conceptual and operational framework of this book. Let's review again one important point. The primary purpose of the field of recreation and parks is to provide opportunities for people to engage in leisure behaviors that will enrich their lives. That is where the concept of "delivery of leisure services" comes in. Agencies use their resources of places and personnel, legislation and finances to deliver leisure services. But in what way is this a system?

The Field of Recreation & Parks

The Leisure Service Delivery System

A system implies that certain elements and processes are required to produce a service or a product. Further, it implies that these elements and processes are not independent; rather they are interdependent. They influence each other. When one changes, it is likely to have an impact on one or more of the others. In our field, personnel and places can be thought of as the elements an agency can deploy to provide leisure services. Personnel use various processes. These may include leading, teaching, planning, organizing, supervising, and managing. If these elements and processes are part of a system, then a change in one will influence the others. An example or two will show how this happens. An agency needs a budget, or money, to hire personnel and to operate and maintain facilities. Here we have three elements: money, personnel, and facilities. All are required to produce the product, leisure service. Suppose that the agency's budget is reduced for some reason. That might require the agency to lay off some personnel. You can see the influence that would have on the opportunities provided for the agency's public. Suppose we are talking about a city recreation department, specifically about a summer swim program. With less money to employ lifeguards and pool attendants, the department would need to cut the hours of operation. Or suppose a new state law is passed that requires all lifeguards at public pools to participate in at least two hours of in-service training each week. This probably would necessitate spending additional money from the pool budget. What happens to one of the basic elements, money, personnel, areas and facilities, or law, usually influences the remaining elements in some way. This is the "system" idea.

But it is only part of the concept. In the broader sense, the elements deployed by leisure service agencies are influenced by the larger society in which agencies operate. Changes in the composition of the population, in economic conditions, or in political philosophies usually impact on all social institutions. For example, when birth rates change, public schools feel the impact. During economic recessions, people tend to postpone expenditures that are not necessary; this impacts business communities. If a new governor is elected, many state services may be changed to reflect a different approach to governmental responsibilities. This may impact such things as social services and transportation facilities.

Take the example of a ski area in a remote mountain location. Suppose you are the manager. In what ways could societal changes influence your operation? Assume an economic recession is in progress. A larger number of skiers may use ski areas that are closer than yours because of the costs of getting to your area. Of course this will influence your profit. Suppose that, over the years, the population from which you draw your clientele shifts to include a higher percentage of retired but active adults. This might influence the kinds of services you provide on a midweekly basis or the types of facilities you develop in the future. The shift in population probably would be a factor in the ways you promote the area. Labor laws and equal opportunity practices will influence your employment of staff. Trends in statewide liability claims will be a consideration in how much insurance you will decide to carry. And the development of new lift technology may prompt you to think about upgrading your equipment. We could go on, but the point is that leisure service agencies are a part of society and are influenced by changes in that society. In a sense, a systems relationship exists between society and the agencies that serve it. The various interactive systems represented by individuals, agencies, institutions, and the overall society exist in a mutually interactive relationship.

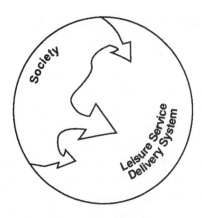

Let's take that last idea a step further. Not only are leisure service agencies influenced by the society in which they operate, they, in turn, impact upon that society. People who use the services change; they learn new skills and develop new attitudes. They may become healthier, less stressed. They may become more open to others and more tolerant of diversity. They may become more supportive of efforts to assure environmental quality, more interested in such things as new park acquisition and development, more demanding in terms of available services. These changes could lead to changes in society—to changes in how people vote, how they spend their money, with whom they associate, and so forth. What seems to exist is an "ecological relationship" between society and the leisure service field. Each influences the other; change in one creates the potential for change in the other.

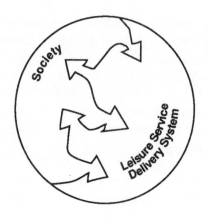

Let's look at another influence on the leisure service delivery system. The field is founded upon a set of beliefs and values. Many beliefs and values are involved, and we want to identify two important ones that influence the leisure service delivery system. Specifically, they influence the behavior of those who are involved in the delivery of services. First, the system is founded on the belief that individuals and groups have rights to leisure opportunities. We assume that all people are entitled, through birth, to a quality of life that includes satisfying leisure experiences. Of course there will be variations in terms of individual interests and selection. And, unfortunately, there are differences in the opportunities possessed by individuals. These exist because of differences in resources, such as time, money, skills, and health. However, the responsibility of the field is to ensure that the right to an enriched leisure life is fulfilled as widely as possible for all people. Second, we believe that recreation is a positive force in our communities and in the nation; and that it has potential for contributing in various ways to the economic and social health of the towns and states in which we live. This does not detract from the concept that we engage in recreation behavior primarily because of the intrinsic satisfaction it provides. It means that, as we do so, a variety of other benefits accrue.

The system concept, then, is based on the idea that the field of recreation and parks, the society within which the field exists, and the people served by the field all stand in a dynamic relationship to each other. The field is a product of society; it is influenced by that society and, in turn, creates changes in people and environments that have potential impacts on communities and the nation. Within the field itself, each of the major elements of money, personnel, areas and facilities, and law also exist in a dynamic relationship to each other. As changes occur in any one of these, the impact may be felt in one or more of the other elements.

The Past and the Future

Our field, as do all other fields, exists in time.

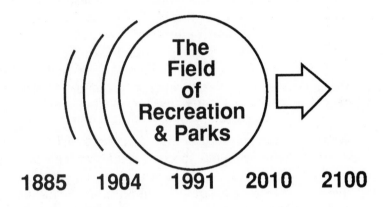

The Field of Recreation & Parks

1885   1904   1991   2010   2100

We can identify its beginnings, the events that marked its evolution, and the social conditions that influenced it through the years. When we do so, we come to a fuller understanding of where we are in the field today: why we hold certain beliefs, do certain things, and so forth. This understanding provides us with a better grasp of the current leisure service delivery system.

The field continues to change; it is not static. Recreation and park professionals work in the field as it exists at the time, and it is hoped that they keep abreast of change and respond to it in appropriate ways. But the rapidity of change forces us to anticipate the future. Adjustments in services and responses to new demands and to changes in the availability of resources require that we look ahead as realistically as possible. Many of our beliefs, structures, and processes have proven to be valid through the years; and some will continue to be valid. But to an extent, what we did in the past will not be appropriate in the future. We need to be ready for change. On occasion, we may need to cause change to occur if we see it is needed. Since we live in a society of continual fluctuation, that also influences the leisure service field, recreation and park professionals must be versatile in serving diverse individuals and groups. Professionals must recognize the multiple roles that are necessary to serve the many needs and interests of participants.

Your Role

We opened this introduction with several questions that you might ask as you begin reading this book. One of these related to your role. What does the leisure service delivery system concept have to do with you? We are going to assume that you are now working in the field of recreation and parks or that you are preparing to do so. The overall concept presented in this text suggests that you must recognize the interrelated nature of the field to maximize your effectiveness as a professional. Specifically, the book suggests that you become more aware of society's impact on what you do, whatever your specialty might be. It encourages you to realize you cannot operate in a vacuum. It suggests that you grasp the significance of leisure: its importance to individual enrichment and community life. It encourages you to see the "ecological" relationships between the people you serve and the kinds of processes you use, to understand that you are working with others' behaviors, and to understand that the professional techniques you use must respond to their needs and interests in appropriate ways. The book prompts you to see how different management processes enable you to do that—to provide effective leisure services. That all sounds simple and logical, and it is. But it is easy to lose sight of the integrated nature of our field and the society in which it operates. You . . . we must not do so if the field is to serve people with maximum effectiveness.

Structure of the Book

The book is structured around three major aspects of the leisure service delivery system.

Part I examines leisure and the conditions in society that influence it.

You will become familiar with the "ecology" of leisure services. The four chapters in this part will provide a basis for developing appropriate values and beliefs about our field and its responsibilities.

Part II is about leisure behavior and the provision of service.

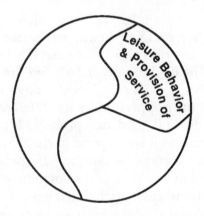

You will be exposed to ideas about the nature of this behavior: what it is, where it occurs, and what factors determine the form it takes. You will read about various considerations in planning and providing for leisure service opportunities. You will also examine some ideas related to professional staff behavior. Overall, the three chapters in this part are designed to increase your ability to apply behavioral understandings in the provision of leisure opportunities.

Part III is a discussion of basic management techniques required in the delivery of leisure services.

These are techniques you will use at whatever level you may be employed and in any of the various specializations that

comprise our field. They are applicable in settings as widely different as the delivery of a single recreation event, such as a teen dance, or the operation of a fully-developed leisure service delivery agency, such as a therapeutic recreation unit in a major hospital.

Our field is a very complex one. Professional practices have evolved greatly in the past few years, in part because of increased research that gives us greater assurance that what we do is what should be done. The field has expanded, and the move toward diversity of services is evident. A wide range of specialized agencies provide leisure opportunities for different constituents. This evolution no doubt is good and probably is inevitable, and will most likely continue if we respond to change appropriately. However, we think there is a danger. If specialization and complexity cause us to lose sight of the common elements in the field and their relationships to each other, we will have lessened our ability to provide the most effective leisure services. Along with continuing development, we need the forces of integration and synthesis. We hope this book contributes in those ways. We hope that when you have read the text, you will have some additional understandings, beliefs, and skills that will enable you to contribute more fully to the leisure service delivery system.

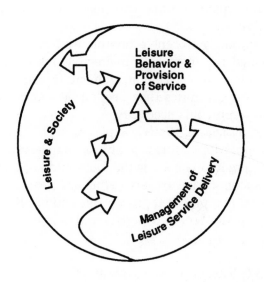

Leisure
Behavior &
Provision
of Service

Leisure & Society

Management of
Leisure Service Delivery

About the Authors

Leisure, once considered a luxury, is now recognized as a necessity. Research shows that everyone, young or old, physically-challenged or able-bodied, not merely wants, but truly needs leisure opportunities. Leisure service managers are responsible for providing customers and patrons with the required access to leisure activities.

Unfortunately, recent economic and demographic trends have revealed the increasing ineffectiveness of traditional approaches to leisure service management. If people are to receive the leisure opportunities they need, a new approach to leisure service management is necessary.

Leisure Systems: Critical Concepts and Applications provides an in-depth discussion of this new approach to leisure service management. Here in one book is the foundation of knowledge necessary for successful leisure service management. *Managing Leisure Systems* contains practical procedures and applications. It is an invaluable tool for both prospective and practicing leisure service managers.

JAMES F. MURPHY is Professor and Chair in the Department of Recreation and Leisure Studies at San Francisco State University. He is a former President of the National Society of Park and Recreation Educators and former Editor of *Schole*, the journal for park and recreation education. His publications include *Concepts of Leisure* (Prentice-Hall, Inc., 1981) and *Recreation and Leisure Service: A Humanistic Perspective* (William C. Brown Publishers, 1975).

E. WILLIAM NIEPOTH is a Professor of Recreation and Park Management at California State University, Chico. He is a former Chair of the Department of Recreation at California State University, Hayward and a member of the National Council on Accreditation (NRPA/AALR). His publications include *Leisure Leadership:*

Working with People in Recreation and Park Settings (Prentice-Hall, 1983) and articles in other texts and journals.

LYNN M. JAMIESON is a Professor and Coordinator of Recreation Administration at California Polytechnic State University, San Luis Obispo. She is a member of the Board of Directors of the National Society of Park and Recreation Educators, and has served on the Board of Regents of the Pacific Revenue Sources Management School. She is co-author of *Introduction to Commercial and Entrepreneurial Recreation* (with John C. Crossley; Sagamore, 1988), has been a contributing author to *Management of Recreational Sport in Higher Education* (Benchmark, 1991), and has written numerous management articles.

JOHN G. WILLIAMS is the former Director of the Department of Parks and Recreation, Sunnyvale, California. He is a member of the National Task Force on the Arts (NRPA), the Board of Directors of the Tri-County Industrial Recreation Council in the San Francisco Bay area, and a past President of the American Park and Recreation Society. He is a co-author of *Productive Management of Leisure Delivery Services: A Behavioral Approach* (with Chris Edginton; John Wiley and Sons, 1978).

Murphy, Williams, Niepoth and Paul Brown wrote the text, *Leisure Service Delivery System: A Modern Perspective* (Lea and Febiger, 1973) that served as a conceptual base for *Leisure Systems: Critical Concepts and Applications*.

Collectively the authors of this text have had broad professional field experiences, in public and non-profit leisure service agencies and in the private sector.

PART I

LEISURE: OVERVIEW

Leisure is an integral part of community life. The continually changing structure of community life, strongly interwoven with leisure service and other community organizations, produces a barrage of evolving values, interests, beliefs, lifestyles, and preferences. Leisure service organizations must be aware of these changes if they are to provide relevant services and programs. Part I studies the key factors that provide an understanding of the basic conceptual, historical, philosophical, and operational aspects of the structure of leisure behavior and leisure services.

The interrelationships of human behavior, leisure, work, and time provide a comprehensive model for understanding the dynamics of how leisure is intertwined with the prevailing mechanistic paradigm or world view. The mechanistic, linear world view, predominant at the outset of the organized Recreation and Park Movement in North America in the mid-nineteenth century, is giving way to a New Age world view. This holistic paradigm provides a promising philosophical, cultural, and operational framework for the delivery of leisure services.

Important developmental phases of the Recreation and Park Movement that are presented provide a foundation for understanding how closely tied the context of service delivery is to the changing nature of community life. Each form of leisure service organization sponsorship—public tax-supported, private non-profit, and commercial— are presented. The range and diversity of professional roles discussed demonstrate the complexity and potential effectiveness of service delivery. Professionalism, a cor-

1

nerstone to any field, is given an expanded definition. There is now recognition, stimulated by New Age thinking and its new insights into human behavior and the organic, holistic dynamics of community life, that leisure personnel must acknowledge that participants need to assume more self-responsibility in meeting their leisure needs. Professionalism, critically important to any discipline or career field, has progressed beyond representing a code of conduct, body of knowledge, and specialized training. Professionalism for recreation and leisure service in the New Age has come to also require recreators to incorporate an interactive style of management that encourages participant involvement, decision making, and choice of leisure options, and political activism to ensure access for all people within the community.

Leisure service agencies, and therefore leaders, supervisors, and executives who work to encourage, facilitate, organize, plan, and manage leisure opportunities, are most effective when they comprehend the totality of interactive human, social, physical, and organizational relationships that exist within a community. Part I of the text provides a background of historical underpinnings, developmental events, and current trends that create a view of leisure service as being an ecologically-based delivery system that uses a holistic, interactive approach to leadership, supervision, and management.

Part I is intended to show that when leisure is defined from a holistic perspective, it blends best with present and evolving patterns of community life. Part II discusses this holistic view merging with progressive developmental interpretations of human behavior. And Part III examines how the holistic leisure service perspective works most effectively with the management and delivery of leisure services. Each of the three parts of the book will present an example in the Overview section from a leisure service agency and discuss key concepts and applications for professional practice. The applications will serve to highlight important concepts and perspectives presented in the chapters.

Holistic Leisure Service Management

Holistic systems management recognizes that each element or subsystem of an organization operates in a dynamic manner within the community system. It also acknowledges the corresponding impact of each decision and action taken by leisure service managers upon all other environments. The following discussion illustrates how a leisure service agency manager (park supervisor) operationalized holistic systems management at Prusch Farm Park, a regional park in the City of San Jose, California Parks and Recreation Department.

Prusch Farm Park

Prusch Farm Park is located next to one of the busiest crossroads in the United States, the intersection of two major interstate highway systems. The forty-seven acre regional park encompasses reclaimed agricultural land that originally served as a dairy farm at the turn of the twentieth century and now is the center of a busy urban community. The surrounding community has a high percentage of Hispanic and Asian residents. On this city of San Jose Park and Recreation Department site is a ten-room Victorian farmhouse, barn, area for small farm animals, rare fruit orchard, community garden, open space turf area, and meeting hall. Soon there will be a multicultural center that will offer opportunities, particularly for Hispanic community residents, to participate in various performing and expressive art activities.

The director's chief duties upon assuming the position, after having previously served as director of the Timpanny Center (a facility that serves disabled persons) and director of a triathalon event for the city agency, were to (1) facilitate access and remove barriers for community residents, (2) gain a sense of the community's wishes for using the farm park, (3) involve community members in decision making related to setting policy, determining programs, and planning for future park development, (4) recognize that there were a number of different roles she should assume in order to best promote and respond to the community's desires for use of the park, (5) encourage community ownership of the facility in order to foster a stronger connection of residents to the park, and (6) create opportunities for different levels of involvement for community members—from direct participation with the community gardens, cooperative department and community association development of self-guided farm equipment displays and a rare fruit orchard, to self-directed operation of the barn that houses a variety of farm animals and services a number of different private association interest groups.

Operational Application

Prusch Farm Park is just one example of a leisure service operation that incorporates a holistic systems mangement approach as its basis for service delivery. To accomplish the many diverse goals and serve the varied populations, the park's director and leisure service personnel took the following actions:

1. They removed barriers so that all community members could have access.

Communities, broadly defined, are structures that enable people to meet needs that cannot be met individually. It is important for leisure service personnel to identify with the community. At Prusch Farm Park, community members were invited to implement programs at the park via newspaper articles, flyers distributed in two languages throughout the surrounding community, and through attendance by the director and staff members at council meetings.

2. They learned about the community's wishes on a periodic basis.

Communities change because of shifts in demographic makeup, evolving economic, social, political, and conditions, value shifts, and other factors. The director went out into the community and attended a number of meetings to elicit concerns, desires and learn past history regarding the development of the park. Community members were invited to come to the park to hold events and join planning committees seeking to plan for the park's future.

3. They involved the community members in decision making.

Communities represent systems in that changes in one dimension have potential for influencing all other elements. The leisure service delivery system, a community subsystem, provides for people's leisure needs through a complex of different organizations. Organizations' roles change as conditions change. Two major associations—Future Farmers of America and Four-H were competing groups who claimed proprietary rights over the operation of the barn. The director brought these two factions together and over a period of four months a set of policies and procedures were developed for the governing and operation of the facility. A community board was established and now directs this aspect of the park's operation.

4. They incorporated role versatility in the delivery of services in order to respond to the diverse and ever changing needs and circumstances of community members.

Leisure service personnel must consider embracing a holistic management philosophy, one that incorporates respect for the individual as a total person. In using such a conceptual perspective, personnel recognize there are multiple problem sources impacting human beings in their communites. The holistic philosophy enables leisure agencies to adopt a service delivery continuum, which ranges from prepackaged, direct service to agencies acting as coordinating and information and referral brokers to community advocates for those constituents who lack needed services. This view blends well with an interactive leadership style. It became apparent to the director that from participation in activities and events at the park some residents already knew what they wanted to do and what benefits existed. These individuals and groups helped establish the community gardens, plant the rare fruit orchard, feed the farm animals, and set up the self-guided farm equipment display. Others desired assistance in planning and conducting community events. For example, cooperative arrangements were made to help a group conduct a Native American Tribal Festival. Still others came to advocate for the development of a multicultural arts center on the site. The director listened and deemed it important to work with a strong community-based power group and serve as a proactive leader in helping them gain approval from the department and city administration to construct the facility in the park. She felt that it was, politically, an appropriate decision to make.

5. They worked to foster a stronger sense of community acceptance for individual community members. This was accomplished by encouraging shared ownership of agency programs, facilities, and services with community members.

People's needs, including leisure needs, are best served within the framework of a holistic philosophy based on the innate values to individuals, their right to be self-determining with consideration for the larger framework of society, and their need for continued growth toward well-being. By adopting several different roles, the Prusch Farm Park Director has helped members of the surrounding area of the park invest in the definition of how and why the facility is to be used. She believes she has begun a process that will enable residents to relate better to the park's presence in their community and correspondingly interpret the recreational farm park as an integral part of the community's past, present and future. In an era of rapid change, the park serves as an important and stabilizing part of people's lives.

6. They created opportunities for different levels of involvement for community members in park services. This approach was designed to foster individual development throughout the life span.

People have a need to grow and will exhibit differing needs over their life spans. Such a developmental view of human behavior works well with a holistic management philosophy. As leaders, supervisors, or administrators, professional recreators can assist people in making successful transitions and facilitate growth at each developmental stage. This is accomplished by encouraging people to access leisure opportunities in a variety of ways or at different levels of personal involvement.

The director has endeavored to foster ways in which community members can participate in the use of the park. Some community members identify strongly with the park's community garden as an extension of their home. People come and tend the garden every day. For others the opportunity to demonstrate cultural pride is paramount, and the director ensures their freedom of expression and strengthens their dignity by working cooperatively with several Hispanic residents to see that the multicultural arts center is constructed. Members of the barn council have been able to develop an operating plan that enables a number of groups to use the facility for a variety of animal activities. Still others work as docents and conduct guided tours of the facility and establish the self-guided environmental displays for other residents to enjoy on their strolls through the park. Each of these different residents is able to access the park and participate in an appropriate manner that corresponds to their current level of need, which fosters their development as human beings. This approach is consistent with the philosophical perspective of leisure as an essential element that contributes to overall life satisfaction.

1

NATURE OF CONTEMPORARY COMMUNITY LIFE

Communities typically serve as the focal point for activities (social, economic, religious, education, family, and so forth) that occur within a defined geographical area. The contributions individuals and groups make to this configuration of business, schools, churches, recreation, and leisure service agencies, often depends on the sense of belonging that people feel through their associations with others. The importance people place in their associations in communities is also largely influenced by the sentiments arising from their context and involvement with others through these affiliations.

Recreation and leisure service agencies are one of the elements that constitute the make-up of community life. While recreation and leisure service as an institution grew out of the changing social, economic, and familial conditions of an industrializing nation in the mid-nineteenth century, it has become a primary structure for the enhancement of community life in the latter quarter of the twentieth century. Work activity continues to provide the basis of exchange for communities to function as an economic system; leisure services, as an activity, provide meaning to people in many ways as a social system.

Leisure also increasingly provides individuals a way for transforming themselves—of becoming "free" of other community activities that do not provide support for or encourage diversity of expression. Leisure has become a physical and material structure that serves as a surrogate parent for children and youth, a vehicle for creating opportunities for people to establish social bonds, and a physical resource that provides open space and play areas for communities; but leisure has also evolved into something more.

Leisure owes its roots in Western civilization to Aristotle and ancient Greek culture, where it served as the basis or wellspring of culture. The activities of work, religion, government, and family life were fed by the energy and creativity that grew out of leisure pursuits. The dynamics of community life were fostered by the joyful, intellectual, spiritual, and artistic expressions of people not bound by inherently generalized, limiting, and predictable expectations of toil and labor. Leisure, interpreted in this ancient era to mean "freedom from the necessity of being occupied (at work)" provided a means of continual personal growth. Each individual's quest had limitless continual personal growth and boundaries for expression covering all physical and metaphysical possibilities.

In contemporary North American culture, work's importance is being recognized as a fundamental activity that serves not as the core, but as just one of the many components of community life. Leisure increasingly represents a central concept for human expression that does more than refresh an individual or community collectively for return to labor. The essence of personal well-being is found in sentiments emerging from within each person while consciously or unconsciously pursuing activities, thoughts, or dreams that are important, interesting, alluring, challenging, or magical. Thus the essence of community life becomes more significant and more symbolically meaningful to people through their engagement in leisure. In what they involve themselves in, those who have a higher degree of freedom, are intrinsically motivated, and can personally govern or control their own actions are more likely to be committed to themselves and their associations. Those aspects of community life in which the structure supersedes the individual only serve human endeavor; one's achievements, goals, and dreams become subordinated to the desired goal.

In survival societies, such individual aspirations are normally dependent upon community structures. If people in a culture are not dominated by having to meet basic human needs, they are able to become transformed, not by structures governed or actuated by the external community system, but by their own actions. Thus, the individual, who develops his or her own capacity for solving problems, engaging in satisfying and purposeful activities, and exercising a greater variety of choices, will more likely see a relationship of one's involvement in community life and personal actions. (While all activities that occur in communities do become worthwhile experiences, leisure is the one element that provides a way for an individual to fully express oneself.) To be more totally expressive as a person has become a desired goal of more and more people as we near the twenty-first century.

Changing Perspectives of Community

The segmentation of human relationships (see Table 1.1) in contemporary urban North American society has posed some unique problems and challenges for human service agencies. Urban people depend more upon others for satisfaction of their life needs than rural residents, and thus associate themselves with a greater number of organized groups. However, people living in urban areas are less dependent upon particular persons, and their dependence upon others is confined to a highly fractionalized aspect of the other's day-to-day activities. City life for almost 80 percent of North Americans is thus characterized by secondary rather than primary contacts, and while they indeed may be face-to-face, they are nevertheless often impersonal, superficial, transitory, and segmental.

The Temporary Community

Mobility is a chief phenomenon of our society, resulting in the fragmentation of families, individual disengagement from commitment to social causes, loneliness, and suffering. Approximately one-quarter of the population in America moves every year, disrupting homes, neighborhoods, industries, businesses, and community life. People, in effect, are becoming strangers to each other. This has implications for recreation and leisure service agencies, where our acquaintances tend to stand only in a relationship of utility to us. Wirth (1972) relates:

> whereas . . . . the individual gains, on the one hand, a certain degree of emancipation or freedom from the personal and emotional controls of intimate groups, he loses, on the other hand, the spontaneous self-expression, the morale, and the sense of participation that usually comes with living in an integrated society (41).

Table 1.1 Segmentation of Human Associations

Type of Association	Disintegrating Characteristics	Integrating/Harmonizing Bonds
Work	• Rapid technological change in work environment resulting in displacement of workers due to automation, robotics, computerization • Increase in entrepreneurship, intrapreneurship contributing to less worker pride and commitment to company but more to individual schedules, goals and projects • Rise in flexible work patterns • Increased national "leisure" holidays with no particular symbolic significance • Rise in craft vocations, blending work & leisure, resulting in secondary nature of work	• Opportunity for sharing with colleagues • Employee recreation/fitness/wellness programs • Doing interesting work • Alternatives and flexible work schedules • Day care at work/recreation centers
Neighborhoods	• High cost of homes making it difficult to live in neighborhoods of choice • One-quarter of all workers commute across county lines to work • One-fifth of the U.S. population moves every year • Development of specialized housing/settlement patterns for singles and young married couples with and without children, etc. resulting in segregated residential patterns • Shopping malls serving as surrogate neighborhood community centers	• Neighborhood clean-up or development projects • Backyard gardening/landscaping • Block parties • Crime watch • Neighborhood recreation associations

Table 1.1 *Continued*

Type of Association	Disintegrating Characteristics	Integrating/Harmonizing Bonds
Family	• Disengagement of nuclear family and traditional kinship groups • More non-married couples living together • More single parent households • More families postponing having children until later • Variety of experimental/nontraditional living arrangements • Less emphasis on whole family interests and greater emphasis on individual interests • Little communication between family members	• Eating together • Family leisure outings, vacations • Resource awareness and skill development by family mentors • Intergenerational programs
Leisure	• Taking work home • Leisure often confined/relegated to after school, after work and weekends, or two weeks during summer • Has to fit within linear industrial work pattern • Perception one needs money to play, recreate • Leisure has less and less meaning to people whose lives no longer reflect this mechanical pattern	• Integration/fusion of whole interests through leisure and vice versa • Self-selected activity choices reflective of life-style; fosters shared interests and mutual compatibility • Leisure awareness programs/service delivery that fosters high degree of freedom, challenge, choice, commitment and personal control

11

The segmental character and utilitarian accent of interpersonal relations in the city have resulted in the rapid growth of specialized tasks occurring within an institutional framework to handle the needs of people. The family has been altered considerably as a unit of social life. Individual members have been emancipated from the larger kinship group, characteristic of the nuclear family, to pursue their own divergent interests in work, education, religion, recreation, and political life. The functions of various community services related to health, to methods of alleviating hardships associated with personal and social security, and to provisions for education, recreation and cultural advancement have given rise to highly specialized institutions and agencies on a communitywide and even national basis. Because of the relative impotence of the individual in contemporary life, the urban dweller often finds himself or herself being exhorted to join with others of similar interest into organized groups to meet personal needs. In this sense many recreation and leisure agencies serve to provide a means for creative self-expression and spontaneous group association, unavailable within the work, education, church, or family milieus.

Toffler (1970) has noted how our highly technological society has become fractionalized because of high social change and disrupted community life. Figure 1.1 illustrates Toffler's major themes and their relationship to leisure service agencies. Transience is a pervasive theme of Toffler's, as the turnover rate of the different kinds of relationships in an individual's life has perpetuated a nation of rootless people reaching for some degree of stability and permanence. Thus, community life, particularly in urban centers, has disintegrated for a large number of people; our relationships with people and things have become more and more temporary.

The Community of Shared Interests

While contemporary community life has become less secure for many and is subject to the fluctuations and uncertainty of a highly mobile and impermanent population, another form of community has been emerging for the last quarter of the twentieth century. This evolving concept of community has little in common with traditional rural agricultural or even urban industrial work-centered communities but instead is based on a greater degree of

Figure 1.1 Relationships of Concepts of Future Shock and Leisure Service

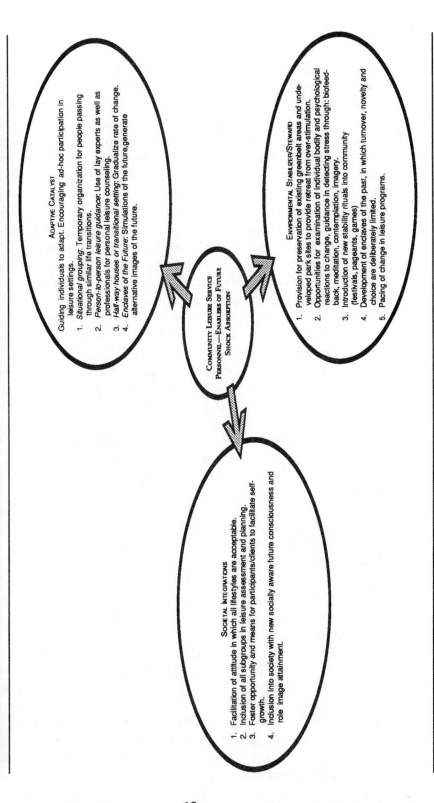

ADAPTIVE CATALYST

Guiding individuals to adapt. Encouraging ad-hoc participation in leisure settings.

1. *Situational grouping:* Temporary organization for people passing through similar life transitions.
2. *Person-to-person leisure guidance:* Use of lay experts as well as professionals for personal leisure counseling. *Half-way houses or transitional setting:* Gradualize rate of change.
3. *Enclaves of the Future:* Simulations of the future,generate alternative images of the future.

COMMUNITY LEISURE SERVICE PERSONNEL—ENABLERS OF FUTURE SHOCK ABSORPTION

ENVIRONMENTAL STABILIZER/STEWARD

1. Provision for preservation of existing greenbelt areas and undeveloped park sites to provide retreat from over-stimulation.
2. Opportunities for examination of individual bodily and psychological reactions to change, guidance in detecting stress through: biofeedback, meditation, contemplation, imagery.
3. Introduction of new stability rituals into community (festivals, pageants, games)
4. Development of enclaves of the past, in which turnover, novelty and choice are deliberately limited.
5. Pacing of change in leisure programs.

SOCIETAL INTEGRATIONS

1. Facilitation of attitude in which all lifestyles are acceptable.
2. Inclusion of all subgroups in leisure assessment and planning.
3. Foster opportunity and means for participants/clients to facilitate self-growth.
4. Inclusion into society with new socially aware future consciousness and role image attainment.

13

individual flexibility, vocational choice and selectivity, and leisure options within a highly mobile society. This new sense of community transcends kinship ties, social barriers, and geography. There are few natural geographical boundaries in the land that give a community identity, and traditional agricultural communities were largely rooted to the land and based on strong kinship affiliation. But contemporary community life has resulted in less overall commitment of people to physical space and greater adherence to an identification with others who represent a compatible lifestyle of shared values and interests. Participation based on shared interests and leisure lifestyle is voluntary and exists as long as individuals are motivated to participate, identify, and relate to others who are similarly involved. Increasingly, people are attempting to reside within commuting distance to work, but near to where they can exercise their avocational-leisure interests.

Community leisure styles of life result from the fragmentation of human associations as reflected by (1) the growing secondary nature of work (represented by the growth of the adjusted and bunched work week, increased absenteeism and worker dissatisfaction, rise in national "leisure" holidays having no particular symbolic significance, earlier retirements, increase in craft vocations that seemingly integrate work and leisure, growth in the number of communities sponsoring festivals to celebrate eroded customs and indigenous artisan talents), and so forth, (2) disengagement of nuclear family and transitional kinship groups (represented by a number of experimental living arrangements, including contractual marriages and single parent households, and a rise in specialty villages, including communities for singles, young marrieds, and retired people), and (3) disruption of neighborhood life (transience resulting from one-quarter of the population moving each year).

Essentially, leisure lifestyles, as opposed to work, neighborhood, or kinship associations and ties, are emerging as the framework for community participation by those seeking to preserve individual identity and integrity in the midst of a highly mobile and segmented society. This is occurring because of an exponentially changing social, cultural, political, and economic environment. Recreation personnel will need to facilitate human association in spontaneous settings where people congregate and serve as enablers of human interactions that are immediate, intense, and without traditional props, rituals, and distancing mechanisms. This seems to be a necessary step because by the time the individual arrives at this "where-is-the-real-me" state, one may be on the move again. Individuals are looking for a way to become attached to others who share similar interests. But since traditional community vehicles for identity seem remote or cumbersome, processes that create less formal procedures for association are more likely to generate participation and involvement.

Factors Contributing to the Reshaping of Community Life and Leisure Behavior

North American culture is redefining itself and has fostered a number of changes that are impacting on structures and elements that make up the subsystems of communities. Naisbitt (1982) comments on trends that are precipitating the restructuring of American society:

1. Economy increasingly based on the creation and distribution of information;
2. Development of balance between impersonal high technology and meaningful human interaction;
3. Movement from isolated, self-sufficient, national economic system to being a part of highly interdependent global economy;
4. More consideration being given matters in favor of long-term rather than short-term time frame;
5. Rediscovery of decentralization—the ability to act innovatively and to achieve results—from the bottom up;
6. Shift from institutional help to more self-reliance in all aspects of our lives;
7. Movement toward participative democracy, as people are demanding a direct say in the decisions that affect their lives;
8. Giving up dependence on hierarchical bureaucracies to horizontal linkages (networking) based on convenience and need;
9. Shift from smokestack industrial region of the North and Midwest to Sunbelt states in South and West, and;

10. Movement from narrow, either/or society with a limited range of personal choices, to multiple-option society (see Table 1.2).

These trends identified by Naisbitt are causing a number of changes in the social milieu that have corresponding implications for leisure service. Some important ones include: demographic shifts, attitudes toward health, work, leisure, technological developments, and basic values.

Table 1.2 Application of Megatrends to Leisure

Megatrend	Leisure Implication
1. Industrial Society to Information Society	1. Leisure education. Recognition of power and influence of electronic technology to inform, teach, entertain.
2. Forced Technology to High Tech/High Touch	2. VCRs, home computers, compact laser discs, community festivals, shopping malls, outdoor recreation adventure trips.
3. National Economy to World Economy	3. Global travel, tourism, linkage or language, ethnicity, and technology through leisure.
4. Short Term to Long Term	4. View leisure beyond immediate gratification, as time free from work but as essence of culture. Understand long-term impact of leisure use patterns on physical environment and personal well-being.
5. Centralization to Decentralization	5. More local specialized leisure events organized by grass roots groups with shared interests (e.g., fun runs, chili cook offs, "beat the boss" events, tail gate picnics at athletic events, etc.)

Table 1.2 *Continued*

Megatrend	Leisure Implication
6. Institutional Help to Self-Help	6. Individual and small scale community groups assuming personal responsibility—self-health—linking health, wellness and leisure.
7. Representative Democracy to Participatory Democracy	7. Involvement of consumers, recipients and clients in program and service development and operation of programs and services.
8. Hierarchies to Networking	8. Linkage of individuals and community interest groups together via newsletters, phone calls, workshops, seminars, computers, etc., to share knowledge of leisure resources, opportunities and to improve services and solve problems. Decline of centralized, bureaucratic public/private corporate structures and removal of age, sex, race stereotyping.
9. North to South	9. Shift from industrial, mechanistic dominant work pattern to desire by more people to focus on quality of life—year round (flexible leisure/work/family balanced life pattern).
10. Either/Or to Multiple Option	10. Shift from family, kinship leisure circle to individual and shared interest group through voluntary association as spur for leisure choices. More balanced work-leisure-community life. Less homogeneous, mass activities and more celebration of cultural diversity.

Demographic Shifts

As we near the twenty-first century, there are significant changes in the size, composition, location, and structure of various classifications of people. Studying how segments of the population are likely to change helps leisure personnel do a better job of managing, staffing, and marketing services and opportunities for people. The data listed below highlight certain characteristics of the American population:

- Approximately one-third (over 80 million people) of the population is between the ages of 15 and 35.
- One-half of the population (120 million people) is over 32.
- One in four of the nation's 64 million children lives with only one parent (compared with 85 percent who lived with two parents in 1970).
- There are more people over 60 than under the age of 10.
- Females outlive males by five to seven years.
- One-fourth of the population lives alone. By 1995, 27 percent of United States households will consist of single individuals—constituting a market for goods and services far different than that offered to the standard family unit.
- Average size of the family is declining. (The average household had 2.62 people in 1989. This compares with approximately 3 people per household in 1970.)
- There are more women "heads of household" than ever before.
- If current age-specific marriage rates do not change, only 70 percent of American women will ever marry (this compares with 87 percent in 1972).
- More young adults are choosing a career over marriage or delaying marriage until later years.
- In the 1990s, over 50 percent of husband and wife families will work, compared with only 12 percent in 1959.
- Approximately 75 percent of the population lives on 16 percent of the land in the 48 contiguous states.
- Approximately one-fourth of the population changes residence each year. This decreases neighborhood and community stability.

- From 1970 to 1980, 42 percent of the population growth took place in three states: Texas, Florida, and California. The megatrend to sunbelt states suggests more acceptance of overall lifestyle issues rather than work only as a primary criteria for settlement.

Traditional images of the make-up of society and values that supposedly reflect these characteristics are in need of sharp change. Leisure service providers, managers, supervisors, and leaders must keep abreast of demographic and psychographic changes to be able to know who their clients, customers, and participants are, and how they can therefore best be reached and served.

Shifting Attitudes Toward Work, Leisure and Wellness

Work
     The traditional dream held by Canadians and Americans has been rooted in the work ethic. According to the Protestant, industrial view, hard work leads to material wealth and thus to happiness. This rational, materialistic, and deterministic view assumes that the North Americans' potential for economic growth is unlimited. Proponents of this traditional dream believe that economic security and self-esteem that accompanies it are available to anyone willing to devote enough time and energy to his or her work. This view has been amended according to Yankelovich (1981), who contends that the newest version of the American dream has the following characteristics:

1. Growing acceptance of the idea that there are realistic limits to economic growth;
2. Decreasing relative emphasis on material possessions; material well-being does not necessarily equal personal happiness;
3. More emphasis on leisure in the balance between work and leisure;
4. Increasing dissatisfaction with dull, monotonous, and unchallenging jobs;
5. Greater emphasis on quality of life, physical and mental well-being, and personal growth and satisfaction;
6. Emergence of an antiwaste morality.

Does this mean the work ethic is dead? Quite the contrary. Studies reveal that younger workers are committed to hard work and to developing themselves in the workplace (Carrington, 1977). Those who embrace the new work ethic want jobs with challenge and meaning, in addition to good pay and generous employee benefits.

Despite the new work ethic's greater emphasis on leisure, the workweek in the United States has actually been increasing over the past two decades. In 1972 the median workweek was just over 40 hours a week. By 1984 it had climbed to 46 hours a week. Concurrently, leisure hours had been reduced from 25 to 17 hours a week in the same time period. Solomon (1986) comments:

> The 40-hour week, protected by federal law for nearly 50 years, is fiction for many wage earners. Professionals and managers worked an average of 45 hours a week (in 1985) while manufacturing employees put in an average of 43 hours. And they have less vacation time—an average of two weeks a year—than do their counterparts in every industrial country except Japan. (10)

Manufacturing workers in the United States have combined paid vacations and public holidays that compare with their counterparts in Great Britain and Japan. However, the Japanese work longer hours and more days during a week. The West Germans and French work considerably fewer hours during the year and exceed the Americans, Japanese, and British in paid vacations and public holidays.

There are more people in the workforce than ever before and with couples delaying or abstaining from having children, household income is increasing. But in contrast to the new work ethic's de-emphasis on material wealth, happiness is still largely equated with material success and therefore one has to work long enough to secure an ample income to be able to "pay for pleasure" in the 1990s.

Work and Leisure

Though work has not diminished leisure's character, for many, leisure seems to mirror the frantic part of work. Leisure for some has meant rigorous activity—jogging, aerobics, racquetball, squash, body building, and so forth. The fitness boom has helped promote a positive attitude toward personal health and wellness. This fad has resulted in more corporations trying to pare costs and increase productivity, encourage their employees to either initiate a leisure wellness and fitness program onsite (incorporating risk and stress management, self-responsibility, nutritional awareness, fitness, and environmental and lifestyle sensitivity and awareness), or offer subsidies for health club memberships and adult education courses.

In some cases companies hope their employees will become more mentally, physically, and spiritually fit so that they might be more adventurous, confident, and risk taking on the job. For example, employees from Esprit de Corps headquarters office in San Francisco are encouraged to pursue outdoor recreation adventure experiences (e.g., rock climbing, white water rafting, wilderness trekking, sea kayaking). It is believed that these experiences provide physical and mental challenge that entail self-awareness, choice, and commitment. As a result of these adventures, the participant, it is felt, becomes more confident in his or her abilities. While broadening their outdoor recreation knowledge and skill level, employees are learning to develop a positive leisure lifestyle. At the same time, they work on team-building processes. As the group works together to solve problems while on outdoor adventures, they develop trust and support, thus improving their ability to work together in a more open and constructive way on the job.

Those inclined to risk taking do so both in work and leisure. According to Dr. Frank Farley, as many as 30 percent of Americans possess a "Type T" trait of thrill-seeking personality (Skrzyeki 1987). Such individuals seek higher levels of stimulation and uncertainty involved in risk taking in everything from commodities market speculation to sky diving. More individuals are expressing this go-for-it attitude, as Farley documents in the workplace where new business ventures have been increasing by over 37 percent since 1980.

Generational differences help explain the upsurge in how Americans view risk. Baby-boomers, for instance, are more inclined to risk taking than their fathers or mothers—the Organizational Man or Woman who valued security and corporate loyalty. Baby-boomers change jobs—on the average four times every twelve years, take extended leaves to pursue other interests, or simply quit because the politics of corporate life becomes distasteful. But for those who do not need to make decisions where lives or millions of dollars hang in balance, Skrzyeki (1987) comments:

> Millions of people have 'small t' personalities and prefer caution to courage. For them, risk is often a vicarious experience enjoyed through video games, action-packed television shows, automobile ads that promote a sense of speed and excitement and well-planned adventure travel. (67)

For these individuals the way of risk taking is the excitement and goose bumps without the "real" risk.

Leisure and Wellness

In an information society, relying on collaboration and linkage at work and elsewhere, more people are now looking to construct their lives in an integrated manner and are finding society's social, economic, and cultural structures to be irrelevant and even destructive when they encourage segmentation and division of roles, lifestyle options, and opportunities. Instead of wellness, institutions that seek sharp divisions in life may be promoting "worseness" (Ardell 1986).

The adoption of a wellness consciousness among many people is thus a positive step in the direction of changing the linear, industrial work ethic and earned leisure life model. Wellness views the person as an integrative whole, a balance existing between the individual and his or her environment, others, and oneself (McDowell 1983). Wellness encompasses a process in which an individual learns to make self-determined choices toward a successful life. A leisure wellness lifestyle recognizes the dynamics of the social and physical environment and the ever-evolving person. One recognizes that each part of his or her life must be integrated and balanced. Such a lifestyle may minimize one's chances of becoming ill, promote a strong sense of intrinsic satisfaction, and increase the prospects for well-being.

A leisure wellness orientation to lifestyle recognizes and embraces the elements presented by Ardell and others (see Figure 1.2). According to McDowell (1983), leisure wellness is "a measure of how well prepared an individual is to take what they know about leisure and directly assume and maintain to some relative degree the responsibility to try and experience it with a dynamic spirit" (36). He further suggests that each individual has a specific type of leisure wellness orientation that affects his or her relationship to leisure and life in general. Leisure wellness entails four areas of leisure consciousness:

1. The depth of Awareness and Understanding of leisure in one's daily life as influenced by other lifestyle areas (work, family, education, spirituality, community, etc.)
2. One's Coping Ability with certain issues of life and behavior (such as guilt, boredom, chronic habits, apathy, etc.) that may interrupt and affect one's pursuit of leisure and overall wellness
3. The Knowledge of the Breadth and Balance of one's interests, resourcefulness and general fitness
4. The degree to which one accepts through Affirmation, Assertion, and Contemplation his/her responsibility to leisure with direct purpose and joy (McDowell 1983, 36).

Figure 1.2 Ardell Wellness Model

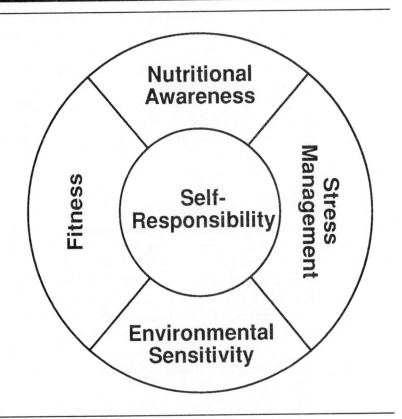

A team of leisure studies educators from San Francisco State University, working with a national corporate headquarters employees group, presented a Leisure Wellness/Lifestyle Enhancement Program over a fifteen-week period. Wellness was viewed as a dynamic process in that the whole individual must be involved in life events—including self-concept, work, primary and other social and work relationships, leisure, and the surrounding environment. The series of seminars and workshops included the following sessions: "Introduction to What Constitutes a Healthful/Satisfying Lifestyle," "Discovering Individual Lifestyle Options," "Exploring New Ways to Live with Time," "Creative Approaches to Developing Lifestyle Options," and "Supporting Individual Lifestyle Choices; Development of Mechanisms for Lifestyle Change." Leisure was identified by its important elements that influence the leisure experience: high degree of personal freedom, internal locus of control, and intrinsic motivation. These factors, when present in an individual, are more likely to lead to satisfaction and well-being at work or at leisure.

The goal of the Leisure Wellness/Lifestyle Enhancement Program team was to assist and guide participants through a process wherein each individual set a personal direction for change—an individual selected a lifestyle option designed to enhance his or her overall well-being. Participants explored not so much what choices to make from an array of activities they could pursue in their leisure, but rather how to get in touch with their outer and inner environment—thereby discovering that the key to high level wellness is not so much what you do but how you feel inside. This awareness of self leads to a deeper sense of spirituality and interconnectedness with the world.

The individual has the capability and must take the responsibility for enhancing his or her own well-being. In a program developed for treating adolescent psychiatric patients, it was reported that a leisure wellness program (one that incorporated elements similar to Ardell) served to "open up the possibility of viewing one's self as a resource in improving one's well-being" (Emmerichs and Kofford 1986, 57). Leisure service providers are challenged to facilitate the recognition for well-being not through the conduct of some specific activity or program, but by enabling participants, consumers, and clients to gain some sense of personal responsibility and control.

Technological Developments

Technology, the application of organized knowledge to help solve problems in our society, has created many leisure opportunities and products. The number of new gadgets and mechanisms introduced each year increases our range of options and leads to life enhancement; they not only create new leisure options, but also transform the way activities are pursued.

Expanded opportunities for leisure participation have been spurred by the development of innovations that impact leisure during the winter (artificial ice-skating rinks, snow-making machines, snowmobiles), summer (wind-surf boards, scuba-diving gear), and year-round (video players and recorders, compact laser disc players and recorders, electric wheelchairs and vehicles equipped for the disabled). While new technology is normally welcomed and enriches our leisure, Kraus (1984) notes that its presence is a mixed blessing: "All forms of technological play tend to be commercially produced and marketed; often they are extremely expensive and thus serve chiefly those who have financial resources, excluding the poor" (7).

According to Naisbitt, as more new technology is introduced into society there must be a counterbalancing human response (high touch), or the technology is rejected. For example:

1. People will want to congregate with others—shopping malls, concerts, movies, and festivals.
2. Individuals will need to compensate for technology by being out in nature more often, going to the beach or camping.
3. Those performing mental as opposed to physical tasks, for example the factory workers of the industrial era, will want to balance the constant use of mental energy by using their hands and bodies more in the leisure pursuits, such as cooking, gardening, and home renovation.

The relationship of technology to leisure portends an even greater need for individuals to understand this counterbalancing human response, as more technology is introduced into society.

The Information Age

The postindustrial, information age, with "third wave" technology (emphasis on maximizing personal options, decentralizing production, self-responsibility, networking, and so on), eliminates the industrial concept of leisure as a relatively precise activity occurring at a particular time and place (Toffler 1981). In its place is an integrated, holistic view of leisure that transcends work, family, church, and school structures. Leisure is emerging as a way of life guided by one's internal needs and intrinsic motivation, that is a more flexible, self-paced experience that can occur at any time and any place (Toffler 1981, 277).

The decline of the industrial era and rise of the information era necessitates that North Americans recognize that the metaphors of centralization, standardization, and synchronization, which were applied to work, family life, and leisure, are no longer as appropriate or useful as guideposts for the future. In an era of destandardization, personalization, and multiple options, values that recognize and promote individual capabilities, self-responsibility, differences among people, and multiple processes and outcomes are most helpful. For example, there are increasingly a variety of nontraditional households in the United States and Canada consisting of single parents (typically a woman). The concept of family no longer can be stereotyped or standardized as representing two parents (male and female) and one or two children.

The linear life pattern (see Figure 1.3), that grew out of the Industrial Revolution, is no longer relevant in an information era filled with multiple options. In the information age, the industrial work rhythm of life gives way to a more flexible, interdependent

Figure 1.3 Linear Life Pattern

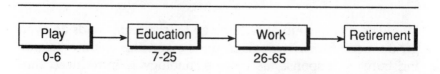

Play	Education	Work	Retirement
0-6	7-25	26-65	

holistic life pattern (see Figure 1.4). There is no designation for retirement, since the idea of being "forced" to disengage from largely self-directed and self-paced patterns becomes irrelevant in an information era of multiple options contrasted with the more limiting either/or options of the industrial era.

The combined effect of flexible work/leisure/education cycles and more egalitarian social roles for men and women within a pluralistic and ethnically diverse demographic context in North America necessitates a new conceptual framework for leisure and other social institutions, including work, family, and education.

Figure 1.4 Holistic Life Pattern

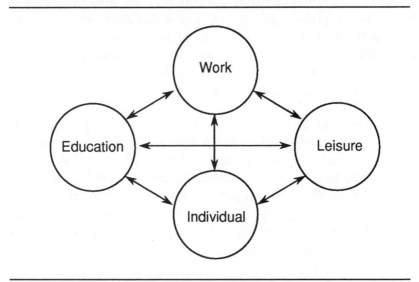

The Physical Environment

The factors affecting leisure behavior are multiple. Certainly the influence of the physical environment, which provides a context for experiencing leisure, is an important ingredient of leisure service delivery. Several megatrends discussed by Naisbitt and presented earlier in this chapter (see Table 1.2) have particular implications for the physical environment. Some of these are: (1) greater demand for home-based leisure via use of video recorders, computers, and other forms of home entertainment, (2) increased spread of shopping malls, (3) more outdoor recreation adventure trips, (4) population shift to the South and West, and (5) more demand for local community specialized leisure events. These are but a few of the trends that have implications for, or are influenced by, the physical environment.

Natural Resources

With the changing social fabric of the country and more general interest in and use of the physical environment as an integral component of the recreation and leisure experience, leisure service managers' concerns about resource conditions, perceived recreation quality, the quantity of recreation opportunities supplied, and the quality of experiences derived from them have loomed as important aspects of the planning, programming, and evaluating responsibilities of managers. Much research has been conducted on natural resources. Stankey and Manning (1986) summarize some of the findings:

1. Virtually all ecological studies of carrying capacity report a curvilinear relationship between recreational use and impact. Typically, most environmental impact occurs under light levels of recreational use, and additional recreational use causes relatively little additional impact.

2. Complex interactions exist between the various physical parameters that comprise the environment; these can be altered by recreational use.

3. Increasing ecological impact associated with recreation can be difficult to determine what is the most appropriate indicator of that impact . . . . [However] recent studies of high mountain lakes in the Sierra Nevada mountains indicate that recreation impacts are inducing subtle changes in water chemistry that will eventually affect their long-term biological productivity.

4. Many ecological impacts are subject to some degree of management control . . . . Management activities can also affect the timing and location of impacts. The location of trails, for instance, is a powerful influence on where people go and, by implication, the nature and location of impacts. Poor design of recreational areas contributes to many ecological problems.

5. Most research done on resource impact problems has focused on vegetation and soils . . . . An understanding of the full range of impacts associated with recreational use is limited, as is an understanding of the dynamics of the impact process. These shortcomings limit the ability of managers to minimize environmental impacts (47-55).

Leisure Service Management and Resource Recreation Decision-Making

There are several broad techniques or managerial strategies available that can be used by leisure service managers to provide an optimal recreation area working within its carrying capacity: (1) reduce the amount of use through restrictions, (2) accommodate more use by supplying additional opportunities, (3) modify the character of use to reduce its impact, or (4) broaden the resource base to increase its resiliency. These broad strategies embrace many specific actions, including mandatory permits, user fees, information and education programs, regulations, and zoning. Management actions may be categorized as either direct or indirect. "Direct management actions focus on visitor behavior, offering little or no freedom of choice. Mandatory permits and regulations are examples. Indirect management actions attempt to influence visitor behavior while preserving some freedom of choice. Information and education programs and user fees are examples" (Stankey and Manning 1986, 53).

Leisure service professionals need to understand the relationships between ecological and social factors in setting carrying capacities and that making managerial decisions impacts the physical environment just as various factors influence the social environment.

Recreation blends with creation. By preserving and experiencing the outdoors, human beings learn about life in its fullest dimension—a holistic, integrated dimension— by absorbing and encountering the totality of their existence. From such experiences, whether in an urban park, game preserve, seashore, mountain, or desert environment, human beings return re-created. The necessity for leisure service managers to comprehend the totality and mix of human and nonhuman factors in program design becomes more important with each succeeding year.

Additional Trends

The following are some additional trends reported by Godbey (1986) that impact leisure service delivery:

1. Leisure activity is likely to become more highly planned and deliberate. Both natural and human constructed environments are likely to benefit and be affected by people bunched together in shorter time blocks.
2. Qualitative aspects of the recreation and leisure experience will increasingly become more important to the participant. With a better educated, older, more economically constrained population, people will seek high quality in both leisure products and leisure experience.
3. No massive increases in participation in outdoor recreation are likely. More people are traveling to state and national parks and most forms of outdoor recreation continue to increase. However, as baby-boomers age, they are less likely to participate in outdoor recreation. While the recurrence of most forms of outdoor recreation is negatively correlated with age or life stage, Kelly (1978) counters that drops in oil prices, weakened dollar overseas, and more time flexibility will likely increase certain forms of participation in recreation resources-based environments.
4. Tourism and leisure activity involving travel are likely to increase. As the demographic character of the population shifts from two-parent, two-child to single partner, nonfamily households, more individuals are likely to be better able to travel.
5. Leisure services in the public sector must be refitted to meet the needs of the changing demographic composition and social conditions of the public. The increased number of one-parent households, more day-care services and after school programs for latchkey children, and other social services appropriate to single partner families are needed. A reemergence of neighborhood parks and local community centers to counterbalance shopping mall mania seems appropriate, but must be accomplished with more interesting, complex, and multidimensional areas and facilities to accommodate demand and need (1-8).

The Community As a System

As can be interpreted from the dynamic forces that impact on society—socially, environmentally, politically, and technologically—there is need for a useful framework providing leisure service managers with a basis for decision making that incorporates the complexity, ever-changing nature, and interdependence of all elements in community life. A most helpful perspective is a general systems theory of an ecological-transactional framework.

A system may be defined as: "A complex of elements or components directly or indirectly related in a causal network, such that each component is related to at least some others in a more or less stable way within a particular period of time" (Buckley 1967, 41).

The human organism is an example of a biological system. The body is composed of several separate but interdependent parts. While each part or organ works independently, the condition of one affects the condition and behavior of others. All must work in harmony if the human system is to continue to operate effectively. Much like this illustration of a biological organism, the community can be viewed as a social organism composed of a variety of separate organizations and institutions tied together in a widespread, interrelated social network. According to Hill (1971), social systems are characterized by four properties:

1. The tasks they perform to meet the needs and demands of their members and those of their environment.
2. The interrelatedness of positions or the interdependence of component parts that form their structures.
3. Boundary maintenance proclivities that serve to differentiate them from other social systems in their environment.
4. Equilibrium and adaptive propensities that tend to ensure their viability as social systems.

Tasks of Social Systems

The task-performing property of social systems pertains to the functions they are expected to perform. Recreation and leisure service agencies, whether they are public, private and commercial, or voluntary and nonprofit organizations, are expected to provide a myriad of recreation opportunities for people to enjoy. The form the activity takes, perceived benefits, degree of complexity, and desired outcomes vary for each individual, and are largely a matter of participant choice.

Interdependence of Component Parts

The concept of interdependence or interrelatedness of positions that constitute a system refers to interacting and reciprocal positions and roles within a system's structure. Implied in the concept of system position are those roles performed if the system is to fulfill its functions. In recreation and leisure service agencies, each staff member has a function to fulfill. As we present later in Chapter 3, the basic purpose of the leisure service worker is to encourage and facilitate recreation behavior on the part of the participant so that the individual's life is in some way enriched. The professional worker does this directly with the consumer through teaching or leading an activity or event, or indirectly by developing budgets, training staff, renegotiating building permits or leases, or advocating for changes in the community that benefit the consumers or clients with whom one works. Niepoth (1983) provides an illustration of this perspective: "the recreation superintendent might appear before the board of directors of the transit agency to encourage them to offer Sunday bus service, which would permit more older adults to use the city recreation centers" (21).

Boundary Maintenance

The boundary of any system may be conceptualized as the demarcation line that separates the system from its environment. It may be discerned through differences in the nature and intensity of patterns of interaction that take place within the system and between the system and the external environment. Thus, in relation to public recreation and leisure agencies, the boundary pertains to interactive patterns within their relational networks that differ in degree and kind from those occurring between these agencies and their social units and nongovernmental organizations, such as families, workplaces, schools, churches, commercial theme parks, and private health clubs (see Chapter 3 for a more detailed analysis of the difference between public, voluntary nonprofit, and commercial recreation and leisure agencies).

Equilibrium and Adaptation

This system perspective assumes a range of possible states within which a system can function and to which it can adapt. States of equilibrium and adaptation are made possible through negative and positive feedback processes, which can be beneficial or harmful in their consequences. Negative feedback processes operate to reduce the mismatch between information about a system's performance and its basic values, triggering behaviors to bring about a convergence between the two when they diverge. Thus, with respect to recreation and leisure agencies, for example, public outcry from older citizens who state they cannot participate in certain programs offered at the senior citizens' center results in recreation agencies looking elsewhere within the community system, perhaps to the local transit authority, for reduced or free bus fares for older persons. This action serves to trigger one system's behavior (public recreation and leisure service agency) in order to enable a subsystem (older persons within a community) to participate more fully in community life.

Positive feedback, on the other hand, is a deviation amplifying rather than reducing the process, which like negative feedback also begins with error or mismatched information about a system's behaviors in relation to internal system standards or external criteria (Zimmerman 1983). Positive feedback processes are viewed as instructive and system-enhancing, contributing to the maintenance of system viability, and are considered essential to the morphogenic processes through which systems grow and change. In relation to recreation and leisure agencies, for example, overwhelming positive response to a new waterslide in a public park operated by a private vendor, who charges a reasonable fee suggests that the public is willing to support private and commercial ventures in the public domain when they coincide with and reinforce community values and expectations. This situation may well serve to foster an even wider incorporation of private-for-profit recreation ventures in public, tax-supported organizations, such as tennis, racquetball or squash centers, golf courses, fitness complexes, or baseball and softball operations.

The morphogenic process by which systems grow and change can take many forms. Some possible contributing factors are as follows:

1. A dramatic change in intercomponent relationships, such as a corporate employee recreation program linking up with a public recreation agency to use its lighted baseball fields for league play.
2. A change in system values, purposes, and standards, as may occur when the Boys Club officially opens its membership to girls.
3. A change in internal and external input operations, such as the unionizing of county park operations employees and their participation in a variety of work-scheduling decisions or in the case of a President's Commission formed to study the nation's outdoors and make recommendations on the country's future leisure resource needs.
4. The ascendance of components with new and different properties governing and managing the system, as illustrated by the takeover of a large commercial theme park by a city administrative structure.

Interacting Subsystems

The social systems perspective provides a particularly helpful philosophical and operational way to conceptualize relationships and provides a basis for formulating action-oriented methods for enhancing the quality of life within a community. In this context the systems perspective, a social ecological view, is composed of a variety of systems and subsystems (see Figure 1.5). At the core of the overall system is the individual organism. Embedded in the human organism is a number of social systems. The organism has direct interaction with social systems and indirect relationships with others. A number of micro- or subsystems, work, school, religion, recreation and leisure, and family represent a pattern of activities, roles, and interpersonal relations experienced by the developing person in a given setting with particular physical and material characteristics (Bronfenbrenner, 1977).

Figure 1.5 Transactions Between Systems

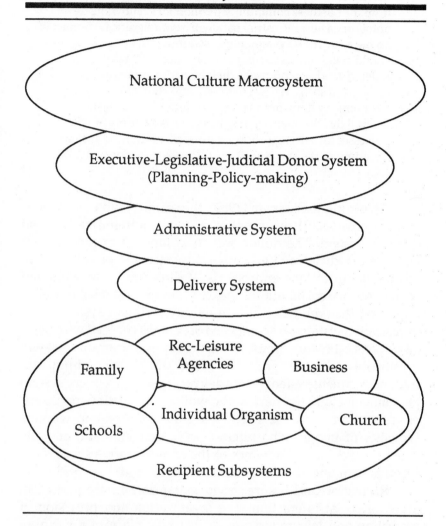

Source: U. Bronfenbrenner. 1979. The Ecology of Human Development. Cambridge, Mass.: Harvard University Press. p. 22.

Together, a group of organisms and particular microsystems constitute the recipient system for specific social policies and programs. This interrelationship of the community subsystem, whether it be leisure services, education, religion, or business, will have some effect, directly or indirectly, on other members of the overall community, as suggested by the following example:

the decision of the city council (government) under pressure from the business community (economic) to allow the development of a new industrial park will have a significant impact on the recreation system. Increased industrial development would mean increased population, soaring land prices, reordered land use priorities, heightened competition for tax dollars and so on. We can see, then, how the desires of people (economic system) are manifested through a subsystem (industrial development) that in turn affects a variety of related processes (urban expansion, land-use planning) and systems, including parks and recreation (Murphy and Howard 1977, 130).

According to Seidman (1983), the national and cultural system (macrosystem) incorporates a donor, administrative, and delivery system. The donor system, composed of government legislative, judicial, and executive subsystems in private philanthropic organizations and boards of directors of business and human service corporations, makes plans and establishes policy regarding the well-being of community recipient systems. Administrative systems are composed of persons charged with overall responsibility for administering the various programs that will presumably solve the "problem." Interacting with the administrative and recipient systems is the delivery system. Delivery system personnel include teachers, social workers, recreation managers, police officers, and the like. This group of first-line workers "consists of people who interact with recipients and actually provide, under the guidelines of the administrative system, the services mandated by the donor system." (Goodman 1973, 87).

Recreation and leisure service organizations are part of an arena of social interaction. The organization and provision of recreation and leisure services do not take place in a vacuum. Leisure service organizations, whether they be public, private, or commercial, are all linked in some form to the larger community system. From such an ecological-systems framework, it would be incorrect not to realize that private and public realms are interdependent. One should recognize that whatever level of analysis or operational input one chooses to intersect (e.g., state or province), it is embedded in a series of hierarchically ordered systems.

There are many stakeholders throughout the system and subsystem levels, and while each has a stake in multiple systems and subsystems, some subsystems exert more powerful influence over people's behavior than do others. It is important to understand the needs, values, and culture of the recipients by those individuals in systems that plan, administer, and implement social policy and intervention. If there is little or no assessment of client-consumer-participant subsystem way of life, there can be little efficacy in the transactions that occur. This information provides the basis for the delivery system and the likelihood of successful implementation, since it is the only direct linkage between the administrative system and recipient system. Obviously, successful implementation is further assured from the degree of support and cooperation of other systems.

Systems Model and Holistic Leisure Service Delivery

The incorporation of a systems approach is deemed the most relevant philosophical and operational perspective for understanding the dynamics of leisure service because leisure ideally represents a holistic integration of a person's physical, mental, and spiritual needs. As will be discussed later in Chapter 4, the leisure service delivery system is best viewed from an ecological-systems perspective. Murphy and Howard (1977) comment on the ecology of leisure service:

> The field has a responsibility to the whole person and can meet it only by recognizing the interrelationships among people in their physical and social environment, and the way these relationships influence, or are influenced by, various social and organizational processes (119).

The elements of the delivery system—social environment, physical environment, clients, consumers, or participants, the leisure service organizations—and the interdependent elements of the community recipient subsystem can best be understood and interpreted from an ecological-social systems perspective. The human organism is a dynamic, interacting composition of many different interdependent parts. This is true for other material and nonmaterial elements that interact throughout society.

Leisure as a Subsystem of the Community System

For a growing number of people, the sense of "community," a feeling of attachment to a community-shared set of goals and way of life, transcends kinship ties, geography, and social distance barriers. The traditional social web of relationships, once embedded in the context of the nuclear family, are being replaced in more North American households by an elastic, and mobile community network based on people's mutual compatibility and shared interests (Gray and Pelegrino 1973).

As related earlier in this chapter, a new sense of community, based on greater individual flexibility for both men and women, with respect to vocational choice, housing relationships and leisure options, has evolved for many people. For those individuals, community life appears to center around commonly held leisure interests and lifestyle preferences. This means that social and political communities will be distinguished not so much by family composition, ethnicity, or geographical orientation, but rather will reflect distinctive lifestyles, including social relationships, housing patterns, dress, and mores emanating from leisure styles and interests.

Given the highly mobile nature of many American and Canadian urban communities, participation is temporary and voluntary. Individuals will stay involved as long as they are motivated to participate in the community and will stop when they are not or when they move on. Such persons are neither rooted to the land as their forbearers were, nor feel a deep conviction to "make the best of it." They seek instead the satisfaction and feedback derived from their self-selected preferences. Their own needs become paramount in decisions involving choice and participation in activities; kinship and work obligations hold less significance. Thus, the recreation and leisure service system—public, private nonprofit, and commercial recreation organizations—in any geographical area serves as the locus of community life and possibly as the primary generator of values and the nucleus of communication, participation, and involvement for more and more people.

New Paradigm for Leisure in Community Life

Individual perceptions contribute to how one views the world, gathers information, solves problems, and defines how one participates in community life. These perceptions have largely been based on a series of assumptions derived from a notion that the external, material world exists independent and apart from the mind and spirit. This mechanistic world view that has dominated twentieth century thinking was formulated in seventeenth century science by Galileo, Descartes, Newton, Bacon, and others. Howe-Murphy and Murphy (1987) give its basic principles:

1. People are viewed in isolation of their environment and can be understood in terms of their 'parts'. That is, individuals are compartmentalized into separate mind, body and spirit components.
2. Phenomena occur along a linear plane and can be explained by cause and effect relationships.
3. The empirical or scientific model is the way to identify cause and effect relationships, thereby explaining phenomena.

These perceptions have influenced most Western traditions and dominated all scientific thought. The mechanistic view of leisure has resulted for the most part in people perceiving that there is a direct linear relationship between the organization of work, steadfast toil, and the existence of leisure in one's life. This materialistic, economic view has served as the basis for the organization of leisure service in community life. Recreation and leisure agencies were organized in the late nineteenth century to provide wholesome, character-building play opportunities and respite from toil for children, youth, and adults. Leisure service and other social and human service agencies were created because an industrial age fabricated a way of life that segmented daily living and created a strong division of labor. One's whole self was not valued as much as one's being able to fill a slot on the assembly line. Natural, biological rhythms so necessary in an agrarian society were replaced by mechanical, artificial rhythms—an industrial work pattern.

The emergence of quantum physics since the turn of the twentieth century, a perspective proposing that mind and matter are intricate reflections of one another, ushered in a new paradigm that brought seemingly disparate areas of physics and spirituality together. This shifting world view perception has been noted by many health, social, behavioral, and natural science scholars (see Table 1.3).

Such a holistic, ecological perspective represents a new vision of reality that will form the basis of our future technologies, economic systems, and social institutions. Howe-Murphy and Murphy (1987) outline the principles of the New Age/Consciousness paradigm:

Table 1.3 Comparison of Mechanistic/Scientific and Holistic/Systems Paradigms[Δ]

Mechanistic/Scientific Paradigm[1]	Holistic/Systems Paradigm[2]
• Tendency toward intervention and uses of technological/scientific approaches to solve problems.	• Desire not to impose solution.
• Techniques become dogma—spontaneity is lost.	• Programmers/managers try to prepare environment for people to work things out themselves.
• Process/experience is secondary. Conclusion/result/product is more important than process.	• Process/experience is primary.
• Programmer intervenes by offering new programs but doesn't look for clues in total environment.	• Programmer extends delivery system roles: facilitator educator advocate.
• Programmer looks for single mechanism to solve problems rather than broadly comprehensive issues.	• World is seen as fundamentally interdependent: mind/body/spirit inseparably connected.

[Δ]James F. Murphy, Department of Recreation and Leisure Studies, San Francisco State University

[1]Mechanistic/Scientific Paradigm: Professional leisure service programmer/manager organizes, structures, and conducts opportunities for participants.
[2]Holistic/Systems Paradigm: Professional leisure service programmer/manager intrudes minimally—creates an environment conducive to self-expression for participants.

Table 1.3 *Continued*

Mechanistic/Scientific Paradigm[1]	Holistic/Systems Paradigm[2]
• Programmers isolate organism from natural/social environments.	• Process of life (mental) takes place in a physical structure (body): *Every movement* is an expression of consciousness.
• Growth is equated with quantitative (GNP), consumptive aspects.	• We use our body as a mechanism to express spiritual consciousness—Growth is a dynamic process that results from balanced expression.

[1]Mechanistic/Scientific Paradigm: Professional leisure service programmer/manager organizes, structures, and conducts opportunities for participants.
[2]Holistic/Systems Paradigm: Professional leisure service programmer/manager intrudes minimally—creates an environment conducive to self-expression for participants.

1. The mind, body and spirit are integrated. This configuration needs to be recognized in every form of human activity.
2. The individual and his or her total environment are interdependent and mutually influence each other.
3. The inner consciousness is connected intricately with global consciousness (44).

This new world view emphasizes the interconnectedness and interdependence of all phenomena. Critical to this new paradigm is the underlying assumption that it is the individual who determines what is intrinsically satisfying and noteworthy (and, therefore, what contributes to leisure experience), not the structure (recreation center, hospital, or park), or the environment induced by others.

Gray (1987, 150-151) states that an emerging paradigm (refer to Table 1.4) is mostly a reflection of members of society and not service providers. In some way this paradigm shift indicates a change in a set of conceptual and operational assumptions for community life. At the core of the new paradigm developed by Gray, recreation and leisure experiences are not viewed in isolation from the rest of a person's life. Rather, the goals of public recreation programs are linked to human development and community-wide needs.

Table 1.4 Old and New Paradigms for Public Recreation Agencies

The traditional paradigm assumes that public reaction agencies will:	The new paradigm assumes that public reaction agencies will:
Provide equal services to all the citizens.	Provide services based on social and economic need.
Provide programs consisting of a series of activities selected from a restricted list of recreation pursuits.	Provide programs of human service that may go far beyond traditional recreation activities.
Act as a direct service provider.	Act as a community organizer and catalyst in matching community resources to citizen need.
Offer programs in department facilities.	Offer programs anywhere in the community.
Provide staff leadership of the activities.	Use staff resources to coach citizens until they can provide their own leadership.
Fund basic services from tax sources.	Fund services from a variety of sources, including fee-for-service, donations, sale of services, contract arrangements, barter, agency partnerships, and cooperation with the private sector, as well as tax resources.
Plan by up-dating the past.	Plan by anticipating a preferred future, organizing services around client groups in response to participants' felt needs and a careful analysis.

Table 1.4 *Continued*

The traditional paradigm assumes that public reaction agencies will:	The new paradigm assumes that public reaction agencies will:
Plan programs with the staff.	Plan with potential clients, community informants, other agencies, political figures, and corporations, as well as with staff.
Encourage participation by publicity.	Develop a marketing approach to operations.
Evaluate results primarily in terms of attendance.	Evaluate services in terms of human consequences.
Motivate the staff to work *for* the people.	Motivate the staff to work *with* the people.
Justify budgets in terms of historical precedent.	Justify budgets in terms of social need and program results.
Require financial accountability.	Require financial and program accountability.
Achieve the ultimate goal of a fine recreation program.	Achieve the ultimate goals of human development and community organization.

Leisure Service—A Systems Model

The emergence of a new model for leisure service is an optimistic development, one that views leisure expression as a fundamental, developmental response of the human organism. Leisure in this context is not perceived as an isolated, primarily physical or emotional release. Instead, each individual is inextricably linked to others in the community.

Thus, from a systems view, each organism and subsystem within the community is seen not in isolation but in terms of relationships and integration. Living systems are not confined to individual organisms and their parts; rather systems are integrated wholes whose properties can be reduced to those of smaller units. The same aspects of wholeness are exhibited by social systems—such as a family or community— and by ecosystems that consist of a variety of organisms and inanimate matter in mutual interaction.

The essence of leisure expression for any human being is holistic, with the specific structure occurring as a result of the interactions and interdependence of each part of the organism. Leisure expression reflects the whole person. Although we can discern individual parts in any system (physical, social, emotional, mental benefits, and so on), the nature of the whole is always different from the mere sum of its parts.

A systems perspective also recognizes the inherently dynamic nature of inanimate matter and living organisms. Each organism is embedded in larger social and ecological systems. Each living system, then, is a part and a whole at the same time, and accordingly has two opposite tendencies: an integrative tendency to function as a part of the larger whole, and a self-assertive tendency to preserve its individual autonomy (Capra 1986).

In a healthy system, a balance exists between self-assertion and integration. Indeed, leisure service agencies ideally provide a full range of opportunities, from agency organized and conducted services to individually encouraged and self-directed expressions, both leading to leisure independence and integration within the larger community. For an organism to be healthy, it has to preserve its individual autonomy, but at the same time must be able to integrate itself harmoniously into the larger systems. Whereas other subsystems of family, neighborhood, and work traditionally provided a symbolic connection of the individual to community life, leisure has grown as a form of self-expression for individuals and a means in which shared interests, representative of one's lifestyle, provide a more appealing and relevant integration with others.

Summary

Recreation and leisure service agencies are one of the components contributing to the make-up of community life. Leisure services have emerged as a primary structure for the enhancement of community life in the latter quarter of the twentieth century.

Leisure, evolving from social, economic, and familial conditions in North American culture in the mid-nineteenth century, is a physical and material structure that serves as (1) a surrogate parent for children and youth, or (2) a vehicle for creating opportunities for people to establish social bonds, or (3) a physical resource that provides open space and play areas for communities. Also, leisure is increasingly being recognized as a central concept of human expression that provides a basis for people to consciously or unconsciously pursue activities connecting them symbolically to each other and thus reinforcing a "moral" sense of community. Thus, through leisure expression, individuals are more likely to be committed to themselves and their associations.

The changing nature of community has evolved from one based on kinship, permanence, and rootedness to the land, to one that is more mobile, with greater adherence by individuals to an identification with others who represent a compatible lifestyle of shared values and interests.

There are a number of factors contributing to the reshaping of community life, including several influencing factors or megatrends identified by Naisbitt. Conditions affected by changes in the social environment that have corresponding implications for leisure service include: demographic shifts, attitudes toward health, work, and leisure, technological developments, and basic values.

Influencing factors impacting the physical environment include: increased demand for home-based leisure, spread of shopping malls, increases in travel, tourism and outdoor recreation adventure trips, population shifts to the South and West of the United States, more demand for local community-specialized leisure programs and services, increased expectation of qualitative, intrinsic, and spiritual experiences, and balancing carrying capacity with recreation use. Leisure service managers need to comprehend the totality of mix of human and nonhuman factors in program design.

The emerging New Age Consciousness paradigm emphasizes the interconnectedness and interdependence of all phenomena. This paradigm is replacing (in general as well as in recreation and leisure service organizations) a mechanistic, linear, and segmental view adopted by North American society in the nineteenth century. The fundamental premises of the evolving New Age paradigm are that the mind, body, and spirit are integrated, and the individual and the total environment depend upon and influence each other. Thus, recreation and leisure experiences are not viewed in isolation from the rest of a person's life.

Leisure service delivery, to be optimally efficient and effective in providing people and communities with worthwhile opportunities for self-expression, should be viewed and operationally structured from a systems perspective. Recreation and leisure service organizations do not take place in a vacuum. Leisure service organizations—public tax-supported, private nonprofit, and commercial— are all linked in some form to the larger community system. When viewed from a systems perspective, the elements of the leisure service delivery system—social environment, physical environment, participants, and leisure service organizations—provide an operationally sound way of coordinating and optimizing leisure experience. This conceptual management perspective, also identified as a holistic-ecological framework, blends with the individual's natural tendency toward the quest for integration of mind, body, and spirit and the community's desire for moral commitment, association, and participation.

References

Ardell, Donald B. 1986. *High level wellness*, 2nd ed. Berkeley, CA: Ten Speed Press.

Bronfenbrenner, Urie. 1977. *The ecology of human development.* Cambridge, MA: Harvard University Press.

Buckley, Walter. 1967. *Sociology and modern systems theory.* Englewood Cliffs, NJ: Prentice-Hall.

Capra, Fritjof. 1986. Wholeness and health. *Holistic Medicine* 1:145-159.

Carrington, David. 1977. The values of younger workers. *Business Horizons* 20:18-30.

Emmerichs, Jeffrey and Heidi Kofford. 1986. A well-being group for adolescents in an acute psychiatric setting. *Therapeutic Recreation Journal* 20:57.

Godbey, Geoffrey. 1986. Some selected societal trends and their impact on recreation and leisure. In *President's commission on Americans outdoors—Leisure review.* Washington, D.C.: U. S. Government Printing Office.

Goodman, L. 1973. Bridging the gap between social research and public policy and welfare, a case in point. *Journal of Applied Behavioral Science* 9:87.

Gray, David E. 1987. Managing our way to a preferred future. In *Current issues in leisure services: Looking ahead in a time of transition,* Joseph J. Bannon, ed. Washington, D.C.: International City Managers Association.

Gray David E. and Donald A. Pelegrino, eds. 1973. *Reflections on recreation and park movement.* Dubuque, IA: Wm.C. Brown Company Publishers.

Hill, R. 1971. Modern system theory and the family: A confrontation. *Social Science Information* 10:7-26.

Howe-Murphy, Roxanne L. and James F. Murphy. 1987. An exploration of the new age/consciousness paradigm in therapeutic recreation. In *Philosophy of therapeutic recreation: Ideas and issues,* Charles Sylvester et al., eds. Alexandria, VA: National Recreation Association.

Kelly, John R. 1978. *Outdoor recreation prediction: A comparative analysis.* Champaign, IL: University of Illinois.

Kraus, Richard. 1984. *Recreation and leisure in modern society,* 3rd ed. Glenview, IL: Scott, Foresman and Company.

McDowell, C. Forest. 1983. *Leisure wellness: Concepts and helping strategies.* Eugene, OR: Sun Moon Press.

Murphy, James F., and Dennis R. Howard. 1977. *Delivery of community leisure services.* Philadelphia: Lea & Febiger.

Naisbitt, John. 1982. *Megatrends.* New York: Warner Books.

Niepoth, E. William. 1983. *Leisure leadership: Working with people in recreation and park settings.* Englewood Cliffs, NJ: Prentice-Hall.

Seidman, Edward, ed. 1983. Introduction. *Handbook of social intervention.* Beverly Hills, CA: Sage Publications.

Skrzyeki, Cindy. 1987. Risk takers. *U. S. News and World Report* Jan 26:60-67.

Solomon, Jolie. 1986. Working at relaxation. *Wall Street Journal* April 21:10.

Stankey, George H. and Robert E. Manning. 1986. Carrying capacity of recreational settings. In *President's commission on Americans outdoors.* Washington, D.C.: United States Government Printing Office.

Toffler, Alvin. 1970. *Future shock.* New York: Bantam Books.

Toffler, Alvin. 1981. *The third wave.* New York: Bantam Books.

United States Congress. 1973. Secs 2(a)1 and 2(3) *Endangered Species Act.* 84 STAT 884.

Wirth, Louis. 1972. Liberalism as a way of life. In *Social change in urban America.* Max Birnbaum and John Mogey, eds. New York: Harper and Row.

Yankelovich, Daniel. 1981. New rules in American life: search for self-fulfillment in a world turned upside down. *Psychology Today* 15:35-91.

Zimmerman, Shirley. 1983. Government and families as integrating systems. In *Handbook of social intervention,* Edward Seidman, ed. Beverly Hills, CA: Sage Publications, Inc.

2

CONCEPTS OF HUMAN BEHAVIOR, LEISURE, WORK, AND TIME

As we presented in Chapter 1, leisure is interrelated with all other elements or subsystems of community life. This chapter provides an overview of the essential aspects of human behavior, leisure, work, time, and world view concepts in nineteenth and twentieth century Western culture (see Figure 2.1).

Views of Human Behavior

The phenomenon of leisure has evoked an immense variety of interpretations among scholars about its origin, meaning, benefits, problems, and place in society. Many of these views offer diverse expressions of the human condition. It is necessary to first postulate how the definer of leisure perceives human behavior. Once this is understood, it is then possible to explore the influence of social, psychological, and environmental antecedents of leisure and be able to make judgments about leisure's varied meanings upon the social and personal worlds of individuals. Chapter 5 also contains information about human and leisure behavior. In this section, we want to set a framework for looking at different views of leisure.

50

Figure 2.1 Dynamic Conceptualization of Time, Work, Leisure, and Human Behavior in 19th and 20th Century Western Culture.

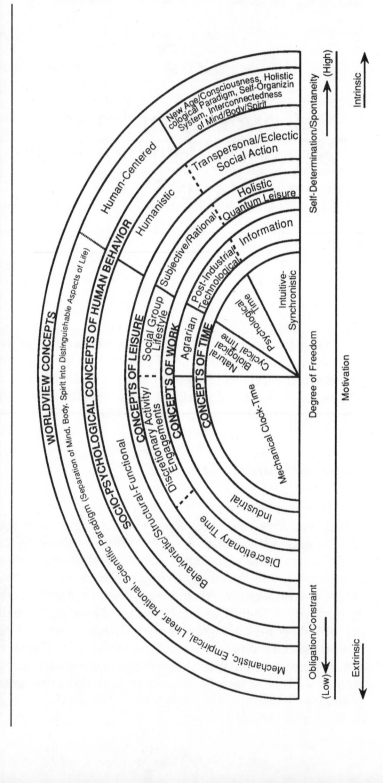

Two of the most commonly accepted perspectives of interpreting human behavior are the structural-functional view, serving as a sociological orientation, and the social-action view representing a psychological model of human nature. The structural-functional perspective emphasizes the importance of institutional and societal forces in shaping and constraining human behavior. The social-action model views the nature of reality from a subjective and experiential perspective "with the greater weight being given the importance of general cognitive factors in determining the outcome of the interplay between Homo Sapiens and the environment" (Murphy 1981, 52).

A structural-functional paradigm suggests that the institutional framework of society provides the social structure for the presence of leisure. One's obligations must first be met, and then leisure becomes a residual reward for work. A social-action model recognizes that an individual's own goal setting and behavior will condition his or her attempts at fulfillment through leisure experiences. Leisure in this perspective suggests it is an integral part of his or her life as a whole, and each individual determines his or her own goals and attempts to realize them accordingly through his or her own way of life.

Growing evidence points to a paradigmatic shift in the study of human behavior (Csikszentmihayli 1976). Most interpretations of behavior incorporate learning theory in that it is generally accepted that organisms modify their behavior in terms of external contingencies of reinforcement (Csikszentmihayli 1976, 6). Such a view determines that control over rewards—and therefore over behavior—resides outside the organism. One would then typically infer that the enjoyment people experience from leisure pursuits is reducible to a chain of conditioned associations originating from an initial set of extrinsic rewards (Csikszentmihayli 1976, 6).

Another more recent view suggests that external rewards become motivating only when they conform to a person's intentions. Leisure from this interpretation provides an open stimulus and arousal-seeking model of human behavior supplanting the purely stimulus-reduction view described above. This more recent study of leisure behavior leads to a conception of human motivation that emphasizes the individual striving to maximize control over increasingly complex challenges in the environment by developing his or her skills.

Mechanistic Approach to Leisure

Scientific determinism and reductionism led to an analytic method of reasoning that breaks up thoughts and problems into pieces and arranges them in their logical order. This approach has become an essential characteristic of modern scientific thought. While this has proved extremely useful for the development of scientific theories and technology, an "overemphasis in the Cartesian method has led to the fragmentation that is characteristic of both our general thinking and our academic disciplines, to the widespread attitude of reductionism is secure—the belief that all aspects of complex phenomena can be understood by reducing them to their constituent parts" (Capra 1986, 146).

In this world view, leisure is seen as a segment of a human's behavior and reducible to interpretation by (1) observing one's overt actions (playing volleyball, hiking, or knitting), or (2) interpreting one's psychological needs by inventorying a person's attitudes toward unconnected nonwork activities or events, or the time when certain events occur. Leisure occurs in this context as a result of earned free time. It is a voluntary expression in which an individual experiences a high degree of personal freedom and is intrinsically motivated. The work rhythm of life provides only a few of these time segments each day, slightly larger blocks on weekends, and longer but interspersed vacations throughout the remainder of the year, so that the leisure experience originates not so much from the free will of the individual, but from the structure and values provided by the mechanistic framework of society.

Ecological-Systems Approach to Society and Leisure

The emerging systems approach to living organisms provides another way to conceptualize human behavior and a holistic conceptual basis for leisure. As presented in Chapter 1, the systems view looks at the world in terms of relationships and integration of all elements, material and nonmaterial. Systems are integrated wholes whose properties cannot be reduced to those of smaller units and whose specific structures arise from the interactions and interdependence of their parts. There are interconnections and an interdependence among all systems levels (community institutions such as family, work, church, and education), each level interacting and communicating with its total environment.

A systems view is an ecological view. It emphasizes the interrelatedness and interdependence of all phenomena and the dynamic nature of living systems. Capra (1986) explains: "A living system is a self-organizing system, which means that its order is not imposed by the environment but is established by the system itself. In other words, self-organizing systems exhibit a certain degree of autonomy. This does not mean that living systems are isolated from their environment; on the contrary; they interact with it continually, but this interaction does not determine their organization" (149).

A strong mechanistic orientation to scientific thinking and everyday application has limited the potential benefits of leisure in specific time blocks. This segmentation of leisure indeed makes it easier to categorize and identify for purposes of scientific inquiry, but does not transmit the core or essence of one's total self because the tools used to gather data and the source of explanation largely represent the material, rational world. The unseen, intuitive, spiritual aspects of a person cannot be rationally observed or documented. A holistic systems approach suggests that meaning is found in the totality of interactions that transcend leisure activities, community events, institutional structures, clock time, and even human understanding. The dynamic nature of human beings can be seen as processes of self-maintenance. Capra (1986) states:

> What makes the understanding of living systems quite difficult is the fact that they have not only a tendency to maintain themselves in their dynamic state but, at the same time, also show a tendency to transcend themselves, to reach out creatively beyond their boundaries and limitations to generate new structures and new forms of organization. This principle of self-transcendence manifests itself in the processes of learning, development and evolution (150).

Philosophical Roots of Leisure

The concept of a free, intrinsically motivated expression of self, leisure, was introduced to Western civilization by Aristotle.

This ancient, classical interpretation was derived from *skole*, referring to a place where one was permitted to engage in scholarly pursuits and where one found respite without distraction. It was viewed as time to oneself, a state of being achieved through learning—a style of existence. *Skole* came to mean the goal, or end, of life. Aristotle believed leisure was essential so that citizens could carry on the business of government, law, debate, culture and contemplation.

The term "leisure" is derived from the Latin word *otium*—or "to be permitted to abstain from occupation or service." This interpretation was a direct reference to the Athenian ideal (*licere*) of absolving a select few citizens from daily physical toil (*ponos* in Greece and *negotium* in Latin) and freeing them to engage in intellectual, cultural, civic and artistic endeavors. Leisure, the essence of culture according to the ancient Greek ideal, had nothing to do with material concern and was strongly linked to individual freedom, self-determination, and an immunity from occupational requirements. Leisure was the basis or essence of culture and therefore of community life.

Askolia, the Greek word for mental toil, is the opposite of *skole*. The parallel ancient Roman term for leisure was *otium*, and its opposite, *negotium*, the term for work. This Greco-Roman perspective of leisure was seen as thus:

> Whether *skole* . . . . for the Greeks or *otium* for the Romans, it was for them a serious business of life. They managed their livelihoods and engaged in politics and political discussion. They learned music and played it and enjoyed the physical areas of war and sport. They were skilled in intellectual conversation, and that consumed much time. But they rarely had an interest in talking about hard work and ordinary labor or even cared to understand its meaning. In their way of life there was no hurry. The scholar or the religious man was quite within the meaning of the notion of leisure if he did nothing but sit and contemplate (Anderson 1964,91).

Leisure in this early context served as the basis for individual freedom and cultivation of a person's total physical, social, intellectual, spiritual and artistic self. But the powerful influence of the Protestant Reformation began to focus all human energy on the secular life. Intellectual wisdom was replaced with material wealth, reason with desire, leisure with work. Many social historians have noted that because of the seventeenth century's scientific thinking and developments spurred by the onset of the Industrial Revolution, a new pattern of community life was created. Galileo, Descartes, Newton and Bacon articulated the transformation that took place in all aspects of community life. Their writings and scientific discoveries led to the mechanization of time, work, and leisure. The incorporation of rational, deterministic, reductionist thinking into every aspect of community life led to a total reformation and redefinition of leisure that gained credibility: leisure as "time free from work." Leisure was to occur only after one's obligations and work requirements had been met.

Culture became the basis of leisure in nineteenth century Western society, in contrast with Greek civilization 2000 years earlier when leisure served as the wellspring of culture. The classical Greek idea of leisure as the contemplative life and the pursuit of the highest human aspects of truth and wisdom was destroyed during developments in Western culture by those seeking to establish labor, in an expanding market economy, as our unique human capacity. This resulted in the promotion of work and humans as primarily economic beings, as the foundation of culture.

Concepts of Leisure

There are three dominant views in behavioral science devoted to the study of human experience. Each uses official theoretical perspectives to describe and interpret why people engage in human activity, including leisure. One dominant view, a behavioral perspective, focuses on observable, objective aspects of human participation. This behaviorist approach holds that the elements of the environment stimulating the individual (and in turn the observable response of the individual to these stimuli) are central to explaining the meaning of human activity.

The second view, an outgrowth of humanistic psychology, provides a more subjective interpretation of human activity. This approach emphasizes the intrinsic, internal states of the individual. Such an approach is devoted to understanding the ways different people perceive things and the influences of their own self-concepts and attitudes (Niepoth 1983).

A third method of conceptualizing human activity, an integrative perspective, focuses on the interrelationships and interconnections between living organisms and inorganic matter. Such a holistic view suggests that leisure is not a unit, but actually many experiences varying in self-perceived commitment, intensity, and duration. Further, in this perspective, leisure may occur in any milieu, whether in work, religious, family, or transpersonal contexts.

The behavioral conceptualization of leisure incorporates the following temporal and functional views: discretionary time, discretionary activity engagements, social group and lifestyle participation. The subjective conceptualization incorporates the classical or Aristotelian view and psychological perspective. The holistic conceptualization includes social-psychological interpretations and New Age/Consciousness interpretations that identify the leisure state, which may occur in any conscious or unconscious aspect of life.

Objective Conceptualizations of Leisure

The conceptualizations of leisure that use objective parameters have been most frequently used by sociologists. Such perspectives are easier to quantify and are amenable to the predominant theoretical models used to explain and predict human behavior—structural-functional and stimulus-reduction.

Leisure as Discretionary or Residual Time

This perspective emphasizes the freedom or discretion of the person in choosing to participate in desired activities. The residual time definitions of leisure are objective and easily quantifiable and as noted by Tinsley and Tinsley (1982), thereby facilitate documentation and research in leisure. But the Tinsleys comment on four disadvantages of the discretionary or residual time interpretations that outweigh the advantages:

First, they define leisure only in terms of the negation of other activities.

Second, these definitions focus on when the activity happens and ignore information about the nature and quality of what happens.

Third, these definitions are not objective as might be supposed, as evidenced by the difficulty in categorizing time when an individual is involved in more than one activity simultaneously.

Finally, these approaches define work and leisure as mutually exclusive, ignoring the possibility that work and leisure may have a similar psychological impact on the individual (4).

As can be seen from the Tinsleys's critique of the discretionary time perspective, such an approach to viewing leisure does not greatly enhance our understanding of the nature of the role, if any, leisure plays in the development of the individual.

Leisure as Discretionary Behavior

This perspective, articulated by Driver and Tocher (1970), incorporates a broader internal representation of leisure as a human experience beyond merely residual time activity characteristics. This view holds that leisure is an experience pursued by an individual during nonobligated time and represents his or her personal free choice. Leisure engagements involve voluntary participant commitment and they are self-rewarding, that is, they are pursued primarily for their own sake (Driver and Tocher 1970). Therefore, leisure experiences in the behavioral sense occur most often where restraints are minimal and the individual's sense of freedom of choice is high.

The leisure behavior perspective is illustrated in Figure 2.2. This model assumes certain environments will result in leisure experience.

Figure 2.2 Post-Satisfaction/Dissatisfaction Approach to Leisure

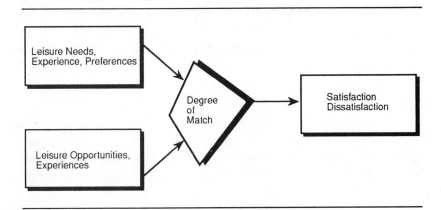

Leisure as a Function of Social Groups and Lifestyle

Social group affiliation and participation provides the most common vehicle for individual leisure experiences. The family represents the most common social unit in which leisure participation occurs. There are three major types of leisure involvement in social groups:

1. Leisure interests (e.g. as reflected in hobbies) cause one to join an existing group with similar interests.
2. Leisure behavior that is central to lifestyle and group formation is based on this leisure interest.
3. Group membership is based on non-leisure factors such as family and friends and demographic identification (e.g., age and gender) that dictate leisure interests and activities.

The norms of leisure behavior manifested through social circles described in number 2 above become reinforced in social worlds that foster certain codes of behavior (Cheek, Field and Burdge 1976). Complete social worlds are organized around leisure interests and are represented by language, rules of behavior, roles, dress code, and even group literature in some cases. Social worlds serve as the environments for social interaction among social groups. They may also have special meanings and symbols that further accentuate differences and distance from outsiders.

Subjective Conceptualizations of Leisure

This conceptual framework of leisure refers to a state of mind or experiential perspective of human behavior. Such a social-psychological orientation focuses particularly upon personal, subjective factors (particularly perceived freedom and intrinsic motivation serving as the basis for leisure experience).

Classical View of Leisure

As discussed earlier, the oldest known view of leisure was derived from Greek culture during the fourth century B.C. and developed by Aristotle. This perspective views leisure as the basis of culture, the end toward which all action is directed. According to this view, leisure is a condition of the soul, a state of being or form of contemplation that involves the pursuit of truth and understanding.

Leisure, according to this classical concept, implies freedom or the absence of needing to be occupied (engaged in work). (Of course, the relatively small number of aristocrats and select citizens were spared from having to engage in toil so that they could freely pursue leisure and engage in intellectual, cultural, civic, and artistic endeavors; this was made possible by a society built on slavery.) In classical Athens, work was understood as the absence of leisure, rather than leisure being understood as the absence of work. In the classical sense, leisure is expressed for its own sake and for no utilitarian purpose.

Psychological View of Leisure

Leisure as a psychological concept refers to an individual's state of mind brought about by an activity freely engaged in and done for its own sake. Neulinger (1976), perhaps the most articulate scholar on the subject comments:

> Leisure has changed from a residual, something inert and negative, to something very much alive, striving, powerful and most certainly positive. It has become a state of mind brought about by a feeling of freedom and a feeling of doing something worthwhile, both highly cherished values in our society. The importance of meaningful personal causation has been seen as an underlying principle of all human behavior (17).

De Charms (1968) suggests that an individual desires to be an Origin rather than a Pawn. The psychological perspective of leisure suggests leisure is not devoted to filling empty time or restoring an individual to a better state of health in order to make him or her a better worker. Rather, the experience of leisure implies that a person's basic needs have been fulfilled and he or she is able to enjoy the satisfaction derived from the intrinsic reward obtained without extrinsic demands.

Leisure, from a psychological view, implies an experience. According to Mannell (1980), it is a transient psychological state, easily interrupted, and characterized by a decreased awareness of the passage of time, decreased awareness of the physical and social surroundings, and an accompanied positive effect (76).

Holistic Conceptualizations of Leisure

A holistic concept of leisure seeks to integrate our understanding of human behavior in that elements of leisure can be expressed in all spheres of life—work, play, education, altered states of consciousness and religion. Since the artificial barriers for demarcation of life are being removed from society (e.g., how and when work must take place, egalitarian social opportunities for all people), the reasons for emphasizing the separation of different aspects of life are no longer necessary to sustain the industrial rhythm of life, nor relevant in explaining the meaning of social relationships.

Social-Psychological View of Leisure

Three prominent interpretations of the social-psychological perspective of leisure are represented by Iso-Ahola, Csikszentmihayli and Tinsley and Tinsley. We will refer to Iso-Ahola and Csikszentmihayli again in Chapter 5.

According to Iso-Ahola (1980) leisure involves situational and social factors and personal experiences that influence the individual's subjective definition of leisure. Further, the individual's definition of leisure and situational factors influences the person's actual leisure behavior. The reverse is also true; one's leisure behavior influences the situational and social factors and one's personal experiences. This view of leisure has three important considerations:

1. The individual and social world in which one experiences leisure behavior is constantly changing.
2. These changes result from an interaction of personal experiences and social influences.
3. The individual is a cognitively active agent in this process.

As articulated by Iso-Ahola, the most important attributes of leisure from a social-psychological perspective are perceived freedom and the need for optimal arousal or incongruity. Iso-Ahola believes that activities primarily engaged in for extrinsic motives will typically be classified as work, and activities primarily pursued by individuals for intrinsic reasons regarded as leisure.

According to Csikszentmihayli (1975), leisure is a state achieved whenever a person optimally interacts with the environment. He identifies this state of playfulness or "flow" with the simultaneous presence of four conditions:

1. The individual is free from obligation.
2. The activity is pursued as a voluntary choice.
3. Participation occurs in a pleasurable pursuit.
4. Activity pursued is culturally recognized as leisure.

Leisure can occur in a shower, on the job, while writing a poem, driving a car, or planting flowers in the garden. According to Csikszentmihayli (1975), flow experiences are momentary, episodic states characterized by: (1) centering of attention on a limited stimulus field, (2) total involvement resulting in a loss of self, 3) loss of anxiety and constraint, (4) disorientation in time and space, (5) enlightened perception, and (6) enjoyment.

Csikszentmihayli contends that we need to understand more about the nature of intrinsic rewards. We spend countless resources motivating people to do things they do not like doing or to keep them in line with social controls. Artificially imposed motivation obliges them to do things at school, work, or play that they really do not enjoy, and so they need to recuperate in leisure activities from the meaningless routines that fail to provide intrinsic motivation. By understanding how intrinsic motivation rewards work, "it might become possible to incorporate flow into normal nonplay life activities, to make the roles available in society more playful and therefore, more free and creative" (Csikszentmihayli 1976,6).

According to Tinsley and Tinsley (1982) , the leisure state or experience resides in the individual, not the activity. The leisure experience involves a constellation of cognitive (e.g., thoughts, images) and affective (e.g., feelings, sensations) attributes experienced by the individual; these cognitive and affective attributes can vary. There is not one single leisure experience but a continuum of leisure experiences that vary in intensity, from those barely perceived by the individual to intense experiences identified as the leisure state. The Tinsleys offer the following characteristics of the leisure experience:

1. Absorption or concentration on the ongoing experience;
2. Lessening of focus on self;
3. Feelings of freedom or lack of constraint;

4. Enriched perception of objects and events;
5. Increased intensity of emotions;
6. Increased sensitivity to feelings;
7. Decreased awareness of the passage of time (18-19).

In order for a person to experience leisure, Tinsley and Tinsley report there are four necessary conditions:

1. The individual's perceived freedom of activity choice is personal rather than a result of external coercion.
2. The individual is engaged in an activity to obtain benefits intrinsic to participation in the activity.
3. The individual experiences an optimal level of arousal.
4. The individual is committed to fulfill his or her potential through engagement in the activity (32-39, 51-52).

The perception of freedom of choice is a fundamental determinant of the leisure experience, and so the experience of leisure commonly occurs when a person is engaged in a leisure activity. However, according to Tinsley and Tinsley's holistic view, the leisure experience may occur in all aspects of life, including work and other life functions, where there is objective evidence that external demands to pursue various activities have been made to the individual. A person's perception of his or her motivation for engaging in an activity may vary over time in the activity. A round of golf or set of tennis arranged for business reasons may end up a leisure experience as the individual's perception of why he or she is engaging in the activity may change from external motives to internal desires and intrinsic motives.

The Tinsleys (1982) have developed a causal model that depicts the benefits of experiencing leisure or the leisure state (see Figure 2.3). The model does not distinguish between types of activities the person engages in, but concerns itself with the person's experiencing these activities. Thus, according to this model, individuals experience leisure in many activities, including work.

Experiencing leisure has a reciprocal causal effect on need satisfaction (a physiological or psychological requirement for the well-being of the individual). Thus, whenever an individual experiences leisure some of his or her needs will be satisfied. "Con-

Figure 2.3 Causal Effects of Leisure Experience

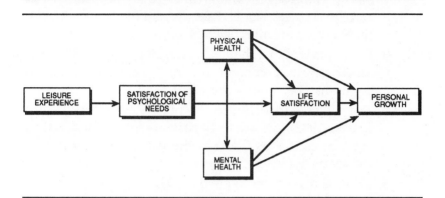

versely, the nature of the individual's needs influences the individual's interpretation of his or her experience while engaged in an activity, and thereby influences the probability of the individual experiencing leisure" (Tinsley and Tinsley, 26). The Tinsleys provide a most helpful link in showing the relationship between participation in a leisure activity and need satisfaction.

New Age/Consciousness Conceptualization of Leisure

The social-psychological or holistic leisure perspectives have not demonstrated that the source of need satisfaction lies in the leisure experience rather than in the mere act of engaging in an activity culturally recognized as leisure. Thus, from the standpoint of these perspectives, scholars conceptualize leisure within a mechanical world view, even though they combine behavioral and humanistic psychological interpretations of the human condition.

The New Age paradigm has manifested itself in many ways. (Howe-Murphy and Murphy 1987):

1. The exploration of both hemispheres of the brain and the various levels of brain functioning suggest that we carry within us ancestral wisdom (Houston 1982).

2. It has been discovered that some individuals have control over parts of their functioning formerly thought to be under the control of the autonomic nervous system (Pelletier 1977). The use of biofeedback, imagery, hypnosis, medita-

tion, yoga and other alternative modalities in treatment of physical illnesses, including cancer, diabetes, heart disease and other stress related diseases, and the management of chronic pain are all reflections of these discoveries.

3. Transpersonal psychology, including the acknowledgment of spiritual emergencies evolved as a way of explaining human behavior (Grof 1986).

4. The potent work of Elizabeth Kubler-Ross (1969), Stephen Levine (1982), and others have increased the understanding that conscious dying is the natural evolution from conscious living.

5. There is a growing interest in and body of literature in wellness (Ardell 1986; Howe-Murphy and Witt 1986; McDowell 1983).

What each of these manifestations has in common is the recognition of personal, individual perception, observation, and interpretation of world conditions and the human experience. This emerging holistic approach extends the work of Iso-Ahola, Csikszentmihayli, and Tinsley and Tinsley to recognize that individuals do exercise influence, even total choice, in finding meaning in their lives through their intuitive capacities.

Kaplan (1981) pointed the way in raising questions about the limitations of viewing leisure from familiar sequential patterns of stages and age images, instead of variations of flexible patterns and settings. Kaplan calls for leisure's conceptual framework to be integral to the comprehensive, holistic view of all matter that quantum physics calls for. This view fosters a philosophy of organic and inorganic interrelationships; everything in the universe, including leisure, is a part of all else; no element exists alone. Leisure, from this premise, could not be studied apart from all other elements or systems.

McDowell (1981) has presented a holistic consciousness conceptualization of the leisure experience, characterized by:

1. A perceived sense of freedom, autonomy, or unboundedness;

2. Self-determination of what is desirable to experience;

3. Intrinsic motivation resulting in a feeling of relaxation;

4. A feeling of timeliness;

5. An intuitive focus on the subjective experience and what one is becoming, as opposed to a rational analysis or awareness of the activity in which one is engaged and what is being accomplished.

From McDowell's perspective, the leisure experience is transitory (i.e., an individual may move in and out of the leisure state while engaged in a single activity) and irrational (i.e. the individual cannot logically explain the factors that cause entry into the leisure state). Mannell (1980) too, speaks of the leisure experience as "a transient psychological state, easily interrupted, and characterized by a decreased awareness of the passage of time, decreased awareness of the incidental features of physical and social surroundings, and accompanied by positive effect" (76). He acknowledges that this interruption may encompass experiential phenomena that scholars would not classify as leisure (e.g., aesthetic, humorous, sporting, and spiritual experiences). Other scholars suggest the leisure experience is similar to a variety of heightening psychological experiences, including mystical experiences, peak experiences (Maslow 1943), and flow (Csikszentmihalyi 1975). The leisure experience is seen as transitory in nature and individuals are believed to experience leisure at many levels of intensity across a continuum—the most intense or engrossing of the leisure experience is identified as a leisure state, that can have a profound effect on the individual.

The Johari Window Effect on Conceptual Development of Leisure

We will discuss the Johari Window again in Chapter 7, and relate it to the functioning of staff members. Here, it will serve as another helpful bridge to understanding irrational, subjective, nonmaterial, and holistic aspects of the human experience (Luft 1969).

The use of the Johari Window model of human interaction incorporates an understanding of consciousness and awareness. Consciousness refers to what is felt within oneself and awareness to that which is felt outside oneself. These states of knowing are uniquely human and central to any interpretation of human interaction (see Figure 2.4).

The four quadrants represent the total person in relation to other persons. The basis for division into quadrants is awareness of behavior, feelings, and motivation. The following are definitions for each quadrant:

1. Quadrant 1, the open quadrant, refers to behavior, feelings, and motivation known to self and to others.
2. Quadrant 2, the blind quadrant, refers to behavior, feelings and motivation known to others but not to self.
3. Quadrant 3, the hidden quadrant, refers to behavior, feelings, and motivation known to self but not to others.
4. Quadrant 4, the unknown quadrant, refers to behavior, feelings, and motivation known neither to self nor to others.

Figure 2.4 The Johari Window

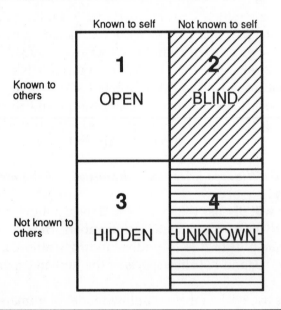

In typical efforts to assess, categorize, and explain leisure behavior, scientists and scholars most often focus their attention on what they can directly see or observe. Most leisure concepts evolve from this segment of human interaction (see Figure 2.5).

Figure 2.5 The Johari Window—Exploring Leisure Behavior

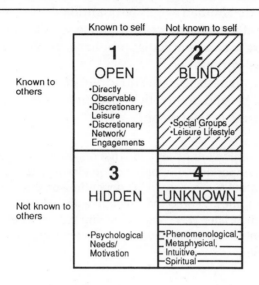

Quadrant 2 also provides a resource for others to assess us. While each of us is unaware of certain things in ourselves, others can capture clues about our behavior. These expressions and behaviors are often revealed through social group interaction. But because individuals are reluctant to share what is most important to them, what people are thinking and feeling is not often understood and therefore not reported in scientific research. Some investigators have developed better tools to assess psychological needs and sensitive feelings. This has helped to uncover a little more of the picture of what constitutes the leisure experience.

Perhaps what is most important to New Age/Consciousness conceptual development is the irrational, nonmaterial, phenomenological, and intuitive contributions to human interaction. This area of largely unknown activity serves to limit overall explanation of day-to-day behavior and life events. It also may be the richest source of ultimate explanation for what enhances personal growth and leads to living organisms interconnecting with each other and the rest of the universe. What we do not know should not curtail our quest to discover it. Most existing devices designed to measure human behavior and conceptual orientations used to formulate hypotheses for assessing individual and group behavior require only that human events be quantifiable, so that we can show cause and effect. This process, of course, enables lay persons and practitioners to solve particular problems, provide service or treat individuals' various needs.

Luft (1969) suggests that the quadrant of unknown human behavior, feelings, and motivation (Quadrant 4) contains the untapped resources of the person:

> What we inherit in our genes and what remains as yet unrealized is an important component of quadrant four. Latent talent may grow at any time in life depending on conditions and opportunities. People may bloom with extraordinary abilities in their later years, and as the life span is extended more persons have the opportunity to develop their Q4 resources (66).

According to the New Age paradigm, intuitive perspectives are helpful for creating an environment and establishing order in the world. But an individual's feelings, emotions, and intuitions are not typically incorporated into considerations that form institutions, structures, and services. This condition has magnified the separation of mind, body and spirit from how we engage in life. Practitioners in many helping professions—medicine, social work, education and leisure—often have suspicion and serious doubt whether spiritual, mystical, and irrational expressions have any relationship to individual growth, development, and well-being. They do not know how to document this type of experience, since it falls outside the existing parameters that explain behavior.

New Age thinking, in concert with systems application and a holistic conceptual framework, calls for a reconstruction of the philosophical foundations, knowledge base, and service delivery for the leisure profession. As reference points for developing professional practice, the hierarchical, mechanistic, culturally monoethnic, patriarchal, and external relation and reductionist perspectives require a 180-degree turn in thinking. The New Age paradigm suggests that the individual's own inner dimensions of reality are the essential ingredients for defining meaning in life, including the recreation and leisure experience. Leisure is relevant to the degree that the individual perceives his or her experience as emanating from within oneself and connecting with the universe. The recognition that it is the individual who imparts creativity and order to institutional and environmental structures provides the basis not only for leisure service professionals, but for all human service providers.

A holistic conceptual perspective which captures social psychological and New Age thinking, is an integrating conceptual view of human and leisure behavior. Most studies of the human organism suggest that the key elements of freedom of choice and intrinsic motivation are learned in the context of the person-environment interaction. However, there is increasing evidence that viewing leisure as a segmented category of life for individual pleasure and well-being, made available principally by the structure of work, is not only naive but lacks scientific support. Such a structural-functional and objective view not only limits the importance of leisure to merely being a residual choice of activity from an environmentally-induced engagement determined by others, but it also underestimates the innate growth potential inherent in all human beings (Tinsley and Tinsley 1982). Emerging holistic models based on research of the human condition suggest that it is the needs of the person (conscious and unconscious) that determine what will be intrinsically motivating (and therefore what defines the leisure experience), and not the structure of the environment (playground, community center) or stimulus (leadership, announced benefits) induced by others.

Concepts of Work

Work is the dominant rhythm of North American culture, and leisure is valued as a reward for people who earn it through gainful employment. Other elements of community life, including the family, church, and education, are defined mostly in this relation to the work requirements of our culture.

The linear, sequential pattern of living in North American culture (illustrated in Chapter 1, Figure 1.3), influenced by second wave technology, is oriented around the mechanistic, industrial rhythm of life. The institution of work dictates social arrangements and becomes the critical determining factor or variable from which all other elements of life are measured. In an industrialized society, work came to be sharply differentiated from other aspects of community life. Industrialized societies are characterized by occupation specialization and a sharp division of labor.

Work justifications in industrial America were not seen as intrinsic to the activity and experience, but were religious rewards. The Protestant work perspective was perhaps appropriate for an industrializing nation of immigrant factory workers, who found opportunity for good pay and improved standard of living and gladly accepted a subordinated role at the workplace.

In preindustrial, agrarian societies, work becomes largely subject to the laws of nature. While there is less demarcation between work, family, and leisure roles, one's energies are primarily physically expressed in labor. Kaplan (1979) states:

> in pre-industrial (agrarian) societies there is a difference, for them one's work is holistic: the whole farm is cultivated, whole shoes and whole dresses are made. The pre-industrial worker does not find himself in an assembly line, with fragmented responsibility and only a fragmented car fender to guide through a machine process (17).

Currently, work is going through a transformation wherein the work-leisure dichotomy (created by industrialized societies) is decreasing. Technology makes it unnecessary to segment individual identity and self-expression in any sphere of life. More people are seeking opportunities for self-expression in work and in all community and personal spheres of life. Since they are not constrained by economic security or physical survival, those working in a postindustrial era desire more autonomy, participation in decision making, and use of all of their abilities.

The information age boosted by third wave technology, an outgrowth of the postindustrial society, has fostered a reunification of work-leisure-time into a holistic cultural framework. (At this stage it is impacting only a small segment of the population. Most of the world is still pre-industrial or industrial.) In this view, the individual's participation in community life is as a whole person. One interacts in all milieus from a self-directed perspective, linked inextricably to others within the universe. Satisfaction can occur in any realm, and one is optimally aroused through a variety of internal and external novel experiences.

Concepts of Time

Time is a dimension that serves as an important index in which all aspects of social phenomena are measured. There are several kinds of time; four of these will be presented—natural, mechanical, psychological, and cosmic/synchronistic time.

Imagine the enormity of the types of time that exist even though most community systems in Western civilization are obedient to mechanical time, ever observant of the hands of the clock moving in arcs around a circle. Time is not just a nonspatial continuum in which events occur in irreversible succession from the past through the present to the future. Houston (1982) observes:

> After we leave the periodicities of twenty-four-hour-around the day time or the astronomer-measured passages of star time, we enter into the phenum of the temporal kaleidoscope: atomic time, galactic time, relativity time, biological rhythms, body time, being-in-rage time, wasting time, fear time, anxiety time, pain time, pleasure time . . . . a five-year-old's time, a seventy-five-year-old's time, borning time, dying time, creative time, meditation time, focusing time, timeless time. Ecstasy and terror have their own temporal cadences and, in mystical experience, the categories of time are strained by the tension of eternity (148).

Natural Time

According to the ancient Greeks, physical time was known as *chronos*. Aristotle (1929) spoke of elliptic motion of celestial bodies as eternal. In this sense, eternal meant periodic or recurring. Similarly, the nomadic hunting life was conditioned largely by the rising and setting of the sun. There were no clocks to divide the day into hours, minutes, and seconds. The nomadic, preindustrial, primitive life was oriented around daily, monthly, and seasonal rhythms of the natural universe. Nomads understood the summer solstice and the vernal equinox, and the spring, summer, fall, and winter seasons to be circular conceptions of time that were constant and recurring. Green (1968) states: "According to this image, time is measured in relation to the constant and recurring passage of the sun, the fluctuations of the tides, the stages of the moon, or even the cycles of the seasons" (49).

Time was never lost or wasted; according to this conception of time, the periods of the day were not seen as linear, sequential divisions. The image of time was based on the repetition of activities, both social and natural:

> In this case, time repeats itself, so that one cannot speak of 'wasting time'. The time that has passed is never really lost; it will come again . . . . Time is not cumulative—that is, the idea that one might now undertake something that will reach its completion at some time in the future is not dominant (Green 1968, 49).

Circular, eternally returning time provides people with a strong sense of belief and commitment to the natural world. Ecologically, a person understood his or her relationship to the physical world and was able to live harmoniously in his or her natural surroundings. De Grazia (1962) notes that the ancient Greeks delightedly accepted the eternal harmonious order that could be discovered through contemplation.

The Hebrew term *chronos* was quite different from the Greek and traditional nomadic concept of time, although it also referred to mechanical clock time and measured the hours to the day. The Greeks used *chronos* as a parameter or secondary concept—the planets projected their images in the "receptacle" (the order of things) in constant recurrence. The Hebrews used *chronos* as a primary term, a series of successive linear moments. The "coming age" occurs as an expected, urgent, important future, but it comes only in the fullness of time. In opposition to *chronos*, the term *kairos* refers to a special time, the time of a very special chronos. It is not eternity as suggested by the Platonic model in that nature gave all things their regulatory structure. *Chronos* has a content that is different from other moments of *chronos*. Jesus tells us that no man knows the time (*chronos*) or the seasons (*Kairos*) of salvation (Acts 1:17).

The Greek metaphysical perception of time tried to locate time in the order of things, in the receptacle. The Hebrews tried to locate things in the "world of space moving through time, from the beginning to the end of days" (Herschel 1951, 97).

Mechanical Time

Hunting, food gathering, play, and rest occupied the daily lives of nomads and preindustrial people in a total life rhythm. Living by cyclical, natural time inherently fostered introspection. The mechanization of time occurred when nomads and food-gatherers with specific work tasks needed to meet others to engage in barter and trade goods and wares. This required a more finite division of time between sunrise and noon, noon and sunset. The death of cyclical time and the notion of recurrence vanished with the triumph of Christianity.

Mechanical clocks are known to have existed in the thirteenth century, but the earliest survivors belong to the fourteenth century (Priestly 1968). The week is an arbitrary division, simply a convenient time period between the day and the month. The Greeks divided the month into three ten-day periods, and the Romans had an eight-day week between market days.

In the industrial world time is generally viewed as linear, without beginning or end, never pausing or veering off course. Nels Anderson (1964) states: "The time by which most of us regulate our lives is called mechanical because it reflects the interdependence of man and the rhythm of his machines" (106). According to this image of time being regulated by the clock, it becomes possible to speak of wasting time, letting time escape, and putting in time. De Grazia (1962) writes:

> In this conception, time linear rather than circular; every moment of time is new, and therefore also contains the possibility of something new. A time can pass, and when it passes it cannot be recovered. One can therefore plan to achieve something in the future that is indeed genuinely new .... One must plan for the future, for the span of a lifetime is brief enough, and what shape it will take is not given, but can be contrived (310).

The acceptance of artificial timekeeping devices diluted Homo Sapiens' biological rhythm of movement through space and oriented it to the mechanical beat of the clock. By varying the years, months, and days, it seemed possible to arrange for more optimum work and play schedules.

Mechanical time came into existence because, among other reasons, the industrial civilization has demanded more precision, promptness, and regularity than natural time can provide. Anderson (1964) comments:

> It is mechanical time the engineer must use in planning or directing a project, and the same must be used by the mechanic to measure the speed or output of a machine or the coordination of machines in a series. When the scientist would measure relationships between durations and other abstractions (space, distance, momentum, volume) he must use mechanical time (106).

It is interesting to note that the environment of mechanical time, which demands precision, punctuality, regularity, and reliability is mostly human-made: buildings, paved streets, water systems, sewage systems, lighting and communication networks, even parks, recreation centers, and human service establishments, are all made by human beings. In this environment, the rhythms of natural time are disregarded and typically suppressed: "Technology has continued severing the ties between people and nature. Extreme daily fluctuations have been eliminated by electric lights and temperature control systems. Jet travel allows for climate change as well as providing seasonal variations in diets. Natural environments have even altered the lifecycles of birth and death" (Bammel and Burrus-Bammel 1982, 89). Each of the natural types of time has its own tempo and environmental interpretation.

The human-made environment of mechanical clock time reinforces the artificial rhythms of the industrial workday, communications networks, transportation systems, and scheduled routines of schools, churches, offices, and recreation facilities. Without the clock, free time as we know it in industrial society would not have emerged. Work and leisure, fused in preindustrial society, have become opposing conceptions in our high technology, information age. The contemporary arrangement of time has become rigorously circumscribed by industrial work time. Because work time needs to be filled with productive occupation, leisure time is typically viewed as time that should be devoted to rest, relaxation, and recuperation for work, not as time that is innately meaningful for the intrinsic growth of the individual. Time pressure appears to be closely related to age. Older people are more content with the amount of time they have to do what they need to do. Younger people, who represent the majority of the workforce, report that time spent off the job is more enjoyable than that spent on the job. Sixty percent of workers say they enjoy nonworking time most (Gallup Poll, 1990).

Psychological Time

Time is also a reflection of individual perceptions or inner sense of the passage of events. Each one of us has differences in our temperament. Jung (1923) first described four personality types: thinking, feeling, sensation, and intuition.

Thinking and feeling are opposing ways of evaluating an object or a situation. Thinking accomplishes this through principles such as "true or false;" feeling evaluates through emotional responses such as "pleasing" or "distressing." Intuition and sensation are also opposites; both are ways of perceiving the world. Sensation is the relating function in which the sensory mechanism is used to determine the presence or absence of an object. Intuition is perceived by the consciousness and is a method of relating to the world through hunches and guesses. As with the other opposing functions, those people having sensation as a primary function would tend to be weak in intuition, and vice versa.

These personality functions can be either predominantly extroverted or introverted. All extroverts have in common their willingness to respond quickly to external stimuli, although the way in which they respond will depend on their primary function. Such people tend to be gregarious, and on the whole they are oriented toward action rather than toward introspection or reflection. All introverts tend to exhibit a certain hesitancy about re-

Figure 2.6 Personality Function

Personality	Function
Sensation Type	Tells us something exists.
Thinking Type	Tells us what something is.
Feeling Type	Enables us to make a value judgment about this object.
Intuition Type	Enables us to see the possibilities inherent in the object.

sponding too quickly to external stimuli, requiring time to integrate them before responding overtly. Introverts enjoy being
alone and find satisfaction from occasional seclusion.

Any typology is an abstraction of reality. Everyone has
potential for all four functions:

> However, each person has a hierarchy in functions and a
> natural predisposition to one of the attitudes. The more nearly
> balanced the two attitudes are, the greater the individual's
> potential for experiencing both the joys that derive from the
> inner spheres and the pleasures that come from the external
> worlds.... bringing all four functions into conscious control
> is extremely helpful for optimal functioning (Mann, Siegler
> and Osmond 1972,147).

One might argue that the skills of the feeling and intuitive
types of personality will become important attributes in an information-based society. With more of a blend and interaction of
different structures and systems, there will develop an expectation to encourage people to value their intuition and feelings along
with their orientation toward process, time flowing, and inspira-
tion of the anticipated future. Western society has largely been
oriented toward the functions of sensation and thinking and has
tended to undervalue the skills of those who related primarily
through either feelings or intuition.

Many people feel constrained by the one-way temporal
process epitomized by industrial time clocks. They yearn to escape
the artificial entanglements of work time and explore more fully
the natural world unbound by stoplights, the six o'clock news,
school buzzers, alarm clocks, sirens, and factory time clocks.
Indeed, nearly eight in ten Americans, 78 percent, report that
time seems to move too fast for them (Gallup Poll, 1990). Most
people say they don't have the time to do the things they really
want to do. Psychological time is concerned not with the specific-
ity of quantitative time, but rather with quality. Priestly (1968)
observes:

> No matter how the empirical self adapts itself to the concept
> of passing time, a one-way horizontal track, the essential self
> (that expects something different and better) tries to escape
> from the contradictions, the ruthless opposites, and knows

nothing but a sense of frustration, a profound dissatisfaction (173).

Cosmic and Synchronistic Time

Individuals are seeking to know how to perceive time and space as an opportunity to add to their experience and knowledge through a broadening and deepening consciousness. The New Age/Consciousness paradigm suggests that each individual is interconnected with all other organic and inorganic matter in the universe, throughout all time. Cosmic time is derived from the Hebrew word *cosmos*, meaning world peace or universe. Some people say they are guided by magnetic fields from the universe and that their body rhythms reflect this arrangement of things in the world.

There is no regularity or uniform pattern with a cosmic sense of time. In fact, one may experience a number of sensations, feelings, intuitions, indeed a leisure state, outside what we normally consider mechanical time. It is often said we carry with us ancestral wisdom. We can experience what our ancestors did outside of a particular linear temporal period. At the deepest levels of our consciousness (theta or delta) time does not exist: no-time. Individual organisms are most at one with the universe and themselves when transcending clock time, natural time, or other forms of time—there is a sense of timelessness.

The traditional Western conceptualization of time is linear; it uses past, present, and future terminologies and includes birth, life, death, thesis, antithesis, synthesis, origin, process, recapitulation, and so on. But it must be realized that this linearization of time is only one possible conceptualization of social process. The traditional Chinese view of time, for example, a cyclical temporal pattern, would not fit our Western model at all. There are alternative views of the human experience of time, and rates of behavior have variant speeds, accelerations and decelerations, and variations in the uniformity of these patterns.

Time and Consciousness

One's awareness or lack of awareness of time, in work or leisure, points to the significant link between time and consciousness. In order to understand the phenomenon of consciousness, scientists use electroencephalographic (EEG) measures. Our brain continuously gives off electromagnetic pulsations that can be measured by an electroencephalograph. There are EEG levels, called beta, alpha, theta, and delta, that represent different rhythms along a complete spectrum (Gioscia 1972).

These levels of consciousness, according to Adair (1984), provide insight into how awareness of our own consciousness is linked to culture. One might place beta consciousness at the top of the brain, with the other levels of consciousness—alpha, theta and delta—residing in the deeper portions, The deeper levels of consciousness experience reality holistically. Adair (1984) comments: "They do not separate things; they make connections. They do not categorize; they make things whole. They are not critical, nor do they order things in a linear manner. Instead they experience reality in images, patterns and sensations" (10-11).

Characteristics of the four levels of consciousness

1. In Western culture we are most familiar with beta consciousness because it occurs at a level that is rational and is therefore valued. It is the only aspect of our consciousness we have been taught to use. Reading, writing, and arithmetic are all beta functions, as are cause and effect thinking, goal orientation, and our experience of clock time.

    Beta consciousness pertains to linear thinking that is particular and critical. In beta one is able to deal with lots of particulars at the same time in a logical, goal-oriented manner. It fits appropriately with much of contemporary urban living. Beta consciousness separates elements of the whole, ordering them in a linear manner.

2. Alpha consciousness is induced with any rhythmic activity such as running, weaving, or dancing. The alpha levels feel much more flowing. When dancing, for example, you may lose the beat if you stopped to think about something and had no idea what led to that thought.

3. Theta and delta consciousness are active when an individual's focus is in one place. The theta level is an extremely receptive state of consciousness because one is only aware of what is happening at the moment and has no concept of anything else. Adair (1984) explains: "It does

not divide things up, nor categorize things; it simply experiences. Since theta is exclusively focused on what is occurring in the moment it is not linear or goal-oriented" (13).

4. The range from beta to delta is simply one of focus and concentration of awareness—at beta it is spread out, at delta it is completely concentrated. At beta, awareness is particular, at delta it is holistic. Adair (1984) explains:

> In the material world things take time to happen. Time and space create limits and maintain themselves within linear and logical progressions. The inner world is altogether different; as it's holistic, and sequence is not something within its experience—it operates in simultaneous patterns—time is meaningless (Adair, 1984,77).

Csikszentmihayli's discussion of flow, a holistic sensation individuals feel when they act with total involvement, resembles the theta and delta levels of consciousness. According to Csikszentmihayli (1976) one has the ultimate leisure experience when the following are present:

1. Centering of attention on a limited stimulus field;
2. Unconscious awareness of control of actions and the environment;
3. Disorientation of time and space;
4. Merging of awareness, behavior and the environment;
5. Loss of anxiety and constraint; and
6. Enjoyment.

The flow experience is the state of optimum balance people experience when they feel in control over their environment. It is a motivating force independent of external rewards. In this optimum state, individuals develop as holistic, organized systems aware of their total existence.

Csikszentmihayli's research actually has roots in EEG levels and subjective states of consciousness, and has stimulated an interesting development in the study of leisure. Most leisure research and thus practice is based on the active, linear beta consciousness that is readily observed.

Conclusions on Time and Leisure

There are many varieties of time and interpretations of how one experiences events and moments. We live in an era in which many of us feel traumatized by the stress of living in a highly technological environment. The time clock and the rule of machines over the rhythms of daily life, have, for many, served to fragment and disassociate the flow of living and natural rhythms. The technologicalization of the work rhythm of life has emerged as an abstraction from the ordinary life focus and provides a new framework for existence. While this framework of mechanical time provides efficiency, it brings with it an accompanying loss of a sense of past and future. It can be argued that with abstraction of space and time, and loss of a sense of the stages in any operational process, there is also an inevitable loss of a sense of duration. Says Houston (1982): "When the rule of life is 'no sooner said than done,' the whole temporal fabric of existence becomes warped. Warped too, becomes the necessary lag in duration between wants and the satisfaction of those wants" (148).

Clearly there are many ways of perceiving and engaging time and it is important to recognize the extraordinary range and capacity of temporal experience. Leisure may have many more unique gifts for individual enhancement if we begin to explore the powers of time by acknowledging and exploring alternative temporal domains.

Incorporating Leisure Concepts

The task before leisure service professionals is to facilitate opportunities for people to experience enjoyment, personal growth and development, and overall well-being. Leisure service providers, no matter the form of sponsorship (public, private, non-profit, or commercial) attempt to enrich individual and collective community life. While commercial leisure enterprises charge a fee and expect to make a profit, their business would not be frequented and survive unless customers believed that their lives were enhanced and they received some form of benefit. While public and private voluntary agencies may charge minimal fees in order to recover costs that exceed tax, grant, or donation support, their services and programs similarly must meet the declared and anticipated needs of people.

The leisure service profession is learning (from over one hundred years of existence as part of the system of organized recreation provisions and the advancement of scholarly inquiry into the human condition) that the leisure experience occurs in a myriad of forms and impacts individuals in different ways. Therefore we do not know why individuals come to do what they do except in generalities. So we have to provide for a wide range of activities and experiences.

Most scholars who interpret human behavior from a social-psychological perspective view the leisure experience as representing an internal, personal response of the organism free from external stimulus. Individuals engage in leisure for the purpose of obtaining intrinsic benefits, and it is increasingly believed that individuals experience leisure for personal reasons. Leisure experiences range from barely recognizable to intense episodes. The individual may not be consciously aware of all or any aspects of such an experience and its effect on their personal growth. Since most measures of leisure focus on the quantifiable aspects, subjective measures lag in their development.

Experiencing leisure, like any meaningful activity, is linked to improvement of overall well-being. In order to understand the more complete ramifications of leisure, leisure service must be viewed from a systems perspective. Such an approach incorporates the total person as being the initiator and the essential interpreter of the experience, which represents a multitude of needs, emotions, and benefits. Leisure service personnel will become more astute and relevant providers of leisure opportunities as they come to recognize the primacy of the individual as participant, client, or consumer who can best interpret and express the meaning of activities. As professionals, leisure service personnel must come to appreciate that they cannot be detached from those individuals they serve. They must comprehend that leisure is a subjective state in which individual needs and personal goals are most likely to be fulfilled if they can create an environment for the participant to determine how, where, and when leisure experiences occur. This will then foster innate, individual desires to participate in community life, which happens when one is intrinsically motivated and has a high degree of freedom to choose what one wants to do.

Summary

This chapter presented a dynamic conceptualization of human behavior, leisure, work, and time in the nineteenth and twentieth centuries. Two predominant views of human behavior are structural-functional and social-action. Structural-functional emphasizes the importance of institutional and societal forces in sharing and constraining human behavior. The social-action model recognizes that an individual's own goal setting and behavior is more important in determining the result of the interaction between people and the environment.

Leisure is most often viewed from an objective and behavioral perspective that focuses on observable, quantifiable aspects of human participation. The most common objective conceptualizations of leisure are: discretionary time, discretionary behavior and engagements, and social group or lifestyle. Subjective definitions provide a second way of defining leisure. This approach emphasizes the intrinsic, internal states of the individual. Prominent subjective leisure concepts are classical or Aristotelian and psychological. A third method of conceptualizing human activity is the holistic view. It focuses on interrelationships between living organisms and inorganic matter. Two such views are holistic and New Age/Consciousness conceptualizations of leisure.

Work concepts have primarily been linked to the nature of the methods of production. These include industrial or mechanical, agrarian or cyclical, postindustrial, technological and information. A strong thrust of information-based economics involves the reunification of work-leisure-time with a blended life pattern through the lifespan.

Time is most often categorized as natural or organic, mechanical and linear, psychological, and cosmic and synchronistic. Natural time, largely a perspective experienced in ancient civilizations but still in existence in rural societies, refers to the constant and recurring passage of events based on the natural daily, monthly, and seasonal rhythms of the natural universe. Mechanical time is based on the artificial time-keeping devices—clocks—that divide the day, week, month and year into linear, never-to-be-experienced-again segments. Psychological time is a reflection of individual perceptions or inner sense of the passage of events. Cosmic and synchronistic time is based on intuitive, conscious awareness of the relationship of an individual with all other organic and inorganic matter in the universe.

Most approaches to conceptualizing human behavior, leisure, work, and time during the last two centuries have been primarily influenced by the mechanistic, empirical, linear worldview that evolved in the seventeenth century. This approach is based on more material, scientific, and objective measures of human experience. The emergence of a New Age/Consciousness world view, which emphasizes a holistic, ecological, and self-organizing systems approach of human and nonhuman endeavors, provides a blend of mechanistic and nonlinear paradigms. This new world view suggests that work, leisure and time need not be segmented and isolated, but rather all organic and nonhuman matter are interconnected and operate best when designed to interact cooperatively.

References

Adair, Margo. 1984. *Working inside out: Tools for change.* Berkeley, Calif.: Wingbow Press. New York: David McKay Co., 1964, 91.

Anderson, Nels. 1964. *Dimensions of work: The sociology of a work culture.* New York: David McKay Co.

Ardell, Donald. 1986. *High level wellness.* Berkeley, Calif.: Ten Speed Press.

Aristotle. 1929. *Physics.* H. Wickshead and F.M. Conford, trans. New York: Loeb Classical Library.

Bammel, Gene and Lei-Lane Burrus-Bammel. 1982. *Leisure and human behavior.* Dubuque, IA: W.C.Brown Publishers.

Capra, Fritjof. 1986. Wholeness and Health. *Holistic Medicine* 1:146.

Cheek, Neil H., Donald R. Field and Rabel J. Burdge. 1976. *Leisure and recreation places.* Ann Arbor, MI: Ann Arbor Science Publishers.

Csikszentmihayli, Mihaly. 1975. *Beyond boredom and anxiety.* San Francisco: Jossey Bass.

Csikszentmihayli, Mihaly. 1976. What play says about behavior. *The Ontarion Psychologist* 8:5-11.

DeCharms, R. 1968. *Personal causation, the internal effective determinants of behavior.* New York: Academic Press.

DeGrazia, Sebastian. 1962. *Of time, work and leisure.* New York: The Twentieth Century Fund.

Driver, B.L. and S. Ross Tocher. 1970. Toward a behavioral interpretation of recreation engagement, with implications for planning. In *Elements of outdoor recreation planning*, B.L. Driver, ed. Ann Arbor, MI:University Microfilms.

Gallup Poll. 1990. People feel time is running out. *San Francisco Chronicle* Nov. 5:E1-3

Gioscia, Victor. 1972. On social time. In *The future of time*, H. Yaker, H. Osmond, and F. Cheek, eds. New York: Anchor Books.

Green, Thomas F. 1968. *Work, leisure and the American schools*. New York: Random House.

Grof, Stanislov. 1986. Psychology and consciousness research. *Revision: Journal of Consciousness and Change* 9:47-49.

Herschel, A.J. 1951. *The Sabbath*. New York: Frarrar, Strauss and Young.

Houston, Jean. 1982. *The possible human: A course in extending your physical, mental and creative abilities*. Los Angeles: J. Tarcher.

Howe-Murphy, Roxanne L. and James F. Murphy. 1987. An exploration of the New Age/Consciousness paradigm in therapeutic recreation. In *Philosophy of therapeutic recreation: Ideas and issues*, Charles Sylvester et al., eds. Alexandria, VA: NRPA.

Howe-Murphy, Roxanne L. and Peter Witt, eds. 1986. Wellness and therapeutic recreation. *Therapeutic Recreation Journal* 20:(2) Whole Issue.

Iso-Ahola, Seppo. 1980. *The social psychology of leisure and recreation*. Dubuque, IA: W. C. Brown Publishers.

Jung, C.C. 1923. *Psychological types*. London: Pantheon Books.

Kaplan, Max. 1979. *Leisure: Lifestyle and lifespan*. Philadelphia: W.B. Saunders Co.

Kaplan, Max. 1981, Oct. 23. *Leisure scholarship: Some unfinished tasks.* Academy of Leisure Sciences, Minneapolis, Minnesota.

Kubler-Ross, Elizabeth. 1969. *On death and dying*. New York: Macmillan.

Levine, Stephen. 1982. *Who dies? An investigation of conscious living and conscious dying*. New York: Anchor Books.

Luft, Joseph. 1969. *Of human interaction*. Palo Alto: National Press Books.

Mann, Harriet, Mirian Siegler, and Humphrey Osmond. 1972. The psychotypology of time. In *The future of time*, H. Yaker, H. Osmond and F. Cheek, eds. New York: Anchor Books.

Mannell, Roger. 1980. Social psychological techniques and strategies for studying leisure experiences. In *Social psychological perspectives in leisure and recreation*, Seppo Iso-Ahola, ed. Springfield, IL: Charles C. Thomas.

Maslow, Abraham. 1943. A Theory of Human Motivation. *Psychological Review* 50:372-396.

McDowell, C. Forest. 1981. Leisure consciousness, well-being, and counseling. *The Counseling Psychologist* 9:3-32.

McDowell, C. Forest. 1983. *Leisure wellness: Concepts and helping strategies.* Eugene, OR: Sun Moon Press.

Murphy, James F. 1981. *Concepts of leisure,* 2nd ed. Englewood Cliffs, NJ: Prentice-Hall, Inc.

Neulinger, John. 1976. The need for the implication of a psychological conception of leisure. *The Ontarion Psychologist* 8:17.

Niepoth, E. William. 1983. *Leisure leadership.* Englewood Cliffs, NJ: Prentice-Hall, Inc.

Pelletier, Kenneth R. 1977. *Mind as healer, mind as slayer.* New York: Dell Publishing.

Priestly, J.B. 1968. *Man and time.* New York: Dell Publishing Company.

Tinsley, Howard E. A. and Diane Tinsley. 1982. *Psychological and health benefits of the leisure experience: a theory of the attributes, benefits and causes of leisure experience.* Carbondale, IL: Southern Illinois University.

3

THE LEISURE SERVICE PROFESSION

As discussed in Chapters 1 and 2, the emergence of leisure in contemporary North American society owes its heritage primarily to the Industrial Revolution, which created an altered form of community life. Prior to the industrialization of the economic structure in the United States and Canada and the resulting social patterns, community life in rural towns was geared primarily to handcraft trades and farming. Families were rooted to the land. Larger cities were gathering places for banking and commerce, but each country's chief social network existed within the homogeneous extended family context.

By the middle of the later 1880s, with the establishment of a mass production factory system, opportunities for work became more prevalent in urban centers. This development resulted in an exodus of individuals from the isolated and small network of families and friends residing in the countryside and towns to larger, more densely populated urban areas. With this geographical shift came social and psychological changes stimulating the development of an altered form of community, work, and family life.

The highly individualistic nature of the rugged pioneer family member that epitomized the national character in North America began to give way to a new social interaction pattern—both in family and community life. The self-sufficient economic unit, the family, largely dissolved with the introduction of mass production, which necessitated the use of functionally interdependent but autonomous parts to sustain the industrial factory system. This broke up the relatively stable, economically independent family unit and created a gap in social control and support for dependent family members—children, youths, and older adults. This economically and socially tumultuous period in our country's history precipitated the call by socially conscientious citizens, particularly in urban areas of the northeastern part of the United States, to set aside supervised play areas for children. As a result, the organized Recreation and Park Movement was initiated.

Background of the Recreation and Park Movement

The Recreation and Park Movement has progressed through eight phases of professional development. While the Recreation and Park Movement is treated here as an overall social development, each of these areas grew out of separate issues. Later in the twentieth century they became more closely interconnected.

First Phase

The Recreation Movement was spawned in the late 1880s because social workers, social reform leaders, and interested lay citizens saw an imperative need to provide constructive recreation and leisure opportunities for children and youth living in urban slums, and a need to build facilities and play areas for city dwellers no longer free to roam the less inhabited and uncluttered countryside.

This initial development of organized recreation and leisure service in the United States was begun by spirited, socially concerned individuals, including Joseph Lee in Boston (considered to be the father of the Recreation Movement in the United States), Jacob Riis in New York, and Jane Addams in Chicago (Nobel Peace Prize recipient and founder of the Hull House). These pioneers of the Recreation and Park Movement were primarily motivated by the deleterious conditions of urban living and the need to provide underprivileged youth constructive leisure opportunities amidst crowded and impoverished living conditions. According to Neumeyer and Neumeyer (1958), the initiation of the play movement (as it was then called) in the late nineteenth century grew out of the following factors impinging upon urban life:

> It grew out of a situation of need owing to such factors as technological developments, particularly the introduction of modern machinery of production with its monotonous and nerve-racking work; urbanization, especially the overcrowded living conditions in sections of cities; changing home conditions and family disorganization; the speed of living, including increased mobility and daily rushing about; and the increase of leisure (64).

The first specific development is credited to the Boston Sand Garden in 1885, where a coalition of public-spirited citizens, representing a cross section of the community, converted a sand pile and animal grazing area into a much-needed play area in a working class district. Similarly, other recreation areas were developed by socially conscious individuals in rundown neighborhoods. Butler (1970) states:

> The conscience of civic leaders and social workers such as Jacob Riis in New York City and Jane Addams in Chicago was stirred into action by the slum conditions and their effect upon the children and youth living in blighted neighborhoods. Joseph Lee was shocked to see boys arrested for playing in the Boston streets, and George E. Johnson was moved at the pathos of the attempts of little children to play in the narrow, crowded alleys of Pittsburgh (v).

Thus, the first phase of the Recreation and Park Movement, spurred by the discontinuity of community life in an industrializing culture, was oriented to the disadvantaged, poor, and underprivileged children and youth. The energy and resources for development of play opportunities came from the voluntary efforts of social workers and citizens who provided leadership and funds for the establishment of the first playgrounds, community centers, and settlement houses.

The efforts of the early pioneers were instrumental in establishing a frame of reference for organized recreation in this first phase: an orientation to character-building activity. This impetus led to the formation of the YMCA, Boy and Girl Scouts, Boys' Clubs, and local governmentally-supported recreation programs. Sessoms (1971) comments:

> Recreation activities were thought of as a means of building character, instilling values, and providing formal teaching. The philosophy and programs for this period were distinctive; recreation was a means to an end – the building of better citizens (435).

Recreation was thought to be an important, wholesome, social, and personal outlet for young people exposed to undignified and cheap forms of entertainment and unlawful activities in crowded metropolitan and urban slum areas. Butler (1940) indicates the several related issues that inevitably led to the formalization of an organized recreation movement in 1906:

> Bad housing conditions resulting from the growth of tenement slum areas, the great influx of immigrants, the rising tide of juvenile delinquency, the increase in factories accompanied by the evils of child labor and unsanitary and unsafe working conditions, the spread of commercialized amusements that were often associated with vice—all helped to create a condition that made the provision of wholesome recreation a necessity (60-61).

The provision of community recreation came to be seen as a surrogate for families—providing informal, age-related opportunities for children and youth that normally occurred within the home, a respite for individuals seeking diversion from the mindless but physically arduous tasks demanded of factory workers, and a new institutional form that supplied a socially acceptable means for instilling values and behavioral traits desirous in the emerging industrial society.

The formation of the Playground Association of America in 1906 with President Theodore Roosevelt serving as the association's first honorary president was the culmination of some three decades of concern and served to unite the various scattered attempts of communities to provide organized recreation, leadership, equipment, and facilities for people. It was at this stage in the development of community life in America that the importance of recreation as a necessary part of normal life was recognized, and the belief developed that local government should assume responsibility for the provision of recreation.

Second Phase

At a time actually earlier in the nineteenth century, a few decades before social workers and community-minded citizens were initiating urban recreation programs, the evolution of the Park Movement had begun as a result of the work of conservationists and park planners. Some of these individuals had the visionary ability to set aside open space, creating natural park areas, primarily in eastern urban centers of the United States, to provide pleasant, passive surroundings. Such ecologically interconnected areas (e.g., Olmstead and Voux's Central Park in New York, Franklin Park in Boston, and Fairmont Park in Philadelphia) were designed to link the natural landscape with urban community life. Parks were developed to give city dwellers an opportunity to enjoy country living amidst an urban milieu.

The late 1880s saw the beginnings of state and national outdoor recreation areas. Forest preserves, forerunners of the present national forests in the United States, were first established in 1891. Congress created the U.S. Forest Service in 1905. Legislation making Yellowstone the first national park was passed in 1872; creation of the National Park Service came later in 1916. Other federal agencies, with later responsibilities for outdoor recreation resources, appeared about the same time. State park systems also began in this period.

Third Phase

The third phase in the development of the Recreation and Park Movement is marked by local governments assuming responsibility for the provision of organized recreation. This stage of development, characterized by recreation being recognized as an integral part of community life, occurred following the end of World War I. Local public authorities were pressured to assume responsibility for providing recreation. High government officials, prominent organizations, citizens, and economists voiced the collective opinion that public parks and recreation centers were, like schools, essential to the health, safety, and welfare of the community. State legislatures passed enabling laws empowering municipalities and counties to conduct recreation activities:

> The development of public, tax-supported recreation services was primarily a northern urban phenomenon; a response to overcrowding, inadequate housing, and generally deleterious social conditions arising from the Industrial Revolution. The welfare-motivated leaders of the play movement in America were not primarily concerned about the needs of blacks and other nonwhite minority groups. The early propagation of play in urban areas was a consideration for the needs of white immigrant slum children (Murphy 1975, 44).

The specific interest in providing recreation opportunities for nonwhite minority groups was a consequence of World War I, that resulted in greater numbers of racial minorities migrating to the northern urban communities. For the first time blacks were brought into contact and competition with whites for employment, education, housing, and recreation. The expanding concern for race relations necessitated a change in the provision of public recreation service, resulting in a specialized attempt to meet the leisure needs of black citizens through the Bureau of Colored Workers of the Playground and Recreation Association of America, the major professional agency of the Recreation and Park Movement. It provided consultation services aimed at assisting racially segregated community recreation programs until World War II. The prevailing separate but equal doctrine (a result of the *Plessy v. Ferguson* 1896 Supreme Court ruling), dictating the nature of relations between blacks and whites, was also applicable to recreation during the first half of the twentieth century.

The influence of World War I and the War Camp Community Service Act was particularly important to the Recreation and Park Movement, inasmuch as over 600 recreation programs were established in communities near military bases. For the first time in many parts of the country, recreation activities were conducted for all family members, and it was this broadening role of recreation in community life that led to an improved image. The "Recreation for All" slogan became a symbol for the wider and more representative recreation opportunities organized and developed for all members of a community.

Fourth Phase

During the 1930s and early 1940s and due to the Depression, enforced unemployment, impoverished conditions of most people, and a surplus of "free time," recreation became recognized as a diversionary instrument of community life to help break up the monotony of poverty. Because of the reduction in the workweek and high unemployment, recreation received more attention during the Depression from the federal government. "The resulting increased demand for recreation and decreased supply of opportunities available caused federal agencies to try to take up the slack, giving the recreation movement more impetus than it ever had before" (Carlson, Deppe, and MacLean 1972, 44-50).

The Recreation Division of the Works Progress Administration provided direct leadership and guidance in offering recreation activities in over 23,000 local communities during the 1930s. Other federal programs, including the National Youth Administration and Civilian Conservation Corps, provided service to communities and outdoor areas by constructing various kinds of recreation facilities, including picnic grounds, camps, parks, trails, swimming pools, and playgrounds.

Fifth Phase

With the advent of America's involvement in World War II, the government renewed its emphasis on recreation. Several services, the Welfare and Recreation Section of the Bureau of Navy Personnel and the Recreation Service of the Marine Corps, promoted programs on the battlefields, in hospitals, and in camps. The Federal Security Agency's Office of Community Service set up a new recreation division that assisted in the construction and operation of child-care centers and recreation buildings, several of which were taken over by cities as tax-supported recreation departments. World War II had an impact on accelerating the growth of a comprehensive community recreation system. Sessoms (1971) notes: "This movement toward comprehensive organized recreation was accelerated during World War II, when the need to get away from the tragedy of war increased the demand for activities of amusement and diversion for all groups" (435).

Sixth Phase

During the 1950s and 1960s organized recreation had a marked impact on community life. The growing movement was advanced by an increasing concern for physical fitness, programs for the ill, aged, and disabled, an upsurge in outdoor recreation and park development, involvement in the arts, professional education, unification of the parks and recreation professional organizations, and the impact of civil unrest and youth dissent. During the 1960s, two major developments influenced the structure and form of organized recreation and leisure delivery systems. First, the tumultuous period of the 1960s was marked by a period of civil unrest and social upheaval and this activity stimulated a return of organized community recreation agencies to issues of social concern. Community recreation agencies began to give special attention to the complex needs of the poor, disabled, and elderly—especially nonwhite individuals living in urban slum areas. It was only after several riots and civil disorders in many of the nation's cities that the needs of the inner city residents were brought forcefully to the attention of the public. Many of the efforts initiated by municipal recreation departments were typically oriented to providing special summer "crash," cooling-off programs, and were partially or totally subsidized by the former federal government agency, Office of Economic Opportunity.

During this time recreation and leisure service came to be seen as a *threshold* activity that drew participants to other forms of involvement for the purposes of improving community life, organizing neighborhoods for socially constructive activity, and actualizing human potential through leisure expression. As a result of the social upheaval and the application of recreation services by local government and private agencies to social problems, and as recognized by the Kerner Commission Report on Civil Disorders, the delivery of leisure services came to be seen as an opportunity system to improve the quality of life, reduce social pathology, build constructive values in citizens, and generally make communities better places to live.

Outdoor recreation participation also increased. It was precipitated by the expansion of state, provincial, and federal provision for additional camping and water sports opportunities and the promotion of vacation travel. In the United States the development of the Outdoor Recreation Resources Review Commission in 1958 served as the catalyst to this phase of the Recreation and Park Movement in the 1960s. The establishment of the now-defunct Land and Water Conservation Fund and the Bureau of Outdoor Recreation, later known as the Heritage Conservation and Recreation Service, spurred increased federal support for conservation and open space development. The state planning and accelerated municipal land acquisition phase later merged with the environmental movement at the beginning of the 1970s to widen the scope of understanding and sensitivity to the natural world and its contribution to society.

Seventh Phase

A human development phase, encouraged by civil and human rights legislation, emerged at the onset of the 1970s. Recreation and leisure service had a role to play in improving inadequate recreation opportunities and contributing to the total person. This period has been characterized as an *extension* and *linkage* of organized leisure services into the total fabric of community life. Commercial recreation became more prevalent via theme parks, small entrepreneurial business ventures, and tour vacation package operations. Voluntary, private nonprofit, and public recreation agencies began to incorporate a broader human services perspective in an attempt to respond to the total person's needs. Essentially, a new social character developed, one in which an individual, whether that person be able-bodied or disabled, old or young, male or female, white or nonwhite, could grow and develop throughout the life span. New avenues were paved during the 1970s with landmark legislation providing the disabled with similar civil rights won by blacks a decade before. Women, older persons, and working class individuals progressed socially and personally through social legislation and efforts by individuals and groups to integrate the whole of their lives. Such a holistic view of life seems on the threshold of becoming a stable, enduring perspective of more individuals who seek to balance work, leisure, and family throughout their lives.

Recreation and leisure services came to recognize that there are a wide variety of individual needs. Therefore, those who sponsored organized leisure services were encouraged to accept divergent lifestyles and avoid imposing highly standardized and uniform programs upon everyone. Similarly, community agencies found it incumbent to view recreation opportunities within a total network of human and social services that interact ecologically with living organisms.

Eighth Phase

By the end of the 1970s and beginning of the 1980s, more individuals were seeking to integrate work, leisure, family, and education in their lives. Such a holistic, ecological perspective views leisure agencies as being an interdependent part of the entire community system. Agencies are concerned with interrelationships among people in their total (physical, social, and spiritual) environments and the ways these relationships contribute or hinder their ability to realize their human potential.

This new strategy of service is seen as a more active, responsive approach to human service in an effort to satisfy human needs and minimize problems *before* they occur. Weiner (1971) suggests that the community leisure service worker:

> must view himself as the key recreation strategist in the community using all of the following alternative approaches to achieving recreational goals: (1) direct execution of a program; (2) stimulating community interest in a program by offering 'seed' money; (3) guidance, counseling, training and encouraging innovation; (4) providing information services and general support; and (5) determining interests/needs and identifying new resources (167).

This era has also been characterized by a revolution among citizens who have questioned whether recreation and leisure service was a public necessity. More individuals seek autonomy and control over additional aspects of their lives, including leisure. Tax-cutting initiatives, which arose in the late 1970s and early 1980s, were primarily attempting to control growth and excessive spending and bring certain government services under private control. Sessoms (1987) comments:

> Fueled by a new wave of social and political conservatism, Americans began to reassess the role of government and the relationship of government to the private sector. Government was viewed at all levels as being too large, too involved in the private lives of individuals, and too restrictive of free enter-

prise. Could not many of the programs and services of government be better handled by the private sector? Why should there be a local recreation and park agency when there are spas, private racquet and swim clubs, amusement centers, employee recreation services, family entertaining (e.g., TV, computer games, VCRs, etc.) to do the job? How can parks and recreation serve those who see themselves and their private associations, not local public agencies, as the primary providers of recreation services? (169-170).

While each phase of the Recreation and Park Movement signaled a new era of expansion of leisure opportunities, the delivery of community leisure services has been characterized by major contradictions in the profession's approach to leisure. As Kraus (1986) reflects on the emergence of leisure in community life:

We have viewed its expansion as critical to the development of a higher level of creativity and cultural arts in the community at large; yet, our largest single consumer of free time is television and related forms of passive entertainment. We argue that sports build character and positive personality traits; yet, we tolerate and support the wholesale exploitation of college athletes for unjustifiable purposes. We promote fitness and wellness through a popular wave of health-related programs; yet, alcohol and drug abuse represent major forms of recreational participation in our society. Indeed, state and municipal governments alike sponsor or profit from such marginal leisure-associated enterprises as gambling, the sale of liquor, or even more or less prostitution (2).

Further, Kraus (1986) indicates that the movement has been characterized by six philosophical perspectives that stem from our leisure value systems:

(1) traditional 'quality-of-life' approach, which sees recreation and leisure chiefly as amenities, without significant social purpose but nonetheless deserving community support; (2) the 'marketing' approach, which dominates our literature and professional dialogue today, and that urges that recreation be viewed largely as a commodity to be merchandised with a minimum of social goals or constraints; (3) the 'human-service' approach, which views recreation as a critically important life need, to be provided along with other key social

services, often within an umbrella-like agency structure; (4) the 'prescriptive' approach, in which recreation is administered for rehabilitative purposes or to bring about behavioral change; (5) the 'environmental/aesthetic/preservationist' approach, which applies chiefly to resource management and has limited concern with people-based programming as such; and (6) the 'hedonist' approach, which stresses the search for pleasure and sensation as leisure experiences (2).

The growing desire of the private sector and more neighborhood recreation associations wanting to operate and control their own activities mostly reflected a population seeking greater self-determination. People were weary of bureaucracy and standardized, packaged programs. This development during the late 1970s and decade of the 1980s was principally an effort by individuals to connect to the wider community. Kelly (1985) comments on some of the sociopolitical changes that have had an impact on the growth of private leisure enterprise:

> First, there is a shift away from the concept of a service society. A number of demographic and economic factors including rising federal government debt burdens, increases in the proportion of the population retired from production-related incomes, consequent rise in the cost of various welfare and support programs for older people, and a failure to move toward full employment of those seeking work will increase the pressures on government budgets. Sources that can be defined as secondary or unnecessary are not likely to gain vastly increased budgets at any government level.
>   Second, there is a general recognition that government bodies are operating on a condition of scarcity. Just because a service or program is desired or used will not be an adequate justification for its provision by the public sector. In general, opportunities that can be provided by the market sector will be left for private enterprise. It is likely that the dependence on business as a recreation provider will increase rather than diminish (449-450).

These sociopolitical developments are also buttressed by value-orientation changes that have contributed to a shift from government to voluntary organizations serving as the source of role modelling for members of the community. Kelly (1985) indicates that the following trends are influencing this change:

1. Traditional voluntary associations, especially the churches, are a diminishing influence. The role of the church and youth-serving organizations, like Boy and Girl Scouts, as a major modelling force in the society appears past.

2. Social solidarity now seems more than ever based in the immediate communities of family and household. The face-to-face relationships claim priority rather than larger institutions. Life tends to be organized around places owned and controlled by the people with whom one has direct and immediate bonds.

3. A greater emphasis on personal expression and development is found among the highly educated and upwardly mobile younger population groups.

Kelly continues:

Relationships, activities, investments, and even work may be chosen with personal gratification as a central aim. If they do not produce the personal satisfaction anticipated, they may be discarded. For example, marriage is to yield companionship, not just the security of home and family. Work is to offer opportunities for personal development, not just financial security and a place in the society. And leisure is to afford individual development and expression, not just a pleasant filling of leftover time (451).

These developments have raised the degree of individual commitment to producing salient experiences in community life that bring about a positive effect on personal well-being. Since we live in a more affluent society, more people have the financial means to purchase electronic, sport, fitness, or personal growth gadgets, or to create opportunities for leisure expression through travel, dining, spectating, and participation in a myriad of events and activities on their own. The medical, technological, scientific, and economic advances have created more opportunities and choices for all people. Thus, leisure on the threshold of the twenty-first century has grown to become a significant form of human expression, whereby predominant institutions, organizations and family units within the community *must* reconceptualize, restructure, and reform the mechanisms and processes that service their members, employees, clients, customers, and relationships.

With the close of the eighth phase of the Recreation and Park Movement, the newly emerging ninth phase has in just a short span of time begun to provide society with a service delivery system amenable to integrating and blending the leisure experience with other aspects of community life. This development means that leisure will not have to be viewed simply or singularly as a reward, method of punishment, or even a treatment for a social, physical, or psychological malady or dysfunction; it can be recognized as a normal, fundamental aspect of one's total being.

In the 1990s, the emergence of holistic leisure, synchronistic fusion of mind, body, and spirit, means that leisure's attributes exist everywhere. One can be at leisure at any given time or place. Thus, one does not have to postpone gratification, creative insights, diligent intellectual quests, or feeling good. The recognition that it is not the economic, familial, religious, political, and governmental structures that alone produce leisure opportunities is a significant development at the close of the twentieth century. It marks the beginning of a stage of synchronization of all life events—conscious and unconscious, material and nonmaterial, scientific and unscientific, causal and noncausal—and the possibility that everyone can feel the pleasure and exercise their innate ability in participating fully as an individual and a member of one's community, society, and universe. The eighth phase of the Recreation and Park Movement coincides with the second century of organized leisure service in North America. The second century of organized recreation and leisure service should result in agencies and businesses creating more flexible leisure options for participants, consumers, and clients, with leisure experiences becoming more likely perceived as normal, desired expressions of the total self.

Structure of Leisure Services

Leisure opportunities are activated, coordinated and managed by public, private nonprofit and commercial leisure enterprise organizations. Collectively, they comprise the community recreation and leisure system as depicted in Figure 3.1.

Leisure service agencies, then, exist to provide opportunities for people, individually and collectively, to engage in leisure behavior in order that certain personal and social goals can be satisfied. By manipulating the human and physical environments

Figure 3.1 Community Recreation and Leisure Service System

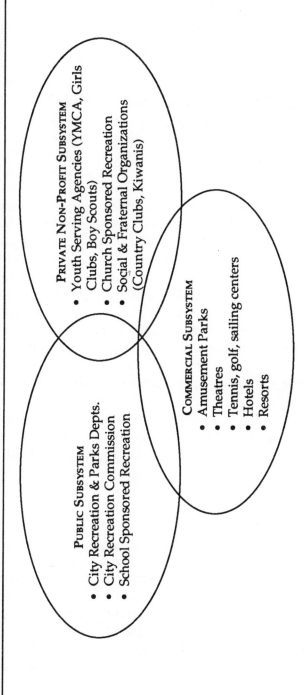

PRIVATE NON-PROFIT SUBSYSTEM
- Youth Serving Agencies (YMCA, Girls Clubs, Boy Scouts)
- Church Sponsored Recreation
- Social & Fraternal Organizations (Country Clubs, Kiwanis)

COMMERCIAL SUBSYSTEM
- Amusement Parks
- Theatres
- Tennis, golf, sailing centers
- Hotels
- Resorts

PUBLIC SUBSYSTEM
- City Recreation & Parks Depts.
- City Recreation Commission
- School Sponsored Recreation

1. Today a variety of representative agencies from all three sectors, private non-profit, public and commercial, can be found in most communities.

2. Collectively, they comprise the community recreation systems.

3. While all three are involved in the provision of formal, organized leisure activities, each is sufficiently different from the others, with respect to philosophy, objectives and finances.

that are part of their operation, agencies structure opportunities that elicit various kinds of recreation behavior. While all three types of community leisure service organizations (see Table 3.1) provide formal, organized leisure activities, each is sufficiently different from the other with respect to philosophy, objectives, and financing to allow for their independent classification.

The responsibility of providing park and recreation services in community settings rests mostly with local government. In accordance with traditions, the primary role of state and federal government is to provide technical and financial assistance in support of local community recreation. Beyond the local community, these state and federal agencies furnish a wide variety of outdoor recreation resources. These resources range in size from relatively small state parks to the vast acreages of parks such as Death Valley National Monument and Multi-Use Lands administered by the U.S. Forest Service and the U.S. Bureau of Land Management. They range in state of development from high density campgrounds to wilderness areas.

There are many different organizational forms through which recreation, park, and leisure services are delivered. Three broad categories we will discuss include public tax-supported (recreation and park agencies, schools, and human resource agencies), private nonprofit (nonsectarian youth-serving organizations, sectarian youth-serving organizations and religious social agencies, settlement houses, and special interest organizations), and commercial enterprises (self-directed activity, entertainment, instruction of personal enhancement, retail manufacturers and suppliers, and travel and tourism).

Public Organizations

The three main types of public community agencies, whose almost exclusive mandate is to provide recreation and leisure services are: special recreation and park districts, separate recreation and separate park departments, and combined recreation and park departments. Howard and Crompton (1980, 209-227) delineate the different aspects of each:

Special Recreation and Park Districts

These have a defined geographical service area and are governed by a body composed generally of three to seven elected

Table 3.1 Comparison and Contrast Study of Public, Private (Voluntary Agencies), and Commercial Recreation

Philosophy of Recreation

Public   Enrichment of the life of the total community by providing opportunities for the worthy use of leisure. Nonprofit in nature.

Private   Enrichment of the life of participation members by offering opportunities for worthy use of leisure, frequently with emphasis on the group and the individual. Nonprofit in nature.

Commercial   Attempt to satisfy public demands in an effort to produce profit. Dollars from, as well as for, recreation.

Objectives of Recreation

Public   To provide leisure opportunities that contribute to the social, physical, educational, cultural, and general well-being of the community and its people.

Private   Similar to public, but limited by membership, race, religion, age, and the like. To provide opportunities for close group association with emphasis on citizenship, behavior, and life philosophy values. To provide activities that appeal to members.

Commercial   To provide activities or programs that will appeal to customers. To meet competition. To net profit. To serve the public.

Administrative Organization

Public   Governmental agencies (federal, state, county, and local).

Private   Boy Scouts, settlements, Girl Scouts, Camp Fire Girls, "Y" organizations, and others.

Commercial   Corporations, syndicates, partnerships, private ownerships. Examples: motion pictures, television and radio companies, resorts, bowling centers, skating rinks.

Table 3.1 *Continued*

Finance

Public	Primarily by taxes. Also by gifts, grants, trust funds, small charges, and fees to defray.
Private	By gifts, grants, endowments, donations, drives, and membership fees.
Commercial	By the owner or promoters. By the users: admission and charges.

Facilities

Public	Community buildings, parks (national, state, local), athletic fields, playgrounds, playfields, stadiums, camps, beaches, museums, zoos, golf courses, school facilities, etc.
Private	Settlement houses, youth centers, churches, play areas, clubs, camps, and others.
Commercial	Theaters, clubs, taverns, night clubs, lounges, racetracks, bowling lanes, stadiums, and others.

Leadership

Public	Professionally prepared to provide extensive recreation programs for large numbers of people. Frequently subject to Civil Service regulations. Volunteers as well as professionals. College training facilities growing.
Private	Professionally prepared to provide programs on a social group-work basis. Employed at discretion of managing agency. Volunteers as well as professionals.
Commercial	Frequently trained by employing agency. Employed to secure greatest financial returns. Employed and retained at the discretion of the employer. No volunteers.

Table 3.1 *Continued*

Program	
Public	Designed to provide a wide variety of activities, year-round, for all groups, regardless of age, sex, race, creed, social or economic status.
Private	Designed to provide programs of a specialized nature for groups and in keeping with the aims and objectives of the agency.
Commercial	Program designed to tap spending power in compliance with state and local laws.
Membership	
Public	Unlimited—open to all.
Private	Limited by organizational restrictions, such as age, sex, religion, and the like.
Commercial	Limited by: law (local, state, and federal), social conception regarding status and strata in some places. Economics—limited to those who have the price to pay.

or appointed board or commission members. Special districts have revenue-producing powers—they enjoy fiscal independence and do not have to compete directly with other community tax-supported services to obtain funds.

Separate Recreation and Separate Park Departments

Parks departments historically have been concerned with horticulture, landscaping, and gardening activities; recreation departments have been concerned primarily with providing programs and leadership rather than maintaining and acquiring park space. There are still examples of each of these types of operations. They are justified because both are unique functions and, therefore, should be given more visibility by having distinct departmental status.

Combined Recreation and Park Departments

Surveys taken in recent years reveal that over two-thirds of local authorities who deliver recreation or park services now use a consolidated organizational form. There are two major advantages to combining recreation and parks into a single department. First, the increased size gives it an increased budget and enhanced prestige and visibility. Second, the centralization of responsibility and authority offer the opportunity for improved overall efficiency.

School Provisions of Recreation and Leisure Services

There are three principal types of relationships between recreation and leisure services and local schools: (1) school administration of community leisure services, (2) community education programs, and (3) joint education and leisure use of facilities.

School Administration of Community Leisure Services. Under enabling laws granted to local school boards, approximately 2 percent of communities have the authority to administer leisure services.

The advantage of this organizational form is that there are necessary facilities and trained leadership present to manage and conduct effective community leisure programs. The disadvantage is that leisure services, as a secondary function, will be vulnerable; if they experience budgetary restrictions, recreation will be the first to suffer reductions.

Community Education Programs. This approach used by some school districts is intended to expand their role by offering a variety of education and leisure classes in the evenings and during school vacations. Over 2000 districts throughout the United States use this approach. The goal of community schools is to make them the center of neighborhood education, recreation and cultural opportunities. A community education program represents integrated community involvement, rather than merely a joint provision.

Joint Education and Leisure Use of Facilities. This approach involves shared use of facilities by both school districts and local community recreation and leisure agencies. The involvement can range from limited school sharing of playing fields and indoor recreation facilities to fully developed joint school district and leisure service agency planning, capital and operating cost outlay, and use of facilities.

Human Resource Department Provisions of Recreation and Leisure Services

We indicated earlier that during the 1970s a number of recreation and leisure service agencies altered their traditional provincial role of direct service recreation to incorporate broad-based human needs. This organizational form has principally been adopted in California, Texas, and New York. Cities have either (1) expanded and transformed the traditional recreation and leisure agency, in both organizational configuration and service role, into a new human service department, or (2) reorganized and consolidated existing social service agencies into a single community human service agency.

Expanded Recreation and Leisure Service Agency. Recreation and leisure service agencies in cities have increasingly recognized that in order to meet the leisure needs of their constituents, they must provide other forms of social and human services. This broadened mandate has been actualized in such diverse services as drug and alcohol counseling for youth, information and referral, delinquency prevention and family service programs, social security, Medicare and health clinic services, job training and placement, and nutrition and hot meals.

Consolidation of Social Service Agencies. This form has typically resulted in recreation and leisure services being assimilated into a larger comprehensive human service agency. The intent of such consolidation is to enhance the coordination and effectiveness of a city's traditionally independent and fragmented social services programs.

The development of human service configurations within local, tax-supported community agencies reflects a holistic approach to respond to and service the whole person. Whether it be an expanded role for a leisure agency or an amalgamation of leisure with other social services in a community, a human resource department is designed to integrate several aspects of community life, rather than separating and treating them as independent and disparate entities.

Private Nonprofit Organizations

There are several voluntary nongovernmental agencies that are a part of each community. Kraus (1983, 191-237) describes four principal types: (1) nonsectarian youth-serving organizations, (2) sectarian youth-serving organizations and religious social agencies, (3) settlement houses and community centers, and (4) special interest organizations. They rely on public contributions supplemented by membership fees and charges for participation. In some cases agencies have pursued special projects and received government grants.

These organizations, which evolved mostly during the first and second phases of the Recreation and Park Movement, have sought to serve the poor, the disabled, and the culturally deprived with a variety of social and educational services and programs. In the 1960s and 1970s many of these organizations undertook an expanded role of human services. Many voluntary agencies do not see themselves as being primarily leisure service organizations, though provisions for leisure experiences often serve as the single largest component of their programs. However, in contrast with most public and commercial organizations, voluntary agencies view leisure not as an end in itself, but as a means through which to obtain other agency objectives (Kraus, 1983, 193).

Nonsectarian Youth-Serving Organizations

The most notable examples of these organizations include Boy Scouts and Girl Scouts, Boys' and Girls' Clubs of America, Camp Fire, Police Athletic League and 4H Clubs. Boy Scouts (1910) and Girl Scouts (1912), and Boys' Clubs (1906) and Girls' Clubs (1945) of America, while exclusively serving members of one gender since their inception, have been opening their membership to others of the opposite sex. These changes are mostly due to the removal of sex-role stereotyping, which dictated that certain activities were not appropriate for boys or girls. Additionally, these four organizations have undergone marked changes in their overall operations by modifying their goals and revamping program objectives to reflect contemporary society. These organizations are keyed to provide character-building experiences for youth and are oriented toward overall enhancement of community life.

In years past this orientation meant assuring that moral and ethical programs that strengthened individual character would result in building good citizens. But the era of Vietnam, civil and human rights, the women's movement, and increased awareness of the inequities for members of our society (in some cases the primary participants in non-sectarian youth organizations), led to more socially-oriented programs focusing on improvement of neighborhood slums, environmental awareness, child care, health and fitness, alcohol and drug prevention, job training, delinquency prevention, and increased efforts to serve the disabled and poor. Today nonsectarian youth-serving organizations are still committed to providing traditional character-building experiences but have also continued to respond to the health, fitness, and plethora of social needs of an expanding constituency.

Sectarian Youth-Serving Organizations and Religious Social Agencies

Voluntary organizations serving a great number of individuals are agencies affiliated with major religious denominations, both on a local and national basis. Kraus (1983) notes two broad purposes of local churches or synagogues in providing leisure programs:

1. to provide recreation for their own members or congregation in order to meet their leisure needs in ways that promote involvement with the institution; and
2. to provide leisure opportunities for the community at large or a selected population group in ways that are compatible with their own religious beliefs (198).

We would include another purpose, that of influencing community values and attitudes as they relate to leisure behaviors.

Perhaps the most notable national organizations are Young Men's Christian Association (YMCA), Young Women's Christian Association (YWCA), Catholic Youth Organization (CYO), and Young Men's and Women's Hebrew Association (YM-YWHA). These organizations provide a network of facilities and programs. In the case of the Ys and CYO, their orientation toward promoting religious ideals of living are geared toward meeting leisure needs of members.

Settlement Houses and Community Centers

Located mostly in inner city neighborhoods in the eastern part of the United States, the settlement house or community center has historically provided extensive leisure service programs and other social work, health, counseling, education, and cultural enrichment programs to poor and minority group members. Many of the earliest forms of organized recreation and leisure service emanated from the settlement house programs. The philosophy of service viewed that the mission of each community center was to meet the total needs of neighborhood residents. While such programs were costly to operate, they often were the hub of each neighborhood where they were located.

Special Interest Organizations

The fourth major voluntary type of agencies, special interest organizations, tend to offer specialized leisure experiences and work as catalysts and advocates in promoting these interests. The list of voluntary special interest, leisure-related organizations include: Sierra Club, Appalachian Club, America Youth Hostels, Little League, National Rifle Association, Arts Councils, and service and fraternal clubs. Special interest groups have significance for their members' nonwork lives.

Commercial Leisure Enterprise

The growth of spending for commercial leisure products, experiences, and services has been steadily increasing. Commercial leisure enterprise represents organizations and businesses in which the participant or consumer pays for the product, event, or service and the purveyor intends to make a profit. This category of community leisure services represents the largest category of financial outlay by the public for leisure opportunities, ranging from instruction, gambling, and entertainment to self-directed participation, products, and services.

Types

There are different ways of classifying commercial leisure enterprise. One is by type of resource or facility, and another by type of activity or experience.

Commercial Leisure Resources:

Shopping Facilities (retail stores, shopping malls, mail order catalog)
Food and Drink (cafes, fast-food and sit-down restaurants, bars, nightclubs, mobile food cart, food and beverage stores)
Stadiums and racetracks
Museums, gardens, and parks
Hotels, motels, and resorts
Amusement parks
Campgrounds
Camps and schools
Products and services

Commercial Experience and Consumption Orientation (Kraus 1983, 230)

1. *Facilities and areas for self-directed activity.* These include golf courses, swimming pools, ski centers, bars and taverns, ice rinks, bowling alleys, billiard parlors, riding stables, boat marinas, driving ranges, campgrounds, and fish and game preserves. The participant initiates the activity in these settings.

2. *Enterprises providing entertainment.* The participant is generally entertained in a positive manner at theaters, indoor and outdoor movies, concert halls, nightclubs, commercial sport stadiums, circuses, amusement parks, race tracks, carnivals, and so forth.

3. *Enterprises providing instructional services.* These opportunities involve commercially-operated programs that offer instruction (for self-improvement, enhancement of abilities) by health centers and studios, or schools that give instruction in music, voice, dance, drama, physical fitness, riding, swimming, and so on.

4. *Manufacturers and suppliers of leisure equipment.* Many leisure activities do not require special facilities for instruction but do involve the purchase of special equipment or

materials. Some products include: musical equipment, tape recorders (phonograph records and players, and instruments), toys, games, gardening equipment, books, magazines, radio and television sets, VCRs, compact disk players, and special leisure clothing.

5. *Travel and tourism.* The largest area of commercial leisure enterprise includes the operation of motels, hotels, commercial campgrounds, amusement complexes and theme parks. It also includes the management of tours, cruises, airline charters, and the like.

Growth

The growth of the $350 billion leisure market has been influenced by four primary factors:

1. Increased affluence. In general people have more discretionary money to spend on leisure products, experiences and services.

2. Availability of more discretionary time or blocks of time. While the amount of leisure has not increased in the last two decades, people are offered more three-day weekends, variable work shifts, and split work assignments.

3. Increased development of technology. The introduction of so many technological advances in travel, gadgets and equipment, and overall improvement in mechanisms that are considered necessary for survival such as household appliances, make it easier for individuals to engage in leisure pursuits.

4. Changed attitudes toward leisure. People are more accepting of free time and the pursuit of activities and experiences that provide enjoyment and promote health, cultural awareness, physical exercise, and educational enrichment.

Spending for leisure products has increased steadily. And while the adult worker is actually averaging more hours of work per week since 1973 (Harris Poll 1986), leisure is being incorporated into work through corporate and business sponsored fitness and employee recreation.

Approaches to the Delivery of Community Leisure Service

Changing events in community life since the 1960s have signaled an end to passive professional roles in many human service organizations. There has been an increase in the desire for more indigenous participation in services provided to neighborhoods in many North American communities. Citizens have initiated petitions against and voiced a disappointment with many traditional city hall or voluntary agency executive board-based program and service decisions. Community residents wanting a chance to direct the destiny of communities in which they live, have started demanding more control over decisions that would affect their neighborhoods. In one example, the Prusch Farm Park formation, in San Jose, California, as detailed in the overview to Part I, has been made operational and more meaningful to community residents through their direct participation in the park's programming and arrangement. (See also "My Philosophy of Service" by Liz Stefanics, executive director, New Mexico AIDS Services, which underscores this operational concept.)

My Philosophy of Service

It is rather crucial as people get involved in providing social/human services that an identity is created with an entire community holistic approach. Too often in recreation, parks, and leisure services, professionals only align themselves with other like professionals or systems (i.e., park and recreation departments).

If we were to be totally successful in providing and coordinating services to the community (whatever group we have identified) then we need to be integrated into all of the groups that serve that specific community.

If I ran a therapeutic recreation program for a city I could not possibly ignore the local Human Services Coalition or the Area Agency on Aging or the Association of Retarded Citizens, etc. Usually a few of these agencies jump into our faces to become involved... because it might be their clients who take part in our services, but the local Human Services Coalition might not receive direct services from my program and I probably would overlook them.

It is this political awareness or political need that our students are not taught to address in the communities that they serve. Often we teach park and recreation students that the services we provide are nonpolitical and that we should maintain a stand that is apolitical. When we do follow those old time generic rules we let the rest of the world pass us by. We lose our funding, we affect the services our constituents receive, and we forget to be their advocates.

If we believe that leisure services [are] a right in this country then we should be addressing what our specific advocacy role would be. In fact we would train/educate students or professionals not only to be public speakers but how to be change agents and subsequently [how] to be elected officials. Many a director of a recreation and parks department has the visibility and the understanding of a community to be its next mayor.

I have had strong experiences in the past two years working through systems to acquire services for constituents and firmly believe that without these formal networks we would not have made as great strides as we have. Some of these systems were in place such as the City Council, the State Legislature, the County and the State Human Services Coalitions, but others still need initiation and building.

A new organization that I started was the AIDS Consortium of New Mexico, that pulled together agencies, organizations, and individuals that provide direct and indirect services around AIDS. Original inception of the concept was to submit a statewide grant to the Robert Wood Johnson Foundation that included proposals from fifteen different agencies. Probably some of the agencies were not interested in signing on for a long term stint with the Consortium but it quickly grew as people learned what occurred when everyone sat in the same room together to plan and share information.

The AIDS Consortium of New Mexico currently has 150 members and has been extremely successful in a number of its goals. Not only have agencies worked together developing new programs, and have shared information and resources, but they are recognized as an important group with some clout. It could be that the public gives us more power than we planned or thought. The Consortium has to date had public dialogs with the State Secretary of Education, Corrections, and Human Services, that [have] created policy changes within the state. The Governor respects our requests with proclamations as appropriate for special programs and legislators seek us out to give input, support or nonsupport to all introduced legislation.

It is this process that we are not taught the importance of in our studies. Internal advisory councils are not the same medium that we are discussing here, I am discussing and proposing that the entire community needs to come together to offer support for services to be holistic in nature.

Liz Stefanics
Executive Director
New Mexico, AIDS Services, Inc.
Albuquerque, N. M.

Service Delivery Continuum

It had been customary for most public and private nonprofit agencies to approach delivery of leisure programs and services by using principles, planning, and service delivery techniques of the professional staff or agency that almost exclusively determined programs for their constituents. With commercial agencies, participants pay for primarily passive leisure experiences. At the same time, though, commercial leisure enterprises find that they must survey potential customers to determine their wants and then build and modify offerings accordingly.

As with other elements within the community system, leisure service organizations interact with other subsystem elements. Recreation and leisure agencies function fully and reach potentially more individuals when they recognize that leisure can occur at any time, any place, and anywhere. By recognizing the myriad of conditions and circumstances that contribute to one's awareness and interest in pursuing leisure experiences, leisure service professionals are more likely to reach participants, consumers, and clients.

We live in a pluralistic society, meaning that there are a variety of lifestyles that are representative of individuals within each community. Lifestyles represent personal interest emphases for defining a way of life, rather than representing a national cultural interpretation. In this sense, individual identity is linked through leisure expression to subcultural identity.

Leisure service organizations, no matter the particular form of sponsorship, best respond to participants, consumers, and clients by incorporating a full and diverse array of professional roles that fall along a service delivery continuum—from direct service to information-referral and enabler to advocate. A leisure professional has an immense task to just develop, conduct and manage programs and services. The professional must also be aware of the factors that intersect with people's lives and contribute to the likelihood that leisure may or may not occur for someone. As discussed in Chapter 2, leisure experiences reflect a variety of internally motivated needs that become manifest, consciously or unconsciously, as one interacts in the environment.

While the direct agency provision of activities, programs, and services will accommodate a large number of people, there are a host of conditions, both internal and external, that can interrupt or impede, and deny some individuals from meeting their leisure needs. Four widely recognized approaches are used by professionals in communities to promote enhancement of optimal leisure expression and overall well-being (refer to Figure 3.2).

In a social climate characterized by complexity, diversity, and rapid change, professional leisure service role flexibility is essential if the agency is to satisfy the divergent needs and demands of its customers. The professional roles to be discussed represent four options available to leisure service agencies in carrying out their service responsibilities. Elements of all four service delivery methods can be employed interchangeably as changing circumstances and conditions demand.

It is recognized in all areas of leisure service that there are multiple professional roles that can be employed to respond to diverse populations. The concept of a service delivery continuum denotes developmentally designed and ecologically connected services, programs, and opportunities. Howe-Murphy and Charboneau (1987) explain:

> To be responsive to individuals with varied activities, motivations, aspirations, personal lifestyles, and personal interpretations of play and leisure, there must exist a wide range of meaningful leisure opportunities. These opportunities can be best provided along a continuum ranging from totally segregated to totally integrated settings. This does not imply

Figure 3.2 Continuum of Leisure Services: Maximizing Opportunities.*

Roles of Service Providers

DIRECT SERVICE	INFORMATION-REFERRAL	ENABLING-FACILITATION	ADVOCACY
Centralized agency approach; agency produces programs; agency relies heavily on staff's expert opinion; agency assumes individual readiness and knowledge of the recreation experience.	No one agency can exclusively provide all recreation services and oportunities; recognizes entire community as part of the leisure service system; suggests knowledge of resources, services, etc. are not static.	Cooperative role of agency and participant; less emphasis on "packaged" programs and more on developmental activities; synergistic programming; leisure education—does not assume that all persons know how to recreate.	Agency becomes involved as an active representative of its constituency; recognizes that recreation is important to community life and an inherent right of all citizens; includes role as mediator of citizen problems and interpretor of discriminatory or unlawful practices.

*Source: James F. Murphy and Dennis R. Howard. 1977. *Delivery of community leisure services: An holistic approach.* Lea & Febiger.

a predetermined set of programs in which an individual is 'placed' but rather a creative, flexible response both to developing human beings and changing social conditions (186).

The continuum concept implies a progression of the person from dependence toward independence. The continuum suggests that the desired state of the participant is for him or her to have a high degree of freedom in selecting leisure experiences, and the service provider's ultimate role is to assist the individual in achieving full participation in the environment of his or her choosing. The leisure service professional also has responsibility for removing barriers that hinder, block, or in any way impede or restrict leisure participation of individuals in communities they serve. Thus, the recognition of a continuum of services underscores the idea that leisure is not simply a reward for remunerative work, but is a fundamental inalienable right of the individual. One may even argue, as we have presented, that it serves to bring wholeness to one's life and enhance well-being.

Service Delivery Roles

The application of multiple service delivery roles for leisure service professionals is predicated on the following three beliefs:

1. No one agency relying exclusively on its own resources can possibly meet all the leisure needs of a community.
2. For leisure services to remain viable, they must work toward alleviating barriers to participation and intervening social and physical environmental constraints that impede the ability of many individuals to experience leisure.
3. Each professional role should function to assist an individual to progress from one type of experience or degree of leisure independence and from one setting or experience to the next. Through each experience one may develop skills, behaviors, interests and an awareness that can be used meaningfully in the same, similar, or entirely new settings.

Direct Service Provider

In the direct service role, leisure service personnel select, plan, and organize leisure activities and services for people. This approach is characterized by a centralized agency-determined estimation of what programs and services participants, consumers, and clients want. A ready-made array of leisure opportunities are preassembled by professional staff and offered to participants to choose, cafeteria style, from a vast assortment of possibilities available.

In the direct service approach a minimum amount of input into the formalization and conduct of programs is required from program recipients. For many agencies this approach has traditionally been the most widely used method since it does not require time-consuming agency effort to query potential participants, evaluate the findings, and then institute service. It is an expedient service-delivery technique. This approach, though, can create a dependence on the consumer because it is largely facility-oriented and assumes that individuals will somehow have the means and ability to attend the activities offered on their own accord.

Information-Referral

The information-referral approach incorporates the use of coordination, referral, and technical assistance. This expanded orientation of service delivery may entail the co-sponsorship of leisure service programs with other agencies (e.g., public leisure service agency cooperating with the YMCAs and the school district to run a fitness program), the initiation of a computerized leisure opportunity system, and the offering of technical and consultative services to community groups. Adopting the information-referral role means recognizing that no one agency can meet all the leisure needs of a community.

Referral "is the process of making it possible for those with whom we are working to receive help from another source, when the nature of the help they need is either outside our areas of responsibility or beyond our expertise" (Niepoth 1983, 225). The referral approach extends leisure service agency responsibilities beyond the boundaries of their own structure and necessarily results in them interfacing with other organizations within the wider community system. While this strategy is deemed more and more important by all human services, certain conditions must exist before agencies can enable others, whom they have contact with, to reach the sources of help people need. Niepoth (1983) says:

> First of all, we [leisure service agencies] need to know where our responsibilities for direct service end; we also need to know the limits of our abilities to provide effective and appropriate help. When these parameters are clear to us, we can be most aware of when referrals are appropriate. Second, to put someone else in contact with sources of help, we need to know the nature of the problem and something about the condition of the person who is experiencing it. Finally, we have to have an adequate knowledge of community resources that are available to which the affected person may be referred (225).

Professionals must decide to make referrals when an individual has his or her leisure options blocked or is seeking information about available opportunities not yet known to the individual. Additionally, as in the case of recreation therapists or counselors, patients might require, following rehabilitation, follow-up to treatment and transitional assistance outside the hospital or clinic. The information-referral process extends the service delivery continuum and helps to link leisure to other aspects of an individual's life and contribute to a more viable sense of community. Thus, each element of community life is more likely to be integrated with each other, resulting in a network that helps foster compatibility and shared interests among residents—the cornerstone of participation in community life (see "Brevard County's Fishing College").

Brevard County's Fishing College

Each year, thousands of retired or semi-retired Northerners drive south to spend their winter in the warm Florida sunshine. Many of them head to Brevard County, the location of Cape Canaveral, but also known for some of the best fishing in Florida. Not surprisingly, one of the favorite recreation interests of the snowbirds is fishing. In response to this interest, Brevard County District 3 Recreation and Parks

Department started, in the mid 1970s, a program titled "Fishing College."

The "Fishing College" met once a week for eight weeks at locations throughout the Melbourne and South Brevard County area. An average crowd of about 100 would come to hear about fishing tips, techniques, equipment selection, fishing hot spots, and so forth. There was no charge to attend because there were no costs incurred by the recreation department. Each Fishing College instructor was a volunteer, and each was an expert from a commercial establishment: sporting goods store, fishing charter boat, freshwater fish camp, a bait and tackle shop, etc. Cooperation from the commercial operators was achieved by offering them the "opportunity" to meet a hundred enthusiastic potential customers. In addition, weekly radio announcements and newspaper articles credited the business establishments for their help.

Special programs concluded the final two weeks of the Fishing College. First, the Coast Guard Auxiliary conducted a boating safety clinic. The final week was devoted to a fish fry. Again, commercial establishments co-sponsored the event. A fish market donated the fish, while a local grocery donated the coleslaw, hush puppies, and drinks. All the instructors returned the final week to act as chefs and to mix informally with the attendees. Each participant who attended all seven of the previous programs was officially "graduated" with a diploma from the Fishing College.

After several seasons of conducting the Fishing College, enough information had been generated to compile a short brochure titled "Guide to Fishing and Camping in Brevard County." This publication was distributed throughout the Parks and Recreation Department, the Chamber of Commerce, the local hotels, and of course the commercial fishing businesses.

Brevard County's Fishing College was a program that accomplished several objectives. It served the interests of an important client group without costing them or the recreation department anything. It also gained the support of the business community who benefited from the publicity and market contacts. It is also interesting to note that this successful program was developed by a recreation supervisor who knew nothing about fishing! It is more important that a recreation programmer know how to spot interesting oppor-

tunities and then find the resources to make the programs
work.

John Crossley
Department of Recreation and Leisure
University of Utah
Salt Lake City, Utah

Enabler

The enabler role incorporates a facilitation process in which professional personnel guide individuals to allow them to make self-directed choices and to gradually transfer (where possible) full responsibility for leisure planning and programming from professional to participant. Murphy and Howard (1977) explain:

> By adopting the facilitative approach, the recreation agency transcends a preoccupation with the development of its own programs to emphasize providing services that enable individuals and other organizations to expand and improve their own leisure opportunities. In doing so, the recreation agency makes great progress toward increasing the leisure self-sufficiency of its clientele as well as maximizing the limited resources it has at its disposal (75).

Another important and increasingly beneficial attribute of the enabler role is leisure education. All leisure personnel are viewed in this context as working to improve the community's attitudes, knowledge, skills, and awareness of community resources for actualizing leisure interests and meeting personal needs. Similarly, leisure service professionals, as they interface with all organizations and services that contribute to community life, are able to assist individuals in drawing a relationship between leisure and wellness.

The process of enabling or guiding individuals to understand what leisure is, helps to foster greater personal freedom and locus of control, two critical ingredients for leisure involvement. This self-recognition leads to increased possibilities for engaging in leisure that have a significant impact on psychological and physical health:

Empirical research leaves little doubt about the fact that intrinsically motivated leisure is positively and significantly related to psychological or mental health. Those who are in control of their leisure lives and experiences and feel engaged in and committed to leisure activities and experiences are psychologically healthier than those who are not in control over their leisure lives and feel detached and uncommitted (Iso-Ahola and Weissinger 1984, 52).

Therefore, a leisure service professional who works within a community context recognizes that there are conditions and barriers affecting one's ability to meet certain leisure interests.

According to Tinsley and Tinsley (1986) (see Figure 2.3) people's psychological needs influence their interpretation of their experiences, thereby influencing the probability of experiencing leisure:

Satisfaction of a person's psychological needs has a salutary effect on his or her mental health, physical health, and satisfaction with life, that in turn, have a salutary effect on his or her personal growth. Failure to satisfy one's psychological needs is detrimental to the physical and mental health of the person and results in a reduction of life satisfaction and a lack of personal growth (21).

By taking a holistic perspective (one that views the totality of the elements of community and life that impact on a person), leisure becomes a meaningful form of expression and a more viable option. The enabling approach facilitates people being able to develop a commitment to and engagement in community life (see Calgary, Alberta Department of Parks and Recreation *Community Development—A Rationale* for an explanation of why leisure service professionals acting as enablers, help foster a greater sense of community involvement and ultimately more significant citizen appreciation of leisure).

Community Development—A Rationale
City of Calgary, Alberta, Canada
Department of Parks and Recreation

Definition
    Community development can be summed up by the United Nations' definition (1955):

A process of social action in which the people of a community organize themselves for planning and action; define their common and individual needs and solve their problems; execute their plans with a maximum reliance upon community resources and supplement these resources when necessary with services and materials from governmental and non-governmental agencies outside of the community.

The term 'community' applies both to geographical areas (neighborhoods) and to 'communities of interest' having a regional or city-wide influence.

Why has the Department Committed to the Community Development Approach?

1. Because we value communities and believe that recreation can serve as an ideal vehicle/means to bring a community together.
   a. To assist groups of people to develop economically and socially viable communities that strengthen personal and family growth.
   b. To develop a sense of community to enhance the quality of life.
   c. To maximize individual and community potential by encouraging citizens to work together to fulfill collective needs.
   d. To encourage a 'self-help' philosophy that will transcend all aspects of community life.

2. Because community work/involvement is an excellent leisure pursuit for a caring/concerned citizen.
   a. To provide individuals with the greatest possible opportunity for personal growth through sharing and community service.
   b. To provide individuals with a range of social opportunities and a strong sense of community interaction.
   c. To provide individuals with the opportunity to develop and exercise their personal leadership skills.

3. Because we believe that a motivated, self-supportive community is most capable of determining and planning for its own needs.
   a. To assist groups in identifying and responding to the unique needs of their own community.

    b. To assist community groups to respond to all segments of the population without discrimination.
    c. To encourage individuals and groups having direct contact with the community to become directly involved in decision making and determining program interests and needs.

4. Because we believe that a motivated, self-supportive community is capable of 'doing more with less'.
    a. To bring forward resources within the community that might not otherwise be available to the public (financial, volunteer, expertise/experience, etc.).
    b. To work with groups to provide recreational opportunities at the lowest possible cost to users consistent with the quality objectives or standards that have been set.

5. Because community involvement in recreational programming frees government tax-based dollars for other activities, therefore increasing the number and range of leisure opportunities available.
    a. To encourage and motivate self-supporting community groups to help themselves.
    b. To attempt to reduce the cost of any city programs through involvement of the community volunteer in the planning and/or implementation.
    c. To encourage participants in city programs to consider the possibility of 'adopting' the program and continuing to run it either on their own or in cooperation with the City or another group/agency.

6. Because community development work provides an ideal opportunity to acquaint citizens with the significance of leisure and leisure services in their lives.
    a. To take advantage of opportunities for 'leisure education'.
    b. To ensure that groups fully appreciate the significance of leisure/recreation in their 'community' and in relation to their mandate.

Some of the Benefits/Outputs of Community Development

• Increased opportunities for recreational activity in the community and throughout the City.

> - Increased sensitivity to user need/preference within each program or community.
> - Increased likelihood of fee structures appropriate to the individual community or interest group.
> - Increased flexibility and speed of response to identified need.
> - Stronger, healthier communities.
> - More involved and satisfied.
>
> Ken Balmer
> Department of Parks and Recreation
> Calgary, Alberta

Thus, leisure service workers contribute to overall individual and community well-being. As several studies have shown, perceptions of social support are associated with reduction of medical complication and death rates in stressful situations. That is, as Iso-Ahola and Weissinger (1984) indicate, high social support appears to help people deal with stresses; low social support seems to increase susceptibility to illness:

> Those who are not engaged in or committed to life are not taking an active role in their social lives and are, therefore, less likely to have social support. Social support can facilitate feelings of control; there are others with whom to share distress and additional resources with whom to combat the stressor. This commitment to life, in general, and engagement in social life, in particular, clearly demonstrates the potential and the importance of leisure in providing resources to fight off stresses and illness induced by them. Leisure can be a means to create social and friendship networks to build 'resistance resources' (54).

Leisure experiences provide a linkage of individual participants with each other and their community through perceived social support from neighbors. Thus, leisure serves to connect one with others and facilitates stress reduction and therefore overall enhancement of well-being. As Iso-Ahola and Weissinger (1984) put it: "Stress-resistant people have a specific set of attitudes toward life: an openness to change, a feeling of involvement, and a sense of control over events" (55).

The enabler role helps move the individual closer to leisure independence. Leisure contributes to personality predisposition toward intrinsic motivation—making a person become more oriented toward challenge, commitment, and control. The interactional effect of an individual becoming more in touch with his or her own needs and intrinsic motivation results in more cognitive flexibility, which contributes to psychological, physical, and spiritual well-being.

Advocacy
This role, increasingly used by leisure service personnel, is characterized by an intervention approach in community social processes designed to change current conditions, status, level of service, or existing laws to enable individuals to realize more personal freedom of expression. This role initially involved professional personnel directly representing the interests of alienated, deviant, or disadvantaged groups. The right to personal fulfillment is influenced by the availability of the means to participate, a feeling of self-worth to provide necessary impetus and sense of free will in order to engage in leisure experiences, and a leisure opportunity system that responds to the whole person. Efforts of leisure service professionals, serving as advocates, have helped produce equal rights legislation for the ill, elderly, and disabled. The 1990 federal Civil Rights Law for the disabled benefited from professional recreators.

The information-referral process assumes that various helping services are available, somewhere in the community. It further assumes that the barriers to taking advantage of those services are lack of information or ability to use them. While most leisure service delivery approaches involve some form of direct involvement with participants and community constituents, the advocate role expands the professional beyond the structure of the organization. Within communities there are certain conditions that are themselves barriers to people's abilities to enjoy their leisure:

> For example, the absence of a public transit system can be a serious detriment to older adults who no longer drive their own automobiles, and who have no one upon whom they can depend for transportation. In such a situation, even if extensive recreational programs for seniors are provided, some individuals will not be able to use them. Architectural barri-

ers often deny access to disabled persons. As an illustration, a multistoried recreation center with no elevator denies opportunities for use to those confined to wheelchairs (Niepoth 1983, 231).

Thus, the advocate views problems as community conditions rather than individual inadequacies. The mechanistic model, exemplified by Newtonian reductionism and Western medicine, assumes most problems emanate from the individual; direct service and information-referral roles are most appropriate and commonly used in these situations. But the public transit and architectural barrier examples suggest a different model similar to a systems perspective and social action model. Lawrence (1977) comments:

> In contrast to the defect-within-the-individual model, the community organization model places the defect with society – its institutions, practices, and organizational patterns. According to this model, the quality of human life services to people can be optimized most effectively by intervening at the level of social institutions and organizations (68).

The professional roles represent two types of services — *direct* and *indirect*. The direct service program role, which uses the social planning model of community organization, suggests that community leisure service personnel use their

> professional training and knowledge to diagnose the needs of the environment and to intervene in order to provide services. The second type of service, indirect, is based on the application of the locality development model of community organization. The role of the programmer in this strategy is to enable or encourage the participant to assist his or her own skills in the initiation of programs and services that he or she feels will meet his or her needs (Edginton, Compton, and Hanson 1980, 69).

The indirect approach is designed to encourage self-help through collaboration between the leisure service professional and the community resident. The leisure service professional, primarily in public and private non-profit agencies, will use the enabler and advocate approaches to serve constituents:

The bases for recreation and park personnel to be involved in advocacy are very similar to the reasons why they are involved in referral. If our objective is to enable people to make the best use of free time in enriching ways, then we need to be concerned about eliminating or minimizing the barriers that prevent it. In some cases, the barrier is the individual's inability to use existing resources. In these cases, referral is appropriate. In other situations, resources are not available to those who need them (Niepoth 1983, 234).

As previously discussed in an example of lack of transportation for older adults and inaccessible public community recreation centers lacking elevators and ramps, such physical conditions make it difficult or impossible for certain individuals to exercise leisure options. The facilities and resources are not only inaccessible, but they are unavailable.

In these conditions, the challenge is not to provide information about resources to the would-be user or to help that person take advantage of such resources. Instead, it is to change existing conditions in ways that benefit citizens with whom we are concerned. In referral, the primary focus of our efforts is the individual with the problem. In advocacy, the focus is more upon the condition or barrier causing the problem. More specifically, the focus is on the decision maker, who can eliminate or minimize problems (Niepoth 1983, 235).

The advocate role becomes a logical extension of the repertoire of service delivery approaches used by the professional. By incorporating an ecological and systems perspective, agency professionals recognize that there are many interacting aspects within a community that impact on the agency's ability to deliver program opportunities to people. In direct service and enabler roles, the professional's efforts are primarily *internal*, that is, the service provider relies on and uses resources that exist within the agency. In information-referral and advocate roles, the professional's efforts are directed *externally* toward other agencies and personnel.

Interchanging Service Delivery Roles

The service delivery continuum is a continuous open loop (see Figure 3.3). At any time a leisure agency may be the target of

Figure 3.3 Interacting Leisure Service Methods for Optimizing Leisure and Well-being

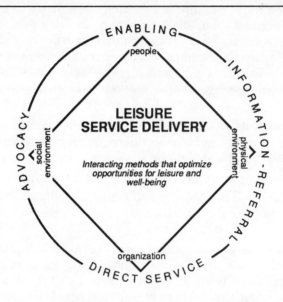

referral or advocacy efforts by personnel in other community human service agencies or by community residents. All service delivery approaches may be viewed within an interactional perspective. Such a model involves three major elements—the individual, his or her physical and social environment, and the interaction that occurs between them. Thus, with service delivery intervention (using information-referral, enabling, and advocacy) the professional seeks to facilitate change in the individual and the environment. "Any intervention strategy is designed with the understanding that there is a direct and reciprocal relationship and subsequent interaction between the individual and the environment" (Howe-Murphy and Charboneau 1987, 198).

Ultimately, for the relationship between the professional and the participant, consumer, or client to be most effective, it must be based on a belief in the individual to make self-determined choices: "Although the level of this ability varies with each person, the fact that we all possess this ability on some level needs to be acknowledged and included in any intervention strategy" (Howe-Murphy and Charboneau 1987, 199).

Thus, while the direct service approach is often the most convenient method of providing leisure opportunities, it may represent the weakest developmental strategy. Leisure program or event planning and delivery are determined by the agency. Participants, consumers, and clients only have to show up to experience programs and services. This approach typically takes place in highly authoritarian-operated organizations. In all other service delivery approaches that may be used, the intent of the professional is to increase options for the growth and development of individuals within the community. Leisure agencies that incorporate the full range of service delivery approaches are more likely to successfully intervene and enhance opportunities for leisure expression among all members of the community. This process points to the interdependent relationship that is fostered between professional and participant, consumer, and client. *This process recognizes recipients of services and programs as collaborators in their own growth and development.* This is the key to distinguishing between recreation professionals and those who only provide "activities for pleasure."

Operationally, the previously discussed professional roles can be suitably implemented based upon the circumstances and needs existing in a given community. By employing a full range of professional roles, leisure personnel extend service delivery to more individuals and make leisure expression more relevant within a wider network to prospective participants. *By using all possible service delivery approaches interchangeably as changing circumstances and conditions dictate, recreators assume responsibility for understanding the impact and relationship of their decisions on the community as a whole.* We will review these various approaches to service delivery, and the roles they suggest for agency staff members again in Chapter 6.

Changing Role of Leisure Service Agencies

The changing composition of communities throughout the United States and Canada reflects a more heterogeneous, diverse population. Community households particularly in the East, West, and Sunbelt states of the United States are reflective of increasingly nonwhite, older, single individuals. All types of leisure service agencies—public, private nonprofit, and commercial leisure enterprises, historically have oriented their programs and services to the majority culture (white, middle-income individuals and families).

Leisure services agencies will increase their constituencies by embracing the entire continuum of service delivery methods and by incorporating a pluralistic model of society with their philosophy, program, and marketing model. Leisure service organizations must recognize that there are many diverse forms of leisure expression and that these differences have less to do with matters of socioeconomic and demographic characteristics (age, sex, income, occupation, education, race, and so forth) and more to do with interest, cultural, and developmental differences that emerge from the mix of personal and environmental variables affecting each of us.

Pluralistic Culture and Leisure

The diversity of racial, ethnic, and cultural groups that inhabit North America significantly contribute to and shape leisure values and behavior. Godbey (1980) illustrates the effects of cultural pluralism, the result of many ethnic, religious, and political minority groups who maintain their identity rather than becoming completely assimilated in the majority culture on the leisure behavior of a postindustrial society.

In a pluralistic society, leisure represents an expression of personal interest or "lifestyle" rather than one's culture. While this is characteristic of our information-fed postindustrial society, the emergence of different, nonuniform, seemingly unrelated forms of leisure expression are not a result of lack of adherence to a more standardized cultural form, but an awakening of awareness and consciousness. On the one hand, this awakening creates planning and programming dilemmas, particularly for agencies accustomed to fitting as many people as possible into a common structure (ballet classes, sports leagues, pottery instruction). On the other hand, personal revelation of one's innate abilities opens up the prospect that more individuals will achieve a level of personal growth—achievable through satisfaction of psychological needs in which an individual's experiences are a reflection of his or her self-determined needs. As discussed in the case study of Prusch Farm Park presented in the overview of Part I, ethnic pride swells when people are able to represent their culture in community activities and are invited to participate in the planning and development of programs and services.

Leisure service professionals have an important obligation to respond appropriately to a pluralistic culture. Godbey (1980) states:

> Our pluralistic culture makes it difficult for leisure service agencies to 'create' culture. Rather, they must reflect the many cultures around them. This cannot be done without the intensifying of formats. . . . [M]aintaining cultural pluralism requires that a delicate balance be maintained between ignoring differences in culture to the extent that those with specific subcultures are either alienated or surrender their identity and recognizing such differences to the extent that members of society have little in common. Leisure service agencies must seek this balance (175).

While the dichotomy may not be as severe as Godbey suggests, leisure service agencies cannot afford to be ignorant of public opinion and diversity of subcultures. One's commitment to a certain lifestyle, which represents and preserves critical aspects of one's race, ethnicity, sex, age, interests, culture, and morals, is not a divisive way of fragmenting the national culture. It is, rather, a way of life and source of identity not represented for various individuals and subcultures in the generalized ideal national character and culture. Leisure, as we have seen, not only promotes life satisfaction, mental and physical health, and personal growth, it provides a meaningful link (through shared interests and mutual compatibility) for people to others in the community.

The Benefits of Leisure Experience

As leisure becomes more acceptable as a personal, intrinsic, and integrated part of the human condition, people come to embrace its possibilities and implications for life fulfillment. As Tinsley and Tinsley's model of causal effects of leisure experience (see Figure 2.3) indicates, the dependence of physical health, mental health, life satisfaction, and personal growth on the satisfaction of the individual's psychological needs must exceed a threshold before effects occur. As people have come to recognize what the leisure experience is and how it profoundly impacts their life, it has become a central life issue. Leisure is a major source of value development. That is, intrinsic motivation, high degree of personal freedom, and a deep sense of personal choice, challenge, commitment and control (which characterize the conditions fostering leisure expression) are desired throughout all aspects of a person's life.

Leisure service personnel have the following immense challenge: shifting from a view of themselves as being the primary determiner of service delivery activities and programs that are designed to meet constituent leisure needs to a view that sees the participant, consumer, or client as having the primary role in assuming a large measure of self-responsibility in meeting their own leisure needs.

Professional Development in Recreation and Leisure Services

The recreation and leisure service field has grown to become an important element of community life and blossomed into a diverse profession. The recreation and leisure movement as described earlier in this chapter has progressed through over one hundred years of development and become an accepted, integral part of the organizations that exist to promote human development and life enrichment through leisure experiences.

Leisure professionals are employed in very diverse categories of human services—rehabilitation and hospitals, armed forces, local, state, provincial, and federal parks and recreation, corporate and employee recreation, commercial leisure enterprise, nonprofit youth and adult agencies, and campus leisure programs. The rich tradition in professional settings represents the range of leisure expression and acceptance of leisure service as an integral part of community life.

If one were to imagine a large, fully developed tree with roots spread out in many directions, yet all contributing to its stability and strong physical and aesthetic presence, it would be similar to an illustration of the recreation and leisure profession's evolution. The recreation and leisure profession has been rooted in several interrelated fields—social work, landscape architecture, horticulture, physical education, and the behavioral science fields of sociology and psychology. Recreation and leisure represents an amalgamation of diverse professions and disciplines all aiming to achieve one purpose: to enhance the human condition and improve the quality of life. We will present additional information about professionalism, as it relates to the responsibilities of service providers, in Chapter 7.

The Professional and the Profession

As Kraus (1983) notes, the term "professional" does not simply imply a person who receives pay for work conducted: "Instead, the term suggests that a professional is one who has a high degree of status and specialized training, and provides a significant form of public or social service" (296). A "profession" must generally satisfy five essential criteria (Hartsoe, 1973).

1. Have a *systematic body of knowledge;*
2. Possess *professional authority* based on *specialized preparation;*
3. Have the *sanction of the community* enforced through *credentialing individuals for professional practice;*
4. Have incorporated a *regulative code of professional ethics;*
5. Have a *professional culture* based on professional organizations, shared values, and traditions.

In each of these five areas that signify professional identity and recognition, recreation and leisure services, in all three primary areas of organizational structure (public, private nonprofit, and commercial leisure enterprise), represent diverse avenues of individual expression.

The leisure service profession is recognized by COPA (Council on Postsecondary Accreditation), the singular body that certifies professional accreditation of college and university disciplines in the United States. COPA recognition was granted to the profession through the National Council on Accreditation. The Council is sponsored by the National Recreation and Park Association, in cooperation with the American Association for Recreation and Leisure.

Systematic Body of Knowledge

The field of recreation and leisure is both sophisticated and complex because it draws upon many diverse aspects of knowledge, both conceptual and applied, related to life enrichment. Kraus (1983) comments:

Conceptual knowledge consists of information about the historical and philosophical roots of leisure and recreation; the social and economic significance of leisure and recreation in the community and nation; the role of play as a phenomenon of human development; and other specific theoretical understandings about environmental issues and processes, the interaction of government and other social forces, and the functions of recreation with the handicapped and other special populations.

Practical or applied knowledge relates to the specific skills needed by recreation practitioners. Depending on the agency and population served, these may include skills of direct leadership and program development, or managerial functions, such as personnel management, fiscal operations, facilities planning and maintenance, public relations, research and evaluation, and similar tasks.

All of these areas of knowledge—while they may involve content taken from other scholarly disciplines or fields of practice—are formulated in terms that are specifically applicable to the recreation field (298).

The explosion of literature—both conceptual and applied—has contributed to scholarly development of the recreation and leisure service profession. There are numerous books, reports, journals, pamphlets, and other materials, including video and audio cassette tapes and films, that represent all elements of the study and practice of recreation and leisure.

Specialized Preparation

The growth of recreation and leisure service fields has resulted in a concomitant growth of college and university undergraduate and graduate curricula offering specialized study. While less than one-third of all curricula are accredited, the demand for more professionally-oriented programs in higher education is testimony to the emergence of the field.

Curricula offerings are provided in two-year community colleges, four-year colleges and universities, and graduate education at the master's and doctorate levels.

Two-year curricula furnish both transfer and terminal programs. Terminal programs provide students with skills suitable for immediate employment. The focus is on paraprofessional status with the assumption that various job opportunities are suitable for direct leadership, rather than supervisory or administrative roles. Additionally, two-year programs offer transfer programs with a mix of general education and specialized recreation courses, which enable the student to progress to a four-year university program.

Four-year curricula provide students with a combination of general education, support or allied discipline courses, and professional leisure education. The basic premise of baccalaureate professional education is to give students an understanding of the contribution the recreation and leisure service occupational field makes to the individual and society. The mix of conceptual and applied professional skills and knowledge is designed to enable graduates to function as employees of all types of leisure service agencies.

Master's and doctoral programs are geared to individuals seeking to advance the knowledge of the discipline and pursue specialized areas of service. Most master's degree students go into upper levels of management; graduates of doctoral programs are predominantly employed as faculty or research scientists in higher education.

Credentialing Individuals for Professional Practice

The process of credentialing is "generally referred to as the practice of establishing qualifications that must be satisfied through a formal review process before one is permitted to engage in professional practice in a given field" (Kraus 1983, 301). There are a number of different standards and screening processes that have been established: (1) registration, (2) certification and licensing, (3) civil service requirements, and (4) employment standards for nongovernmental leisure service agencies.

Registration. This is the process of identifying educational and job experience requirements that applicants must meet in order to be designated as being qualified to serve as practitioners. Various professional societies initiate such voluntary steps; registration is applied typically in government positions with the intent of encouraging the upgrading of professional employment standards. These plans, enacted at the state level in the United States,

usually define personnel standards for each job level, including the duties and distinguishing features of the position, the knowledge and abilities required to carry it out effectively and the minimum education and experience required for eligibility (Kraus 1983, 301).

While registration is not legally binding, many government agencies have developed standards. The first registration procedure in leisure services was developed by the Council for the Advancement of Hospital Recreation (CAHR) in 1956. These standards known as the National Voluntary Registration Plan for Hospital Recreation Personnel were instrumental in paving the way toward acceptance of recreation personnel in hospital and clinical settings.

Certification and Licensing. These terms, often used interchangeably, "refer to the process of evaluating the credentials of persons in occupational or professional fields and giving them legal permission to practice" (Kraus 1983, 303). *Licensing governs the scope of professional practice.* It defines the specific services that may be provided, the populations served, and other factors that impact on a profession. *Certification governs the use of a professional title.* This procedure is designed to protect a field and the public against an unauthorized or untrained practitioner. So while its intent is similar to registration, certification provides *legal protection* for professionals. It gives recognition to such individuals who have qualified and guarantees to employers that certified professionals have attained stated educational and experiential qualifications. In 1981, the National Council for Therapeutic Recreation Certification (NCTRC) was established. The NCTRC has certified over eleven thousand individuals and deems that its certification activities are necessary in the professionalization of the field.

Civil Service Requirements. Civil Service involves a comprehensive set of procedures that screens applicants for employment and provides a job classification system, eligibility examination and opportunities, probationary periods, and promotion, separation, and personnel rights and benefits. It is used throughout local, state, provincial, and federal government recreation and leisure services in the United States and Canada. As Kraus states:

Civil Service is a general descriptive term that applies to many different agencies, boards and personnel systems that attempt to provide a politically neutral method of employment under which individuals are hired because of their formal qualifications rather than because they have political 'contacts' or influence (Kraus 1983, 304).

Civil Service position qualification requirements vary in how stringent they are relative to reflecting state-of-the-art knowledge of the field, related work experience, and skills and competencies deemed necessary for tasks to be performed. The Civil Service standards vary from municipality to municipality, province to province, and federal agency to federal agency.

Employment Standards for Nongovernmental Leisure Service Agencies. Personnel in nongovernmental agencies, those represented by commercial enterprise, private nonprofit youth-serving groups, and corporate employee leisure services, are not typically scrutinized as systematically as governmental agencies relative to professional standards. This is not to say that these agencies have less qualified individuals. Most of these agencies establish standards for employment on a national level that are recommended to local branches or units.

All of the types of standards—registration, certification, licensing, Civil Service, and nongovernmental organization-recommended standards—are viewed by many professionals as needing to have higher expectations and be more stringent and more selective. This practice will result in improving the quality of service to people.

Code of Professional Ethics
The fourth criteria that establishes an occupational field as a profession is the existence of a code of ethical behavior and responsibility. Most professional organizations in recreation and leisure service have such a code of ethics. In most influential professions practitioners who violate their codes often forfeit their right to practice. Fain (1989) comments:

Those professions the public perceives as having great potential for doing harm are the ones with the strongest codes and methods for enforcement. Not only is this essential to protect the public against unethical professions, but it is critical to the profession that its members guarantee to the public they can be trusted (197-98).

There are, however, typically no procedures for enforcing codes. In some highly specialized areas of the profession, in therapeutic recreation, leisure counseling, and gerontology, there is additional concern because professionals are working with more emotionally vulnerable individuals. Further, where research is undertaken using individuals, the withholding of treatment that is considered to be beneficial could be seen as a violation of providing the best care. The enactment of an enforceable code of ethics is seen by a growing number of practitioners and educators to be critical to the motivation of the leisure service profession. Without the kind of trust representative of a code of ethics, professionals undermine their sanctions to practice.

Existence of a Professional Culture

The recreation and leisure service field is represented by many organizations that seek to advance the profession and promote improvement in the quality of life. The prominent professional organizations are the American Association for Leisure and Recreation, National Recreation and Park Association, Canadian Park and Recreation Association, Commercial Recreation and Resort Association, and National Employee Services and Recreation Association. Kraus (1983) notes that professional organizations have been established to:

1. Regulate and set standards for professional development;
2. Promote legislation for the advancement of the field;
3. Develop programs of public information to improve understanding and support of the field;
4. Sponsor conferences, publications, and field services to improve practices; and
5. Press for higher standards for training, accreditation, and certification (288).

Most professional organizations exist to provide their membership with the most current, up-to-date information that pertains to professional practice. At the same time, they provide various services, information, and support community agencies desiring to enact a program.

Conclusions on Professional Development

Professional standards pertaining to employment, education and training, and development of a body of knowledge may not represent the entire scope of the field or discipline. For example, authors of this text suggest there is a range of service delivery approaches that all professionals in recreation and leisure should be aware of and be prepared to use to enhance leisure participation. The ecological perspective that we use in this text implies that it is appropriate for professionals at times to intervene within the various subsystems of a community to be able to ensure the development of individuals. Howe-Murphy and Charboneau (1987) further state that:

> This intervention enables us to improve the transactions between the individuals and the environment. If this concept of growth and change is to become a reality, it is imperative that we no longer just adapt to existing organizational and social systems and maintain traditional roles. We are challenged to expand our roles to implement innovative functions that respond to the dynamic needs of individuals and their environment (26).

Some have doubts about the progression of development that leads to certification of professional personnel in recreation and leisure service—the intensified push toward advancement of the profession should not forsake the participant, consumer, and client. Indeed, the enabler and advocate service delivery roles suggest that the goal of service delivery is not merely to provide quality programs and services but to facilitate change in community life, making it possible for more people to experience leisure and make self-directed choices about how to enhance their own living. So:

> a change agent can be perceived as a person who encourages other people and the community they live in to make favorable changes. Change agents acknowledge that the people they are involved with are ultimately responsible for changing themselves. From this perspective, change agents recognize that change is a developmental process and that they are participants in the process (Howe-Murphy and Charboneau 1987, 36).

The professionalization of the recreation and leisure movement must not be viewed as a static set of criteria of what it takes to attain recognition from one's colleagues or the community. Rather, it must be viewed as a developmental process designed to foster the continuous upgrading and improvement of professional education, training, and standards of practice.

Ultimately, each constituency within a community must make its own decisions about program philosophy and direction, appropriate techniques for service delivery, and appropriate organizational structures to administer professional service. What then is professionalism? What should professionals do to meet their obligations in providing opportunities to their constituents? What is the basic commitment of the park and recreation professional to provide high-quality services and programs that create opportunities for the meaningful use of leisure? (Sessoms 1987, 174)

What all professionals can do is be equipped to deal with social change; it overrides both wants and experiences as a determinant of service. The social-technological changes discussed earlier in this chapter and in Chapter 1 suggest that old patterns do not necessarily fit the new circumstances for all segments of the population. The major changes—"megatrends"— outlined by Naisbitt and presented in this text, coupled with a desire by more people to incorporate leisure in their whole lives, have profound consequences for professional practice and recreation and leisure service organizations. It is becoming more essential for all leisure service providers to "involve in our decision making those we serve or those we want to serve. This should be done at both the macro and micro levels; that is, the community at large should be involved in decisions that affect the overall patterns of services, but each interest group and neighborhood must also have a say in the content and delivery of services" (Sessoms 1987, 177).

This is necessary because the leisure experience is a highly personal matter. Leisure has become more acceptable and accessible to more individuals, and leisure service programs and services must reflect the diversity of the population. This concern has been articulated by Lord, Hutchison, and Van derBeck (1980) who caution that a social distance can be created between the participant and professional, reinforcing the idea that consumers need services that are best provided by experts:

In essence, this is a political relationship, since it legitimizes
the professional in the role of policy and decision maker for
the client. Rather than fostering a sense of shared responsibility for the problem, the professional behaves in ways that are
designed to maintain awe and respect for the profession (231).

What is suggested by Sessoms and by Lord *et al.* is that the
leisure service profession must stay abreast of the
sociotechnological and political changes occurring in everyday
life, and that professionalism may need to incorporate a new
model of practice in which leisure service practitioners learn to
collaborate more fully with participants, consumers, and clients,
rather than plan and deliver programs and services for them. With
the adoption and incorporation of the ecological service delivery
philosophy and operational and management systems perspective by professionals in leisure service organizations, it is more
likely that a collaborative professional-participant relationship
will occur, and thus individuals' lives are more likely to be
enhanced and community life enriched.

Summary

The Recreation and Park Movement has progressed through
eight phases of professional development. During the first or
initiation phase, organized recreation was seen as an imperative
need to provide constructive play opportunities for children and
youth living in densely populated urban areas in the northeastern
part of the United States. The first efforts at organizing such
programs and services were largely the result of social reformers,
social workers, and interested volunteers. During the second
phase parks were developed in urban centers to provide pleasant,
passive surroundings. The third phase saw the development and
institution of responsibility for the provision of organized recreation by local government. The fourth phase of organized recreation occurred between World War I and World War II. Recreation became recognized as a diversionary instrument of community life to break up the monotony of poverty. During the fifth
phase the government renewed an emphasis in recreation. Several federal level services promoted recreation during World War
II. These developments helped to accelerate growth of a compre-

hensive community recreation system. During the 1950s and 1960s, community recreation expanded to include more programs for the elderly and disabled. An upsurge of interest in outdoor recreation, the arts, and professional education also took place at this time.

Also during the course of the 1960s, as a result of civil unrest and social upheaval, leisure service came to be seen as a threshold activity. This concept of recreation as a social instrument suggested that recreation could provide a means for people to become involved in programs that improved community life, organized neighborhoods for socially constructive activity, and enabled opportunities to actualize human potential through leisure expression. The seventh phase, which took place in the 1970s, and was spurred by civil and human rights legislation a decade earlier, saw the development of leisure services into the total fabric of community life. The eighth phase, principally a phenomenon of the 1980s, became focused more on self-help. More individuals, dissatisfied with stagnant, segmented, or indifferent services, sought more autonomy and control over all aspects of their lives, including leisure.

Leisure, while not as plentiful for some as it is for others, is seen by more people as a way to realize personal growth, release tension, or learn a new skill. Leisure can even be integrated with one's full-time profession—it is no longer necessarily linked to one having earned it. The potential for leisure expression exists within each individual and permeates all aspects of living. The decade of the 1990s, the beginning of the ninth phase of the Recreation and Park Movement, promises to be a dynamic period in the continuation of merging leisure into the totality of people's lives—at home, at work, and at play.

The provision of leisure opportunities is represented by three forms of organization sponsorship—public, private nonprofit, and commercial enterprise. Public recreation is primarily the responsibility of local, county, and state government, with some federal participation. Private nonprofit agencies include four principal types: nonsectarian youth-serving agencies; sectarian youth-serving and religious agencies; settlement houses and community centers; and special interest organizations. Commercial leisure organizations represent businesses in which the participant or consumer pays for the product, event, or service and the purveyor intends to make a profit.

Leisure service professionals can best respond to participants by incorporating a full array of service delivery roles that fall along a continuum and suggest a progression from dependence to independence for participants. Four kinds of professional roles were presented: direct service, information-referral, enabler, and advocate. In direct service, leisure personnel select, plan, and organize leisure experiences and services for consumers. Information-referral incorporates the use of coordination, referral, and technical assistance. The enabler role employs a facilitation process of professionals providing guidance to individuals to allow them to make self-selected choices. As advocates, leisure service professionals become active representatives of their constituents. This role is characterized by an intervention approach in community social processes designed to change current conditions, status, level of service, or existing laws to help individuals realize more personal freedom of expression and fuller participation in community life.

Leisure service agencies are being challenged to change their customary practice of misconstruing professionalism with high standards of direct service and thus assuming that if they are the primary determiners of constituent leisure needs participants will be better served. A new definition of professionalism is beginning to develop: a concept of service recognizing that recipients of programs and services should assume more self-responsibility in meeting their own leisure needs. Professional recreators gain esteem by helping to facilitate participant choice, awareness, and understanding of options available and by ensuring that reasonable access exists for all people in settings where recreation experiences occur.

There is increasing recognition that as leisure becomes equated more as a personal, intrinsic, and integrated part of the human condition, people will come to embrace it as an integral aspect of overall life fulfillment. Leisure represents an extension of personal interest and lifestyle for more people. Leisure professionals have a responsibility to respond to the diversity of subcultures, lifestyles, and racial and ethnic enclaves that, when put together, represent the majority of people in North America.

The recreation and leisure field has emerged as a full-fledged profession in its second century of organized service. Recreation and leisure represents an amalgamation of diverse professions and disciplines, all aiming to achieve one purpose—enhance the human condition and improve the quality of community life for everyone.

References

Butler, George. 1940. *Introduction to community recreation.* New York: McGraw-Hill.

Butler, George. 1970. A fair share. In *Recreation and leisure service for the disadvantaged.* John A. Nesbitt, Paul D. Brown, and James F. Murphy, eds. Philadelphia: Lea & Febiger.

Carlson, Reynold, Theodore Deppe, and Janet MacLean. 1972. *Recreation in American life.* Belmont, CA: Wadsworth Publishing.

Edginton, Chris, David Compton, and Carole Hanson. 1980. *Recreation and leisure programming.* Philadelphia: Saunders College.

Fain, G. 1989. Ethics and the therapeutic recreation profession. In *Issues in therapeutic recreation: A profession in transition.* David Compton, ed. Champaign, IL: Sagamore Publishing.

Godbey, Geoffrey. 1980. Leisure in singular and plural cultural societies. In *Recreation and leisure: Issues in an era of change,* Peter Witt and Tom Goodale, eds. State College, PA: Venture Publishing.

Harris Poll. 1986, April 21. *Wall Street Journal,* 2D.

Hartsoe, Charles E. 1973. Recreation — A profession in transition. *Parks and Recreation. 8(6): 33.*

Howard, Dennis R., and John Crompton. 1980. *Financing, managing and marketing recreation and park resources.* Dubuque, IA: Wm. C. Brown Company Publishers.

Howe-Murphy, Roxanne, and Becky Charboneau. 1987. *Therapeutic recreation intervention: An ecological perspective.* Englewood Cliffs, NJ: Prentice-Hall.

Iso-Ahola, Seppo, and Ellen Weissinger. 1984. Leisure and well-being: Is there a connection? *Parks and Recreation* 19:52.

Kelly, John R. 1985. *Recreation business.* New York: Macmillan.

Kraus, Richard. 1983. *Recreation and leisure in modern society,* 3rd ed. San Francisco: Scott, Foresman and Company.

Kraus, Richard. 1986, Oct. 19. *Recreation and leisure in post-industrial society: Transformation in values.* Anaheim, CA: National Congress for Recreation and Parks.

Lawrence, Mark A. 1977. Developing program models for the human services. In *Developments in the human services,* Herbert S. Schulberg and Frank Baker, eds. Vol. II, 2nd ed. New York: Human Services Press.

Lord, John, Peggy Hutchison, and Fred Van derBeck. 1980. Narrowing the options: The power of professionalism in daily life and leisure. In *Recreation and leisure: Issues in an era of change,* Peter Witt and Tom Goodale, eds. State College, PA: Venture Publishing.

Murphy, James F.   1975. *Recreation and leisure service: A humanistic perspective.* Dubuque, IA: W. C. Brown Publishers.

Murphy, James F., and Dennis R. Howard. 1977. *Delivery of community leisure services.* Philadelphia: Lea & Febiger.

Nesbitt, John A., Paul D. Brown, and James F. Murphy, eds. 1970. *Recreation and leisure service for the disadvantaged.* Philadelphia: Lea & Febiger.

Neumeyer, M. and E. Neumeyer. 1958. *Leisure and recreation: A study of leisure and recreation in their social aspects.* New York: Ronald Press.

Niepoth, E. William. 1983. *Leisure leadership.* Englewood Cliffs, NJ: Prentice-Hall.

Sessoms, H. Douglas.   1971. Recreation — Theory and practice. In *Encyclopedia of education.* New York: Macmillan.

Sessoms, H. Douglas.   1987. Reassessing the role of public leisure services. In *Current issues in leisure services,* Joseph J. Bannon. ed. Washington, D.C.: International City Managers Association.

Tinsley, Howard and Diane Tinsley. 1986. A theory of the attributes, benefits and causes of leisure experiences. *Leisure Sciences* 8: 21.

Weiner, Myron E. 1971. A systems approach to municipal recreation. In *The municipal year book.* Chicago: International City Managers Association.

4

ECOLOGY OF LEISURE SERVICE—AN INTERACTIONIST-DELIVERY MODEL

The relationship of the various subsystems that interact, contribute to, and exist in dynamic relationship in community life is best understood from an ecological perspective. In this sense, leisure experiences occur within society and influence other activities, behaviors, and values, and in turn are influenced by the same sources, thus creating an ecological relationship. Changes that occur elsewhere among the various elements—participants, social environment, physical environment, leisure service organizations—will affect each component. Gist and Fava (1964) relate the concept of human ecology (as we use it in this text as a basic premise of the nature of leisure service):

> [It] is . . . . concerned with interactive relationships between individuals and groups and the ways these relationships influence, or are influenced by, particular spatial patterns and processes. It is concerned with cultural, racial, economic, and other differences insofar as preferences and prejudices associated with these differences serve to bring people socially or spatially together or keep them apart. It is concerned with social organization insofar as the organization of human activities influences, or is influenced by, the spatial distribution of people or of institutions. Above all, it is concerned with the dynamics of the social order insofar as change in the structure and functions of institutions, or changes in patterns of human relationships, bring about ecological changes, and vice versa (96).

Within such a holistic model, the leisure service professional assumes a more comprehensive and flexible role. The ecological, interactive systems model requires that agencies accept a responsibility for the whole person; this can best be fulfilled by the leisure service professional recognizing the interrelationships that exist between people and their social and physical environments and the way these relationships influence, or are influenced by, various social and organizational processes.

Ecological Model of Leisure Service

The elements of the leisure service delivery system are the participants, social environment, physical environment, and leisure service organizations. Each element is an integral part of the overall delivery system and functions in a unique and interdependent manner. This process recognizes the dynamic relationship that exists between human beings and the social and physical environments   (see Figure 4.1).

Figure 4.1 Ecological Relationship of Elements of the Leisure Service Delivery System

As presented in Chapter 1, we believe agencies that adopt a holistic philosophical and operational perspective will best be able to respond to all community members. The holistic framework provides a more elastic and flexible organizational planning and service delivery management process, since leisure service professionals will be better able to recognize changes that occur continuously within a community. For example, leisure service personnel will be more adept and knowledgeable when they encounter changes in new leisure interests (participants), ethnic mix (social environment), transportation issues (physical environment), and revised goals and objectives instituted by the Parks and Recreation Commission (leisure service organizations). Leisure service personnel will know that each element of the delivery system existing within every community cannot be viewed in isolation of others and that each contributes to the successful implementation of programs and services.

Any change within the community system will have a corresponding impact on all other subsystem elements. The leisure service professional, whether the individual is a leader, supervisor, or top level administrator, must view all elements—participants and nonusers, social and economic issues, natural and physical structures and elements, and the leisure service organization—when making decisions, developing programs, establishing user policies, or designing areas and facilities. Any action related to one element has a corollary relationship and implication for each of the other components of the leisure service delivery system.

As presented in Chapter 1, the adoption of a systems perspective is seen as an appropriate direction for the recreation and leisure field to take because system implies wholeness, integration, and synergy—all elements or subsystems are interrelated, and when viewed as a set of interdependent components of the whole, they may well provide a comprehensive method of understanding how each aspect of community life exists in relationship to each other.

The various elements of the delivery system are outlined in Figure 4.1. Each element is presented independently, as each has a separate set of conditions and processes, but all function with each other in an interdependent manner. The ecological perspective of leisure service delivery provides a useful operational design for agencies. This perspective encompasses the full spectrum of possible service delivery approaches and integrates enabling and advocacy strategies. These *external* approaches provide a way for leisure service professionals to extend the service delivery continuum beyond the normally defined parameters of an agency. They are able to reach out into the context of the community to either facilitate leisure opportunities for individuals requiring assistance, or intervene on behalf of the agency's constituency to remove barriers that restrict or prohibit participation in leisure experiences.

By incorporating an ecological model in leisure services, managers become more aware of each element of the community that provides programs and facilities. And by looking at the elements as a whole, they recognize that many residents lack the means or opportunities to pursue leisure. As such, leisure managers are able to draw upon several possible service delivery roles to maximize opportunities, information, resources, and legislation to ensure access and fair treatment for all individuals. "The selection of a given strategy is based upon the three-fold goal of improving the adaptive capacities of individuals, improving the supportive qualities of the environment, and improving transactions between people and their environments" (Howe-Murphy and Charboneau 1987, 19).

The ecological perspective presents a different model for leisure practitioners. It suggests that multiple participant behaviors can occur in the leisure milieu. These behaviors will require that diverse service delivery approaches be used to best connect individuals to their desired goals. The ecological model embraces advocates and change agents who act not only to facilitate growth and development of individuals, but intervene within the community as a whole. In encouraging the use of this model, Howe-Murphy and Charboneau (1987) offer this challenge to therapeutic recreation professionals:

> This intervention enables us to improve the transactions between the individual and the environment. If this concept of growth and change is to become a reality, it is imperative that we no longer just adapt to existing organizational and social systems and maintain traditional service roles. We are challenged to expand our roles to implement innovative functions that respond to the dynamic needs of individuals and their environments (26).

The ecological concept of adaptation assumes that individuals are cognitive, growth-oriented, and goal-seeking beings. The social climate that pervades our information-oriented society is constantly changing. Individuals continuously attempt to adjust and attain an acceptable balance with the environment. An ecological perspective encourages opening up new leisure options for individuals and eliminating others that restrict or inhibit participation. In order for each human being to achieve maximum control over his or her life, he or she must achieve a mutual interdependence with each of the interacting elements within the community system.

Underlying Principles

The leisure service profession has a philosophy, a set of values, goals, and a knowledge base that people embrace to support their goals and desires, enabling them to seek leisure opportunities that will contribute to their overall life satisfaction. The following are principles that extol an ecological perspective as related to leisure service:

1. The relationship between leisure service personnel and the participant, consumer, or client is based upon mutual respect and reciprocity, authenticity and openness.

2. While the total person, including current abilities, limitations, interests, and needs, is recognized, progressive forces, those that enable individuals to move toward a state of well-being, provide a focal point for leisure service personnel.

3. Problems, liabilities, and deficits are a result of multiple variables. Single-factor causes are not helpful in understanding human behavior, faulty interactions, or inadequate environments.

4. Individuals are concerned with issues of personal control and self-determination. Environments that are least restrictive and that provide maximum support are the most helpful in enabling humans to attain a healthy interdependence with their environments (Germain, 1979).

Participants

Recreation and leisure opportunities will yield a variety of individual behaviors. As discussed in Chapter 2, the relative degree of freedom and intrinsic motivation experienced by an individual serves as the cornerstone of conditioning elements that foster leisure expression. "The freedom to choose is a function of both environmental factors (the relative presence or absence of opportunities) and personal variables (availability or lack of such resources as time, money, health, and skill)" (Niepoth 1983, 60).

There are a number of personal factors that influence individuals' leisure behavior. These internal factors combine with the external social and physical environmental elements to form the basis for the leisure environment. Each person is affected by the various environments that intersect with community life. However, no two people are exactly the same; each of us reacts differently to the same stimuli.

Personal factors that influence leisure behavior will be discussed in greater detail in Chapter 5. Some include personality, perceptions and attitudes, knowledge and skills, age and stage in the life cycle, and goals and aspirations. The components of an individual's make-up are influenced by all of the stimuli that exist within the environment. But these stimuli, in turn, are motivating only when they conform to a person's intentions and may become aversive if an individual interprets the stimuli as a sign of someone trying to be manipulative.

This perspective contrasts with the learning theory suggesting that human beings modify their behavior in terms of the external social and physical environmental contingencies of reinforcement. The theory that control over rewards (and hence behavior) resides outside the organism has been replaced with a holistic, human developmental model. Therefore, a new interpretation of leisure emphasizes that one can control increasingly complex challenges in the environment by developing one's skills. As people develop skills, they seek a state of optimum balance during which they feel in control over their environment. This state, known as flow, is a motivating force independent of external reward. Leisure, from a holistic interpretation, is an interactional state that a person is most likely to experience with total involvement.

Those who deliver leisure services in a community must be expected to meet an interrelated set of individual differences occurring in a leisure setting. Leisure experience is influenced by a number of interrelated organizational, social, and physical environmental factors, and individual considerations combine to influence recreation and leisure behavior. While leisure service personnel generally seek to promote enjoyment, personal growth, and overall quality of community life, they must always be aware that each participant, consumer, and client requires a unique approach in order that their individual needs be met. And the fulfillment of these needs is intended to result in a personally satisfying leisure experience.

Social Environment

Community life also represents various social elements that contribute to the livableness of an area—housing, occupations, transportation, sanitation, distribution of income, education, race, religion, and social class. The differential impact of these social aspects results in varied conditioning circumstances for members of the community. Leisure choices and preferences and forms of ethnic, class, sex, age, and racial expression, while influenced or even dictated by the majority culture, are primarily a reflection of individual motivation and needs.

However, certain cultural, economic, and religious influences may enhance or deter participation in leisure offerings because of social pressures, attitudes, motives, public opinion, or discrimination by other social groups in the community. The social factors that affect leisure behavior are complex. Some of the influences are readily observed, while others are more subtle and not easily recognized.

There is an emerging lifestyle that provides an alternative perspective to the traditional mechanistic model that has influenced work, leisure, and family and provided an industrial rhythm of community life. Chubb and Chubb (1981) offer an illustration of how lifestyles that society considers acceptable can play a major role in determining leisure participation patterns:

> At least until recently, American society has encouraged its members to aspire to lifestyles characterized by professional

employment and a sizable gadget-filled house on a large lot in the suburbs, with two large late-model automobiles providing unlimited transportation. To achieve this lifestyle, many have been willing to take additional jobs or even borrow large sums of money, thereby further reducing their free time or the proportion of their salaries that could be used for recreation (142).

The Chubbs argue that this situation has existed for many because society has endorsed individuals spreading out to considerable distances from urban centers. While this was considered socially or environmentally desirable, it resulted in individuals having to commute one or two hours a day to work.

The shape of the accepted household and marital patterns has similarly had an impact on people's leisure environment. The traditional nuclear family, comprised of a married couple with a number of children, has given way to family units predominated by single-headed households or households comprised of two adults with one or no children.

Nontraditional and varied familial patterns are more commonplace in the 1990s. The combined influences of improved health care, removal of sex and age stereotypic influences in education, business, and industry, and more discretionary income as a result of improved employment opportunities have made it possible for the industrial, mechanistic model of work (a dominating influence in one's overall lifestyle) to be altered to reflect greater personal freedom. Thus, there is a mix of social characteristics within a given community that has different effects on choices people make, attitudes toward work and leisure, opportunities for leisure expression, and overall social, medical, economic, educational, and cultural conditioning that increases or decreases one's proclivity to engage in leisure behavior.

Subcultures and Leisure Expression

There is a set of national characteristics that reflects an overall cultural orientation that influences, even dictates, human behavior. The collection of mores, rules of conduct, norms, values, and belief system together form a basis for guiding human endeavors, including kinship, friendship, work, and leisure patterns.

Within each national cultural context, there are distinctive styles of leisure expression found in various subcultures. Besides the dominant American and Canadian lifestyle behavior pattern representative of white, urban, middle-income, Anglo-Saxon Protestants, there are a number of different subcultures. These subcultures are differentiated by income, geography, ethnicity, religion, age, marital status, political affiliation, and lifestyle preferences, all of which contribute to leisure behavior.

Examples of subcultural groupings are:

1. *Subcultures of poverty.* These include people who live in ghettos or barrios in urban centers and dispersed groups of low-income workers who live in depressed agricultural areas and other non-urban settings.

2. *Subcultures of place.* Locations where people live or grow up—neighborhoods, cities, towns, counties, provinces, or regions—affect attitudes and behavior.

3. *Subcultures of ethnic origin.* One's ethnicity (Chinese, Vietnamese, German, Scottish, Hispanic, etc.) often contributes to the maintenance of a separate identity and distinct behavioral pattern.

4. *Subcultures of religion.* Each religious group (Roman Catholic, Muslim, Jewish, various Protestant sects, etc.) develops its own subculture.

5. *Subcultures of age.* Various age groups, each at a certain stage in the life cycle—children, teen-agers, young adults, middle-age adults, and the elderly—form separate subcultures.

6. *Subcultures of principal activity.* Groups of people who have a similar life situation—those who do the same kind of work, are unemployed, independently wealthy, or retired—often have a unique subculture.

7. *Subcultures of marital status.* Singles, married, widowed, and divorced, constitute groups with similar social circumstances.

8. *Subcultures of politics.* Political parties of Democrats, Republicans, Communists, Socialists, and so forth, form distinct groups.

9. *Subcultures of lifestyle and special interests.* Individuals who participate with others having similar interests, such as surfers, hunters, youth gang members, antique collectors,

women's movement participants, and human potential enthusiasts, typically exhibit similar participation patterns (Chubb and Chubb 1981, 145).

Many individuals tend to be involved in more than one subculture; and these associations represent a diversity of beliefs, values, mores, and behavior patterns. Memberships in one subculture will take precedent over others. These patterns pervade the activities of such subcultural groups and influence their lifestyles.

While common elements prevail throughout society, subcultures are found to vary within a common societal framework or develop completely independent and self-contained lifestyles. As people attach greater meaning to leisure experiences and lifestyle becomes a more desirable reflection of their central life interests, leisure service professionals will need to understand the nature of diverse subcultures. This is particularly important as it relates to minority groups, who, through their subordinated role in society and various subcultural traditions and adjustments to discrimination and intolerance, have had to evolve leisure lifestyles that have often been seen as "deviant" and outside the mainstream of society. Chubb and Chubb (1981) explain how participation in one of these several subcultures has an effect on an individual's leisure behavior:

1. Within a subculture, the individual is influenced by the beliefs and behavior of the other members. Individuals may prefer certain kinds of leisure experiences because they are so well integrated into their everyday life. They tend to unconsciously take part in activities similar to other members of a subculture.

2. Membership in a subculture may require strict adherence to clearly specified behavior patterns. In some subcultures, particularly certain ethnic, religious, and some special interest groups, members desire to retain a unique identity, to perpetuate certain attitudes and behavior patterns. There is even an attempt to avoid "contamination" by outside ideas and practices, and a well developed set of guidelines and rules are carefully taught. Members of these subcultures "may have access to many unique

recreation opportunities because of their membership, but they may also feel obliged to refrain from many of the recreation opportunities open to them through memberships in other subcultures connected to age, place, or principal activity" (145).

3. The size of a particular subculture may allow its leisure behavior patterns to coexist alongside the majority culture. However, some subcultures, particularly certain ethnic, lifestyle, or special interest groups may be harassed or restricted in their efforts to express their principal beliefs and way of life. This has been true for subjugated ethnic minority groups, such as black, Hispanic, and Asian subcultures, gays and lesbians, and certain special interest groups like off-road motor vehicle enthusiasts.

It was not until the 1960s that a wave of civil and human rights legislation began to dismantle archaic laws that discriminated against various ethnic and racial lifestyle subcultures from participation in certain recreation facilities and public leisure experiences. The recognition that leisure expression has an ecological framework has given rise to interest in certain special interest subcultures (surfers, airstream trailer campers, country and western dancers, etc.), since there is a greater understanding of the consequences of some forms of leisure expression altering or damaging the natural environment.

Advances in technology have increased leisure opportunities for the disabled and elderly by means of assisted devices leading to expanded leisure options (e.g., wheelchair accessibility to hiking trails and ramps and curb cutouts providing access to many previously unavailable recreation places). But technological innovation has also left certain fragile natural environments vulnerable to dirt bikes, mountain bikes, and snowmobiles, for example. There are emerging conflicts among competing users of certain leisure places. These conflicts reflect different philosophical perspectives in the nature of leisure experiences. Some may only see the consumptive or direct use of a given milieu while others recognize the long-term consequences to certain types of use—overuse negatively impacting the carrying capacity of a resource, motorized or otherwise nonhuman impact of vehicles on certain terrains, and redesign and alteration of natural settings.

Leisure participation exists in an ecological relationship with the natural or physical environment. Some forms of leisure expression may need to be controlled, thereby requiring individuals to understand more acutely the relationship of leisure, a measure of personal freedom and psychological, physical and spiritual well-being, to the rest of the elements contributing to the quality of community life.

Therefore, while some subcultural groups (particularly those discriminated against) require encouragement in their leisure expression, others may require guidance and laws that will lead to better balance between leisure expression and environmental impact. As various forms of leisure expression become more evident in our culture and greater opportunities become available for all subcultures, leisure service professionals must understand how leisure is interwoven into the total fabric of community life.

Physical Environment

The provision, quality, and accessibility of open spaces, park lands, and recreation areas and facilities no doubt influence their use by various groups and individuals in society. The environment, places and settings where leisure behavior occurs, is an important contributing element to availability and the meanings assigned to them by particular sociocultural groups. Further, "the physical environment is important for maintaining orderly relationships because it serves as a repository of meanings for symbolizing relationships and also provides a spatial field in that social life can be organized" (Cheek, Field and Burdge 1976, 32).

Environmental settings can be identified by particular symbolic, ritualistic, or functional meanings given to them by social groups. Cheek and Burch (1976) developed a taxonomy of *leisure locales*, places where people engage in behavior not ordinarily associated with instrumental or work aspects of existence. Each leisure locale or setting has its own particular social value, design and structural features, and constraints. They are characterized by three main factors.

1. *The specialized moral order:* the type of social value placed on a particular locale.
2. *The physical design:* the set up and arrangement of a locale.

3. *The social structure:* the composition and social organization of the locale—whether people are in groups or alone and whether the groups are composed of friends, kin, or strangers.

Each of these factors serves to ensure particular behavioral responses. The classification of leisure locales developed by Cheek and Burch (1976) is as follows:

1. *Transitional.* This group is characterized by theaters, waiting lounges in airline terminals, train and bus stations, other transportation depots, and courtrooms. They are representative of strangers coming together either to rejoin or dissolve human associations.

2. *Integration.* These locales, such as swimming clubs, tennis centers, and playgrounds, serve as central interaction places and symbolic focal points of certain social groups who frequent such locales; the ecology of the places allows these groups to be spatially and temporarily segregated.

3. *Bonding.* The locales here refer to large open space locations — sports stadiums, zoos, parks, beaches — where large groups of strangers are organized into small intimate social groups.

4. *Solidarity.* These indoor open space locales, characteristic of museums, galleries, and specialized shows, bring together bonded pairs and organized groups, such as school children and tour groups. These locales "reaffirm the larger social order through the display of artifacts that give physical shape to collective representations of myths" (156).

5. *Custodial.* These settings refer to golden age clubs, youth clubs, scout camps, and day-care centers. They provide leisure opportunities for social groups and serve as a means of managing certain populations by occupying them in useful activities.

6. *Exchange.* Exchange locales represent a wide variety of indoor functional places, including singles' bars, shopping malls, post offices, and unemployment offices. In these locales "personal futures are traded and exaggerated claims assume a certain currency" (156).

7. *Fantasy.* Characteristic fantasy locales, such as fairs, circuses, and amusement parks, provide settings for make-believe and vertigo for bonded pairs and kins.

Each of these leisure locales has its own particular design and activity cycle constraints. The leisure locale provides unique, emotion-filled experiences that are set apart from our normal routine of life. These experiences provide the substance for reaffirming one's identity. No one form of leisure agency sponsorship is able to meet each behavioral form of expression characteristic of various social groups (although one leisure locale—the shopping mall—has emerged as a complex environment that facilitates a number of behavioral responses, including transitional, solidarity, exchange, and fantasy).

Leisure Resource Carrying Capacity

Physical leisure resources are a source for supply of leisure opportunities. Leisure resources, each with different characteristics, derive identity from human needs. Each resource-based setting has certain physical, biological, psychological, and emotional characteristics that relate to an area's ability to support individuals using it. A lake, for example, will have certain physical and biological factors—size, depth, water quality, and available parking space—as well as psychological factors: color of the water and sand, density of users occupying the beach area, and age, ethnic origin, and exhibited lifestyle of users. These factors will affect the perception of the user experiencing the leisure resource or setting. Carrying capacity refers to the "number of recreation opportunities that a specified unit of a recreation resource can provide year after year without appreciable biological or physical deterioration of the resource or significant impairment of the recreation experience" (Chubb and Chubb 1981, 292). While this is an imprecise definition, it does suggest that a leisure resource is affected by a large number of factors.

The leisure service manager must respond to these problems of user conflicts and carrying capacity because it is expected that the degree and number of potential conflicts will increase in the future. Leisure service managers, then, must not only be concerned about what personal characteristics affect leisure behavior, but also what environmental resources exist to support individual and group desires. Leisure managers may be able to reduce the effects of high density in some leisure locales and resources by redesigning the facilities, changing operation policies, and upgrading the maintenance procedures. They may also need to activate a leisure education program that teaches participants to adapt their behavior to suit overextended resources.

Some suggestions for reducing user conflict without necessarily reducing the total number of opportunities existing at a given resource, are offered by Chubb and Chubb (1981):

- Separating different kinds of users on a time basis; for instance, a lake may be reserved for fisherpersons during the early morning and evening hours and be available for use by powerboats and water skiers during the rest of the day.

- Spatially separating less compatible users by including buffer zones in a facility's design so that activities do not conflict or by zoning an area, such as a lake, so that incompatible activities do not overlap.

- Setting up one-way systems at exhibitions and on trails, drives, and canoe routes so that more people can enjoy the experience while having fewer contacts with other users.

- Providing alternative resources that will divert some of the users from an overused fragile environment to one that is capable of carrying the additional load. For example, people who are using unique scenic, biological, or cultural resources in state or national parks for activities typically undertaken at community and regional parks may be diverted to new county parks or commercial developments if they are placed at strategic locations and cost about the same (673).

The leisure resource itself may have to be modified and participants may have to alter their typical behavior patterns to balance carrying capacity and reduce user conflict. Leisure service managers will have to advocate for changes in other subsystems that have traditionally revolved around the mechanistic, industrial rhythm of life—the restrictive economic perspective that focuses work activities in concentrated periods results in lopsided demands for recreation resources in evenings, on weekends, and during holidays. Further, people have tended to bunch their leisure around the linear work rhythm and thereby exacerbate the threat to resource carrying capacity and increase user conflicts among participants seeking varied use of leisure settings.

Leisure managers not only have a responsibility to teach skills, provide opportunities for potential users, and administer programs and services but they must ensure that vulnerable individuals, lacking quantity and quality of leisure experiences, are assured their rightful opportunity to participate fully within their community. A leisure policy must be developed and articulated that calls for the integration within city planning of comprehensive plans of industrialists, environmentalists, politicians, and lay public—as a central component—essential to the assurance of high quality community life.

Leisure Service Organizations

Community leisure opportunities are activated and coordinated by public, private nonprofit, and commercial organizations. Collectively, they comprise the community leisure service delivery system (see Chapter 3, Figure 3.1). Leisure service agencies exist to provide opportunities for people, individually and collectively, to engage in leisure behavior in order to satisfy certain personal and social goals.

Agencies structure opportunities that elicit various leisure behaviors by manipulating the human and physical environments that are part of their organization and delivery system operation. The human environment includes agency staff and participants, and the physical environment includes natural resources, developed land and water areas, facilities, and equipment and supplies. These two environments are inseparable. One affects the other, and together they act upon the participant.

The leisure service delivery system is based on the agency's commitment to provide opportunities that encourage and facilitate selected kinds of leisure behaviors; the specific nature of the behaviors depends upon the goals, objectives, and delivery approach of the particular agency and the human and physical resources that are available. Agencies are likely to be more effective when they comprehend the totality of interactive human, social, physical, and organizational relationships that exist within a community.

An ecologically-based delivery system works most effectively with a holistic view of management. "This concept rejects the idea that managerial functions such as personnel supervision or facilities design and maintenance can be understood or dealt with effectively in isolation" (Kraus and Curtis 1982, 13). An ecological perspective suggests that each element or subsystem of the leisure service delivery system is interrelated with all other elements. A holistic management approach requires that each managerial function—organizing, planning, directing, staffing and evaluating—must be handled in relationship to one another. Kraus and Curtis (1982) comment that:

> all managerial functions must be seen as closely interwoven and dependent on each other, in a highly integrated system. To illustrate, it would be impossible to consider developing new programs without considering their personnel requirements, or the facilities that would be used to house them. Similarly, the ability to raise funds to supplement tax allocations is heavily dependent on an agency's public and community relations efforts (13).

Each managerial function, no matter what level in the organization—center director, program supervisor, personnel officer, chief administrator, or executive director—requires understanding of each separate area of responsibility and functioning along with full awareness of its relationship to all of the others.
For leisure service agencies to be most effective, they must structure, coordinate, and create opportunities for individuals within an ecological-systems framework. Agencies interface with the social and physical environments of a community in order that programs and services will fit individual needs and expectations. Leisure opportunities provide the context for individuals to participate in a myriad of satisfying and growth-enhancing experiences. These experiences contribute to individual well-being and facilitate social bonding for social groups, which results in improving the habitability and quality of community life. Those contributing and interdependent elements of community life— the ingredients of the delivery system, the physical environment (topography, transportation, housing, environmental impact, etc.), the social environment (culture, ethnic groups, education, health, etc.), and human concerns (motivation, needs, individual experi-

ence, self-concept, competencies, etc.) — that are acted upon in an integrated, interactive manner bring about the most meaningful participation. This occurs through effective holistic organizational management, recognizing how each element or subsystem operates in a dynamic manner within the community system, and the corresponding impact each decision and action has upon all other environments.

Since participation in community life encompasses and represents variations of human expression, leisure service agencies must necessarily be committed to respond to diverse forms of experiencing leisure with a delivery system structure that promotes optimal human expression. Agencies will be most effective when they are cognizant of the whole network of human activity and interacting elements within the social and physical environments of community life. Each element or subsystem within the overall organization of community life mutually modifies the other, an interaction that exemplifies the dynamic, synchronistic process that contributes to community life.

Leisure service is not a static entity of social organization. It is both an organizational structure and process of human development that fosters self-growth, group identity, and overall sense of community for individuals and groups through their activities and experiences. Leisure agencies facilitate opportunities that can lead to awareness of one's overall sense of connectedness to others and the environment. Leisure agencies accomplish this through recognizing what the resources and staff of the agency can provide and supplying leadership that enhances an individual's well-being in *all* venues and in any conscious or unconscious state, activity, or life experience.

Leisure Service as Expectation of Programs and Services

Most leisure service agencies have tended to offer available resources and provide opportunities for expressing a wide variety of leisure behaviors. Agencies emphasize programs or services that they deem as the most appropriate and desirable in attracting participants, consumers, and clients. As discussed in Chapter 3 and with more emphasis in Chapter 6, leisure agencies provide opportunities for leisure that extend along a continuum, from direct service at one end to enabling and advocacy at the other. With the direct service approach, agency personnel determine and make assumptions about people's leisure interests and desires.

Leisure service agencies have typically adopted a singular delivery perspective and used the expertise of the professional staff's program planning and development skills to provide direct service to customers and clients. This has been most characteristic of public, tax-supported agencies and some private, nonprofit organizations. In contrast, with the enabling approach leisure service providers recognize that individuals should be guided and encouraged to choose their own leisure pursuits. The advocacy role extends the leisure service professional beyond the agency's structure to interact more forcibly within the community to remove barriers that restrict participation, lobby for consumer rights, and work to generally legitimize leisure expression for all members of a community.

Expectation of Benefits from Participation

In the late 1960s and 1970s, leisure agencies began to embrace a more complete spectrum of delivery approaches in offering programs and services to people. Used principally in commercial leisure enterprise, a marketing perspective was adopted by all forms of leisure organizations to reach customers and clients. The marketing orientation attempts to first determine what client groups want and then to provide services that meet those wants (refer to Table 4.1).

The marketing perspective suggests that an agency is more likely to succeed if it looks through its "customer's eyes." That is, a marketing leisure service orientation entails delivering services and programs that people want and will readily support, as opposed to a direct service product orientation that tends to be more concerned with delivering the services or programs the agency deems appropriate.

The marketing orientation also differs from direct service in that it recognizes people expend their money and time with the expectation of receiving benefits, not the delivery of services themselves. Crompton and Lamb (1986) emphasize that:

> Citizens don't buy programs or services; they buy the expectation of benefits. Programs themselves are not marketable.

Table 4.1 Fundamental Difference Between a Direct Service Product (Selling) Orientation and a Marketing (Customer) Orientation

Selling	Marketing
1. Emphasis is on the program	1. Emphasis is on what client group wants
2. Agency first develops the program, then figures out how to attract people to participate	2. Agency determines what client groups want, and how to efficiently develop and deliver a service to satisfy these wants
3. Internal agency orientation	3. External market orientation
4. Emphasizes agency's wants	4. Emphasizes potential user wants
5. Success is measured by number of clients	5. Success is measured by level of client satisfaction achieved

Source: Howard and Crompton 1980, 319.

> Only their benefits have a value to client groups. A service or program itself is simply a vehicle for the user benefit it conveys (10).

According to this view, the business of leisure service should be defined in terms of customer wants. Crompton and Lamb distinguish between "needs" and "wants." They suggest that leisure service agencies have traditionally been concerned with what they think people should have, that is, what they need. This product or direct service approach is likely to fail because people may not want what is provided. If leisure service agencies provide what people indicate they want, a marketing concept, they are more likely to support the program. Thus, recreation and leisure service agencies develop and offer services and programs that respond to participant, consumer, and client wants. It is important that these services and programs are consistent with participant, consumer, and client wants. Participants purchase benefits; the programs and services are a means to an end. Leisure agencies must then determine potential customer wants so that these aspirations can be incorporated into programs and services that are likely to provide benefits (for example, relaxation, challenge, excitement, prestige, adventure, fantasy, novelty, companionship, and acquisition of knowledge).

There are a wide range of programs through which people's wants may be met. If leisure agencies define their service or business orientations in terms of specific programs, they may miss opportunities to serve customers.   Crompton and Lamb (1986) offer four implications of leisure agencies focusing on client group wants:

1. It ensures that we retain our focus on client groups and do not become preoccupied with programs, services, or the agency's internal needs.

2. It encourages innovation and creativity of programs and services by suggesting there are many ways to service similar client group wants.

3. It stimulates an awareness of changes in client group wants as they occur, and hence services are more likely to remain relevant.

4. It will probably lead to a broader definition of the role of the agency and thus contribute toward keeping its services abreast of society's wants (11-12).

Embracing such service delivery orientation reinforces the idea that a leisure agency must periodically redefine its mission and scope by assessing whether its programs are the *best* medium for serving client group wants.

In order for leisure service agencies to best incorporate a customer perspective, the marketing component should be reflected in the agency's internal organization and coordination efforts. Such an integrated approach requires that the actions of everyone in the agency should be guided by potential client wants and demands. Therefore, the delivery of services to satisfy wants means that all departments of the agency should be consumer oriented: "Primary concern is not with how many participate, but rather with providing the desired target market with a satisfying experience" (Howard and Crompton 1980, 335).

The essence of the marketing concept is focusing on the wants of potential customers whenever decisions regarding an agency's programs, services, prices, location, and promotion are being considered.

Interactive Process of Recreation and Leisure in Community Life

The leisure service delivery system encompasses an ecological, philosophical, and operational perspective that recognizes the interrelationships of people and their surrounding social and physical environments. Such a perspective recognizes that agency personnel should be aware of the ongoing interaction between people and their environments. This type of organizational strategy is best facilitated by an *interactive leader*. The interactive leader comprehends the totality of the contributing subsystem elements in community life (people, social environment, physical environment) and is able to use the full array of service delivery approaches to respond to client wants. This New Age service provider responds intuitively and balances these impressions of client wants with the rules, regulations, and policies of an organization to better understand what is necessary to serve members of the community. Benest, Foley and Welton (1987) explain further:

> The interactive leader seeks change rather than ignores it, encourages colleagues to exercise individual creativity rather than succumb to structural regularity, and actively places human and community concerns first rather than institutional concerns. And, in times of change, problems, concerns, and even crises are perceived as opportunities that can be seized for the benefit of all (154).

Entrepreneurial Approach to Leisure Service

This interactive style of leadership promotes entrepreneurship in an organization. Entrepreneurs, acting alone or with others, seek to seize new opportunities to deliver services in unorthodox ways to existing or new clients—and to generate the revenue to pay for it. Entrepreneurs would rather not perpetuate tradition. Instead, they look to develop opportunities that will foster change, make things happen, and create a better living environment.

The entrepreneurial perspective does not stand apart from the rest of the service delivery approaches; it merely extends and opens up the process whereby leisure service personnel are willing to risk security to promote improvements in service delivery that will benefit customers.

The entrepreneurial approach, which is drawn from the private commercial sector, has mostly been associated with revenue production. While its success is well documented in the burgeoning leisure industry, some argue that the entrepreneurial perspective may undermine the public sector's approach to financing leisure services. Therefore, the traditional approach to financing leisure should also continue to be used. Sessoms (1987) notes that:

> . . . . extensive use of the entrepreneurial approach by local park and recreation systems will cause the public to expect the system to be self-supporting. The hard-earned place of local park and recreation systems as an essential element of government would be lost—and difficult to regain should this entrepreneurial approach fail to meet the public's needs and expectations.
>
> [also] . . . . critics of the entrepreneurial approach note that socially and economically disadvantaged individuals would experience even greater inequities if local park and recreation systems were to rely extensively on the free-enterprise model. Persons with low incomes would be unable to purchase recreation opportunities or would be forced into the position of having to be declared "poor" in order to gain free or reduced admission to various activities and services (173).

Sessoms (1987) argues that there is a middle ground, a combination of approaches that public and private agencies should employ:

> The most critical element in the success of a local system is the congruence between what the public wants and expects from its park and recreation system and the system's ability to meet those expectations. The expectations should be viewed in terms of (1) the services rendered and (2) the means by that these services are rendered. In other words, program content and organizational policies are equally important (173).

Importance of the Interactive and Ecological Approaches to Leisure Service

Though many changes are occurring in society, not every community is changing at the same rate or in the same direction. Yet all the changes impacting together on society as outlined in Chapter 1 are contributing to the formation of a new culture. Public, tax-supported recreation, that grew out of the industrializing northeastern United States, is seen by many as primarily a surrogate parent for families. Its growth in North America may be attributed to the effective manner in that it has served its constituents, particularly low-income, disadvantaged groups and those without an abundance of personal resources, enabling them to assume total responsibility for their own leisure activities and experiences.

Leisure service must come to recognize that it is not inextricably linked to the mechanistic rhythm of the industrial work schedule. It does not exist as it used to—essentially incorporated into the community system as a way to provide children and youth opportunities for leisure removed from the urban industrialized family. Leisure service has inherited many different justifications for its existence within community life, not the least of which is that it serves as the primary consumption-oriented industry in the United States. While public leisure service is a strictly local matter, its private commercial counterpart ostensibly extends beyond neighborhoods. Further, people have suggested, by virtue of their expenditure patterns, that they desire more efficient, diverse, flexible, risk-oriented, and higher quality programs than what some agencies have typically offered.

Sessoms (1987) comments on the dilemma faced by public, tax-supported agencies in changing from their typical direct service delivery approach to the interactive leadership and ecological and systems approaches *despite* dramatic changes in community life:

> it is difficult for local park and recreation systems to assume roles that are unfamiliar to the public. If the public expects the local park and recreation agency to be a direct provider, then the agency is somewhat handicapped if it wishes to adopt another role, say that of facilitator or technical assistant, even

though such a role would be consistent with the public's current desire to be more in control of its recreation activities and organizations (176).

Leisure service delivery has become not only an extension of government to provide individuals with opportunities for enjoyment, skill development, and overall enhancement of lifestyle, it has emerged as an important vehicle for self-identity and modality for making changes unavailable or denied in other life spheres. Thus, approaches to leisure service delivery may logically extend from ready-made, prepackaged agency-organized and conducted activities for consumers to leisure service styles that accommodate a more versatile form of leisure experience. These delivery approaches have become a more acceptable and necessary part of leisure services because they recognize that participants are more sophisticated in their tastes and have a well-developed repertoire of skills and interests that they desire to organize and manage on their own.

The broadening of leisure service roles also recognizes what became clear in the 1960s and continues to impact the lives of the urban and rural poor and culturally and socially disadvantaged—that leisure service provides threshold experiences that allow individuals to be supported and meet their basic existence needs (such as child care, hot meals, job counseling, blood pressure testing, and transportation to programs). Leisure service should not be conceived as a single form that serves only one type of individual, those who understand what they want, know how they are going to participate, and desire the direction of professionals to satisfy their leisure interests. While this approach is most convenient for the agency, because it can focus on its structure (rules, policies, facilities, schedules, and programs) instead of each individual, the approach does not provide sufficient latitude to respond to the ever changing social, political, and economic situation in a community. But, leisure agencies that comprehend all the dynamics of community life—participants, social and physical environments, and leisure organizations—will be most flexible and adaptive to changes continually impacting the community. The increased variety of service delivery roles also correspondingly results in agencies being able to accommodate more individuals by being sensitive to their life situations. As Sessoms (1987) states:

Each segment may require a different approach, sometimes for the same activity and service. Or, all may expect the same approach. Some groups may want the local recreation agency simply to provide facilities and technical assistance, while others expect the agency to give instruction, supervision and direction. Each local system must decide for itself to what extent it will play the role of facilitator; offer technical assistance and grants to provide recreation association; encourage and rely upon the private sector to provide quasi-public services; provide leisure education and leisure counseling; implement entrepreneurial strategies; or support particular positions on a range of social and public policy issues (176-177).

The trend of public and private nonprofit agencies shifting toward this broadened role will necessitate a more ecological orientation toward community life, leading to holistic planning and solutions. Tindell (1987) explains:

Limited public funds necessitate an approach different from directly serving constituents. Park and recreation resources — facilities and staff — should be fully utilized in cooperative problem-solving and programming with local agencies and residents . . . . Park and recreation staff must continue to take responsibility for maintaining access to leisure experiences for citizens, often shifting from the previous role of direct providers to that of community catalysts/facilitators.

Citizen coalitions can be assisted with incorporating themselves as nonprofit, public benefit corporations to take over operations of community centers that local governments can no longer afford to support. City staff can then serve as trainers, consultants, and monitors of these new provider groups. Citizen groups can be used to do special fundraising and provide extensive voluntary support for maintaining public facilities by sponsoring "Adopt a Park" park cleanup, tree planting, and park watch programs (164).

The information-referral, enabler, and advocate roles will require different and special training beyond program planning and development, which typically serves as the core of direct service approach:

Skills to be developed include knowledge of formal/informal political processes; means of volunteer recruitment and man-

agement; how to establish nonprofit, public benefit corporations; citizen involvement/human motivation techniques;
means of assessing community needs; ways of organizing
neighborhood associations; group processes; conflict resolu-
tion/mediation; strategic planning/problem-solving; and
citizen action training (Tindell 1985, 164-165) .

These nontraditional public leisure service skills and delivery approaches have been used in other allied leisure service
organizations.

We find ourselves in the midst of a continuing transition from
an industrial to an information society. Though technology has
altered values about the acceptability of leisure as a legitimate
expression of human behavior not needing to be sanctioned by
religions, work, familial groups, or institutions, leisure service
providers must always see themselves as "advocates of quality
and style of life, decided not by us, but rather by the people who
live it" (Tindell 1985, 2).

Implementing the Interactive Process in Leisure Service Delivery

The interactive model used in leisure service changes the
perspective of the leisure service worker from a central but
narrow view to a broader view recognizing all the dynamics—
subsystems—within community life. The interactive leader works
to create opportunities for each individual to define what he or she
wants. The leader also determines what service delivery approach can best be used to either refer, coordinate, facilitate,
inform or instruct about, or advocate for programs or services that
will most accurately reflect participant, consumer, and client
desires.

The director of Prusch Farm Park in San Jose, California
presented in the overview to Part I serves as an example of a
leisure service manager using a variety of professional roles to
facilitate diverse forms of leisure expression, thereby contributing
to the enhancement of community life.

Benefits to the Social and Physical Environments

Leisure service agencies provide an important context and
experiential process that connects people with their environment.
It is often stated that recreation and leisure facilities and the

programs and services provided in these settings enhance the overall quality of people's lives. Indeed, these are positive impacts of leisure that benefit a community. Some of the economic benefits attributed to leisure services include:

1. Leisure service organization (public, private nonprofit, and commercial) payrolls provide jobs, and whole salaries generate income tax revenues for federal, state, and some municipal governments.
2. Well-maintained and managed park, recreation and leisure facilities often increase the assessed value of adjacent property, which in turn generates income tax revenue for local government.
3. Recreation and leisure-related consumer expenditures stimulate local businesses, which in turn generate sales tax revenues, employment opportunities, and additional production of goods and services.
4. Quality leisure opportunities are a major drawing card for location of new industry and large businesses, which in turn bring investments and enhance the local tax base (*Winning Support for Parks and Recreation*, 1983).

Of course, recreation and leisure experiences provide other developmental benefits to people and a community. As previously mentioned, leisure opportunities:

1. Improve a person's fitness and overall physical health;
2. Lead to emotional well-being and contribute to a positive state of mind;
3. Promote skill development, self-confidence, and social interaction;
4. Contribute to people having a balanced lifestyle.

The list of benefits is endless. This very small sampling, however, does suggest that recreation and leisure experiences have economic, resource, and human consequences deemed important for communities and people. Because people's life circumstances are continually changing, there is a concomitant social and leisure behavior evolution occurring in communities. Leisure service agencies must necessarily have a management style that fosters a flexible, ecologically sensitive organizational approach which creates an infrastructure capable of responding and adapting to change.

Sources of New Programs

Leisure service personnel must constantly be aware of new sources for program development. "If it is to retain life and growth, an agency must have a stream of modified or new programs to replace older programs that offer decreasing want-satisfaction potential to client groups" (Howard and Crompton 1980, 389).

All leisure personnel, no matter the form of each of their agency's sponsorship, can be alert to consumer demands. By virtue of client orientation throughout the organization, such agencies will be more likely to pick up cues from the human, social, and physical environments that suggest the need for new program development. New and improved programs hold the key to the survival and growth of leisure service agencies. The ongoing changes in client groups and leisure opportunity suppliers, together with new technologies, "have combined to make the introducing of new programs a vital element in agency strategy and planning" (Howard and Crompton 1980, 389).

Each agency must have an established procedure for systematic program idea search, screening, and development. This concept is also referred to as entrepreneurship—providing employees freedom to experiment with new ideas to keep the organization current and in concert with the changes in the community.

Howard and Crompton (1980) describe circumstances in which new clientele may emerge and become apparent to a leisure service agency:

- There may be an obvious gap in the existing provision of traditional leisure opportunities available in a community, for which there is client support, that the agency could usefully provide.

- Introducing a program that is entirely new to the community (where there may be only a small core of enthusiasts but known to have clientele support in other communities).

- Unfilled newly emerging wants arising from changes in the desires and lifestyles of a clientele may suggest new directions (preference patterns are hard to predict over a period of time, but because of increased discretionary income and expanded leisure opportunities for individuals, clientele may desire and be willing to spend more to buy services that more precisely fit their wants).

- Emergent new technology, capable of producing new want satisfactions or of substantially improving the satisfaction of wants now partly appeased, may facilitate new programs.

- New client groups may emerge for existing services. For example, the influx of female and older people now interested in aerobics and jogging represent client groups very different from young adult males who traditionally were the target market for fitness programs.

- A clientele may not change, but sometimes increased understanding and insight into their wants provide recognition of the potential of a new want satisfying program. For example, adoption of the marketing concept means that attention focuses from the recreation and park service agency as a resource supplier to a personalized concern with people's leisure interests (379-390).

Conclusions

We are only beginning to understand the significance and influence of the leisure experience. Leisure represents a wider sphere of life than it used to. The leisure service profession interfaces with a more diverse clientele and now includes interactions with attorneys, accountants, entrepreneurs, corporate officers, computer programmers, marketing and advertising experts, and consultants. Delivery of community leisure services also incorporates new partnerships with a myriad of community agencies as participation expands.

Leisure services provide the most qualitative description of the *livability* of a community. Leisure agencies are essentially trying to satisfy individual and group demands. This is accomplished both through the provision of opportunities that take the form of programs or services and nondirect action designed to remove social, physical, and psychological barriers to participation and advocate for the legitimate place of leisure in community life. There are community contexts in which certain forms of leisure expression are inappropriate; yet the same expressions would be acceptable in other contexts. And local customs and history may dictate that certain types of leadership and management styles are more or less acceptable for various segments of the population.

Leisure service agencies that incorporate an ecological-systems approach to delivering opportunities for their customers will best understand how to relate to the mix of interests, lifestyles, social and political changes, and the dynamic interrelationships that exist among all elements of community life. The array of leisure settings or locales in communities should provide a full range of leisure experience opportunities for the individual that might typically involve spontaneous and self-selected uses of the physical environment. The complex of services and programs that constitute the agency's contribution to the leisure delivery system must be perceived in its totality, so that the individual can explore and take advantage of all possible opportunities for human growth and self-fulfillment.

Summary

Elements of the leisure service delivery system are the participants, the social environment, physical environment, and leisure service organizations. This configuration for organized recreation and leisure service is a holistic, ecological, and systems model. Each element is an integral part of the overall delivery system and each functions in a unique and interactive manner. Such a philosophically and managerially holistic organizational framework provides professional personnel with a more useful operational model to meet the leisure needs of individuals and communities.

There are a number of diverse subcultures that exist in North America. Subcultures may be differentiated by income, geography, ethnicity, religion, age, marital status, political affiliation, and lifestyle preferences. Each represents distinctive styles of leisure expression and suggests that diverse approaches are necessary in serving community members.

A number of elements influence the physical environment, including population density and settlement patterns, transportation, and technological developments. Leisure locales, places where people engage in leisure behavior, may be characterized by the influence of three principal factors: (1) specialized moral order (social value), (2) physical design, and (3) social structure. These factors provide a basis for developing a classification system of leisure locales: transitional (theaters and airline terminals); integration (playgrounds and tennis centers); bonding (sports stadiums and zoos); solidarity (museums and galleries); custodial (youth clubs and day-care centers); exchange (bars and shopping malls); and fantasy (fairs and amusement parks).

With the growth in demand for recreation experiences, leisure service managers must respond to problems related to user conflicts and carrying capacity (number of recreation opportunities that a recreation resource can sustain without biological or physical deterioration of the resource or diminishment of the recreation experience).

Leisure service agencies are most likely to be effective when they comprehend the totality of interactive human, social, physical, and organizational relationships that exist within a community. An ecologically-based delivery system uses a holistic view of management. Each managerial process—organizing, planning, directing, marketing, staffing, and evaluating—no matter at what level performed in an organization (center director, program supervisor, or executive director), requires understanding of each of the other managerial areas of responsibilities.

Regardless of the form of organization sponsorship, an emerging agency responsibility is marketing. The marketing orientation differs from a direct service product orientation in that it recognizes people do not buy programs or services, but they do buy (or desire to experience) the expectation of benefits from participation.

The interactive leader or manager is seen as an important new professional role for leisure service professionals. This role implies that the leader or manager comprehends the totality of the contributing subsystem elements in community life (people, social environment, and physical environment) and is able to use the full array of service delivery approaches to respond to client needs. The interactive style of leadership and management promotes entrepreneurship. Entrepreneurs, acting alone or with others, seek to seize new opportunities to deliver services in unorthodox ways to existing or new clients – and to generate the revenue to pay for it.

Society is in constant change. Leisure services must continually be responsive to new aspects within each community that impact the quality of life and opportunities for individual participation. Leisure service agencies must necessarily employ a management style that fosters a flexible, ecologically sensitive organizational approach which creates an infrastructure capable of responding and adapting to change.

References

Benest, Frank, Jack Foley, and George Welton. 1987. The interactive leader. In Joseph J. Bannon. Ed., *Current issues in leisure services.* Washington, D.C.: International City Manager's Association.

Cheek, Neil H., Donald R. Field, and Rabel R. Burdge. 1976. *Leisure and recreation places.* Ann Arbor, MI: Ann Arbor Science Publishers.

Cheek, Neil H., and William R. Burch. 1976. *Social organization of leisure in human society.* New York: Harper and Row, Publishers.

Chubb, Michael, and Holly R. Chubb. 1981. *One third of our time. An introduction to recreation behavior and resources.* New York: John Wiley and Sons.

Crompton, John L., and Charles W. Lamb. 1986. *Marketing government and social services.* New York: John Wiley and Sons.

Germain, Carel, ed. 1979. *Social work practice: People and environment, an ecological perspective.* New York: Columbia University Press.

Gist, Noel, and Sylvia F. Fava. 1964. *Urban society,* 5th ed. New York: Thomas Y. Crowell.

Howe-Murphy, Roxanne L., and Becky Charboneau. 1987. *Therapeutic recreation intervention.* Englewood Cliffs, NJ: Prentice-Hall.

Howard, Dennis R., and John L. Crompton. 1980. *Financing, marketing, and managing recreation and park resources.* Dubuque, IA: Wm. C. Brown Publishers.

Kraus, Richard G., and Joseph E. Curtis. 1982. *Creative management in recreation and parks,* 3rd. ed. St. Louis: C. V. Mosby.

Niepoth, E. William. 1983. *Leisure leadership.* Englewood Cliffs, NJ: Prentice-Hall.

Sessoms, H. Douglas.   1987.   Reassessing the role of public leisure services. In *Current issues in leisure services*. Joseph J. Bannon, ed. Washington, D.C.: International City Manager's Association.

Tindell, J. 1985. *Community development and urban leisure opportunity: A resource guide.* San Jose, CA: Department of Parks and Recreation.

Tindell, J. 1987. Grass roots community development of leisure opportunity. In *Current issues in leisure services*. Joseph J. Bannon, Ed. Washington, D.C.: International City Manager's Association.

Winning Support for Parks and Recreation. 1983. State College, PA: Venture Publishing.

PART II

SERVICE: OVERVIEW

The recreation and park field exists to deliver leisure services for its various constituents. In essence, what the field does is provide opportunities for people to engage in leisure behaviors. These behaviors, and the services that facilitate them, exist within society. They influence and are influenced by that society. Part I looked at leisure dimensions of society. The concepts we presented there provide a framework for the content included in this section of the book. Here we want to consider some ideas about leisure services, about the behaviors these services facilitate, and about the service providers.

Leisure behavior is expressed in an extremely wide variety of ways. When we examine these, we find common elements. Some of these elements are found in all behaviors, and some are more characteristic of those associated with leisure. Part II will look at these elements and characteristics. We will examine factors that influence leisure behavior, and will present some information about such key concepts as life stages and lifestyles. We do this because we believe that it is possible for recreation and park personnel to deliver effective leisure service only if they understand something about leisure behavior.

Leisure services include four major categories: delivering or enabling activity opportunities, providing recreation and park areas and facilities, facilitating recreation behavior through such services as leisure educating, and promoting leisure in communities. When we talk about delivering leisure services, we often use the term "programming." Traditionally, this term has been limited to the provision of activities. We see it in a broader sense.

There is much in traditional programming that is sound and valid and addresses today's needs. But innovation is also required.   Public demands and societal conditions change.   In delivering program services, we must recognize these changes and respond appropriately. We have not always done so in the past. Sessoms (1985) observes that change has been slow:

> The activities and services offered by various park and recreation systems today are not too different from those provided a half century ago. Granted, there have been some innovations in the delivery of services and the content of programs but, for the most part, recreation and park agencies continue to do what they have done in the past (221).

He notes that the innovations in service delivery that have occurred have often been based more on budgets and financial circumstances than on our insights into leisure behavior and the profession's responsibilities in contemporary society. He contends that the field needs to take a broad approach to service delivery, one that recognizes the great diversity of the constituents we serve. We agree.

We believe that, as we plan and deliver leisure services, we must keep in mind what we know about leisure behavior and good programming techniques. To be effective, we must be sensitive to the holistic nature of behavior and aware of the influences of life stages and lifestyles. We must assess needs accurately and respond appropriately to changes in public interests and expectations. The concepts presented in Part I of this text provide the framework for doing so. In Part II we will identify some general approaches and techniques.

We will also look at some considerations related to service providers. In Part III we will present detailed information about staffing and other personnel considerations in the delivery of leisure services. Here, in Part II, we will discuss some background information about service providers in general. In this field, as in all of the human services, staff members use their unique talents to bring about the professional objectives they seek. We will look at the idea that staff members are "instruments" for achieving agency objectives. And we will examine the concept of competency and review some dimensions of professionalism.

In Part II we will focus on service: the provision of opportunities for leisure behavior. An examination of many recreation and park organizations would allow us to illustrate concepts presented in this section. We have selected one that is especially appropriate: Do-It Leisure in Chico, California.

Do-It Leisure

Do-It Leisure is a private, nonprofit agency that was established in 1973 to serve the needs of disabled persons. The initial emphasis was on "mainstreaming" special populations into recreation opportunities available to all citizens in Butte County, California, and on community education to build acceptance and understanding of the disabled.

These purposes still exist, but the organization has expanded its program. Do-It Leisure's primary purpose now is to "make it possible for persons who are physically or mentally challenged to utilize personal and community resources to improve the quality of their lives" (Do-It Leisure 1986). The organization operates as a division of the Work Training Center, another nonprofit agency that emphasizes services for the developmentally disabled. The center provides insurance coverage, accounting services, and other support functions for divisions under its umbrella.

Do-It Leisure's intent is to serve all disabled persons in Butte County. It provides a wide variety of programs through the efforts of a director, four core staff members, nine full-time therapists, several part-time workers, and 50 to 60 volunteers. About 700 disabled persons receive direct services from the organization, which is funded from private sources, such as United Way, and the Butte County Department of Mental Health, and from three public recreation and park districts in Butte County. In addition, participants pay nominal program fees.

Application of Concepts

We will look at four major concepts and briefly comment on their application in Do-It Leisure.

1. *A leisure service organization achieves its purposes by providing opportunities for its constituents to engage in leisure behavior.*

Do-It Leisure's purpose is to help disabled persons use personal and community resources to improve the quality of their lives, mainly by involving clients in leisure opportunities. Through these leisure-oriented experiences, the organization works to meet more specific goals such as the development of independent living skills and expansion of social contacts.

2. *Recreation and park personnel are able to plan and deliver leisure services more effectively when they know about leisure behavior.*

Do-It Leisure begins with the premise that people who use its services have purposes in mind when doing so. In its efforts to attract clients to programs and in actually delivering the various services, the organization makes some assumptions about the clients' goals. Staff members confirm or correct these assumptions through interactions with individuals and groups. Staff members also consider the physical and sociopsychological circumstances of each client when they plan and deliver programs. What kinds of activities will meet individual interests? What skills will be needed? What kinds of promotional efforts will encourage participation? How do individual circumstances influence transportation needs? Knowledge of behavior helps staff members to answer these kinds of questions.

3. *A leisure service agency will deliver those services that are consistent with its constituents' needs, characteristics, and circumstances, and with the agency's philosophy and resources.*

Do-It leisure provides the four major types of services: provision of activities, provision of facilities, facilitation of leisure behavior, and promotion of leisure. The *provision of activities* includes opportunities such as out-of-town trips and live-band dances. "Teens in Action," an activity program for adolescents in group homes, helps to create more of a family atmosphere and provides appropriate adult role models. "Senior Outreach" is a service for older adults in care facilities. One staff member is developing a creative dramatics program.

An example of *facility provision* is a drop-in center for the mentally ill. *Facilitation of leisure behavior* is a major Do-It Leisure effort. Therapists work with individual clients in areas such as mobility training, independent living skills, and leisure counseling. It also includes a broad program of training to develop skills in fifteen different sports.

Promotion of leisure in the community occurs in many forms. For example, Do-It Leisure staff members represent the needs of the disabled on a communitywide, 10-year master plan committee, convened by the Chico Area Recreation and Park District. The organization itself is a member of a nonprofit agency network, organized by the Chico Chamber of Commerce. Do-It Leisure also supports "People First," a group of disabled persons that advocates more effective services for people with special needs. Staff members refer clients to other agencies, when appropriate, for health care, legal consultation, or similar services.

Do-It Leisure's programs also represent different approaches to providing services. The dances, excursions, and Senior Outreach, for example, are direct services. Other programs represent more of an enabling approach. For example, a group of mentally ill persons expressed a need for an activity program for their own group. Do-It Leisure helped the group get going, but the clients themselves organized it and now provide the leadership. For some programs, Do-It Leisure defines rather precise objectives. Mobility training is an example; the purpose is to help people learn to use transportation resources so that they can get to recreation programs, visit friends, go shopping, and use other community services. The objectives for other programs tend to be more general.

4. *Organizations deliver services through staff members who become more competent when they increase self-awareness, develop effective interpersonal relationships, and accept certain professional responsibilities.*

Do-It Leisure provides opportunities for its clients through the efforts of the professionals and volunteers who make up the staff. This is especially apparent when therapists and specialists work with individuals and groups. It is evident also in the work of all other personnel who make program services possible.

The director and core staff members represent the organization in the community. Their relationships with other community members enhance the ability of Do-It Leisure to attract participants, generate funding, cooperate on mutual concerns, and create favorable impressions about the agency. Staff meetings and various in-service training efforts encourage personnel to become more aware of the role of interpersonal relationships in their professional work. Staff members improve and maintain competency in various ways. They participate in professional organization workshops. The director and two core staff members are pursuing graduate degrees. One member teaches leisure courses at California State University, Chico. And three are conducting research related to agency program services.

In the three chapters that follow, we will expand upon these four major concepts, as well as others. We will present many ideas related to leisure service that we hope will encourage you to think about applications in other situations.

References

Do-It Leisure. 1986. *Mission statement*. Chico, CA.

Sessoms, H. Douglas. 1985. Lifestyles and life cycles: A conceptual programming approach. In *Recreation and leisure: Issues in an era of change*, pp. 221-243, Thomas L. Goodale and Peter A. Witt, eds. State College, PA: Venture Publishing.

5

LEISURE BEHAVIOR

If we asked you to think about your most recent recreation activity, you probably could describe it in reasonable detail: where it happened, when it happened, what you did, and perhaps why you engaged in that particular activity at that particular time. You could most likely identify the beginning of the activity and the end of it: "We went skiing early Saturday morning and came home Sunday evening," or "I played volleyball between my one o'clock class and my chemistry lab at four." From your point of view, your participation was an experience, probably an enjoyable one.

Others might see your participation in different ways. The friends who went skiing with you may have noticed that you were skiing better on Sunday than you usually do. One of the ski instructors, on the hill, perhaps observed your technique in terms of the class level she felt you would be in if you took a class. A vacationing ophthalmologist, riding on the chair lift, might have been aware that you were not wearing dark glasses even though it was a very bright, sunny day. The proprietor of the ski shop in the lodge may have noticed you walk by on the way to the lift and wondered when you were going to replace that old ski jacket you were wearing. The perceptions of those who observed your behavior were influenced by such things as their relationships to you and their professional orientations.

Recreation and park personnel are interested in behavior because they work with it all the time. For example, when a ski area is designed, planners consider the kinds of behavior that occur at ski areas. Those who are responsible for marketing and promoting the area devise strategies based on a variety of facts and assump-

tions about the behavior of those they want to attract. Lift operators, patrol personnel, ski instructors, rental shop operators, food
service workers, and others work daily with the behavior of
patrons. This involvement with behavior is true for almost everyone working daily with the behavior of patrons—it is true for
almost everyone who works in the field of recreation and parks.

Basic Concepts of Leisure Behavior

This chapter will identify some concepts about behavior that
should enable you to plan and deliver leisure services more
effectively. Leisure behavior (or "recreation behavior;" we will
use the terms interchangeably) is a complex phenomenon, a
dynamic, fluid, on-going process. There are different dimensions,
such as motives, individual differences, social relationships, and
attitudes and beliefs. However, these elements do not operate
independently of one another: they are integrated. Here, we will
separate out different aspects in order to examine them, but the
separation is artificial. To truly understand behavior we must
recognize the holistic nature of it.

Let us begin by restating one of the major concepts defined in
the Overview to Part II, the one that applies directly to this
chapter. *Recreation and Park personnel are able to plan and deliver
leisure services more effectively when they know about leisure behavior.*
The overall purpose of the field is to provide opportunities for this
kind of behavior. This can best be done when we are aware of why
people engage in recreation and the factors that influence their
choices. Let us look at four other broad, important concepts and
several more specific concepts related to each of these four.

People Engage in Leisure Behavior to Achieve Certain Goals

For the most part, behavior is purposeful and goal-oriented,
not random. The nature of our goals and their influences on our
behavior fall into the area of motivation theory.

Intrinsic Motivation

Leisure occurs in free time, time that is relatively unobligated:
we feel a sense of relative freedom. This differentiates leisure

behavior and work or work equivalents. The reason for using "relatively unobligated" time and the term "relative freedom" is that we often assume obligations in recreation. Suppose you told some friends that you would go to a concert and that you would drive. Haven't you accepted an obligation? Yes. Does this mean that going to the concert is recreation behavior? Yes and no; it depends how you feel about it. If you are looking forward to going, expecting to enjoy it, and the driving doesn't detract from those feelings, then attending the concert would be recreation, though you still would have the obligation to take your car. However, if you really did not want to go but did so because you promised to drive, the experience probably would not be recreation. The key here is the degree to which you feel a sense of freedom from external obligation.

In work, we usually obligate ourselves to complete a task for which we receive some kind of extrinsic reward, typically money. In work equivalents, the payoff may be something else. For example, in many cases going to school can be thought of as a work equivalent. The reward is further education that leads to some other goal, such as a new job or a promotion. Assume, however, that you took a class in woodworking or history, not because you wanted to become a cabinetmaker or a history teacher but simply because you enjoy these subjects. Is that a case of "work equivalent"? Probably not. In the first case, the motivation was something other than the activity itself. You were preparing for a job, and the class was a means to that end. In the latter case, you were intrinsically motivated; satisfaction came from the class, not from the expectation of a deferred reward.

Freedom, Competence, and Arousal

When intrinsically motivated, you do something because of the enjoyment associated with the doing—you enjoy the activity for "its own sake." That idea can be clarified. Intrinsic satisfaction seems to come from activities in which you have both a sense of freedom in participating and a sense of competence, and when there is "optimal arousal" (Iso-Ahola 1982). Perhaps you like to go white-water rafting. In terms of intrinsic motivation, "like" means that you go because you feel a sense of freedom while rafting, you believe you are good at it, and it provides just the right amount of excitement. It is neither so scary as to be uncomfortable, nor so tame as to be boring. This last idea is related to "optimal arousal", that internal state between distress and boredom that is optimally exciting for an individual (Ellis 1973). Ellis contends that people engage in leisure behavior to maintain this optimal level through recreation, when they can exercise relative freedom of choice. Csikszentmihayli (1975) describes a "flow" concept that has similar elements. Csikszentmihayli notes that in certain leisure activities, individuals become completely absorbed. Concentration is high and attention is centered. There is a feeling of being competent and in control, and so the involvement is intrinsically motivating. This state occurs when the capabilities of the individual are in balance with the demands of the situation. If the demands are too high, there is anxiety; if they are too low, there is no interest.

Internal Self-Attributions

Self-attributions (Iso-Ahola 1980) are inferences we make about our own causes of behavior. We can attribute what we do to either personal or environmental and situational factors. Personal attributions are internal. When you say, "I went rafting because I'm good at it," you are making an internal attribution. Another example would be " I like to go to concerts because I understand the music." In both cases, you are attributing your participation to your competence. If you made the comment, "I went to the concert because I told my friends I would drive my car," you would be making a situational or external attribution.

Internal self-attributions are associated with a feeling of being in control, being able to determine your behavior, or choosing what you want to do. This feeling of self-determination contributes to perceived freedom; external attributions reduce the sense of freedom.

For some theorists (Iso-Ahola 1980; Neulinger 1981), perceived freedom is the most important characteristic of leisure. In Neulinger's paradigm, if there is a sense of constraint the activity is work or a work equivalent, even though it might be intrinsically motivating. On the other hand, if there is a sense of freedom, leisure may occur with extrinsic motivations or a blend of both intrinsic and extrinsic motivations. Satisfaction may come from the consequence of the activity rather than from the activity itself. Home maintenance and exercising to keep fit are examples. The key is whether or not the individual freely chooses to engage in the particular activity. However, the category of "pure leisure" in Neulinger's paradigm is reserved for those experiences where both perceived freedom and intrinsic motivation are present. Others (Kaplan 1975; Roadburg 1985) place emphasis on enjoyment as the essential characteristic of leisure.

Specific Goals Individuals Seek. Within the framework of intrinsic motivation, there are different specific reasons for participating. These reasons differ from time to time for the same person. Even so we can identify some reasons that are fairly common, for example, to enjoy the company of others, to escape the pressures and routines of everyday life, and to sense accomplishment or mastery. Ragheb and Beard (1980) identify six dimensions of satisfaction that suggest the kinds of benefits people seek in recreation: psychological, social, educational, relaxational, physiological, and aesthetic.

Leisure Needs and Satisfactions

Some leisure needs are "activity specific" and others are "activity general" (Tinsley, Barrett, and Kass 1977). For any given individual, some needs can be met only by specific activities, while others can be met by any leisure activity. One activity may provide multiple satisfactions for an individual. For example, a ceramics class might provide companionship with others who have similar interests, and a sense of achievement when classmates and the instructor admire work completed.

The satisfactions most people seek in leisure tend to be immediate ones, sensed at the time of participation. However, some individuals might be motivated by more distant goals as well as the immediate ones. A golfer may see practice on the putting green as a way to improve future scores, but he also practices because it is fun. A skier might jog to keep in condition for the slopes, but she also runs because she enjoys it.

Psychological Conflict. Suppose you wanted to go surfing with friends, feeling that this would meet your need for companionship. You probably wouldn't express it that way, but that would be your goal. However, you might also feel a need for security or to be safe from harm. If your surfing skills are not too sharp, or if the surf is heavier than you are comfortable with, you might experience psychological conflict. In one way, you want to go; in another, you don't. The feelings are about equally weighted. Another example would be the beginning sport parachutist about to make his first jump. He perceives the potential for exhilaration and achievement, as well as the possibility of equipment failure or faulty technique. The junior high school student considering going to his first dance might experience a conflict between his emerging interest in girls and his fear of looking foolish in front of friends. Another kind of conflict involves two different activities, occurring at the same time. For example, suppose a physicist loves to play tennis and enjoys foreign films. She receives an invitation to attend a foreign film festival on the same weekend she is entered in a local tournament. She wants to do both but can't, and so she experiences psychological conflict.

Some Needs Have More Influence. Maslow's scheme (1943) is often cited in recreation and park literature. While there is some suggestion that the theory has been applied uncritically (Iso-Ahola 1980), it does provide useful ideas about relationships between different needs. Maslow contends that needs exist in a hierarchical arrangement, from survival needs on the bottom, security, belonging, and esteem needs, to "self-actualization" on the top. Lower needs have more potency for influencing behavior. Higher needs do not become operative until those lower in the hierarchy are met to the individual's satisfaction. In regard to the earlier example, in terms of Maslow's theory, you might want to go surfing with friends to meet an unsatisfied need for companionship, but decide not to go because you don't think you can handle the heavy surf conditions. In a sense, the thought of going creates an unsatisfied need for safety or security; by not going you meet this need. Notice that there is no psychological conflict because one need is more potent.

Success and Failure
Obviously satisfaction should contribute to our overall feelings of well-being, or the general quality of our lives. Consistent successes or failures in achieving our goals probably will influence our confidence and feelings about ourselves. Success tends to build self-esteem. In terms of any specific activity, whether or not we succeed might be a determining factor in our decision to engage in the activity again. For some of us, failure will be discouraging and we will quit. Others will try harder. In general, success and a sense of achievement lead to further participation.

Success contributes to feelings of competence, and these are part of the concept of intrinsic motivation.

Level of Aspiration

What does it take for you to experience satisfaction in an activity? What must happen for you to feel competent? Questions such as these bring up the concept of "level of aspiration," the idea that different individuals may have different expectations for the same goal. Let us say that you and a friend go bowling. She bowls 147, and you bowl 129. Will she be satisfied with her score and will you be pleased with 129? That is another way of asking if what you bowled meets your level of aspiration. Remember the physicist who likes tennis? She might be satisfied if, in a tournament, she plays well enough to win one set; or she might only be happy if she wins her division. Intrinsic goals involve states we hope to achieve, such as feelings of accomplishment, excitement, or relaxation. Level of aspiration deals with the degree to which the state must be present for us to feel satisfied.

Using Information about Goals to Plan and Deliver Services

First of all, remember the characteristics of intrinsic motivation. Try to provide activities that enable people to feel a sense of freedom, to experience success and feel competent, and to be appropriately excited. Be aware of the typical reasons why people engage in leisure behavior, but remember that there is variation from individual to individual and from time to time. Get information about people's specific interests through surveys and individual contacts. Ask people what they want to achieve; find out what will lead to satisfaction and enjoyment. If you can talk to some people who do not use agency services, try to find out why they are non-participants.

Keep in mind that asking people what they want to get from their recreation participation may not produce enough information to be useful. You may need to probe a little in appropriate ways. For example, if I tell you that I'm looking for enjoyment, that doesn't give you much to plan for because enjoyment is not very operational in and of itself. Of course, what you know about intrinsic motivation suggests that I'll enjoy something when I feel a sense of freedom and competence and when the level of excitement is right for me. But if you find out that I enjoy being with other people, that I like to accomplish things, and that I don't like pressure, then you know something more useful about my interests and needs and have much more to work with.

Recognize that you will be making inferences about people's goals. A couple of examples will illustrate this. Assume that you are a recreation center director. You really will not know why one of the teen-agers who uses the center is playing basketball today rather than shooting pool, unless he tells you. Similarly, you will not know for certain what will attract his interest tomorrow or next week. You can make some guesses; and the more you know about this individual, about adolescents as an age group, and about recreation behavior in general, the more accurate your guesses should be. You can confirm these guesses by asking for information and making careful observations. The inferences you make, based on the information you have, will influence how you structure the program you offer at the center. Let us say you infer that this teen-ager enjoys competition and "staying in shape." Assume further that you believe the other adolescents who are playing basketball today have the same goals. This might cause you to put more emphasis on scorekeeping to enhance the competitive aspect, and perhaps you would set up fifteen-minute quarters rather than ten-minute periods to provide more exercise. However, if the teens' objectives were mostly social, to enjoy the company of others in a friendly game, your emphasis on competition and exercise would be less likely to foster satisfaction. If this were the case, you would want to structure the situation differently—make sure players get to know each other and provide opportunities for social interaction after the game. The challenge would be to make your initial inferences as accurately as possible, to check them as service progresses, and to make changes when needed and possible.

Other Factors Influence the Nature of Leisure Behavior

The actual goals we pursue, the ways we seek to meet them, and our responses to the degrees of our success are influenced by a variety of factors. Some of these are associated with individual characteristics, and others are related to the situations within which leisure behavior occurs.

Individual Differences

There are some characteristics we have in common with other individuals whose backgrounds are similar to ours, and other characteristics we share with all other human beings. Yet in a sense each of us is a unique individual (Brill 1978). We differ from others in our personalities, attitudes and beliefs, self-concepts, and other similar psychological factors. We also differ in terms of biological and physiological conditions, such as cardiovascular functioning, coordination, and visual acuity. Most of us have different background experiences: we grew up in different places, had different family circumstances, lived in different communities, and encountered different social institutions. Through these experiences, we developed different values; these are social or cultural variations.

Individual variations such as age, sexual identity, ethnicity, educational background, occupation, and income level do explain some differences in leisure behavior, but the relationships are relatively weak (Burch 1969; Kelly 1985). Some of the influences are fairly obvious. Older adults tend to have less physical energy than the young. Elementary school age children are likely to have less freedom from parental supervision than adolescents. These age differences involve both biological and cultural or social considerations. Variations in physical energy probably are physiologically based; differences in independence tend to be culturally prescribed. Occupational differences create variations in income level and influence the amount of free time people have and when they have it. Income levels influence the leisure choices we make, at least to a degree. Differing levels of education expose us to different leisure activities, and education influences our awareness of activities and our skills. You probably can think of some other individual factors and the ways they might relate to recreation behavior. These individual factors do not operate independently. For example, construction work is not just an occupational category. The individual who holds this job is also a certain age, has a certain educational level, is either male or female, and lives in a specific location. The influences of these conditions are interactive.

Other People

Humans tend to be social organisms, for much of our behavior occurs in groups. Typically we are born into a family situation that includes at least one other caring person. We first learn social skills in the family setting. These skills are expanded in schools and in other social institutions such as churches and leisure service agencies. From early childhood on we develop friendships. Some theorists contend that the need to be affiliated with other persons, to belong, and to experience companionship is a basic human motive (Kretch, Crutchfield, and Ballachey 1962). Some of our social contacts are fairly casual; others are more intense; and some are intimate. In all cases they have potential for influencing behavior.

We feel the influence of other people in two basic ways. These ways can be illustrated by a couple of questions. First, think about some favorite recreation activity of yours. Now answer these questions: How did you become interested in this activity? Do you participate in it alone or with other people? It is possible that your answers might be different, but chances are you first were exposed to the activity through family or friends and that you engage in it with others. Most likely socialization and social motives were involved at some point.

Socialization

Socialization is the process through which an individual learns the values and behaviors considered important by the society in which he or she lives. The person learns what is needed to function as a social being. He or she internalizes these learnings, making them part of the self. Socialization occurs through interactions with parents, teachers, recreation leaders, other people, recreation and park agencies and other social institutions. Although the literature on socialization tends to focus on childhood and adolescence, socialization happens throughout one's life (Iso-Ahola 1980).

Socialization influences recreation behavior in many ways. One example will serve as an illustration. When Suzzane was a child, her mother and father often took her to art galleries. She observed her parents' behavior, noticed the things they liked, heard them talk about different artists. They told her about painting and taught her some things about terms and techniques. They also taught, directly and by example, proper social behavior in galleries—things to do and not to do. In these ways Suzzane learned about different kinds of paintings, developed the ability to identify different styles, was encouraged to express her own likes and dislikes, and learned to enjoy going to galleries. She found she could converse with others, besides her parents, about painting and painters. And she felt comfortable in a gallery. The socialization process included the development of knowledge, values, and behaviors. It happened in the family setting, but it could have happened at Suzzane's school, with a teacher, or in any number of other settings with other people. Instead of gallery visiting, the socialization process could have been ice-skating, camping, or volunteering to help at a convalescent hospital.

Social Motives

In later years, Suzzane might go to art galleries with friends. Much recreation behavior occurs in social or group settings. The satisfactions of interacting with friends and companions are powerful leisure motives. Iso-Ahola states that the empirical evidence for this is "strong and unambiguous" (1980, 242). Individuals sometimes seek relative isolation in leisure, such as in wilderness use. However, even here the typical backpacker makes the trip with at least one other person. In many leisure activities that we would not consider primarily social, participants experience satisfaction from interacting with other participants as well as from the activity itself (Buchanan and Burdge 1980; Crandall 1979).

Other Social Influences

Iso-Ahola (1980) notes several other social influences. Many leisure activities can be done only with others. Obvious examples are team sports, most card games, and many forms of dancing. Also, you may do something simply, or in part, because other people are doing it. If all of your friends learn to cross-country ski, it is likely that you will also want to learn. Observations of others might influence your perceptions of competence in an activity—you compare your skill or performance to that of performers who are, in your opinion, at about your level. And your perceptions of competence in the social relationships associated with leisure activities are sources of satisfaction.

Settings and Situations

Leisure behavior takes place in settings that include physical and often human elements. Tennis is played on a court, with a clay, lawn, asphalt, or other type of surface. The court is marked with appropriate lines and divided by a net. Usually a fence surrounds it. The court is located somewhere: near a major street, or in a residential neighborhood. The surroundings might be noisy or quiet. There are weather differences. Some days may be hot, other days windy. There will be other people: an opponent or opponents, a partner if the game is doubles, and perhaps spectators.

These elements influence behavior. For example, a poorly surfaced court will produce different responses from players than one that is in excellent condition. The presence of spectators may cause different behaviors than if only the players are there. Either the presence or absence of spectators might influence an advanced player differently than a beginner. A less experienced player might play better against an advanced player; the advanced player may let down, mentally, and not play as well. Both might become irritated with the condition of an inferior court and agree to some temporary rule changes to compensate for the poor surface; they will play an unusual bounce over if it occurs on a serve and will serve from and receive in the better court on either side rather than alternate courts.

More may be involved than a one-way relationship when the environment influences the individual. Often the participant causes changes in the setting. Unbroken powder snow encourages certain kinds of skiing behavior. However, the first skier down the hill changes the slope for those who ski later. Subsequent runs by more skiers continue to create changes. The hill becomes packed; eventually moguls may develop. These changes cause other changes in skiers' responses. We could provide many other examples, but these illustrate the basic idea that there often is a reciprocal relationship between recreation behavior and the situations within which it occurs.

But we respond only to those parts of the environment that we are aware of, and we respond in terms of the reality we perceive. Perhaps we are skiing and waiting in line for the chair lift. Suppose the lift is about to have a malfunction develop in the electric control circuitry, and this will cause the lift to stop unexpectedly sometime in the next four or five minutes. Repairs will take about fifteen minutes, during which time the lift will not operate. If we knew this we probably would not get on the lift for the next ride; we would avoid the possibility of being stuck on the lift while it is stopped. But we are not aware of this condition. The reality is that the lift will malfunction and stop. But since we do not perceive this condition, it is not a reality for us and so it does not influence our behavior.

Using Information about These Other Factors

This may seem obvious, but you should get to know as much as possible about the people you hope to serve. How old are they? What are their educational backgrounds? Where do they work and live? Perhaps there are past records in your agency that provide information about your clientele. You might get relevant demographic data from governmental entities, such as city and county planning departments. Spend some time in the community; note where people live and talk to them in informal settings, such as shopping malls, school athletic events, and church services. This will give you some feeling for the overall nature of your service population. Remember that you will need to individualize your overall perceptions. The specific retired male who shows up at one of your programs will probably have some different interests other than the ones he also shares with most other older adults. Of course this takes time (and you may not have much of it), but you have a better chance of serving people effectively when you know your clients as individuals.

Structure your services to include opportunities for social interaction. Recognize that some people will come to programs in pre-existing social groups; others may appreciate help in developing new friendships.

Be aware of the socialization processes that might be occurring through the services you offer. What kinds of behavior are you encouraging? What values and attitudes will these opportunities promote? Are these the behaviors and values you want to encourage? Are they compatible with individual, community, and agency expectations?

Consider that it might be appropriate to facilitate the socialization process. This often happens as a routine part of classes we teach. For example, in golf lessons we not only help people learn how to use different clubs, but we also teach proper behavior on a golf course: to replace divots, to not talk when others are hitting, to invite faster foursomes to play through, and other knowledge and skills not immediately concerned with just hitting the ball. These enable students to play comfortably with others on a golf course, and give the beginning golfer confidence that he or she will not behave inappropriately. Teaching proper course behavior "socializes" the individual to the game of golf.

Check the facilities you work with to be aware of their potential influences on behavior. Recognize the effects of such things as proper maintenance and aesthetics. In many cases you will create or modify environments to encourage certain kinds of behavior. In a company lunch room, you might arrange tables to encourage social interaction. At a ski area, you might groom some slopes and let others become more uneven or "mogulled" to facilitate different behaviors from different levels of skiers. If the behaviors you observe at a facility seem not to be what you expect, try to find out how people are seeing them. What are their perceptions?

Psychological States Influence Leisure Behavior

Behavior is a function of the interactions between the internal states of an individual and the external characteristics of the situation he or she is experiencing. We must consider internal or psychological states if we are to understand behavior.

Perceptions
We respond to events in terms of our perceptions and in accordance with the meanings they have for us (Combs, Richards, and Richards 1976). Reality, for each of us, is what we believe it is. The meanings we assign to events and objects can be influenced by many factors, such as our self-concepts, past experiences, hopes and aspirations, fears, values, and biases. Experience may cause us to modify our perceptions to conform more to "external" reality, but the modified perceptions are still perceptions. We behave on the basis of these.

Since perceptions include meaning, beliefs and attitudes are involved. Attitudes are feelings about an object or entity and involve tendencies to respond favorably or unfavorably toward it. We form attitudes on the basis of our experiences. We may adopt a "trial" attitude from something we see or hear, or from another respected person; but we confirm or modify these based on experience. In this sense, behavior influences attitudes. Is the trial attitude verified by the behavior? by the experience? Does it pay off in terms of goals? Does it fit in terms of self-concept? In turn, as attitudes develop and change, they influence subsequent behavior.

Individual Meanings

Behavior occurs in settings. In skiing, for example, the hill, lifts, and other skiers all are parts of the external environment. They exist outside of the individual. However, the individual understands, and assigns meaning to them on the basis of his or her values, attitudes, and perceptions. If you think the day is good for skiing, you will behave as such, unless something occurs to change your perception. For it to be a good day for Marilyn, the snow must be relatively dry, the slopes well-groomed, and the lift lines not too long. Sachiko also likes uncrowded lift lines and slopes, but she doesn't care what the snow conditions are as long as there is enough. She arrives at the ski area, finds that the snow is heavy and wet, and doesn't think much about it. Marilyn gets to the hill, realizes what the conditions are, and decides not to ski. The same snow conditions have different meanings for each of them. Marilyn values dry snow; Sachiko does not.

Let us suppose that the snow is wet and heavy only near the bottom of the hill and that the upper runs are in good shape. If Marilyn thinks the snow on the whole hill is like it is at the base, she probably will not ski. Her perception will be that the conditions are not what she likes. This perception governs her behavior, not the reality of the conditions. Hill conditions, the friendliness of personnel at the area, the price of lift tickets, the quality of food in the cafeteria, and most other aspects of the operation will be known to all skiers through their perceptions. As another example, two people may encounter the same staff member in the rental shop. One person may see the staff member as friendly and helpful; another person sees him as competent but rude. Who is correct? As far as his behavior goes, it does not matter—each customer will relate to the staff member on the basis of his or her perceptions.

Past Experiences

Marilyn might have had a bad fall one time skiing in wet, slushy snow. The individual who felt the rental shop staff member was inattentive might have encountered a rude person the last time she rented equipment. These past experiences can create different meanings for the individuals involved. These meanings will be conditioned, in part, by one's needs, values, and attitudes. If you generally value friendly people, your perceptions of the personality of the man in the rental shop will be more important to you than if all you care about is getting the right equipment and getting out on the hill.

Individual Identities

Kelly (1983) emphasizes the importance of self-concept in our understanding of leisure behavior. He observes that the concept of self is multidimensional. Our identities change over time, and we express different selves in different situations. Leisure provides "an openness to 'play' with role identities, to do more than respond to social norms, to be and become ourselves in the event" (Kelly 1983, 94). This expression of self, the development and verification of identity in leisure, influences style as much or more than the specific activities we choose.

A "role-identity" model (Kelly 1985) brings together the influences of society and the self-determining nature of the individual. It recognizes the central influence of socialization processes and the fulfillment of normative behavior defined by social roles. However, a role-identity model emphasizes that there is much individual expression in terms of styles. Roles provide a framework; our individual identities influence the ways we express ourselves in those roles. Our identities change over time and in different settings. In small and large ways, we are always in the process of becoming something different. We express not only who we think we are, but the self we want to become. The influences on leisure of these two dimensions, social roles and individual identities, are combined and interactive.

Using the Implications of Psychological States

The most important thing to remember is that perceptions create reality and meanings for individuals. To understand other people's behavior, you must try to see things from their points of view. If someone's behavior seems unusual, keep in mind that it probably makes sense to that person. Don't assume that other people will see things the same way you do, or that their interests and values will be the same as yours. Recognize that a person's behavior generally will be consistent with his or her self-concept.

How do you know what another person's perceptions are? As mentioned before, you need to talk to people. Ask them for their views; get feedback; listen to people; develop rapport. People will be more likely to let you know how they feel and what they are thinking if they trust you. Observe behavior and try to make accurate inferences.

Leisure Behavior Changes Over Time

A fundamental human characteristic is change. We change through developmental processes. Children grow; under proper circumstances, they mature, learn useful skills, and develop new attitudes. As adults, we can continue to learn, develop new knowledge and skills, and change or develop new attitudes and beliefs. Some change is inevitable. Eventually, and with much individual variation, we experience reduced energy levels when we get old. Other changes result from accidental or chance events; you break your leg or see a movie that dramatically alters your attitude about something. And still other change results from purposeful attempts to bring it about or failure to do something. For example, an individual can alter physical functioning through exercise programs or become less fit through lack of activity. Some change is temporary, and some is permanent. When it occurs, it usually influences behavior.

Stages in Life Involve Different Social Roles

A "life course" approach (Kelly 1983) suggests that leisure styles and preferences change over the course of an individual's lifetime. Kelly views the life course as a "journey from birth to death" (53). As we move through childhood, adolescence, young adulthood, middle age, and older age, we encounter different sets of social interactions and contexts for our recreation behavior: family settings, schools, commercial establishments, and others. This journey is somewhat different for each person. However, people born at the same time in the same culture experience much that is common: prevalent economic conditions, political climates, and other major social events.

Kelly (1983) identifies three major life periods: preparation, establishment, and culmination (58-59). Preparation has a future orientation. It is a time when, in the eyes of the society, the individual is preparing for later life—growing up, going to school, developing employment potential, preparing for important long-term relationships. While there is much variation in terms of years, the establishment period typically begins with full-time employment. During this period, we tend to be productively involved in society and have established our place in the social system. For many, work will be an important dimension. Childrearing and family responsibilities will be significant for some. The third major life period, culmination is also difficult to pin down in terms of years. Typically, it is marked by retirement. If there were children, they are grown and gone. This is period in which we recognize that life is different than it was before and there is a limit to what lies ahead. It can be a period of great satisfaction; we enjoy new roles and seek to find meaning and integration in life. For some, it can be a time of loneliness, stress, illness, and anxiety.

The changing social-physical environment we encounter at different stages of life, influences our motivations and perceptions of leisure opportunities. In part this is attributable to role-related leisure. Our social roles change: from child, to student, parent, friend, and others that are appropriate for different stages and settings. These roles have impacts on what we want to do and what we are able to do. For example, recreation behaviors associated with the role of the college student may be quite different than those of the parent. The leisure of young parents often revolves, in part, around their children; playing with them in the home, taking them to recreation facilities and community events, being spectators at activities in which the children are participating, and other role-related activities. College students more typically interact in leisure with others of the same age; attending athletic events, going to parties, listening to music, enjoying outdoor recreation, and other wide-ranged activities. Of course not all leisure is role-related, but some of it is. The satisfaction that comes from role-related leisure results directly from the interactions involved. In part, satisfaction may come from a sense of competency in the role—being a "good" father or mother and fulfilling other social roles in expected ways. Social norms help to define the accepted role-related behavior.

Role identities change over time and in different settings. Behavior expected of a young, second-year college student will be different in some ways from that of a middle-aged adult who returns to finish a degree started earlier in life. The self-identities of each are different. And what is acceptable behavior for the sophomore in the fraternity house will be different for the middle-aged student in his professor's home. It will be different for the older student at home, with a spouse and teen-age children, than for other students in the college snack bar. The meanings of leisure, as well as perceptions of what is appropriate behavior, will change for each individual.

Leisure Opportunities and Meanings Change

Resources and opportunities change during the life course. Young parents, with an infant in the home, have different restrictions on their time than older adults whose children have grown and moved. A retired person typically has fewer external obligations than an individual who is employed. The relative amount of independence people have influences their opportunities, the kinds of places they can go, and the things they can do. Other conditions that influence leisure opportunities include financial resources and health.

The life course approach is related to a "balance" model (Kelly 1985). Here we see leisure preferences change through life in response to and as part of other life developments. The meanings of leisure alter and the outcomes vary at different life stages. Our recreation behavior results from our assessments of which activities are most likely to produce the combination, or balance of satisfactions we seek at different stages of life.

Obtaining and Using Life Stage Information

You can easily make fairly accurate guesses about the ages of your service clientele and can get demographic data (including age categories) for the general population from several sources. You need to know more, however, since age does not directly define life stage. Again, you need to talk to people and be observant. When appropriate, you can also obtain information through surveys. Try to determine the social roles, related to life stages, that individuals value. Create program opportunities for people to express and enjoy these roles. Youth sports, in which parents can serve as coaches or enjoy spectator roles, are examples.

Recognize that individual resources sometimes vary with life stages. Be aware of such factors as lack of time and transportation that might constitute barriers for people at different stages. Work

to offset these through direct service, or through referral or advocacy processes. For example, young parents sometimes feel "tied
down" by the ongoing responsibilities of caring for their children.
By providing programs for preschoolers, or by advocating for the
development of such programs by another appropriate agency,
you might enable young mothers or fathers to enjoy some additional free time for themselves that they otherwise would not
have. Or, you might provide for a cooperative preschool program
that involves parents, in this way you would create additional
opportunities for parents to engage in role-related leisure.

Theories of Leisure Behavior

The concepts discussed in this chapter are not separate,
independent influences—they are interactive. For example, Knopf
(1983) identifies four interacting "systems" of influence: home and
work environments, personality, social forces, and cognitive processes. He emphasizes that these influences are interrelated
and that there are no "simple linear cause-effect relationships"
(226).

Iso-Ahola (1980) also recognizes the varied, interacting nature of influences. He contends that there are different levels of
determinants. The most basic are biological makeups and psychological states rooted in childhood socialization and learning. These
set the stage. They dispose us to engage in some activities and not
others and influence our individual needs for optimal arousal.
Within the framework of these basic influences, we select activities
that are intrinsically motivating. At the highest level, we are
influenced by "leisure needs," what we say we want to get out of
recreation behavior. Iso-Ahola cautions that leisure needs are
only the "tip of the iceberg." Expressed needs are fairly easy to
determine. However, to fully understand recreation behavior, we
must dig deeper and look at lower levels of influence. We need to
also be aware of social environments and situational influences
that operate at all levels.

Kelly (1985) defines three approaches to explaining variations in recreation behavior and adds a useful note about "style".
We discussed his "life course" and "individual identity" approaches earlier and presented ideas about individual differences
(for example, gender and age) that are related to his structural

approach. He suggests that the influences apparent in these three approaches are expressed as much in "style" of behavior as in the selection of different activities. That is, recreation behavior often differs less in terms of what we do than in *how* we do it. For example, eating out is a popular leisure activity; but there are big differences in where and how it is done. Many people travel; the places they go, how they get there, how long they stay, and what they do on-site vary for different travelers. There is a difference between swimming in a pond on a farm and in a heated pool at a resort hotel. In the resort pool, splashing around in the shallow end with friends differs from solitary lap swimming. These are differences in style rather than in activity.

Several other authors have presented theoretical explanations of leisure behavior that illustrate the interacting nature of various influences (Chubb and Chubb 1981; Ellis 1973; Kaplan 1975; Levy 1978; Niepoth 1983; Smith and Theberge 1987).

Summary

In this chapter we have noted some characteristics of leisure behavior. Recreation and park personnel work with this kind of behavior and provide opportunities for it to occur. The different ways that opportunities can be provided will be discussed in later chapters. This chapter should provide a framework for understanding these ways. Our basic premise is that you will be more effective in delivering leisure services if you know something about recreation behavior.

In summary, we can say that recreation behavior is goal-oriented and characterized by intrinsic motivation and a sense of freedom. Some leisure behaviors are fairly common. Beyond these there are wide variations. We are influenced by many different factors: personal, sociological, psychological and environmental. Leisure behavior changes over the life span. The processes of learning, socialization, role fulfillment, and expressions of personal identity influence the things we do, how we do them, and the meanings they have for us. An understanding of behavior provides a basis for our professional decisions and actions. Observations of specific instances of behavior permit us to verify general understandings and make appropriate applications to the individuals or groups with whom we are working.

References

Brill, Naomi I. 1978. *Working with people: The helping process*, 2nd ed. Philadelphia:J. B. Lippincott.

Buchanan, Thomas, and Rabel J. Burdge. 1980. Satisfactions and secondary activities: A canonical analysis. In *Abstracts from the 1980 Symposium on Leisure Research*, p. 11. Arlington, VA: National Recreation and Park Association.

Burch, William R., Jr. 1969. The social circles of leisure: Competing explanations. *Journal of Leisure Research* 1:125.

Chubb, Michael, and Holly R. Chubb. 1981. *One third of our time? An introduction to recreation behavior and resources.* New York: John Wiley & Sons.

Combs, A. W., D. L. Avila, and W. W. Purkey. 1978. *Helping relationships: Basic concepts for the helping professions.* Boston: Allyn and Bacon.

Combs, Arthur, Anne Cohen Richards, and Fred Richards. 1976. Perceptual psychology: A humanistic approach to the study of persons. New York: Harper & Row.

Crandall, Rick. 1979. Social interaction, affect and leisure. *Journal of Leisure Research* 11:166.

Csikszentmihayli, Mihaly. 1975. *Beyond boredom and anxiety.* San Francisco: Jossey-Bass.

Ellis, M. J. 1973. *Why people play.* Englewood Cliffs, NJ: Prentice-Hall.

Iso-Ahola, Seppo E. 1980. *The social psychology of leisure and recreation.* Dubuque, IA: Wm. C. Brown Company Publishers.

Iso-Ahola, Seppo E. 1982. Intrinsic motivation: An overlooked basis for evaluation. *Parks & Recreation* 17:32-33

Kaplan, Max. 1975. *Leisure: Theory and policy.* New York: John Wiley and Sons.

Kelly, John R. 1983. *Leisure identities and interactions.* London: George Allen & Unwin.

Kelly, John R. 1985. Sources of leisure styles. In *Recreation and leisure: Issues in an era of change*, Thomas L. Goodale and Peter A. Witt, eds. State College, PA: Venture Publishing.

Knopf, Richard C. 1983. Recreational needs and behavior in natural settings. In *Behavior and the natural environment*, Irwin Altman and Joachim F. Wohlwill, eds. New York: Plenum Press.

Kretch, David, Richard S. Crutchfield and Edgerton L. Ballachey. 1962. *Individuals in society.* New York: McGraw-Hill.

Levy, Joseph. 1978. *Play behavior.* New York: John Wiley and Sons.

Maslow, Abraham H. 1943. A theory of human motivation. *Psychological Review* 50:370-396.

Neulinger, John. 1981. *To leisure.* Boston: Allyn and Bacon.

Niepoth, E. William. 1983. *Leisure leadership: Working with people in recreation and park settings.* Englewood Cliffs, NJ: Prentice-Hall.

Ragheb, Mounir G., and Jacob G. Beard. 1980. Leisure satisfaction: Concept, theory measurement. In *Social psychological perspectives on leisure and recreation,* pp. 329-353. Seppo E. Iso-Ahola, ed. Springfield, IL: Charles C. Thomas.

Roadburg, Alan. 1985. *Aging: Retirement, leisure and work in Canada.* Toronto: Methuen.

Smith, David H., and Nancy Theberge. 1987. *Why people recreate: An overview of research.* Champaign, IL : Life Enhancement Publications.

Tinsley, Howard E. A., Thomas C. Barrett, and Richard A. Kass. 1977. Leisure activity and the need satisfaction. *Journal of Leisure Research.* 9:110-119.

6

LEISURE SERVICE PROGRAMS

A director of a recreation center sits in a circle of preschool children and tells a story about turtles. Several blocks away, the owner of a ceramics studio works up clay for afternoon students to use. In the same city, a leisure counselor meets with a client to explore interests and opportunities. Miles away, inside Yellowstone National Park, a crew of park aides cleans up a campground area and repairs tables and fire pits. In a small community, many miles east of the park, a physical director provides judo instruction for sixteen teenagers. Farther south, a park planner makes an on-site inspection of a city park that is under construction. In western Alberta, a maintenance crew works on a chair lift at a major ski resort. Three thousand miles away in Acapulco, the food services manager at a large hotel checks on final arrangements for a banquet. In New York, a cousin of the manager works with a small group of hospital patients in a drama program.

One of the major concepts defined in the overview for Part II is that a leisure service organization achieves its purposes by providing opportunities for its constituents to engage in leisure behavior. All of the people mentioned above are working to provide such opportunities; they are engaged in a common task—providing leisure services. Some, such as the physical director and the center director, are involved directly and immediately with participants. Others, such as the park planner and the summer park aides, work more with the physical environments and re-sources that participants will use. We could expand the list of examples to cover all phases of public, private, and commercial agencies, at all levels from local to international.

Basic Concepts

In this chapter, we will discuss three basic concepts and several more specific ones related to leisure services.

Agencies Deliver Services and Provide Opportunities by Using Resources

Each of the individuals mentioned in the first paragraph is part of a delivery system. For example, the campground is one of many in Yellowstone; and Yellowstone is one of the many parks administered by the National Park Service. At each site and in the various subunits within each site, personnel provide opportunities for people to engage in leisure behavior. Similarly, the judo class is one of many programs administered by the local YMCA.

Various Approaches to Providing Service

Some agencies are committed to providing direct service to their publics. They deliver opportunities so that people can participate immediately and directly. When the sixteen teens arrived for the judo class, it was ready to go. The facility was in order and properly equipped, and the instructor was present and prepared. The participants had nothing to do but engage in the activity that was provided.

The preschool program might also illustrate a direct service approach. However, under different conditions, it could grow out of an enabling approach. Let us assume that there was no program in the city for preschool children three months ago. A group of mothers approached the center director and asked about the possibility of starting such a program; they were told that the recreation and park department would help them if they wanted to pursue the idea. With the assistance of the center staff, they developed the program they wanted and they recruited and employed an instructor. The city provided the facility, publicized the program, and handled financial arrangements such as collecting fees, and paying the instructor. In this situation, the participants created the opportunity with the help and support of the agency. The agency enabled the program, but did not deliver it ready-made.

In Chapter 3 we commented on direct service and enabling approaches in terms of the professional roles of staff members. In a direct service approach, participants depend more upon agency staff. An enabling approach fosters more independence. Service is enhanced when recreation and park personnel are able to use both approaches, depending upon the needs and expectations of the public and upon the philosophy and resources of the agency.

Different Specific Objectives of Agencies

In Yellowstone, the intent of the interpretive center staff is different from the purposes of the personnel responsible for campground maintenance. The overall mission of the superintendent of Yellowstone will be somewhat different from the missions pursued by the superintendents of Cape Cod National Seashore, Arches National Monument, or Lake Mead National Recreation Area. True, the general objectives of preserving the resources and heritage and providing for the enjoyment of people are common purposes. However, the nature of participation will differ somewhat from site to site and, therefore, the specific purposes of each superintendent and staff will differ. At the ski resort, the maintenance staff has specific objectives different from those of the ski school staff or the personnel of the rental shop, even though the common intent is to provide opportunities for resort patrons to ski.

Some agencies set fairly general objectives. They may strive, for example, to provide wholesome recreation opportunities for all ages; or they might attempt to provide the resources so that people can use their leisure time constructively. In either case, the agency's intent is to offer a range of opportunities for the public it serves. Except for providing the general framework, the agency does not try to directly control the specific values that the individual receives from participation. The typical municipal recreation and park department is an example. It offers a wide range of opportunities for different ages, different interests, and different levels of skill. The agency structures the opportunities so as to minimize or eliminate hazards to the health, safety, and welfare of participants, and avoids encouraging or permitting activities that are contrary to major community values and expectations. It assumes that participants will benefit, sometimes in similar ways, but often in unique ways.

Another approach is to work consciously for the development of certain specifically defined benefits and values. Agencies doing so often have an ethic or a creed that serves as a basis for their operations. Or they may serve special populations. Examples of the former would be the various councils of the Boy Scouts of America, which foster behaviors and values consistent with the scout oath. Illustrations of the latter would be hospitals and treatment centers where recreation therapists seek certain specified benefits for patients and clients. Some agencies will use a combination of approaches, depending upon clientele and specific programs. For example, a veterans' administration hospital may offer activities for short-term, convalescing patients with the objectives of simply reducing boredom and enriching the normal hospital routine. However, activities provided on the neuropsychiatric ward of the same hospital may be designed to achieve specific objectives developed by a medical team for individual patients.

Human and Physical Elements in Agency Resources

To provide opportunities for people to engage in recreation behavior, each agency commits its resources of legal authority, finances, personnel, physical facilities, and land and water areas. The agency organizes and manages these elements to achieve the objectives it has for the particular unit, facility, site, or program.

Let us say, for example, that a municipal recreation and park department wants to provide opportunities for city residents to play golf. Obviously the department will do such things as acquire land and develop a golf course. The department will employ personnel to maintain the course and keep it in an attractive condition. It will also employ personnel to offer lessons, regulate play so that it proceeds efficiently, and provide food services and equipment sales. The department will train and supervise these employees so that appropriate service is provided. And it probably will use mass media to make the public aware of the golfing opportunities.

Planners, landscape architects, construction supervisors, park maintenance workers, gardeners, custodians, and other similar individuals are immediately concerned with the creation and manipulation of physical environments. So are the center director and the judo instructor. When the judo instructor arranges mats, makes sure that the showers are clean, and puts a display on the club bulletin board, he is manipulating the physical environment. He does so with the reasonable expectation that it will encourage certain kinds of behavior from the teens. He also manipulates the human environment, of which he is a part. He directly influences club members through teaching and leadership. He encourages them, and the group itself may serve as an encouraging element. The YMCA executive director and the program director are also concerned about the human environment; they recruit qualified staff members, provide in-service training programs, give supportive supervision, and establish overall guidelines for the behavior of members participating in activities.

The human environment includes agency staff and participants; the physical environment includes natural resources, developed land and water areas, facilities, equipment, and supplies. These two environments, physical and human, are somewhat inseparable. One affects the other, and they act upon the participants as a combined influence. For example, the way a leader responds to a group is influenced by the facility in which she is working. The same art instructor will behave somewhat differently in a well-equipped studio than in a poorly equipped one. On the other hand, an imaginative instructor can make much better use of an inadequate facility than can a leader who is less well qualified.

The Opportunities an Agency Provides Constitute Its Program

Our definition of *program* is broader than the more traditional definition, which includes only organized activities for participants. Judo instruction is part of the program of the YMCA; providing campgrounds and visitor centers is part of the program of the National Park Service; and planting catchable trout is part of the program of a state department of fish and game.

In providing programs (opportunities), the agency is delivering leisure services. The agency's public is in direct contact with some of the services. The preschoolers and their parents are in an immediate relationship with the center director and with the physical environment of the center. However, the preschool program also depends on other energies and resources not directly experienced by the youngsters and their mothers. A custodial staff keeps the center attractive and ready for use, an area supervisor supports the activities of the director, and the central administration sets the financial framework for the center's operation. These efforts are also part of the leisure service delivery system.

Every recreation agency presents a complex of opportunities for the public it hopes to serve. For some agencies, the range of opportunities is very broad and diversified; for others, it is highly specific. The number of services offered by a typical tax-supported recreation and park department in a large municipality and the specialized services of a commercial ceramic studio illustrate the contrast.

Programs Encourage and Enable a Wide Variety of Leisure Behavior

Obviously not all leisure behavior occurs under the sponsorship of a recreation and park agency. For example, when friends drop by for a visit in your home, you feel no agency influence. Yet much of our leisure is influenced directly or indirectly by some agency. If you watched television while your friends were at your home, a commercial enterprise probably provided the programming. If you and your visitors went for a walk in a neighborhood park, this experience was influenced by the fact that somebody developed the park initially and now maintains it. A self-initiated hike in a wilderness area may be facilitated by diverse organizations. Some agency administers the area; assures appropriate uses, assists visitors, and carries out related activities. You have to get to the site. That requires a car, which requires gas. Or you must use public transportation, go with a friend, or get there some other way. You might need equipment such as hiking boots, a pack, or rain gear. Maybe along the way to the site, you might stop for lunch, so perhaps the food service industry will contribute to your experience. The point is that, while some leisure behavior is completely without external support, much of it is facilitated by leisure service agencies.

Various Kinds of Behaviors

We discussed the nature of leisure behavior in the last chapter. Here, we want to give you an idea of the various kinds of behaviors that agency programs encourage and enable. We could describe several schemes, but the following provides a good overview.

Socializing Behaviors

Some recreation behavior is centered around the process of relating to other people socially. Examples are dancing, dating, going to parties, and visiting friends. In these activities, we are in the company of people we like, and we relate to each other with a minimal consciousness of social role. That is, we relate to people as people rather than as instructor to student, clerk to customer, physician to patient.

Associative Behaviors

Another type of behavior encouraged by recreation and park agencies is people getting together around common interests through groups such as car clubs, stamp collecting groups, and gem and mineral societies. Frequently this kind of behavior includes developing an organizational structure, holding meetings, and electing officers, in addition to actually participating in the common interest (rebuilding cars, collecting stamps, doing lapidary work). Kaplan (1960) used the term *associative* to identify these types of activities.

Role-Related Behaviors

Leisure involves relatively few social role obligations that are externally imposed. We do conform to many roles in our leisure behavior, but we accept these freely. For example, in a club membership we carry out many roles because we enjoy them— being the president or treasurer or a committee chairperson. Even if roles are not taken on voluntarily, they may still have leisure dimensions. Society expects certain role behaviors of parents. Some of these are leisure related, as illustrated by the father who takes his son fishing or serves as a Little League coach. As suggested in the last chapter, effectively fulfilling role expectations often provides part of the enjoyment associated with an activity.

Acquisitive Behaviors

Some recreation participation is manifested in collecting things such as old bottles, matchbook covers, dolls, toy soldiers, and antique furniture. This often leads to associative behaviors as well; bottle collectors frequently join a club and find added enjoyment of their interests in the company of other collectors.

Competitive Behaviors

This category includes the whole range of sports and games. Competitive behavior usually occurs within the context of a set of rules or procedures that define what may and may not be done. Also, there is an opponent, either actual or implied. In gin rummy, the opponents are actual (the other players); in solitaire, the opponent is implied. In competition, the essence of the activity is to outscore or in some other symbolic way to defeat the opponent. In all cases, some types of skills and strategies are involved.

The diversity of sports and games is immense. Included are team sports, low-organized games, and table games. In some sports, the competitive element may not be readily apparent or may not be present at all. Examples are hot air ballooning and fishing. These may involve competition in the usual sense: a bass fishing contest with prizes for the biggest fish, or a distance race for balloonists. Otherwise, there is competition only in the sense that we try to overcome gravity or outwit the fish.

Cooperative Behaviors

In contrast to competition, some games are characterized primarily by cooperation. "New Games" and several similar movements (Michaelis 1985) promote activities that emphasize working together, playfulness, creativity, participation, and a sense of community.

Testing Behaviors

Testing behaviors are similar to sports and games. Here, we test our skills against some criterion or some environmental condition. In small-bore rifle competition, the marksman not only aspires to shoot better than his opponents, but may also want to shoot a perfect score. He may mentally test his performance against this standard. The mountain climber frequently stakes her life on her skill, as well as on her equipment. At a much less hazardous and less spectacular level, the crossword puzzle buff also tests his skill.

Risk-Taking Behaviors

Many recreation pursuits involve considerable risk. In sport parachuting, the jumper assumes a life-or-death risk with each jump. Obviously the participant, when measuring the risks, assumes that she has a reasonable chance for success and safety. The great popularity of gambling casinos in Reno and Las Vegas rests in part on the attractions of risk taking, with a different loss or gain at stake.

Explorative Behaviors

A fairly large percentage of the motorists on the nation's highways at any time are engaging in what we might call explorative behavior. Sightseeing and travel, as well as scuba diving, spelunking, and hiking, allow the participant to discover new environments or to rediscover the finds of past adventures. For the amateur biologist, the explorations might be with a microscope, or for the hobby archeologist, in the sifted dirt of an exposed hillside. For many people, reading can be an exploration.

Vicarious Experiencing

Reading is also an illustration of vicarious experience, as are television viewing, movie attendance, and spectator sports. Fantasy and daydreaming might fall in this category.

Sensory Stimulation

Vicarious experiencing involves sensory stimulation, as does all recreation behavior to some degree. However, some experiences seem more dependent than others on this factor. Enjoying the taste of new foods in a gourmet cooking group, experiencing the visual excitement of a light show, and listening to certain types of music are examples.

Physical Expression

Physical expression and movement also seem to involve some sensory elements. Often there is joy, in the simple act of running or jumping. Frequently skills will be involved, as in diving, skiing and many dance forms.

Creative or Expressive Behaviors

All of the arts are related to expression in a creative sense, usually through some medium—clay, paint, the spoken and written word, musical instruments, the camera, and countless other elements; or, as in dance, through movement itself.

Appreciative Behaviors

Creative behavior is participatory. That is, people do things; they paint, they sculpt, they write, they act. The outcomes or results of such activity are often observed and enjoyed by others. The settings are concert halls, museums, art shows, and living rooms with stereo sets. Appreciative behavior also is participatory; and in some cases it may be creative, as when two people viewing the same abstract painting enjoy a different experience. However, in appreciative behavior the participant usually responds to the product or result of the creative process, rather than interacting directly with the material as does the artist. Appreciation may be involved in other types of leisure behavior; for example, seeing a sunset or experiencing the beauty of an underwater reef.

Cognitive Behaviors

All of the behaviors described in this section include cognition or thinking. However, for some leisure behaviors mental activity is the essential element. Participating in a discussion group or solving a crossword puzzle are examples.

Variety-Seeking Behaviors

Much of what we do in our free time probably involves an element of change from life's normal routines. The city dweller going to the mountains, the accountant playing tennis, and the personnel director taking solitary hikes in the woods are examples.

Personal Growth Behaviors

Most leisure activity promotes personal growth in some way. However, some kinds of behavior do so specifically, as the individual intends, yet the behavior is often motivating and satisfying in itself. Learning for its own sake is an example—taking a history class or studying a foreign language merely for the pleasure of doing so and the feeling of accomplishment and competence that result. For some, jogging may fall into this category; fitness is a motive, but the activity itself becomes pleasurable.

Service-Oriented Behaviors
Volunteering in all its various dimensions frequently has the characteristics of leisure behavior. Once commitments are made, there is a sense of obligation, but the obligations are taken on freely. And volunteering often is based on intrinsic motivation.

Anticipatory and Recollective Behaviors
Jensen (1985) among others suggests that the recreation experience includes anticipatory and preparatory phases and a reminiscence phase, in addition to the actual participation. The former two include looking forward to the experience, planning, getting any needed equipment ready, and other preparatory activities. The latter includes talking about the experience, seeing photos and slides, and showing souvenirs to friends. While these dimensions are part of the total experience, they also might be viewed as recreation behaviors in and of themselves.

The preceding behaviors are not mutually exclusive. For example, mountain climbing may involve risk-taking, testing of self and equipment, appreciation of scenery, association with members of a climbing club, and physical expression. Volunteering might include elements of socializing, variety-seeking, role-related behaviors and personal growth.

Programs Encourage Different Kinds of Behavior

As indicated earlier, the resources of recreation and park agencies are devoted to providing opportunities for one or more of the behaviors we just discussed. The opportunities may encourage either highly skilled behavior or behavior that involves only basic skills. The comparison between scuba-diving classes and swimming lessons for beginners is illustrative. Some opportunities will involve one-shot behaviors, such as a trip to Europe. Others provide for frequent participation, for example in teen drop-in centers and on playgrounds. Time and distance are factors when we compare the opportunities provided by the National Park Service, for example, with the opportunities provided by municipal recreation and park departments. The national parks readily accommodate most vacation types of uses. Car camping, backpacking, and related pursuits usually require more than an afternoon of free time; and the parks usually are located some distance from most users, so travel time is also involved. On the other hand, one can drop in at the aquatic center at the local high school for a quick swim any summer day after work and before dinner. Leisure opportunities involve many other differences: individual or group participation, the amount of equipment required, the intensity of participation (as in tournament bowling versus a bowling date for a young, single couple).

Agencies Deliver Different Kinds of Services

Another major concept is that a leisure service agency will deliver those services that are consistent with its constituents' needs, characteristics, and circumstances and with the agency's philosophy and resources. Overall, recreation and park agencies provide several kinds of program services. Some offer activities in the form of classes, tournaments, special events, clubs, and other opportunities for leisure behavior. Some provide areas and facilities, environments within which leisure behavior occurs. These include basketball courts, swimming pools, craft studios, auditoriums, libraries, ski resorts, marinas, wilderness areas, and restaurants. In addition to these two basic types of service, some agencies facilitate leisure behavior through such things as leisure education and similar services (Edginton, Compton, and Hanson 1980; Howe and Carpenter 1985). Kraus (1985) suggests that another kind of program service is the promotion of recreation opportunities by providing technical assistance to other organizations and jointly sponsoring programs. Many agencies offer a combination or all of these program dimensions. Let us take a look at each one.

Provision of Activities

In offering activities, agencies provide opportunities for leisure behavior. Earlier in the chapter we described several types of leisure behavior. We also suggested that various other classification schemes exist.

Classifications

Many recreation and park agencies use categories that describe the types of activities offered. These commonly include aquatic, arts and crafts, drama, dance, music, outdoor recreation, sports and games, and social recreation (Corbin and Williams 1987; Edginton, Compton, and Hanson 1980; Farrell and Lundegren 1983; Russell 1982). Occasionally different names are used for the categories. The term performing arts might designate such activities as dance, drama and music (Kraus 1985). These three plus arts and crafts are sometimes combined into one category of *cultural activities* (Tillman 1973). This category might be expanded to include festivals and other special events that focus on ethnic, national, or regional heritage (Howe and Carpenter 1985). Sometimes other types are included: hobbies, travel and tourism, and mental or literary activities.

Farrell and Lundegren (1983) suggest the different methods that we can use to classify activities. The one described above is the functional approach. We can also categorize by the areas and facilities required, by the number of people needed for participation, or by the age groups served. Agencies frequently publicize their programs by seasons and times available: spring-summer, mornings, evenings, and other time designations. Farrell and Lundegren also suggest that programs might be classified according to the motives and interests they serve.

Formats

Agencies use several basic formats for providing activities (Edginton, Compton, and Hanson 1980; Farrell and Lundegren 1983; Russell 1982). Competitive formats are appropriate for many sports and games. Class formats, including seminars and workshops, provide for learning and enable associative behaviors. Agencies use special event formats for festivals, art shows, concerts, and company picnics. We find open or drop-in formats in a wide variety of leisure settings. Here, agencies provide a facility and people use it on a drop-in basis, rather than at scheduled times or in an organized manner. Overall, the range of open format service is very wide; restaurants, swimming pools, regional parks, and sporting goods stores are examples.

Farrell (1987) identifies spectating as another format. This includes situations where people go to the event, as in attending a professional soccer match, and situations where the event comes to the viewers, as in televised travelogues and game shows. You could consider these as special events, but they tend to be presented on a frequently recurring basis. Agencies in the private enterprise sector often use this format.

Not all leisure service opportunities fit neatly into one of these formats. A combination is often used. For example, a bowling alley accommodates drop-in use. It also provides classes, tournaments, and occasionally special events such as demonstrations. Visitors to a national park use it on a drop-in basis, but they may also attend scheduled campfire programs or go on nature hikes led by rangers. Some agencies use outreach formats (Bannon 1973; Edginton, Compton, and Hanson 1980). They take program opportunities to people in an attempt to serve populations who typically would not, or could not, come to the agency. Examples include inner-city youth, home-bound older adults, and immigrants who have not yet expanded their community contacts beyond their own group. Trips and outings and voluntary services are other types of formats (Russell 1982).

Activity Analysis

Analysis permits the programmer to assess the potential of an activity to contribute to objectives. To analyze an activity, you break it into its various parts or components so that you can understand it better and make some judgments about the influences it might have on participants. Farrell and Lundegren (1983) describe several ways of analyzing activities. Analyses may be based on the different kinds of social interactions that occur, the relative emphasis on different learning domains, or other schemes. The analysis might focus on the presence or absence of specific dimensions such as elements of chance, rules and rule complexity, time requirements, suspense, competition, role functions, necessity for decisions, and uses of props. Analysis sometimes involves clustering activities into groups that have similar characteristics or provide similar outcomes. Clustering facilitates the substitution of one activity for another when there are restrictions on what might be offered.

Sometimes we analyze activities as part of an effort to modify or adapt them to enhance their potential for achieving desired objectives. Therapeutic recreation personnel often do this. Having said that, we want to point out another consideration. When leisure services are provided for disabled persons, there are many advantages to "normalization" and "mainstreaming" approaches (Howe-Murphy and Charboneau 1987). In normalization, we provide activities and other leisure services in forms that are typical; that is, not adapted for any special group. Mainstreaming means to maximize people's abilities and minimize the effects of their disabilities. You can see that these approaches are related. Both are based on the assumption that disabled persons' lives are enriched more if they can participate as normally as possible, without disadvantage, in the ongoing flow of everyday life.

Provision of Areas and Facilities

Activities occur in some place. If you want to go swimming, you have to have water—a pool, a lake, a stream, or the ocean. When you paint with watercolors, you perhaps do it in your home, but maybe in a studio or a classroom. Backpackers typically hike in wilderness areas. Actors usually perform on a stage in an auditorium or theater. Sightseers go places to see things—the seashore or the redwoods, migratory birds in a state refuge, historic buildings in a metropolitan area.

A second major program service is therefore the provision of areas and facilities. For some agencies, this is their major service. They do relatively little in terms of offering scheduled activities led or supervised by agency personnel. For others, areas and facilities serve primarily as sites for scheduled activities. In either case, the provision of areas and facilities includes planning, development, maintenance, and operational responsibilities for leisure service personnel.

Classifications

Areas and facilities can be classified, but there are few widely used schemes for doing so. The classification system developed by the former Outdoor Recreation Resources Review Commission (ORRRC 1962) is one example. The system includes six different classifications based on the nature of use at the area and the presence or lack of development or unique features. Chubb and Chubb (1981) identified several broad categories of resources that are more encompassing. They emphasize that their descriptions are of opportunities rather than of physical properties alone. Undeveloped recreation resources include any site that is relatively "native" in terms of its present condition. A wilderness area is a good example. These areas include different topographic features, surface materials, climatic conditions, usually vegetation, sometimes water, and often wildlife. Private recreation resources, in addition to vacation residences, include the myriad of areas and facilities managed by clubs of various kinds, homeowners' associations, youth agencies, and industries.

The properties range from large open spaces to special facilities such as golf courses, fitness studios, and resident camps. Commercial resources also represent a wide variety of facilities: restaurants, bars, amusement parks, race tracks, theaters, shopping malls, resorts, and other private enterprises. Publicly owned resources are found at local, regional, state, and federal government levels. They include playlots, neighborhood parks, school sites, community centers, regional parks, reservoirs, state parks, and national forests. Cultural resources exist in both the private and the public sectors. Facilities here include museums, libraries, and the various properties that support the performing arts and certain aspects of mass media.

In Chapter 3, we referred to a classification scheme developed by Cheek and Burch (1976) that provides additional understanding about the influences of physical resources on behavior. They identified seven "leisure locales," which are places where people engage in leisure behavior. They are distinct from places where other types of behavior occur. The spatial and physical cues they provide encourage certain kinds of nonwork behavior.

Resource Preservation

Some recreation and park agencies are responsible not only for enabling leisure behavior, but also for preserving the areas or facilities they manage. To a certain degree, this is true for all park agencies. However, the best example is the National Park Service, which has the dual responsibility of preserving parks for future generations while making them available for use by the public. This often causes problems. There is so much use at some areas that the Park Service has difficulty preserving the resource in its natural state. This condition is related to one aspect of "carrying capacity," the ability of a resource to accommodate use without sustaining permanent or unacceptable damage (Knudson 1984; also see Chapter 4). Another aspect of carrying capacity is the degree of use an area can accommodate without an appreciable deterioration of the leisure experience for visitors. This varies from resource to resource. Many people can use a reservoir beach without damaging the recreation experience, assuming that there is no disruptive behavior. In fact, some individuals might come because of the crowd. On the other hand, very few people at a wilderness lake can destroy the experience for a backpacker.

Multiple Uses

Some resources support other uses as well. This "multi-use" concept (Knudson 1984) applies to areas such as forests and reservoirs. Forests may be managed for timber production and watershed use, as well as for recreation. Reservoirs may support many water-oriented leisure behaviors and at the same time provide for the generation of hydroelectric power and flood control. Sometimes these uses are in conflict. For example, logging operations and wilderness recreation uses are inappropriate in the same forest area. Sometimes the conflict is between two recreation uses, as in the case of cross-country skiing and snowmobiling, or waterskiing and fishing.

Accessibility

Recreation and park agencies need to assure that their areas and facilities are accessible to the publics they hope to serve. This is particularly important for disabled persons. A heightened awareness in society of the needs and interests of the disabled, along with the much greater expectations of these individuals for full leisure participation, has led to legislation and to agency intent to provide for accessibility. Ramps, properly sized doors, and drinking fountains and public telephones at an appropriate height facilitate use by people in wheelchairs. Braille signs, audio tapes, and other interpretive materials enable the blind to more fully enjoy scenic areas. Agencies consider a variety of other architectural and equipment needs when developing areas and facilities to make them more accessible.

Facilitation

When agencies offer activity opportunities and provide physical resources, they are facilitating leisure behavior. They also do this in other ways when they enhance the potential for individuals to enjoy leisure. This "facilitation" is a third kind of program service. We will examine four different types: leisure education, leisure counseling, referral, and advocacy.

Leisure Education

Leisure helps people develop useful skills, knowledge, and attitudes. When you teach someone how to play the guitar, you have added to his leisure repertoire. When you give someone who likes to trap shoot some information about where she can find places to do it, you have added to her range of opportunities. When you help someone to understand more fully the benefits of leisure activity, you have increased the chances that the person will participate more often or with greater enjoyment. When you do these things, you are providing leisure education. Schools have many opportunities to provide leisure education, and they do so in varying degrees. Often, however, they do not do as much as they could because of the pressures of other demands on curricula; and there is evidence that educators sometimes are uncertain about what leisure education is and how to provide it (Mundy 1987). Recreation and park agencies also have many opportunities for leisure education. These have been very evident in therapeutic recreation settings and to a lesser degree in communities and the private sector (Mundy 1987).

Leisure service personnel have developed several different models for leisure education (Edginton, Compton, and Hanson 1980; Mundy 1987). Peterson and Gunn (1984) developed leisure education guidelines that indicate typical areas of focus. These include awareness of leisure and leisure resources, and activity and social interaction skills. Mundy's model includes these elements, as well as attention to self-awareness and decision-making processes. Howe and Carpenter (1985) suggest a continuum of leisure education based on the needs of the individual and the involvement of staff members. Some people only need information that tells them what activities are available and where to find them. This is one end of the continuum. Other people who may have psychological or attitudinal problems related to leisure are nearer the other end. Here the need is much different and the interventions are more complex. What the professional does at this level essentially is leisure counseling. In between these two ends of the continuum, leisure education may take the form of experiences that increase awareness, clarify values, or develop skills.

Leisure Counseling

The early impetus for leisure counseling came from recreation therapists. Later, counseling expanded into other community settings. Its purposes are primarily the same as those of leisure education. Many of the techniques overlap those used in leisure education, particularly in terms of exploring interests and developing awareness, skills, and values. However, as suggested above, counseling frequently deals with barriers to leisure that may be fairly deep-seated. And there is greater emphasis on counseling techniques and relatively less on education as such. As in leisure education, several models of or "orientations" to leisure counseling exist (Allen and Hamilton 1980; Edginton, Compton, and Hanson 1980; McDowell 1981). Allen and Hamilton identify five different approaches, ranging from helping an individual explore his or her own interests and then providing information about opportunities, to dealing with general personality problems and emotional states that interfere with leisure functioning. McDowell offers a similar conceptualization. Those who provide leisure counseling require special professional preparation. Except when using techniques that are largely educational, recreation and park personnel should not attempt it unless they have had special training in psychology or counseling (Edwards 1981).

Referral and Advocacy

Sometimes we see people who have problems that interfere with their leisure functioning, but we cannot do anything about them directly. Or the problems we see are so widespread that we consider attacking them more generally than at the individual level. In these cases, we might use either of two additional facilitation processes: referral or advocacy. We use referral when the problems an individual has are beyond either our expertise or our areas of responsibility.

Suppose that you are the director of a city recreation center used by adolescents. One of the teens comes to your office one night and tells you he has a drinking problem. It is getting worse, he is worried about it, he is afraid to tell his parents, but he has to do something because it is "messing up" his whole life. This problem probably is interfering with the teen's leisure as well as other aspects of his life. It might be beyond your expertise, but you do have an opportunity to do something now that he has come to you asking for help. Here is where referral can be used. If you can suggest a place where he can get some help and do what you can to assist him in getting it, you have probably facilitated his future leisure behavior, as well as his behavior in general.

But, let us suppose the problem is bigger than this one teen. There is a lot of adolescent drinking in town. You and many other concerned adults know that underage youth get beer all the time. This might be a place for advocacy. You cannot do anything directly to stop teenagers from drinking, but you can stir up interest in the problem and work with others to find out what is going on and what can be done about it.

Another problem might be that many senior citizens cannot attend recreation center programs because city buses stop running at 9:00 p.m. You could appear before the local transit authority board to ask, on behalf of seniors, that service be extended to a later time. You might get several older adults to go with you to increase the impact of your request. This is a form of advocacy.

Witt (1985) suggests that leisure service personnel have not done as much with advocacy processes as they could. He notes that, in using leisure education and leisure counseling, we have focused more on clients' or participants' problems than on the environments that might have caused the problems. He says we have a tendency to "blame the victim" rather than blaming the environment. We help individuals to cope with barriers to leisure, to change or develop appropriate values, attitudes, skills, and knowledge. But we give relatively little attention to changing the social conditions that might be the cause of problems. He suggests efforts to remove barriers, make opportunities more available to all, and create more humane environments. Advocacy processes can contribute to these objectives.

Recreation and park personnel can use referral and advocacy processes to address many problems that interfere with people's leisure. There are several different techniques involved, and there are considerations to keep in mind (Edginton, Compton, and Hanson 1980; Niepoth 1983). You should know when and where these processes are appropriate and how they should be used.

Promotion of Leisure

We have said that recreation and park agencies provide opportunities for people to engage in leisure behavior. These are leisure services. We often call them programs. These include scheduled activities, as well as areas and facilities that people can use on an informal or unscheduled basis. Helping people develop their capacities to enjoy leisure more fully is also a program service; we   have described this as facilitation. In what way is "promotion" a leisure service? Later in the book, we will talk about promoting programs, engaging in activities that help inform people about our services and encouraging their participation. Here, we are talking about promotion in a broader sense (Kraus 1985).

Working with Other Agencies

One aspect of promotion is working with other agencies in the community or area to assist them in their efforts to provide leisure services. Maybe a local church wants to start a Saturday morning exercise program for young adults, or the chamber of commerce is trying to organize a communitywide ethnic celebration. They turn to you, as a leisure service professional, for help. Or maybe a state forestry department would like to contract with a local recreation and park agency to develop and run a junior ranger program. All of these illustrate ways that agencies extend leisure opportunities for people, in addition to the other ways we discussed earlier.

Acting as a Catalyst

Another aspect of promotion is acting as a general catalyst for leisure services. This is promotion in the broadest sense. It occurs when an agency creates greater community awareness of the importance of leisure or helps the public understand more fully the benefits to be obtained. Perhaps the agency persuades public officials to declare a communitywide "Fun for the Family Week." Or maybe the agency convinces local television and radio stations and newspapers to highlight leisure opportunities in the community during a particular month. The "Life: Be in It" program, borrowed from Australia and used widely in the United States, is an illustration of this kind of promotion.

Provision of Nonleisure Services

The new paradigm for public recreation agencies, described in Chapter 1, suggests an additional dimension of service. We also commented on this dimension in Chapter 3, in a discussion of different types of leisure service agencies. This is activity that contributes to people's ability to enjoy leisure by assisting with nonleisure problems.

Nonleisure Services

Suppose, for example, that a relatively high percentage of older adults in a community is not receiving proper nutrition. This may be because of disabilities that make it difficult to prepare meals, or limited incomes, or lack of knowledge, or lack of motivation to eat properly when alone. Given this situation, a local, public recreation agency might decide to offer a low-cost, high nutrition lunch program at a neighborhood center. In addition to basic humanitarian motives, the agency might do so because a poor diet detracts from the older adults' abilities to enjoy leisure.

We suggested earlier that behavior is holistic, that leisure behavior is influenced by other dimensions of the human condition. People who are hungry or lack energy because of inadequate diets are not likely to be enthusiastic participants in leisure service programs. Providing at least a partial solution to this problem facilitates older adults' leisure participation. The agency might do this through referral or advocacy efforts, by referring older adults to an agency that offers such services, or by encouraging some other organization to develop a nutrition program if these services are unavailable. If the leisure service agency offers the program, it might also provide recreation activities before or after the lunch period. The center director might know the neighborhood well and be able to encourage participation. Center personnel may have the appropriate skills needed to plan and administer such a program. Kraus (1985) identified this "non-recreational" service dimension and noted such illustrations as substance abuse counseling, housing and legal assistance, and family services, as well as nutrition programs.

Appropriateness of These Services

Some would argue that recreation and park agencies should not provide these kinds of services, saying that we do not have the needed expertise or a public sanction for doing so. Much of the debate over the human service responsibilities of our field center on these two points: expertise and public approval or expectations. Several years ago, a major position paper at a National Recreation and Park Association Congress called upon the field to broaden its perspective and recognize its larger human service obligations and opportunities (Foley 1977). While there was much support for that position, it was not unanimous.

Most leisure professionals would accept the idea that nonleisure conditions affect leisure. The question is: how should our field respond? The options range from directly providing nonrecreational services at one end, to confining our efforts to traditional leisure services at the other end. In between are the options of referral and advocacy efforts and taking the role of a coordinating agency. Our general position in this text is that agencies should do what is needed to enhance people's leisure lives. If agencies have personnel with the necessary expertise, and if their constituent bodies sanction it, agencies should take advantage of opportunities to provide nonrecreation services that enhance people's leisure. If these conditions are not present, agencies should provide referral services or engage in appropriate advocacy when they have opportunities for doing so.

One form of advocacy is to work within political structures to influence legislation. Laws often are proposed that could have direct effects on policy development and operational practices in our field. Recreation and park personnel have opportunities to work for the passage of favorable laws and to help defeat unfavorable ones. We need to be sensitive to how we go about this kind of activity, and we need to consider how our professional interests and our responsibilities as private citizens differ.

Summary

In this chapter we have looked at leisure program services. The basic purpose of our field is to deliver these services, which enable the expression of leisure behavior. Agencies achieve this general purpose by meeting specific objectives. These differ from agency to agency. In pursuing their objectives through the delivery of leisure services, agencies make use of both human and physical resources. This encourages and enables a wide variety of recreation behaviors.

We examined four basic kinds of program services. The *provision of activities* includes such things as classes, tournaments, and special events. The *provision of areas and facilities,* in addition to making resources available for use, may include responsibilities for resource protection and multiple-use management. *Facilitation of leisure behavior* includes leisure education, leisure counseling, and advocacy and referral. *Promotion of recreation* generally is a fourth type of basic service. In addition to these, agencies may provide nonleisure services that contribute to people's ability to benefit from recreation opportunities. When we deliver these types of services, we can think of them as *programs*. Recreation and park personnel have tended to use this term primarily with activity services, but it may be applied to the other services as well.

References

Allen, Lawrence R., and Edward J. Hamilton. 1980. Leisure counseling: A continuum of services. *Therapeutic Recreation Journal* 16: 19-21.

Bannon, Joseph J. 1973. *Outreach: Extending community service in urban areas.* Springfield, IL: Charles C. Thomas.

Cheek, Neil H., Jr., and William R. Burch. 1976. *The social organization of leisure in human society.* New York: Harper & Row.

Chubb, Michael, and Holly R. Chubb. 1981. *One third of our time? An introduction to recreation behavior and resources.* New York: John Wiley and Sons.

Corbin, H. Dan, and Ellen Williams. 1987. *Recreation programming and leadership.* Englewood Cliffs, NJ: Prentice-Hall.

Edginton, Christopher R., David M. Compton, and Carole J. Hanson. 1980. *Recreation and leisure programming: A guide for the professional.* Philadelphia: Saunders College Publishing.

Edwards, Patsy B. 1981. Leisure counseling: Recreators keep out! *Parks & Recreation* 16: 43.

Farrell, Pat. 1987. Leisure programming. In *Recreation and leisure: An introductory handbook,* Alan Graefe, and Stan Parker, eds. State College, PA: Venture Publishing.

Farrell, Pat, and Herberta M. Lundegren. 1983. *The process of recreation programming: Theory and technique.* New York: John Wiley and Sons.

Foley, Jack. 1977. *Human service national policy statement, draft #2, National Recreation and Park Association.* Paper presented at the National Congress for Recreation and Parks, Las Vegas, Nevada.

Howe, Christine Z., and Gaylene M. Carpenter. 1985. *Programming leisure experiences.* Englewood Cliffs, NJ: Prentice-Hall.

Howe-Murphy, Roxanne, and Becky G. Charboneau. 1987. *Therapeutic recreation intervention: An ecological perspective.* Englewood Cliffs, NJ: Prentice-Hall.

Jensen, Clayne E. 1985. *Outdoor recreation in America*. Minneapolis,MN: Burgess.

Kaplan, Max. 1960. *Leisure in America*. New York: John Wiley and Sons.

Knudson, Douglas M. 1984. *Outdoor recreation*. New York: Macmillan.

Kraus, Richard G. 1985. *Recreation program planning today*. Glenview, IL: Scott, Foresman and Company.

McDowell, C. F. 1981. Leisure consciousness, well-being and counseling. *The Counseling Psychologist* 9: 3-32.

Michaelis, Bill. 1985. Fantasy, play, creativity and mental health. In *Recreation and leisure: Issues in an era of change*, Thomas L. Goodale, and Peter A. Witt, eds. State College, PA: Venture Publishing.

Mundy, Jean. 1987. Leisure education. In *Recreation and leisure: An introductory handbook*, Alan Graefe, and Stan Parker, eds. State College, PA: Venture Publishing, Inc.

Niepoth, E. William. 1983. *Leisure leadership: Working with people in recreation and park settings*. Englewood Cliffs, NJ: Prentice-Hall.

Outdoor Recreation Resources Review Commission. 1962. *Outdoor recreation for America*. Washington, D.C.

Peterson, Carol A., and Scout L. Gunn. 1984. *Therapeutic recreation program design: Principles and procedures*. Englewood Cliffs, NJ: Prentice-Hall.

Russell, Ruth V. 1982. *Planning programs in recreation*. St. Louis: C. V. Mosby.

Tillman, Albert. 1973. *The program book for recreation professionals*. Palo Alto, CA: Mayfield Publishing.

Witt, Peter A. 1985. Buckpassing, blaming or benevolence: A leisure education/leisure counseling perspective. In *Recreation and leisure: Issues in an era of change*, Thomas L. Goodale, and Peter A. Witt, eds. State College, PA: Venture Publishing.

7

SERVICE PROVIDERS

One of the basic premises of this book is that the field of recreation and parks exists primarily to provide opportunities for people to engage in recreation and leisure behaviors. In Chapter 5 we examined some concepts about this kind of behavior. In Chapter 6 we presented some information about the leisure services that facilitate it. These services involve the use of various resources—primarily legislation, money, areas and facilities, and personnel. All of these are essential. They are part of the leisure service delivery system. They stand in sort of an "ecological" relationship to one another: changes in the status of one usually influence the status of the others. In this chapter we want to present some basic concepts about one of those major resources—personnel, or leisure service providers.

In later chapters we will present many additional ideas related to personnel—about staffing and directing the leisure service delivery system and about the roles and responsibilities of personnel in organizing, planning and evaluating. The concepts in this chapter will serve as a framework for what is to come later.

Basic Concepts

Personnel who work in the field of recreation and parks do so as full- or part-time employees or volunteers. They carry out a wide variety of responsibilities, some of which are generic; that is, they tend to be found in all agencies at all personnel levels. Others are associated more with the various specialties that make up the field. Whatever their specific responsibilities, most agency staff members work with other people. They work with participants who use agency services, with other staff members, or with both groups. Working with people involves interpersonal relationships. These general conditions related to personnel lead to one of the major concepts that we defined in the overview to Part II. Organizations deliver services through staff members who become more competent when they increase self-awareness, develop effective interpersonal relationships, and accept professional responsibilities. This major concept suggests several other concepts that we want to present.

Sociopsychological Factors Influence Staff Behavior

Turn back for a moment to the beginning of the last chapter. What you will find there are descriptions of some recreation and park personnel engaged in activities related to their jobs. They are providing leisure services. They are engaged in certain behaviors. Many of the things we know about recreation behavior are evident there. The motives might be different, but perhaps they are not. The patients in the hospital drama program might be motivated by a desire for a sense of achievement and for recognition from others. Those same general goals might be desired by the recreation therapist who is facilitating the drama program. It would be more accurate to say that the basic motivations might be similar, but that the means of obtaining them differ. At any rate, motivation or goal seeking is involved in both participant and staff behavior. Various physiological, psychological, social, economic, and geographic conditions influence behaviors; these operate for staff as well as for participants. Staff members plan how to meet their goals, just as participants do. They perceive the results of their actions; they experience satisfaction or disappointment or other emotions in the same way participants do. What we know about behavior generally can help us understand better what staff members do, why they do it, and what influences their behavior. If your responsibilities as a staff member require you to work with other agency personnel, keeping in mind some of the concepts in Chapter 5 will help you be more effective.

Each Staff Member Has Certain Unique Talents

Every staff member is different in some ways from other individuals. It is true that we do have much in common with other personnel. We share many values, goals, abilities, and insights. And the more specialized our work, the more likely we are to be similar, in terms of professional characteristics, to the other staff members with whom we work. However, each of us is unique. Each of us can do some things better than others do them. We have different backgrounds and personalities, different skills and energies.

When we use our talents, both those that are unique and those that we have in common with others, we are using ourselves. We are bringing our personal resources to bear in the delivery of leisure services. Of course, we use the other resources available to us: legislation, money, areas and facilities, and sometimes other staff members. But most of what we do professionally is influenced by, and is an expression of, our personal characteristics.

This concept suggests that staff members are "instruments." This may be an unusual way of putting it, but when you examine the idea further, it is descriptive. Combs, Avila, and Purkey (1978) used a similar expression in a text on basic concepts for those working in the helping professions:

> Professional helpers must be thinking, problem-solving people; the primary tool with which they work is themselves. This understanding has been called the "self as instrument" concept. In the helping professions, effective operation is a question of the use of the helper's self, the peculiar ways in which helpers are able to combine knowledge and understanding with their own unique ways of putting them into operation (6).

Leisure services are delivered through staff members. Staff members plan services, organize services, implement services, work with the public, and work with other staff. When we do this, inevitably we use "ourselves." We use our skills and our knowledge. We are influenced by our beliefs, our attitudes, and our values.

Service Providers Use a Variety of Core Processes

Recreation and park personnel carry out a wide variety of responsibilities, and they assume such roles as enablers, direct service providers, advocates, and suppliers of leisure resources. In Part I we talked about the need for recreation and park personnel to be versatile, to be able to function in different roles at different times, depending upon the situation. To be able to do so is to be able to serve more people more effectively. When personnel function in these roles, they use various professional processes.

Earlier in this chapter we asked you to look back at the beginning of Chapter 6. We suggested that the park and recreation staff members described there are all engaging in behavior. Let us be more specific. They are functioning in different professional roles. In doing so, they are engaging in various professional processes, which are evident in a wide range of situations. We can see that the recreation center director is communicating with preschool children, but all of the individuals described are communicating in one way or another. The physical director is teaching. It is quite possible that the leader of the maintenance crew is instructing also—if not now, then earlier when he taught crew members how to carry out various maintenance operations on the ski lifts. He is probably also engaging in leadership when he gets crew members to carry out tasks. The recreation therapist at the hospital might also be using leadership techniques to motivate patients to participate in the drama program. And like the crew leader, she will be involved with group processes. The park planner, of course, is planning. Probably everybody described in that paragraph is doing or has done some planning. For example, the leisure counselor planned what she wanted to accomplish in the session with her client, and the food services manager is planning the banquet.

We have commented in various places about things that recreation and park personnel do, and there is much more about staff activities and responsibilities in later chapters. For right now, let us take a look at some professional behaviors that occur frequently in most recreation and park settings. We have called them "core" processes because they are used by most staff members at most levels of responsibility (Niepoth 1983). We will examine several of them briefly.

Communication

All of the professional things we do in the field involve communication in some way. We talk on the telephone, write memos, give speeches, hold meetings, teach classes, use word processors to develop reports, listen to conference presentations, recruit volunteers, supervise staff, read journals—the list is almost endless. Communication involves the person sending the message and the intended receivers. In two-way communication, each individual is both a sender and a receiver. Communication also involves the message itself and the means by which it is sent (for example, verbal comment in face-to-face interaction, telephone conversation, written letter). Communication occurs in both verbal and nonverbal forms. Sometimes we forget the importance of nonverbal communication. Our gestures, intonations, facial expressions, and body movements may carry stronger messages than what we say verbally (Tubbs and Moss 1974).

Communication is effective when all the people involved have a common understanding of the meanings of messages. The kinds of things that keep this from happening include problems with the means used to send messages (e.g., a poor phone connection) and language that is not understood by receivers (e.g., use of technical terms or jargon). Psychological and perceptual factors may work against effective communication also. In addition to incongruities between verbal and nonverbal messages, problems may include inaccurate assumptions, anxiety, anger, and status differentials. Obviously you will be more effective in communication when you are aware of the kinds of problems that can occur and when you try to eliminate or minimize them.

Problem Solving

We also spend much time solving problems. Every time we make a professional decision, we engage in problem solving to a degree. Problem solving involves various steps and considerations (Bannon 1981), but in essence we determine what the problem is, what condition we would like to achieve, what alternatives exist, and which one is the best. Sometimes we go through the process very thoroughly and systematically; at other times we do it quickly and without much thought.

Teaching, Leading, Working with Groups

Three processes that most recreation and park personnel use in some form are teaching, leading, and working with groups. All of them involve interpersonal relationships.

We use instructional processes to help participants develop skills and to help staff members improve or maintain professional effectiveness. In public agencies, we often use educational methods to encourage the voting public to learn more about policy issues in our field. We do this in the commercial sector when we help boards of directors and investors to better understand our services and procedures. When we teach, we promote the development of attitudes, as well as learning in cognitive and psychomotor areas. We are interested, for example, not only in teaching wilderness survival skills, but also in developing attitudes that lead to appropriate uses of wilderness areas.

Teaching changes behavior. We also change behavior through leadership. We motivate people to do something. We get staff members to complete assignments, volunteers to help with projects, and participants to plan and carry out different leisure programs. There is no one best style of leadership. How we lead will vary according to our own personal characteristics, the people with whom we are working, and the overall situation. These conditions influence the degree to which a leader focuses primarily on getting a job done or on building rapport with followers. Effective leaders are able to choose the right blend of task-oriented and relationship-oriented behaviors to match the situation in which they are working. There is considerable research about leadership (Stogdill 1974), and several major theories (Fiedler 1967; Hershey and Blanchard 1982). Writers in our field have applied the knowledge about leadership in general to recreation and park situations (Edginton and Ford 1985; Kraus 1985; Niepoth 1983; Russell 1986; Sessoms and Stevenson 1981; Shivers 1986).

Leadership often occurs in groups, and we work with many different kinds of groups in the leisure services: participant groups, staff groups, professional organization committees, community task forces, treatment teams, and others. While groups differ in such things as goals, structures, norms, procedures, climates, cohesion, and sociometric patterns, most have two properties in common: a social dimension and a task orientation. We participate in most groups not only to accomplish some purpose, but also to enjoy the interactions among members. Groups develop in rather predictable patterns and typically encounter such common problems as conflict, apathy, and the inability to reach decisions. A group can improve its efficiency. One of the most productive ways for group members or a group facilitator to help is to provide feedback to the group on how it is doing. The group needs to know if its procedures are appropriate, if its goals are clear, and if members are participating in useful ways (Niepoth 1983; Sessoms and Stevenson 1981).

Other Core Service Delivery Processes

Personnel use the processes of organizing, planning, promoting, and evaluating in different aspects of service delivery. For example, some staff members organize volunteer training sessions, others plan budgets, and others evaluate staff effectiveness. Some manage resources such as physical properties, money, and personnel. The physical properties may be neighborhood parks, major scenic areas, hospital day rooms, theaters, bowling alleys on military bases, lounges on cruise ships, plant life in botanical gardens, scuba equipment and compressed air in a diving rental shop, art supplies, and a great variety of other things. Money can come from tax revenues, congressional allocations, grants, voluntary contributions, membership dues, or fees and charges. Personnel may be full-time staff members, part-time or seasonal workers, or volunteers.

While the processes of organizing, planning, evaluating, and managing resources may be specific to certain jobs, they are also used by almost all personnel in generalized ways. For example, everyone organizes his or her own time and energies. Most professional behaviors are based on or preceded by some kind of planning. We all evaluate our own performance, even if we do not evaluate anything else. And most of us work with some kinds of resources and our work requires the expenditure of budgeted money. We all attempt to work in congruence with agency philosophies and our own personal philosophies. We gather relevant information about the public we work with and the settings within which we work. These are all core processes.

All recreation and park personnel also work within legal frameworks. Every agency operates on the basis of some kind of authorizing legislation. In addition, many types of services are influenced by regulatory laws. For example, state health and safety codes usually require certain procedures and standards in the operation of swimming pools, resident camps, and day care centers. Liability is another legal consideration for most recreation and park personnel. Almost any staff member can be sued. Whether the suit will be successful and a judgment rendered against the staff member or the agency depends largely on whether the staff member acted negligently. This is a complex legal matter involving the professional expertise of lawyers and often the court system. However, we can identify some general considerations. For negligence to be successfully charged, it has to be established that the staff member had a responsibility for doing something, that he or she did not act in a prudent manner in discharging this responsibility, and that the failure to do so resulted in damage or injury (Guadagnolo 1980; Van der Smissen 1968). Much information about actual liability cases involving recreation and park agencies is available (Kozlowski 1984).

Competent Service Providers Capitalize on Strengths and Respond to Situations

People who use leisure services expect recreation and park personnel to be competent. This expectation is also held by the agencies who employ personnel and, typically, by staff members themselves. What is competence? In the most basic sense, it is simply the ability to do something effectively. We talked about competency as related to intrinsic motivation in Chapter 5. Here we are referring to competency in the professional sense. There are at least three components. First, you need to be able to perform certain processes. We have just discussed some of these. For example, in working with people, we use such processes as communication and leadership. At the management level, we engage in budgeting, organizing, and other processes. To be competent, you need to be familiar with the processes, to have experienced them, and to have some feedback about your uses of them. Second, you need to be able to recognize the demands of the varying situations within which you use the processes. These do differ. For example, a park ranger probably would use the process of communication differently in a crowd control situation than in a staff meeting. The ranger would need to be able to assess the demands of each situation and adjust or adapt the actual uses of the particular process. A third aspect of competency is related to personal characteristics, including strengths and weaknesses. For example, one individual will communicate differently, at least in some respects, than another individual. Suppose you are the park ranger. You will have different styles and different talents than those of another person on the park staff. To be competent, you need to be aware of your own styles and strengths to take best advantage of them, and of your weaknesses to be able to adjust and improve.

Most of us aspire to be competent, to be effective in our professional roles. There are both intrinsic and extrinsic reasons for this. We appreciate praise from the publics we serve, recognition from our supervisors, promotions, pay raises, and similar rewards. But many of us also derive a great deal of personal satisfaction from doing our jobs well, from knowing that we are effective.

Competence, then, is the ability to use necessary processes effectively, recognizing both the demands of each situation and one's own individual uniqueness. In our field, it usually involves working with people. This requires some basic understandings about behavior. It requires a sensitivity to interpersonal relationships.

Relationships Influence the Effectiveness of Service Providers

The delivery of leisure services inevitably involves interpersonal relationships. This is most obvious in working with participants. For example, when a sailing specialist at a resort marina teaches basic skills for beginners or provides leadership in organizing a cruise for advanced students, she is relating directly to guests. Less obvious are the relationships among staff members, and when staff members interact with other personnel. When a planner designs an addition to the dock area, he works with the resort manager and with representatives of the local governmental agency. When the resort manager develops the operating budget, she consults with the board of directors. The food and beverage supervisor provides training for new staff members who will work in the resort's restaurants, snack bars, and lounges. The sailing specialist interacts with local representatives of the U.S. Coast Guard to assure that resort boats meet safety standards. The quality of these relationships directly influences the quality of staff members' work and services.

What is involved in professional relationships? Of course, communication is involved. Relationships are established and maintained on the basis of both verbal and nonverbal communication. Perceptions are also involved, perceptions of your own and other people's behavior. Griffin and Patton (1974) suggest that all relationships have three dimensions; the intensity or frequency of the interactions, the question of who is "in control" of what happens, and the emotional climate or presence of such feelings as friendliness or hostility. For example, although a staff member might interact more frequently with colleagues in the same division than with the unit supervisor, the less frequent interactions with the boss might be more intense. The emotional tone might be different in the types of interactions; perhaps it would be more formal with the supervisor. In this example, there might be no question of who is in control, at least in the professional sense. However, when there is ambiguity, those involved usually come to some understanding about control before the relationship develops very far. Of course, in many relationships control is shared.

Effective Relationships Involve Mutual Need Satisfaction, Trust, and Empathy

Griffin and Patton (1974) suggest a couple of useful ideas about perceptions and relationships. When interacting with another person, you tend to be aware of your own needs and the potential for the other person to meet those needs. You probably do not consciously say to yourself, "What do I want and how can this individual help me?" But we behave on this basis. We are all goal-oriented human beings with needs; we work to meet these needs. There is nothing wrong with that. However, Griffin and Patton remind us that, in effective relationships, there are additional considerations: What are the other person's needs, and how can I help with those? We sometimes get so focused on what we want that we fail to remember that the other person also wants to get something out of the relationship.

A key element in relationships is trust. Johnson (1981) contends that trusting and being trustworthy are essential if relationships are to develop and grow. Trust is the belief that another person will not do anything to hurt you—disappoint, ridicule, embarrass, or reject you. It involves risk. You open yourself up to the possibility of harm, but you expect that it will not happen. In professional settings, trust also involves counting on others to do something that should be done, expecting that they will not let you down. Being trustworthy is being willing to respond so that the other person's trust is not betrayed. Trust is based on experience. We are inclined to trust other people when our experience tells us that either they, specifically, can be trusted or that people in general are trustworthy. When trust exists in a leisure service agency, the potential for effective interactions among staff members, and therefore for more effective service is much greater.

Empathy is another aspect of relationships. It is the ability to experience the situation of another person as if it were happening to you; to feel as the other person feels (Katz 1963). There are many significant outcomes to an expression of empathy. It builds rapport. It shows others that you understand. It facilitates communication. These conditions enhance participant satisfaction and contribute to good staff morale and unity.

Closely related to empathy is sensitivity to the circumstances and values of others. This quality helps recreation and park personnel work more effectively in situations where their backgrounds are culturally different from those of the participants or other staff members. This would be the case, for example, in working with tourists from other countries. We can suggest several other possibilities. Immigrants and other newcomers constitute a large potential service group with whom we might work. Military recreation personnel often interact with local, off-base populations overseas. Staff members at resorts in other countries, frequently work with their counterparts from local areas. In at-home situations, agency supervisors encounter and need to be sensitive to the perceptions and expectations of culturally different staff members. This kind of sensitivity is also useful in other ways. When younger staff members, for example, work with older participants, there is a potential for misunderstanding. In a sense, the two groups (staff members and participants) represent different cultures. Instead of age, the differences might be in income levels, educational backgrounds, or general lifestyles. Whatever the specifics, sensitivity to others' points of view and values contributes to effective relationships; these facilitate effective services.

Relationships May Involve Interpersonal Conflict

When people interact, there is potential for conflict. Often it seems to be inevitable (Johnson 1981). Conflict may occur when you want to get something done, but someone else interferes with that happening. The other person obstructs what you do, prevents it, or disagrees with your purpose or your method. We mentioned psychological conflict in Chapter 5 as a condition where an individual has difficulty selecting between recreation alternatives. Here we are talking about conflict between two people.

Roark (1978) suggested that the potential for conflict increases when relationships are more intense or when interdependency increases. These circumstances are often present in staff situations. Conflict can be productive in group efforts (Sessoms and Stevenson 1981). It can help to clarify issues and solutions and can generate action. However, it can also be destructive if the responses of those involved are not appropriate. What are typical responses? You can try to avoid conflict but, as we suggested, this may be unrealistic. You can ignore it. This eventually will be expressed. You might be able to prevent conflict in some cases or minimize its effects in others. And, of course, you can deal with it. Empathy, rapport, good communication, and other attributes of an effective relationship should lessen the potential for it to occur or help to manage it if it does arise. Different writers have suggested methods for conflict management (Johnson 1981; Roark 1978; Sessoms and Stevenson 1981). Implied in many approaches is a "win-win" strategy, in which both parties gain benefits or achieve mutual satisfaction (Gordon 1977). These strategies are in contrast with "win-lose" situations, which often stir up anger or frustration and frequently work against building future relationships.

These last three concepts help us understand professional relationships. They help us realize that if someone like the resort manager focuses on her needs and fails to consider the needs of her staff, the professional relationship will be less effective. As a result, she will be less effective. That is not to suggest that the needs of the organization come last or that the primary goal of a manager is to have a well-satisfied staff. But it stands to reason that good staff morale should lead to better staff functioning. The agency's goals and the goals of the staff need not be incompatible. The concepts help us realize that relationships are built on trust and empathy. An empathetic supervisor will be more aware of staff needs and feelings. This will enable him to work more effectively with them. Understanding contributes to trust; trust builds morale. We will say more about supervision and other processes in a later chapter. The point here is that relationships are important.

Self-Awareness Contributes to Effectiveness

You will be more effective in interpersonal relationships if you have appropriate self-awareness. Some ancient sage said, "Know thyself." Actually, a lot of people probably have said this, and we all know that such advice is good. But how can you know yourself? Who are you, anyway? Do others see the same person you think you are? Luft (1969) provides a very useful way of visualizing these questions and of finding some answers. He developed the "Johari Window", which enables us to look at ourselves in two dimensions: (1) what we know about ourselves and (2) what other people know about us. The four cells of the Johari Window are based on these two dimensions.

To relate the Johari Window to our current discussion, let us look at two people, you and a friend you work with named Carlos. First, you know some things about yourself that Carlos also knows. Luft speaks of this aspect as the "open" part of your relationship. Then, you know some other things about yourself that Carlos is unaware of. Perhaps you have not told him yet, or you are not going to tell him. Luft calls this the "hidden" dimension. Maybe it is something that is unimportant to your relationship. However, if there is something important, Carlos should know about it. Let us say that it bothers you to be interrupted when you are writing a report. Knowing this will help Carlos and others relate more effectively to you in the work situation. Telling Carlos how you feel is engaging in "appropriate self-disclosure" (Johnson 1981).

The "blind" part of the relationship involves those things that Carlos knows about you that you do not know. Wait a minute! Is it possible that another person knows something about you that you do not? Certainly. Suppose Carlos feels that you are inconsiderate, even though you see yourself as being very sensitive to the feelings of others. "OK," you say. "I can see how that might happen. But who is right? Am I really insensitive?" You may or may not be; that's not the point. The point is that if Carlos feels you are inconsiderate, that is "reality" for him. He probably will react to you on the basis of this perception, whether it is accurate or not. We considered the importance of perception in the chapter on behavior. The same principles apply here. To learn more about yourself, you need to be receptive to feedback from others. This involves listening to what is being said, picking up on nonverbal cues, and being sensitive to how others react to you.

The more you share relevant information about yourself and the more receptive you are to feedback, the more open you will be. Luft (1969) and others (Egan 1976; Johnson 1981) believe that openness contributes to effective interpersonal relationships.

There is a fourth, or "unknown," dimension in the Johari Window. This is the part of ourselves that neither we nor others are aware of. This dimension is a bit more difficult to apply to everyday relationships. The idea is that we may have potential, but at present unknown, feelings or behaviors that could become apparent later on in some situation. For additional insight about the Johari Window and its effect on the conceptual development of leisure, refer to our discussion in Chapter 2.

Meeting Professional Responsibilities Contributes to Effectiveness

Professions serve complex social needs. Health care is an example: internists, anesthesiologists, orthopedic surgeons, pharmacists, optometrists, nurses, dentists, psychiatrists, pathologists, and other medical personnel all focus on different aspects of treatment and prevention. Maintenance of health is an important and complex need in society. So is education. To serve this need we have teachers, administrators, subject specialists, psychologists, counselors, and others. We could develop similar illustrations for law, engineering, and other well-established professions. The field of recreation and parks is relatively new as a profession.

Professions are characterized by certain responsibilities. They develop specialized bodies of knowledge through research, applications of methods adapted from other fields, and systematic evaluation of practices. These processes permit validation of techniques and minimize trial-and-error approaches. Professions pass their specialized knowledge on to new candidates in the field through programs of professional preparation. They keep current members of the profession informed through programs of in-service training. Professions develop standards for admission into the field or for identifying competent workers. These standards take the form of systems of certification or registration. Professions regulate their members through codes of ethics to assure that the best interests of the public they serve are protected. To address these responsibilities more effectively, professions form societies for collective action. In Chapter 3, we presented some ideas about the professional development of our field and about its status with respect to professional activities.

Professions carry out professional responsibilities to assure effective service for their publics. This seems reasonable. If we validate our techniques, pass this information on to practitioners, regulate entry into the field or identify those qualified needed to work in it, and define through codes of ethics how practitioners should relate to those they serve, we should be able to give better service. However, some have cautioned that professionalism can potentially be self-serving (Witt 1985). We may seek such status more for our own needs than as a way of assuring our effectiveness. If recreation and park personnel can keep sight of the reason for our existence as a field, it will help to focus professionalism on service. We need to remember what Duncan (1985) called our "radical roots," our heritage of serving people's leisure needs and attacking the barriers that prevent their expression. We need to recognize the values of working closely with our constituents. As we suggested in Chapter 3, professional status should not separate us from the publics we serve.

Given these cautions, it is useful to identify some staff behaviors related to professionalism. These are similar to "core processes" in the sense that they are appropriate in all or most positions. When you work in this field, you should be able to read and understand research findings in order to apply new knowledge when and where it is appropriate. You should be able to evaluate professional techniques and services. When you do this systematically and record the results, you are engaging in a type of research. In a sense, you are contributing to the field's body of knowledge. You should keep current through reading professional journals, attending workshops or conferences sponsored by professional societies, or enrolling in appropriate university courses. These activities will enable you to be more effective as a service provider.

There are a couple of other activities related to professionalism that are appropriate for staff members. When individuals become registered with a state plan, they not only identify themselves as competent workers; they support the plan by participating in it. To the degree that the plan actually identifies competency, supporting it will help the field and the public overall. In the same vein, personnel who are active in their professional societies benefit in direct ways; at the same time they help to do collectively, through the organization, what individuals alone cannot do. They support accreditation of university professional preparation programs, publication of professional journals, the offering of conferences and workshops, and other activities related to improving and maintaining effective service.

Summary

In this chapter we have identified some ideas about leisure service providers. In later chapters we will discuss the kinds of things they do as they deliver services. The purpose here was to look at some staff characteristics and behaviors as a background for these later presentations.

The things we know about behavior in general apply to personnel, as well as to participants. Leisure service providers have goals and are influenced by a wide variety of sociopsychological, geographic, economic, and other factors. When individual staff members behave in the professional sense, they use the unique talents that each of them possesses. They use these talents to bring about the professional objectives they seek. As they do so, they work with people. They develop relationships, which involve different elements and dimensions, such as needs, intensities, emotional climates, and questions of control, trust, and empathy. Sometimes interpersonal conflict occurs. We will be more effective in our professional relationships if we are aware of our own strengths and weaknesses and of our values, beliefs, and attitudes.

Recreation and park personnel aspire to be competent. Competency involves the ability to use professional processes appropriate to the situations in which we are working and in a way that recognizes our individual talents. Many of the processes we use are common to most personnel positions in most leisure service agencies. We have called these "core" processes. Personnel also engage in certain behaviors related to professionalism. These include using appropriate research findings, keeping current by attending conferences and reading professional journals, and being active in professional societies.

References

Bannon, Joseph J. 1981. *Problem-solving in recreation and parks.* Englewood Cliffs, NJ: Prentice-Hall.

Combs, A. W., D.L. Avila, and W.W. Purkey. 1978. *Helping relationships: basic concepts for the helping professions.* Boston: Allyn and Bacon.

Duncan, Mary.1985. Back to our radical roots. In *Recreation and leisure: Issues in an era of change,* Thomas L. Goodale, and Peter A. Witt, eds. State College, PA: Venture Publishing.

Edginton, Christopher R., and Phyllis M. Ford. 1985. *Leadership in recreation and leisure service organizations.* New York: John Wiley and Sons.

Egan, Gerard. 1976. *Interpersonal living: A skills/contract approach to human relations training in groups.* Monterey, CA: Brooks/Cole Publishing.

Fiedler, Fred E. 1967. *A theory of leadership effectiveness.* New York: McGraw-Hill.

Gordon, Thomas. 1977. *Leader effectiveness training.* New York: Wyden Books.

Griffin, Kim, and Bobby R. Patton. 1974. *Personal communication in human relations.* Columbus, OH: Charles E. Merrill.

Guadagnolo, Frank. 1980. Legal aspects of managing recreation and park agencies. In *Financing, managing and marketing recreation and park resources,* Dennis R. Howard, and John L. Crompton, eds. Dubuque, IA: Wm. C. Brown Company Publishers.

Hershey, Paul, and Kenneth H. Blanchard. 1982. *Management of organizational behavior: Utilizing human resources.* Enlewood Cliffs, NJ: Prentice-Hall.

Johnson, David W. 1981. *Reaching out: Interpersonal effectiveness and self-actualization.* Englewood Cliffs, NJ: Prentice-Hall.

Katz, Robert L. 1963. *Empathy: Its nature and uses.* New York: The Free Press.

Kozlowski, James C. 1984. *Recreation and parks law reporter.* Alexandria, VA: National Recreation and Park Association. Published quarterly starting in 1984.

Kraus, Richard G. 1985. *Recreation leadership today.* Glenview, IL: Scott, Foresman.

Luft, Joseph. 1969. *Of human interaction.* Palo Alto, CA: National Press Books.

Niepoth, E. William. 1983. *Leisure leadership: Working with people in recreation and park settings.* Englewood Cliffs, NJ: Prentice-Hall.

Roark, Albert E. 1978. Interpersonal conflict management. *Personnel and Guidance Journal* 56: 400-402.

Russell, Ruth V. 1986. *Leadership in recreation.* St. Louis: Times Mirror/Mosby.

Sessoms, H. Douglas, and Jack L. Stevenson. 1981. *Leadership and group dynamics in recreation services.* Boston: Allyn and Bacon.

Shivers, Jay S. 1986. *Recreational leadership.* Princeton, NJ: Princeton Book Company.

Stogdill, Ralph M. 1974. *Handbook of leadership.* New York: The Free Press.

Tubbs, Stewart L., and Sylvia Moss. 1974. *Human communication: An interpersonal perspective.* New York: Random House.

Van der Smissen, Betty. 1968. *Legal liability of cities and schools for injuries in recreation and parks.* Cincinnati: W.H. Anderson.

Witt, Peter A. 1985. Gaining professional status: Who benefits? In *Recreation and leisure: Issues in an era of change,* Thomas L. Goodale, and Peter A. Witt, eds. State College, PA: Venture Publishing.

PART III

DELIVERY: OVERVIEW

Part I of this book dealt with the philosophical foundations of leisure service. Part II dealt with the concept and structure of leisure service. Part III will deal with the management and delivery of leisure services.

In the management and delivery of leisure services, the holistic view of leisure may be represented through the organization's management philosophy. This philosophy is reflected in every aspect of leisure service delivery. When the philosophy is implemented, delivery becomes a dynamic process that places clients and participants first and responds to their needs.

Recent trends in organizational excellence, public-private cooperation, and reorganization demanded by research in international trends and managerial leadership have just begun to impact upon effective leisure service delivery. Changes in the corporate sector, in global, national, and local economies, in demographics, and in consumer attitude and behavior have been straining the traditional approaches to the management of a leisure service delivery system.

It has been suggested (Benest, Foley, and Welton 1984) that lack of skill may not be the problem in effecting managerial changes in an organization. Rather, the attitude and approaches of current leisure service managers may resist changing from a traditional, bureaucratic, top-down management style to a more adaptive, modular or systems approach so important to effectively manage large-scale and small-scale leisure service delivery systems. While the development of certain basic managerial skills

is imperative, it is also a fundamental requirement upon which the
manager and staff build an organization that is responsive to
continued change, client needs and leisure service demands. The
challenge of adequately responding to client demand for public or
nonprofit and private commercial leisure service delivery is com-
pounded when staff at all levels in an organization are unwilling
to change and are not trained to execute various management
functions.

Many universities that offer degrees in recreation, park, and
leisure studies appear to be doing a good job in preparing students
in the history and scope of the field, philosophy, and program
planning. But some universities may not be adequately preparing
students to manage an organization, particularly when it begins to
grow and become complex. In an age of exploding new technology
and ever-changing dynamics of community life, organizations are
becoming increasingly difficult systems to manage. To know the
right type of program that a particular community or clientele
needs is one matter; to deliver a well-designed program by using
applicable management practices is another. Today's managers
need to be prepared to contend with developing the right kinds of
plans, knowing when to change the organizational structure
because it has grown beyond its present usefulness, hiring and
training the necessary managers, providing the right kind of
motivation for a diversified staff, controlling the operations so that
objectives are met, and adeptly handling political situations.

Part III will not only present the essential elements of the
management process, but will also provide information on how
the manager and staff can effectively respond to changes that
affect the leisure service delivery system. While the principles
may be the same for managing a large or a small organization,
certain unique features of small and large organizations will be
explained. The basic management processes discussed are (a)
futuristic planning based on client-participant needs, (b) an organizational structure that is flexible, (c) excellent human resource
management, (d) delivery of services sensitive to client needs, and
(e) tight monitoring and evaluation systems. An example of a
private commercial recreation organization is presented here to
illustrate a type of contemporary, service-oriented structure that
incorporates these management processes at all levels and acknowledges that managers must be trained to accept change as a
way of life.

Sandestin Beach Resort

Sandestin Beach Resort, located on the northern Gulf Coast of Florida near the town of Destin, is a 2,400-acre, full-service resort. Lodging includes some 1,000 condominiums and homes, the 500-room Sandestin Beach Hilton Hotel, and the 190-room Bayside Inn. Amenities include five restaurants, the Market (an upscale shopping center), two 18-hole championship golf courses, grass, clay, and hard surface tennis courts, a 98-slip marina, a General Store, sail and power boat rentals, a game room, a health club, numerous swimming pools, bike rental operations, and more than a quarter mile of beach on the Gulf of Mexico and four miles of property on Choctoawatchee Bay.

The Sandestin recreation department also offers the following activities for the residents and guests of the resort:

1. Day camp and tot programs: high quality activity programs for children four years of age and older
2. Beach services: umbrella and sailboat rentals, regularly scheduled beach sports such as volleyball, sandcastle building, and treasure hunts
3. Body shop: a full service health club featuring Nautilus exercise machines, sauna and steam rooms, massage therapists on duty, and scheduled aerobics programs
4. Special event programs: from 5K runs and triathlons to 4th of July carnivals, planned for all ages on all parts of the resort
5. Winter resident programs: special programs for winter visitors to Sandestin, including golf outings, field trips, speakers, bridge, and pot luck suppers
6. Conference programs: a wide range of activities for every age group; for example, the Wacky Olympics to promote adult team building and a beach-side hot dog roast for children.

Philosophy of Management

The Sandestin recreation department's philosophy of management grew out of an understanding of the relationship that service has to overall guest satisfaction and ultimately to profit-ability. The concept is simple—recognize who the true "boss" of the operation is. The true "boss" is the consumer, not the depart-ment head or general manager or even the CEO. At the resort the guest who purchases the goods and services is actually the "boss"; without his or her support the entire operation will fail.

When meeting the needs of this "boss," the employees who have the first line of responsibility are actually the line staff. The supervisory and management levels of the organization are there to support the line staff and provide them with what it takes—be it adequate supplies, special training, or just a pat on the back—to best serve the customer.

The line staff is just as important to the successful operation of the resort as is the general manager. The diagrams presented here compare the old view and the new view of the organizational structure that follows this new management philosophy. In Figure 1, the responsibility for success is placed on the CEO, who assigns tasks in a way that will best meet the needs of the people. In this diagram, the consumer as "boss" is not seen.

Figure 1 Traditional Structure

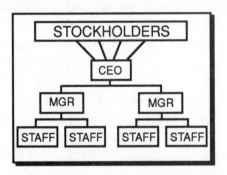

In Figure 2, the client or participant is seen as the head of the organization; line staff members directly communicate with the clients and respond to their needs. Assisting and supporting the staff are the various levels of management, whose job is to make sure that the line staff best serves the "boss."

Figure 2 Service-Oriented Structure

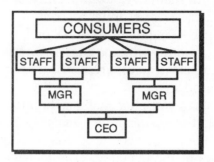

Implications and Examples

The service-oriented structure has new implications for each level of any public-private nonprofit, or commercial leisure service operation.

For the line staff: the responsibility for guest satisfaction at Sandestin is clearly placed on their shoulders. If they are unable to fulfill their duties, they must be able to communicate their needs to their supervisors on a timely basis. For example, health club attendants are running short of towels for the guests. The attendants—not the housekeeping department or the health club manager—are responsible for keeping an adequate supply. Under the service-oriented structure, the attendants would know whom to contact and what to do when towel usage is high. This direct accountability increases response to guest needs and raises the level of guest satisfaction. Providing quality service to the clients and participants served in each type of leisure organization is critical to the success of the operation.

For the manager: A service-oriented structure implies greater communication between the line employees and the supervisor. Thus the supervisor will have greater levels of confidence in the employees. If this is to work, quality employee-training programs have to be conducted. The employees need to clearly understand what is expected of them and how to achieve it. The service-oriented structure also calls for the MBWA (management by walking around) style of management. For the manager to be successful in supporting employees, he or she must actively communicate with them. An example of this is the recreation director who visits each area under his control two to three times a day, each time checking for operational problems, coaching the staff and communicating with the guests. Direct communication among staff members decreases response time and improves the levels of guest service.

For upper management: Recognizing the importance of the line staff in achieving the organization's goals is a factor in a service-oriented structure. Using this concept may challenge many of the traditional views of the manager. The manager has to clearly understand his or her role as a supporter of the staff and has to be as much of a team leader and motivator as a decision maker. The successful manager will take time to talk with the line employees about their operational needs and will help meet them. Rather than reprimanding employees, this manager helps them solve problems so that they can better serve the guests. This reinforces the idea that service to the guests is the ultimate concern.

Advantages of This Idea

The concepts behind a service-oriented structure are not new. Service to the consumer has long been recognized as a key to the success of any organization. But this idea helps focus on the relationships between employees and supervisors and the responsibilities each has toward the client. By using this idea, all employees, from upper management to line staff, should have a better understanding of who the "boss" is and what their real job is.

Application of Concepts

1. *Long-range planning is necessary for any organization and must involve managers at all levels in the agency.* A top manager at Sandestin Beach Resort voices the importance of having line staff input into the planning process. Using information they supply about customer wants and needs aids the

development of goals and objectives in the long-range planning process.

2. *Organizational excellence can best be achieved when organizations recognize that clients and participants need continuing opportunities to voice their input.* The use of an inverted organization chart showing the consumers as bosses represents innovative thinking at Sandestin Beach Resort. In this service-oriented structure staff members are encouraged to be more responsive to their clients than in the typical organizational structure.

3. *The key to human resource management is that all employees recognize how each contributes to the satisfaction of customers.* Valuing all employees for their contribution to greater satisfaction is a major factor in the management philosophy that governs Sandestin Beach Resort. Supporting line staff requires that all personnel mobilize to deal with guest needs regardless of rank or position. This is the holistic/ interactive leadership concept in action.

4. *As managers become more cognizant of all the elements that affect services or programs (e.g., transportation, health of clients, clean and safe facilities, and enthusiastic personnel), the more likely it is that service delivery will result in a satisfying experience for the clients.* Obviously, in this example, all details that surround a positive leisure experience for guests are part of service delivery. Positive response to the guests allows a smooth process of meeting their needs.

5. *Monitoring and evaluating leisure services requires ongoing review and adjusting to the changing circumstances of clients.* Through guest audits and line staff input, changes may be made in the management of this resort. Because the guest is boss, expressed needs are responded to more quickly than in the typical top-down organizational structure.

References

Benest, F., J. Foley, and G. Welton. 1984. *Organizing leisure and human services.* Dubuque, Iowa: Kendall/Hunt.
Holdnak, A. 1989. Philosophy of management. (unpublished manuscript).

8

ACHIEVING VISION: PLANNING FOR CHANGE

For today's managers, the holistic view of leisure needs to be integrated into a management style that provides effective delivery of services. Through understanding the catalyst role of leisure services, a manager ties each of the key work functions together in developing excellence. To this end, several major managerial responsibilities are required for effective service delivery.

Managers in leisure services have a major responsibility for developing plans that will ensure an accurate projection of work, finances, and strategies. Unfortunately, according to current research on the planning process, "Planning tends to be thought of as an occasional exercise leading to a specific plan rather than an integral function of organizational management" (Getz 1986, 17). Planning, however, allows a manager to be proactive rather than reactive in situations requiring expert leadership.

Role of Leadership

Managerial leadership is at the base of all duties described in the following chapters. Through an interactive leadership approach, the manager can develop an organization that projects vision in order to assist future planning.

As such, planning is an essential step in the management process. Other managerial functions (organizing, developing human resources, implementing service, and monitoring and

265

evaluating) depend upon the planning function and how thoroughly it establishes direction.

Busser and Bannon (1987) point to six key tasks of a manager:

1. Keeping up to date on participant-community needs and requirements
2. Formulating budgets
3. Allocating time
4. Looking for ways to improve the functioning of the organization
5. Keeping the general public, board, participants, and other important groups informed about the organizations, activities, plans, and capabilities
6. Taking immediate action in response to crises

To adequately handle those six tasks, managers must use advanced planning techniques. *Therefore, a key role of planning is to develop an appropriate framework to access important information for handling managerial tasks.* According to Koontz and O'Donnell (1980), "Planning is deciding in advance what to do, how to do it, when to do it, and who is to do it" (156). Thus, when a manager executes a task, there should be a planning framework from which information can be consistently drawn, regardless of how many times the task is executed. In other words, the tasks have already been anticipated by setting the goals for managerial work.

Planning is also a key means by which to set targets that may later be evaluated. Therefore, another role of planning is its relationship to the process of evaluation that must take place. To this end, planning and evaluating are dependent upon each other.

Planning Approaches: Creating Vision

The literature in our field identifies many approaches to planning (Corbin, and Williams 1987; Edginton, Compton and Hanson 1980; Tillman 1973). Some focus on the roles of agency planners. In the "authoritarian," "traditional," "current practices," "trickle-down," and "educated guess" approaches, someone in the agency makes the decisions about what services will be offered. The bases for planning are the professional knowledge or perceptions of the individual doing it. What was done last year?

What are other agencies offering? What do I think will be successful?

Other approaches focus on the needs and interests of the intended consumers of the services. Either we ask them or someone who speaks for them what they want, as in the "expressed desires" or "community leadership input" approaches, or we use "identification of needs" and "investigation" approaches to assess more systematically what is needed. A "sociopolitical" approach (Kraus 1985) recognizes the influences of sociological and political factors such as differing needs in various types of communities, pressures for services brought by different needs in various types of communities, and pressures for services brought by different constituencies.

Leisure service professionals should have appropriate knowledge and skills to use in planning; if they rely only on their own judgments, they could be very wrong. Our programs exist for the people who use them, and theoretically we should base what we do on what they want. However, they may not really know what they want. Their perceptions may be limited by past experiences, or they may not know what is possible. Edginton, Compton, and Hanson (1980) identify an "interactive discovery" approach, which recognizes the involvement of both professionals and participants. It emphasizes the ability of people to work together to meet their own needs and the roles of leisure service personnel in facilitating these efforts. These authors see the various approaches existing along a continuum. At one end are approaches like the "educated guess" that emphasize the input of leisure service personnel. At the other end are those that focus on the involvement of the consumers, such as the "interactive discovery" approach. At the one end, we are interested more in direct service delivery and professional control; at the other, we are concerned about participatory planning, controlled by the consumer.

Regardless of the ways that planning is approached, nothing is more effective than the ability to accurately create a vision of what a leisure service agency or business should be—the overriding goal that operates through setting objectives and effective monitoring and evaluation.

The vision so necessary to planning was never more effectively created than in the Magic of Disneyland and the enjoyment it brought to millions of people. Vision, alluded to in Naisbitt and Aburdene's *Reinventing the Corporation* (1985) describes a manager's need to have "powerful vision—a whole new sense of where a company is going and how to get there"(21). That vision is then translated into the concept of shared vision where employees and consumers alike agree with and believe in the direction that the company takes through planning. According to Naisbitt and Aburdene, "The only way to translate vision and alignment into people's day-to-day behavior is by grounding these lofty concepts in the company's day-to-day environment"(27).

Naturally, if the concept of shared vision is important, your management style will affect the approach you take to implement planning at all levels. If you approach planning in an authoritative fashion, the concepts of employee involvement and satisfaction may prevent a unified plan from being implemented. In contrast, a participative management style may produce higher levels of employee satisfaction and therefore greater shared vision (Swidley 1985). This state calls for the ability to involve key personnel and community leaders in decision making.

If an atmosphere that fosters a shared vision is to be created, the following must exist·

1. All employees must be involved in various plans set forth by the enterprise, agency, or organization.
2. A realistic timetable must be determined to accomplish a specified plan or update.
3. All planning documents should be consistent with regard to overall goals and objectives.
4. Planning documents should be tied to an evaluation process.
5. Planning documents should be updated according to a predetermined schedule.

Another part of the planning process involves decision making.

The Planning Process

Policy

An initial part of the planning process has to do with the development of policy. Probably more so than any other single form of plan, policies are open to misunderstanding. Employees think of them in negative terms as a way used by managers to prohibit employees from doing anything enjoyable. On closer scrutiny, however, policies can be considered as plans. They are general statements or understandings that guide and assist managers in the decision-making process. A policy guides decisions toward the implementation of goals and objectives. Policies are forms of plans that help achieve the overall goals and objectives of the organization. They should always be in the best interest of the organization. When thought of in this way, policies tend to be perceived less negatively. Very often they come into being because individuals misuse certain privileges, thus casting policies in a negative light. In many cases, however, policies are implemented in advance to assure that goals or objectives are accomplished.

Most policies are interpreted through the exercise of initiative as well as discretion. Sometimes it becomes necessary to deviate from them when it is in the best interest of the organization and the individuals it serves. Policies should be flexible to reflect the constant change experienced by organizations. For example, in a community with a great number of senior citizens, the hours of operation of recreation centers should accommodate those who prefer participating in activities between 10 a.m. and 4 p.m. However, discretion should be used in deviating from a general policy that has set the hours of operation from 2 p.m. to 10 p.m.

Generally, when policies are altered, it is appropriate that employees deviating from them explain the reasons for doing so to their superiors. In the case of hours of operation, which are ongoing and constant, the explanation should probably be done in writing with approval to make the change permanent.

Another example of a policy is the number of overtime hours that an employee can work during any given pay period. The policy might read: "No employee will work more than 10 hours of paid overtime in any given pay period. All overtime will need prior approval of the district supervisor." Such policies generally are to prevent abuses of overtime. During emergency situations, supervisors and managers can use discretion in deviating from a minimal overtime policy. Again, deviation should be brought to the attention of superiors or, if time permits, approval can be obtained in advance.

Goals and Objectives

A second element inherent in all parts of the planning process is the development of goals and objectives. Regardless of the type of plan being initiated, a general goal statement and more specific objectives statements are the basis on which the planning process takes place.

For example, using programming models described in leisure literature, we can highlight the following basic dimensions of program planning (Corbin and Williams 1987; Edginton, Compton, and Hanson 1980; Farrell and Lundegren 1983; Russell 1982):

1. Stress the needs of those for whom the services are intended.
2. Develop objectives for those services.
3. Plan the program.
4. Promote it.
5. Implement it.
6. Evaluate it.
7. Revise it as needed.

These dimensions apply to all services. Kraus (1985) points out an additional consideration. Because program planners operate within a philosophical framework, they must establish or identify this framework clearly at the outset. These steps constitute what is known as an "interactive" model of service delivery, which is a good example of the many planning processes necessary to effectively provide for a range of leisure services.

In order to establish clear-cut general goals and more specific objectives, a few common points may be made, regardless of the type of plan being implemented. First, goals and objectives are considered ends toward which activity is aimed (Koontz and O'Donnell 1980). Goals are stated in broad, global, general terms; while objectives are specific, narrower, and measurable and are essential to the evaluation process.

Second, goals tend to be centered around the basic purpose of an agency or business. For example, when an agency, department, or organization, either public or private, is established, an authority exists by which it was established. In the case of a public park and recreation department, the goal might be "to provide all citizens of the community an opportunity to engage in a wholesome recreation program during their leisure for the betterment of the individual and the total community." From this broad goal, an agency may then develop more specific objectives that personnel use to plan a work program and evaluate their success in attaining that goal. Another term for goal in this case is *purpose*.

Some examples of broad community leisure service goals are listed below and follow some of the guiding principles for the leisure profession:

1. To develop a sense of community to enhance the quality of life
2. To maximize individual and community potential by encouraging citizens to work together to fulfill collective needs
3. To provide individuals with a range of social opportunities and a strong sense of community interaction
4. To encourage individuals and groups having direct contact with the community to become directly involved in decision making and determining program interests and needs
5. To work with groups to provide recreational opportunities at the lowest possible cost to users consistent with the quality standards that have been set
6. To encourage and motivate self-supporting community groups to help themselves
7. To provide individuals with the opportunity to develop and exercise their personal leadership skills
8. To assist groups of people to develop economically and socially viable communities that strengthen personal and family growth

A manager has nothing to measure, evaluate, or control unless there is a plan with which to compare the results. The effectiveness of the planning process is determined by how well the manager understands the whole management process and can relate it to the individual managerial functions. Many times supervisors plan without realizing the relationships among the parts of the planning process. This type of planning tends to be unsystematic and not well organized. Obviously the manager or supervisor of a leisure service delivery system who approaches planning with understanding, precision, and thoroughness will do a much better job and, in turn, will be more assured of desirable results.

Planning should take place at all levels in an organization, from the top administrator to the lowest levels, including the maintenance worker. Thus another key role of planning is that it organizes all employment tasks, regardless of level. The scope, the depth, and the detailing of the staff's plans will differ, but the process is the same. Without planning, the individual will waste time and accomplish little.

Overall goals and objectives can vary considerably from department to department, depending upon the emphasis of the department. In too many instances, however, departments have no written goals and objectives, although the top administrator can usually state a few general ones. But how realistic they are and whether achieving them is really sought vigorously is another matter. An example of a client goal in a therapeutic recreation setting might be to stimulate the socialization and interaction of participants. This goal is very general, however. Overall goals are best achieved through specific objectives, which can be quantified in terms of their attainment. It is certainly necessary to have the overall goals as stated, but achieving them will most likely happen in stages. A quantifiable objective that would help to achieve socialization and interaction might be to have participants learn and practice *specific* social skills as part of ongoing group membership.

Objectives are specific, realistic, and attainable and lead to accomplishing the overall goal of expanding and strengthening in-service training. Similarly, the overall departmental goal of developing a sound evaluation program may be accomplished by several intermediate, quantifiable objectives, such as the following:

1. Having all participants fill out a questionnaire, indicating their likes and dislikes of all craft classes at the conclusion of the fall classes

2. Employing a research and evaluation team to measure the effectiveness of summer playground programs

3. Hiring an agricultural consultant to determine the proper fertilizing techniques to be used on eight random park areas

Developing a sound evaluation program can also help a department determine how effectively it is implementing its program and using its money and human resources. For example, expanding joint funding and using park and school facilities is a better use of public land and public funds. This overall goal can be achieved, for example, by the following intermediate, quantifiable objectives:

1. Joint planning, construction, and development of the Hilton Park School site and the hiring of an architect by July 1
2. The opening of the new recreation center in the Westwood Junior High School this fall
3. The operation of five summer playground programs and school playgrounds next summer at Washington, Garfield, Irwin, Lincoln, and Jefferson schools

Each of these quantifiable objectives is directed toward accomplishing the overall goal. Without them, however, and without a specific schedule and plan, the overall goal might never be accomplished. In too many cases, overall goals are just words mouthed by administrators.

In the organizational structure in public agencies, the municipal park and recreation manager is responsible for a park function and a recreation function. Each of these functions should have its overall goals implemented by quantifiable objectives attainable within weeks or months. Likewise, through the districts and in individual facilities such as recreation centers and parks, the same procedure should be followed. These objectives and goals should be developed jointly and agreed to by both supervisor and employee. They should be stated in writing with a timetable for implementing them, and then dated when they have been accomplished. Employees should be thoroughly familiar with them so that they know what they are working toward.

In addition, goals and objectives should be measurable so that the person in charge and the employee can determine if they have been achieved. Quantifiable, measurable goals and objectives give employees a sense of satisfaction in a job well done.

Goals and objectives should be realistic so that people in both the upper and lower echelons of the organization can quickly see

possibilities and achievement of success. Goals and objectives that
are merely handed down and are beyond the capability of employees soon lead to frustration. Without goals and objectives, employees may appear to be busy, but actually they may be achieving
little or nothing.

Very fine overall goals may never be achieved because they
are not broken down into attainable, measurable, realistic objectives that can be accomplished by employees at a lower-level.
Organizations may also fail because the lower-level employees
never see how their small objective fits into the overall goals, and
thus may feel useless and nonproductive.

Setting goals and objectives is a very important part of
planning. It requires participation at all levels, practice, work, and
constant revision, but the results are well worth the effort. Effective planning will go a long way to assure success in the other
management functions. According to Getz (1986) "Statements of
an agency's mandate, goals and objectives must be carefully
developed. Specific policies and priorities must follow with built-
in mechanisms for ongoing evaluation, review and revision"(30).

Decision Making

A third step in the planning process is decision making.
Generally it is considered the final step, except when derivative or
minor adjustments have to be made in plans. Decision making is
the actual selection of a course of action from among the alternatives. For all practical purposes, it is the goal of planning. Developing alternatives should not be minimized, however, because
a good alternative usually becomes more apparent during the
decision-making process. Without good alternatives, many managers have found themselves stymied and ineffective.

There are several ways to produce a large number of alternatives. A good technique is brainstorming, which involves several
people familiar with the goals and objectives of the organization.
Many ideas, regardless of their validity and value, are tossed
around. They are examined and combined into alternative courses
of action. Another method is to ask resource people experienced
in the area to suggest alternative solutions.

Selecting from among proposed alternatives is generally
done in three ways (Koontz and O'Donnell 1980): (1) from
experience, (2) from *experimentation*, and (3) from *research and*

analysis. Experience, the most often used procedure for producing and selecting   alternatives, has provided us with the best technique for doing a job. If something has been successful in the past, we usually assume that it will work in the future.   We can sometimes alter the technique slightly to make it applicable to a new situation.

When making decisions based on experience, however, we should evaluate them against challenges in the future. As conditions and times change, our past experiences may need to be modified. This process works effectively when different conditions are carefully analyzed, measured, and evaluated, rather than followed blindly.

The second method, *experimentation*, is another way to choose alternatives. Sometimes this method is rather costly, however, particularly when it does not work and projects need to be done over. The experimentation method should be carefully considered, in the recreation programming phase.

One of the most promising methods of selecting from alternatives is the research and analysis method. This scientific approach to planning has been extremely successful in some professions and industries, although applying it to leisure service, which is more of a behavioral than an exact science, may be somewhat difficult. In the *research and analysis method*, alternatives are broken into component parts, each one is dealt with individually, and they are then fitted back together. Each phase is studied and experimented with more economically and realistically than the whole could be. Many agencies that are establishing programming and research sections are hiring trained people from the fields of psychology and sociology.

An example of this approach is PERT, the Program Evaluation Review Technique (Williams 1972). An entire project is divided into component parts and evaluated in terms of what is to be done, who is to do it, and how long it will take (see Figure 8.1). Finally, all of these parts are combined to give an overall plan of how the project is to be accomplished to obtain a particular goal. This approach has resulted in more effective planning for construction and maintenance. Similar efforts are being made by many colleges and universities to give us more exact ways of making better decisions.

Whatever the method of arriving at the alternatives and selecting from among them, leisure service managers can make

Figure 8.1 PERT Chart with Critical Path for a Typical Park Development Project (No Large Building Construction)

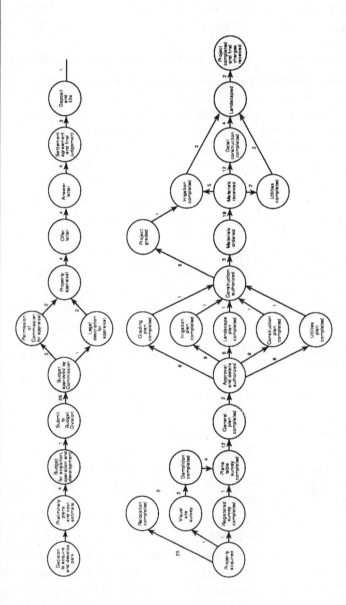

This typical park development project consists of thirty-four activities, work functions or processes. All planning and construction is to be accomplished by parks and recreation department forces. The numbers between activities indicate number of weeks to complete an activity. This is determined from an average of maximum and minimum estimates. This is called the "critical path" because it indicates the longest sequence of activities. When totaled, it gives time to complete the project, 141 weeks in this case, which is equivalent to 2 years and 8 months. This project is assuming that all timetables are met. Missing commission agendas, delays in ordering equipment and involvement with application for federal funding could prolong the project several weeks.

their selection much more easily if goals and objectives are clear. They then can delineate their work and authority and their employees are sure to do a better job when they know what is expected of them and what their limits are.

Procedures

Another part of the planning process is the development of procedures, which give employees details for handling many activities. Procedures are a guide to some form of action. Often a policy will set the stage for certain thinking in an organization, and a procedure will be necessary to implement parts of that policy. But more generally, procedures are important in themselves because they define a course of action, such as how to complete a requisition for equipment. Detailed instructions for doing so might be listed on the reverse side of the requisition itself. The instructions should include, for example, how many copies of the requisition are necessary, who gets which copies, how to specify the quantity of items to be requisitioned, the necessary nomenclature or description of the equipment, and how the requisition is routed through the agency. The procedure will help employees make sure that they supply the information correctly and submit it properly.

Another procedure might deal with the disposal of governmental property, outlining how it must be accounted for when it is declared surplus, how it can be disposed of, and what records need to be kept on it. Again, the procedure is there to guide the actions of employees so that they use the proper method. Often procedures protect employees from making a mistake that could be embarrassing or cause them to be negligent in their work. Procedures should be written and easily available for reference.

Rules and Regulations

Rules and regulations are guidelines governing the means by which the goals and objectives of the department are achieved. They require certain actions or prohibit other actions that are not in the best interest of the public. Rules can seem to be negative, but they serve the interests of the general public by regulating the behavior of those few employees who might become disruptive.

Planning Documents

A manager is responsible for a number of planning documents. This section describes some of them and provides information about how to create a readable document. For our purposes, this form of planning involves the creation of a clearly written document that outlines specific plans. The following documents are those typically found necessary in a public or private leisure service organization.

Comprehensive Plan

One extremely important type of plan is a comprehensive plan. According to Bannon (1976) "Comprehensive community planning is an attempt by a public agency or organization to involve all those individuals and groups likely to be affected by some contemplated action in the decision making that precedes the action"(4). Also known as long-range planning, comprehensive planning is intended to assist professionals with decisions about capital improvements, park and facility development, recreation program development, and growth.

In a case study example of a long-range planning process in the Champaign Park District (McKinney et al., 1986), the following elements were used in developing the plan:

1. Historical content for planning
2. Demographic content and neighborhood analysis
3. Information acquisition and selection: the process of planning
4. Planning meetings
5. Mailed questionnaires
6. Site surveys
7. Policy board interviews
8. Staff questionnaires
9. Planning team
10. Goal-objectives development
11. Recommendations to the board

A document covering such elements should include the above items arranged in a readable format. General guidelines on the preparation of planning documents will be covered later in this chapter.

Programs

Programs are plans in that they are a composite of policies, procedures, rules, assignments, and tasks all put together in an effort to carry out a given assignment. Such programs are generally supported by budgets, personnel, equipment, and other factors in an effort to achieve specified goals or objectives. Some programs are simple and attainable in a short period of time, while others are complex and attainable over a longer period. As mentioned in Chapter 6, programs include various kinds of services. A typical program consists of a group of recreation activities offered during a season or period of the year for the benefit of the participants. Included are arts and crafts, music, dramatics, sports, and games.

Work programs may involve completing a marina, constructing a recreation center, ballfield, or an entire park. A program has all the necessary elements to carry it through to completion. Programs are the results of planning and are a form of plan in themselves in that they are established to accomplish or meet an agency's goal or objective.

Budgets

A budget is a financial plan expressed in dollars and cents. It outlines financial goals to be accomplished. Sometimes it is expressed in dollars, in work hours, or in other units generally associated with dollars. There are operating budgets as well as capital improvement budgets, but in either case the entire purpose is to accomplish the goals of the agency. Budgets become control devices in that they are generally approved by the commission, board, or council authorizing the agency or department program for a given period, usually one year. Once approved by the commission or board, they become legal and binding and require specific actions for which the agency is held accountable. Budgets should therefore be well planned and should include supportive background for justification. They should be followed with as little change as possible. Budgets are prepared in various forms and in varying details, depending upon the given form of organizational sponsorship under which they operate. Table 8.1 is an

Table 8.1 Performance Budget, City of Sunnyvale, California

813 Neighborhood Recreation Activities

Niskanen, James
Rec Supervisor

To provide structured recreation activities for youth (2–19) at city park sites and facilities throughout the year.

Fiscal Year	Work Hours	Total Cost	Equivalent Units	Equivalent Unit Cost	Equivalent Units/Hour	Eq. Unit Cost Constant ($)
1983–84	52,020	539,703	52,011.58	10.38	1.00	10.38
1984–85	58,320	584,913	55,207.49	10.78	.98	10.21
1985–86	57,131	667,942	56,063.08	11.91	.98	10.92
1986–87	59,326	884,429	62,631.41	10.93	1.06	9.59
1987–88	56,861	765,644	71,976.00	10.64	1.27	8.94
1988–89	51,858	718,758	88,798.73	10.45	1.33	8.44
1989–90	62,153	882,516	68,850.87	10.82	1.11	9.94
1990–91	61,135	943,630	75,851.57	12.44	1.24	9.23
1991–92	61,135	993,429	75,851.57	13.10	1.24	9.26
1992–93	61,135	1,043,101				
1993–94	61,135	1,095,258				
1994–95	61,135	1,150,019				
1995–96	61,135	1,207,520				
1996–97	61,135	1,267,895				
1997–98	61,135	1,331,290				
1998–99	61,135	1,397,855				
1999–00	61,135	1,467,748				

NOTE: There are no significant changes to this program. Also, it is not expected that the Community Center Renovation Project would have major impact on this program, with the exception of Special Events.

Table 8.1 *Continued*

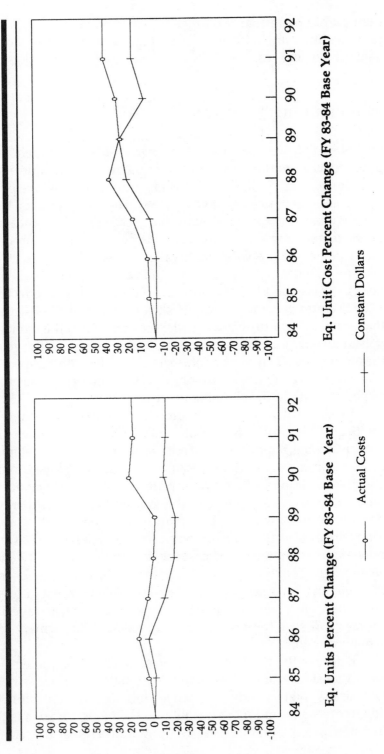

Eq. Units Percent Change (FY 83-84 Base Year)

Eq. Unit Cost Percent Change (FY 83-84 Base Year)

—o— Actual Costs   —+— Constant Dollars

example of a performance budget from the City of Sunnyvale that provides for a method of determining the accomplishment of goals and objectives.

The Planning Technique

Now that we have discussed types of plans and their purposes, it is important to outline the planning technique itself (McKinney et al. 1986). Most of the planning processes take place after goals and objectives have been set. The manager must then put the plans into action. Many times the planning process is directed at solving a given problem. During the planning process, the first step is to properly identify the problem: the solution then becomes the goal or objective. Organizations whose goals and objectives are too idealistic and broad are never very effective. They seem to be unable to establish the intermediate objectives that are necessary to achieve the larger ones. Or if the manager fails to directly identify and solve a problem related to the goals, the employees will never be able to accomplish anything specific. The more exact and precise the objectives, the more precisely they can be set forth in the planning process.

Likewise, if you can really pinpoint a problem or goal, you can begin to formulate a solution. Let's look at an example of in-service training. Suppose we had established the goal of developing a sound, in-service training program to make employees more effective in the implementation of programs. This goal was admirable but broad. To accomplish this goal and to plan further, we needed to break it down into more manageable parts and to establish an objective of a six-week first-aid course, a six-week preventative maintenance course for lawn mowers, and a twelve-week program-planning course for center directors. In so doing, the planning becomes more of a reality. We then begin to set deadlines. Next, we think in terms of personnel to teach specific courses and seek the necessary components to implement and achieve our goal.

Before setting attainable objectives or stating the problem, we had to consider many other things. We felt that there was a need for training. We concluded that our leaders needed more information, more skills, and more insight into their jobs, for such is the first step in the planning process. This was all based on the second step in the process referred to as forecasting. Our premise was that our leaders needed more training because past records showed that, often in the case of injuries and accidents, our leaders did not know what to do; in the case of mowing, larger numbers of breakdowns occurred in our lawn mower operation than were acceptable.

Our next step was to determine alternative courses of action. How could we best set up these training courses? Should we conduct them ourselves with our most skilled personnel, or bring in someone from the Red Cross or a maintenance equipment company? Or could we send our employees to school at the local junior college or try other alternatives?

Then we evaluated alternatives in the light of our premises and goals. We wanted the leaders to know first-aid methods; but it would be rather expensive to send them all to school. The fact that our own leaders might not be as equipped, capable, and competent to teach first aid indicated that bringing in someone from the Red Cross might be the best of the alternatives. In the case of the maintenance crew, a better solution seemed to be send them to the junior college because there were fewer of them. This brings us to our next step: the selection of a course of action. At this point, the plan is adopted and the decision is made. We are well on the way to attaining our goal of in-service training for employees. Quite obviously we will follow the progress of the program with interest. If we see the need for change or a way to improve the program, we will formulate derivative plans.

For the first-aid course, we should have our supervisory personnel do follow-up, on-the-job instruction. Likewise, we might set up an on-the-job follow-up for the maintenance crew. In both cases, we want to assure that what was learned in the courses is implemented.

The planning process as presented in this section has only been outlined briefly, but the essentials are there. The better you understand the planning procedure and expand and improve upon it, the more likely it is that the planning will result in accomplishing the agency's goals and objectives in a timely and efficient manner.

Some of the problems in planning result from lack of accuracy in premising and forecasting, as well as from a lack of flexibility. With so many changes occurring rapidly in the community, our plans are often outdated before they can be implemented. The changes in the political climate and in technology, combined with the lack of funds to carry out our plans, curtail the energy required to carry out proper plans. Even with such limitations and drawbacks, however, one cannot neglect planning as an important management function. It cannot be left to chance. It should take place at all levels of an organization. The planning should be organized and it should be well defined.

Long-range planning should be integrated with a short-range plan. Plans are generally more acceptable when people have been a part of the planning process and when the plans are well communicated up and down the chain of command.

Composing a Planning Document

Some general principles should be followed in composing a planning document that will be followed by an enterprise, agency, or organization. The following characteristics apply to long-range planning, budget, program development, and policy and procedural manuals. This list was adapted from Kelsey and Gray (1985).

1. The cover of the document should be done by a graphics professional and should include the title, the sponsor and art work or photos.

2. The binding selected should be determined by the length of the document. Either plastic spiral binding or velo-binding is appropriate for long-range documents. For shorter-range documents such as a policy and procedure manual, a ring binder is ideal for updating.

3. The copy should be prepared with a word processor and printed on good quality white paper, using black ink for the text and illustrations. Keep the original copy as clean as possible, and use margins of 3/8 inch at top and bottom, and an additional 1/2 inch on the left margin.

4. Charts, diagrams, and figures should be produced on a microcomputer if possible.

5. Appendix materials should include raw data as needed to clarify key points in the document.

6. Consider ways to increase the visibility of certain documents so that they will be used more often. For example, a lengthy policy manual may not be as useful as a sharp-looking, concise summary of policies.

Summary

This chapter has dealt with the importance of planning. The other four management functions—organizing, human resources, implementing, and monitoring and evaluating—are a result of planning and will be no better than the quality of planning itself. *Planning is basically the setting of goals—for the enterprise, organization, division, district, center, or park—and establishing a procedure to accomplish them.*

The planning process described in this chapter is primarily a management function. For the most part, the principles presented here are appropriate for any endeavor or any profession, but we have tried to present planning more specifically as it applies to leisure services.

We have arrived at many basic leisure service planning premises, keeping in mind the philosophical concepts presented in earlier chapters of this book. These premises are the outgrowth of broad goals set forth in the establishing authority, whether state enabling laws, city charters, authority boards of park and recreation, or other boards. These premises give us the basis to plan park and recreation programs. Each setting will be different and will have different needs and requirements. For example, in some settings people might have more free time, less meaningful work, more discretionary income; the population might be denser; there might be less open space. Following the basic premise, we can begin to forecast what needs to be done in terms of planning park and recreation services.

The recreation movement in the United States and Canada has reflected programs geared primarily toward the middle-class citizen. This bias will be overcome only when people in charge of planning recreation programs really understand these premises and incorporate basic leisure service principles in planning their programs.

References

Bannon, J. J. 1976. *Leisure resources: Its comprehensive planning.* Englewood Cliffs, NJ: Prentice-Hall.

Busser, J., and J. Bannon. 1987. Work activities performed by management personnel in public leisure source organizations. *Journal of Park and Recreation Administration* 5:1, pp.1-16.

Corbin, D. H., and E. Williams. 1987. *Recreation programming and leadership.* Englewood Cliffs, NJ: Prentice-Hall.

Edginton, C., D. M. Compton, and C. J. Hanson. 1980. *Recreation and leisure programming: A guide for the professional.* Philadelphia: Sanders College Publishing.

Farrell, P., and H. M. Lundegren. 1983. *The process of recreation programming: Theory and technique.* New York: John Wiley and Sons.

Getz. 1986. Management planning in public recreation agencies. *Journal of Park and Recreation Administration* 7:3. pp.17-31

Kelsey, C., and H. Gray. 1985. Master plan process for parks and recreation. Reston, VA: American Alliance for Heath, Physical Education, Recreation and Dance.

Koontz, H., and C. O'Donnell. 1980. *Principles of management,* 6th ed. New York: McGraw-Hill Book Company.

Kraus, R.G. 1985. *Recreation program planning today.* Glenview, IL: Scott, Foresman.

McKinney, W., C. Burger, R. Espeseth, and G. Dirkin. 1986. Long-range park and recreation planning—A case study. *Journal of Park and Recreation Administration,* 4:4, pp.23-24.

Naisbitt, J., and Aburdene, 1985. *Reinventing the corporation.* New York: Warner Books.

Russell, R. 1982. *Planning programs in recreation.* St. Louis: C. V. Mosby.

Swidley, S. 1985. Participative management employee satisfaction, and innovation in selected public park and recreation agencies. (unpublished doctoral dissertation, Indiana University). 147.

Tillman, A. 1973. *The program book for recreation professionals.* Palo Alto, CA: Mayfield Publishing Company.

Williams, J.G. 1972. Try PERT for meeting deadlines. *Park Maintenance* September, 1972, pp. 10-12.

9

ORGANIZING FOR EXCELLENCE

Perhaps the most sweeping changes being made in management have to do with the function of organizing. The organization of businesses, agencies, and governmental units has traditionally had a rigid, formal structure and an informal or "shadow" structure. In recent research concerning business organizational structure, it has been suggested that traditional organizations may not be the most effective in producing customer, client, or participant satisfaction. Through a leadership approach that allows a manager and key staff to serve as catalysts, the function of organizing is shifting from a task orientation to a system orientation.

This chapter explores both the traditional and the more current methods of organizing leisure services for excellence, and reflects the dynamic changes that affect society, the community, and the setting that delivers services.

What Is Organizing?

Organizing takes into account the formal and informal structure of an organization: the span of management authority, responsibility and accountability, line and staff relationships, centralization versus decentralization, and the synthesis of these factors to make organizations work. Typically a manager is involved with developing a system that allows the organization to carry out an ongoing work program. Each of the above factors requires a manager's attention when making decisions about the work to be arranged and delegated.

Further, organizing is a multifaceted process that involves more than grouping individuals into work units and developing a system to deliver leisure service. Organizing involves developing a team effort and gaining the support and cooperation of personnel, participants, and advisers in order to carry out the goals of the organization. The structure designed to accomplish the tasks (that is, the organization chart) is meaningless without a firm commitment on the part of employee and client to achieve the goals of excellence prescribed by an enterprise, agency, or organization. A manager's understanding of these relationships is key in developing a cohesive unit designed to accomplish goals and objectives. Unfortunately, too much emphasis on the formal organization structure has led some managers to believe that simply having the structure will guarantee results. This reliance on structure has tended to cause revolutionary changes that are a response to societal changes.

As noted by Naisbitt and Aburdene (1985) "The old bureaucratic layers are giving way to more natural arrangements of the new information society" (30-34). Structures that are changing the nature of the formal organization are, among others, small teams, lattices, matrices, and quality circles. These structures exist so that an organization can be responsive to the clients, participants, or consumers who use the service.

Organizational Structures

It is important for any leisure service delivery system to be structured in a manner that suits the unique characteristics of the employees, goals, and type of consumer. Several structures described here may be appropriate for a certain system.

Formal Organization

Whether it is acknowledged by an organizational chart or not, all agencies have a formal organization that is planned and recognized by the members of that organization. There is also an informal organization that is often unorganized and sometimes suppressed by those in a leadership position. But inevitably this has an impact on the total operation of the organization.

As Allen (1958) comments, "The formal organization is a system of well-defined jobs, each bearing a definite measure of authority, responsibility, and accountability, the whole consciously designed to enable the people of the enterprise to work most effectively together in accomplishing their objectives"(60-63). The formal organization is structured officially by management, and it is generally depicted on paper as an organizational chart. The theory is that *the formal organization defines the jobs of all of an agency's managers and component sections and designates authority and responsibility that delineate the work relationships between these individuals.*

The park and recreation organization usually provides for a director or chief executive who heads the organization and is totally responsible for its operation. The other individuals who report to the chief executive are also indicated in the authority relationships and are shown in their positions relative to the carrying out of organizational goals and objectives. These relationships are governed by policies, procedures, rules, and regulations.

The formal organization is activated by the goals and objectives of the organization, which may typically run in a top-down structure. All of these factors are integrated to make the organization function smoothly. When they do not work, it is most likely the result of poor organizational practice. Some of the greatest mistakes made by the formal organization grow out of restrictions in organizational policies that do not grant discretionary power to employees at front-line levels, do not provide them with an opportunity to use their talents, or do not recognize their individual preferences and capacities. However, for a manager to assume that a group of individuals can be brought together in a situation with no direction and little guidance indicates that the manager is unaware of the basic realities of human behavior.

A formal organization is guided by two basic principles. The first is *unity of objectives,* which provides that all individuals in the organization need to work towards the same goals and objectives (Koontz and O'Donnell 1980). To be most effective, these goals and objectives should be well formulated and accepted by all concerned. While not everyone will totally agree with them, it is important that major efforts be directed toward accomplishing them, particularly if the organization expects to achieve much success.

The second principle is *efficiency* (Koontz and O'Donnell 1980). Efficiency calls for very clear-cut lines of authority. Proper balance of responsibility and authority, adequate involvement in the planning and problem-solving processes, and security and status are important factors in the motivation of employees. In addition, the organization must be efficient in getting the most for its effort, spending its dollars and time well, eliminating waste, and encouraging economy. Efficiency will affect the overall organization in accomplishing its goals and objectives.

The concept of rigid, formal organization is changing drastically as corporations restructure for change (Peters 1987). Successful firms in the future may have flatter organizational charts, be populated by more autonomous units, use highly trained, more flexible people, and be more quality and service conscious (Peters 1987). The formal organization as described and modified by Peters may be most effective when combined with the basic mission or goals of the system, using effective, responsive techniques for handling the work plan.

In an era of unprecedented uncertainty, the organization of the 1990s may have the following characteristics:

- Flatter organizational structure
- Service consciousness
- Faster innovation
- More autonomous units
- Quality consciousness
- Oriented towards the creation of market niches (recognition of high differentiation among constituents)
- More response to customers and constituents

In order to achieve greater organizational flexibility, front line personnel need to be given more discretion in making decisions about services provided to participants. In effect, middle-level managers need to emphasize making things happen across functional boundaries. Middle managers in their reward and evaluation systems need to shift away from being rule interpreters who protect functional integrity in the traditional, vertical organization. They must seek to encourage and facilitate activity that allows multiple functions to occur faster by breaking down ("bashing") the functional barriers that they were formerly paid to

protect.   First-line supervisors and managers in this process
become members of self-management teams. Middle-level managers become coordinators, responsible for quality, cost , schedule, and people development. They are trained in (1) participative management, (2) as group facilitators, and (3) problem
solving (see Table 9.1).

Table 9.1 Changing the Nature of First-Level Management

Old Approach	New Approach
1. Narrow span of control	1. Wider span of control
2. Schedule of work	2. Coach and sounding board for self-management
3. Rule enforcer	3. Facilitator
4. Lots of planning	4. Lots of wandering
5. Focused down or up in the organization	5. Focused horizontally, working with others
6. Transmitting middle and top management needs "down"	6. Selling and promoting team ideas "up"
7. Providing new ideas for workers	7. Helping teams develop their own ideas: cross-function

The way leisure service organizations can achieve organizational flexibility is to:

1. *Simplify the structure*: reduce layers and train first-level
   managers to become members of self-management teams.
2. *Change the role of middle-level managers*: switch from the role
   of rule enforcer to bashers of barriers between functions in
   order to reduce autonomy and speed action-taking at the
   front line.

Informal Organization

*The informal organization consists of all groups, cliques, clubs, and
other groupings of employees sanctioned or unsanctioned by the organi-*

zation, that affect the organization to its advantage or disadvantage. In many cases, managers in the formal organization refuse to deal with the informal organization. By not recognizing its existence, managers may endanger the efforts of the agency, as well as detract from its mission. Informal groups are the result of people's basic need to belong and feel important, which the formal structure may not be meeting. These groups interact in numbers of two or three or more. Many times the informal leader is sympathetic to the problems of people within the structure. This sympathy can unite individuals in informal groups that may interfere with the effective functioning of the formal organization and possibly create pressure and conflict for the managers.

Informal groups generally evolve among individuals who work near each other and who have the same interests or common concerns. Such groups can have a great influence on standards and policies for their benefit. The informal organization can affect the success of an agency. By approaching it from an open, sincere standpoint, a manager can analyze their need to organize and can help to integrate their interests and needs into the operation. The informal organization tends to be more prevalent in larger organizations in which a sense of belonging is minimized by the massiveness of the organization. Often, organizations run in an overly bureaucratic manner tend to foster informal organizations that are detrimental to the formal organization.

In many park and recreation delivery systems, center directors or park workers who have common concerns and problems band together to make their desires known. These individuals initiate informal groups during coffee breaks or in bowling leagues where they come together socially. An informal leader often emerges and begins soliciting support among other groups, and eventually they evolve a "formal-informal" organization. In many larger organizations these informal groups are ripe for labor unions or other bargaining agents to pick up their cause. Managers of park and recreation agencies are now realizing they need to be aware of informal organizations as actively functioning parts of the organization. Using this structure for input and support may help achieve the organization's larger goals.

The detrimental effects of the informal organization can be offset by following sound organizational practices. One of these practices is assigning meaningful work that incorporates the task concept (providing an individual with an opportunity to perform a task from start to finish), as opposed to the more common division-of-labor approach (dividing work into separate parts where the employee does not see the whole task or process and, as a result, does not get a feeling of accomplishment). The need for informal organization can also be minimized by creating smaller maintenance teams within a given recreation district, instead of having a centralized maintenance component that services the entire department. Another approach is to place employees as close as possible to where they can see the end result so that they will have a sense of accomplishment and worth. Establishing general guidelines and policies and leaving as much control, decision making, and authority as possible to the lower-level supervisors allow employees to set their own pace and realize their own accomplishments.

The formal and informal organizations can work together and need not be in conflict with each other. Although the organizational chart may show which individuals are supposedly in positions of authority, the real power may be held by someone at a much lower level.

Inverted Pyramid

More recent management literature describes the concept of inverting the organizational structure pyramid and sees the organization from the point of view of customers as bosses (Peters 1987). In this type of structure, input begins with participants as they interact with line staff. Their needs are interpreted and responded to through the organization's manager to the board or authority. This type of structure, alluded to in the Sandestin Resort example (Overview, Part III), represents the concept of an organization with a participant-first orientation.

The Sandestin organizational structure (refer to Part III Overview, Figure 1) represents how an inverted pyramid reflects the customer orientation. This structure has several organizational characteristics that distinguish it from the typical formal organization. Some of these characteristics (Peters and Austin 1985) are shown below and can be related to any leisure service delivery system:

1. Customer support people are "showered with attention."
2. Promises to customers are kept.

3. The customer's perception is what is viewed as most important.
4. "Overkill" complaint procedures are used.

In the inverted pyramid, the manager's activities are focused primarily on supporting participant-consumer needs through the personnel directly involved with them.

Small Team Structure

Another alternative to the formal, bureaucratic structure is the small team. In a small team system, groups are organized according to talent and to tasks that might be accomplished. The teams are then encouraged to be innovative in solving the particular work tasks. Small teams may be generated out of any structure. They may focus on problem solving, long-range projects, or short-term events.

Lattice
In the lattice system, all employees are called associates who interact directly through a "crosshatching of horizontal and vertical lines." Essentially, this structure brings the informal structure out of the closet because no one holds any formal authority.

Matrix
Very similar to the lattice, the matrix approach is an effective organization for leisure service delivery. In this structure, roles and responsibilities shift with work assignments. For example, if there is a special arts event and an employee is assigned responsibility for it, she may assign duties to other staff members. When another event takes place, she may not have any authority. Those in the matrix usually have certain basic tasks, but their level of involvement and responsibility may vary by work assignment.

Quality Circles
This concept of Japanese management has found its way into American management. In this system, people who are actually doing the job are involved in the decision-making process. By gathering the best input from those who are producing and delivering leisure service, problems may be solved more effectively.

Through a variety of mechanisms such as these, the manager can ensure that the goals of the organization will be achieved. As Peters and Austin (1985) suggest, people will automatically work toward excellence when they understand and mutually agree with the goals of the company for which they work.

In this section we have dealt with traditional and nontraditional organizational structures. Whatever the organizational strategy, it is imperative for managers to have an organization that can adapt to change and respond to the participant-consumer who uses the service.

Characteristics of Organizational Structures

Managers of organizations typically give attention to questions of departmentalization and supervision, including "span of control." We will use the example of a local, public recreation and park agency to illustrate these matters. For other less traditional organizations, these principles and considerations must be adapted to meet the unique characteristics of each form.

Departmentalization

As any organization grows, ultimately it will need to be divided into more workable units. This happens when the span of management (or span of control) is increased to the point that managers can no longer efficiently supervise all of the individuals who report to them. The work load must then be divided into smaller or similar functional units and managers placed in charge of each unit in accordance with their ability to supervise (McFarland 1958).

Departmentalization in a park and recreation agency is generally done by geographical area. The city or county is divided when the recreation or park superintendent is no longer able to supervise all of the recreation centers and parks in that area. At this point, district supervisors become responsible for a district within the geographical boundaries of the city. The other method of departmentalization is according to activity or function within a recreation and parks department.

In addition to the agency being divided into geographical areas, it may also be necessary to divide responsibilities according to activities such as swimming, sports, dramatics, and music and to provide a manager for each. Many park and recreation delivery systems are structured into the parks division, the recreation division, the construction division, the special facilities division, and others.

To determine how responsibilities should be divided, the manager of a modern park and recreation delivery system needs to consider many specific items when organizing or reorganizing a department. Some of these considerations are the strengths and weaknesses of the managers, the geographical size to be managed, the number of different types of functions that the department has, and the availability of funds. There are advantages and disadvantages in any type of organization. Two different organization types will be presented to provide an idea of the various structures of contemporary leisure service agencies.

Table 9.2 shows a typical large park and recreation delivery system that is organized by *function* at the departmental level with a parks division, a construction division, a recreation division, and a special facilities division. The parks and recreation divisions are then organized by *geographical* area, while the construction and special facilities are organized on a *functional* basis. The advantage of this type of organization is that a higher degree of specialty is possible when all park functions are under the direction of the park superintendent and all recreation activities under the direction of the recreation superintendent. This type of organization also assures a great deal of consistency throughout the department in policy and program matters.

The functional type of structuring has many disadvantages, however. For example, as Table 9.2 indicates, no one individual is in charge of Central Park. Each of the park, recreation, and special facilities divisions has approximately one-third of the responsibility for the park and its activities. Unless the three lower-level managers can mutually agree on actions or decisions, they are forced upward in the organization to the district supervisors, who must themselves agree when making decisions. The same is true of the superintendents of the divisions. Only at the level of director does a single manager have the authority to make a decision affecting all parties concerned. Common in park and recreation agencies, this type of organization is generally very cumbersome and moves extremely slowly. It also creates a great deal of friction between division and staff and requires many meetings, during

Table 9.2 Functional Departmental Organization with Divisional, Geographical, and Functional Organization

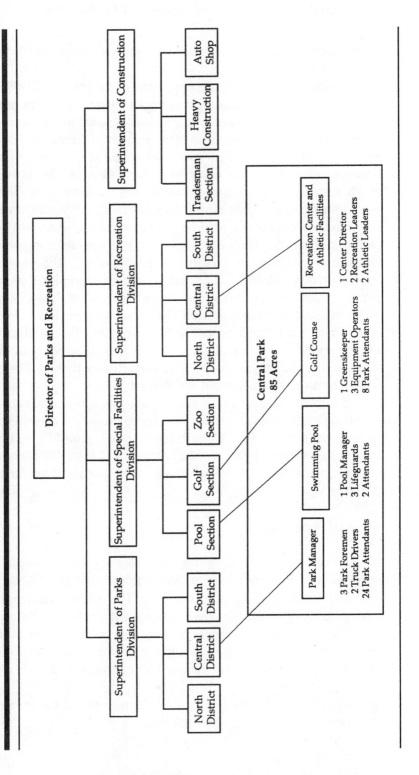

which decisions are worked out by mutual agreement rather than by managers alone.

A geographically organized department is presented in Table 9.3. The advantage of this type of organization is that there is a much clearer line of authority as it relates to decisions at a particular facility. All of the operational functions of Central Park are under one manager. Decisions can be made at the lowest level, closest to where the actual work takes place. They can also be made much faster and with fewer meetings. This form of structure obviously requires a much more versatile manager at each level of the organization, a manager who has technical knowledge of both park and recreation activities. However, this method of organization adheres to more effective management practices than does the functional method. The disadvantages of the geographical organization are that it does not allow for as much specialization, and there is less consistency within the whole department. On the other hand, there will probably be more flexibility within the organization. The construction division, which appears in both forms of organizations, is a service department that will be discussed in more detail later in the chapter.

In summary, departmentalization is designed to divide the organization into smaller units in order to provide more effective managerial supervision. Departmentalization should not, however, be confused with decentralization or the establishment of service departments. These two areas will be discussed later in this chapter.

Span of Control

As an organization grows, the employees are typically grouped into more manageable units. Managers are assigned to lead and direct these units accordingly. The original principle of span of control or span of management (McFarland 1958) dealt with the total number of persons that one manager can supervise—generally four to eight people at the upper levels of management. At the lower levels, a manager can supervise from eight to fifteen. More recent literature suggests flattening the organizational structure, decreasing the number of supervisors, and increasing authority (Peters 1987).

Table 9.3 Geographical Departmental Organization with Divisional Geographical Organization

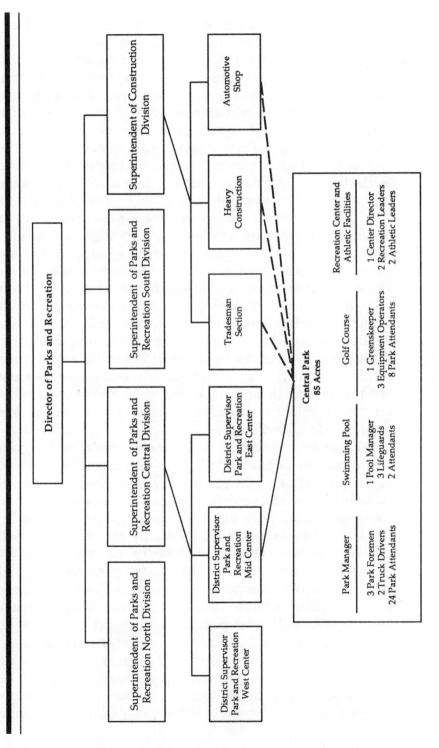

Although the growth of an organization is inevitable, it complicates effective functioning in many ways. The more levels the organization has, the more expensive it becomes to operate and the more managers it must employ. Organizations have had little choice except to add levels and managers, because without proper management, ineffectiveness begins to permeate the organization, resulting in increased costs. One way to decrease the layers of an organization is to decentralize authority.

In addition to increasing the costs of operation, additional levels slow down and complicate communications when there are four instead of three people deliberating about plans. For example, a director of parks and recreation is discussing with the superintendent of recreation the desirability of having recreation leaders wear a specific type of uniform. The superintendent of recreation in turn discusses uniforms with his district supervisors and asks them to investigate the possibility with center directors. At this point, one district supervisor misinterprets the intent of the inquiries from the director of parks and recreation and conveys the idea that leaders will wear uniforms whether they like it or not. When the communication is then passed from the center director in that district to the recreation leaders, it is stated that they have to be in uniform by next week. The intent and meaning of the director of parks and recreation were lost in the communication among the four levels.

When an organization has too many levels, planning and control are complicated as plans are apportioned between the recreation and parks divisions and passed down through the ranks to the lowest level of employees. An effective and responsive organization is structured as simply as possible, with only a few levels. And, as mentioned previously, the managers should direct only as many subordinates as they can supervise effectively.

A factor to be considered in managing employees is their geographical distribution. It is much easier for a manager to supervise people who are all housed in offices within the same building. Obviously this permits the manager to see his/her subordinates regularly, either on a formal or an informal basis.

The complexity of the work assignments of subordinates also affects span of control. Quite obviously the director of parks and recreation or the superintendents of the various divisions supervise individuals who have very complex jobs, so their span of control is limited. However, district supervisors of parks or recreation direct the less complex work of subordinates. Thus a park manager finds it much easier to supervise eight or ten people all doing routine maintenance work.

Another related factor that affects span of control is the amount of coordination necessary. If a great amount of coordination is required, the manager's span of control increases. At the upper level of park and recreation management, there is a great need to coordinate the efforts of the parks, the recreation, and the administrative divisions. At lower levels, except for special events, coordination is limited at the level of the park manager or center director.

Several factors determine how often and how much time the manager must spend supervising subordinates (Koontz and O'Donnell 1980). These include the amount of training that each person has had. Depending upon tasks, individuals with more education and training require less time and fewer contacts. The amount of authority that can be delegated also affects the amount of supervision that subordinates need. The more independently they can work, the less supervision is required. The amount of planning and the number of policy procedures the organization uses may also affect the frequency of supervision, as well as the amount of time necessary to keep up with the latest trends in programming and new facility designs.

The use of objective standards, such as how often the grass needs to be cut and paper picked up, helps to cut down on the need for supervision. In the previous chapter, quantifiable objectives were said to make management more effective, particularly from the standpoint of evaluation. Accurate and precise communication techniques and the amount of personal contact that supervisors have with their subordinates affect the manager's job, and thus the span of control. Each of the factors mentioned and their variations affect how frequently and to what degree the supervisors must oversee their employees.

In any organization, all of these factors must be taken into account in giving each manager a span of control that is reasonable and will assure an adequate job. It is wise to limit the inexperienced or new employee to a narrow span of control. As she proves her capability, the span of control can be increased to a point where she can effectively do a good job.

Management Techniques for Organizing

Elements of Delegation

As Allen (1958) states, "Delegation is the entrustment of responsibility and authority to another and the creation of accountability for performance"(117). The success of an organization depends to a great extent on the manager's ability to delegate authority. The managers who must deal with the principles of organization find that their ability to do so is based on their authority. This authority is paramount and is a key aspect of a manager's job, for it must be used to carry out work through the people who make up the organization. A higher-level manager can use authority to force middle or front-line managers to comply, or the manager can persuade them to carry out their tasks in the hope of attaining economic or social gain. Either way, authority is essential. It is extremely important that the leisure service manager understand what authority is, as well as its relationship to responsibility and accountability.

Responsibility is probably one of the most misunderstood terms of management. *Responsibility is the obligation that the manager has to successfully carry out the task assigned.* Authority, on the other hand, is the power or ability given the manager to carry out the task. *Authority can be defined as the power to act officially, the sanction to command others, to make commitments, to expend funds, to utilize equipment, and so forth.* In any case, the manager has the authority to perform a task. Because of his limited ability, whether it is of a technical, temporal, skill-related, or informational nature, particularly at the upper level and middle level of management, it is impossible for one person to do all of the tasks necessary.

The director of a leisure service agency cannot single-handedly run all of the recreation centers, swimming pools, and parks, make the day-to-day decisions so that they can function properly, answer all of the correspondence, or deal with all of the public. Therefore, the director must rely on others to help with an assignment. This is accomplished by first employing subordinates, grouping them according to the organizational principles previously discussed, and then delegating to them the authority to carry out their assigned tasks. Total effectiveness will depend upon how well the director can delegate authority.

Although managers can delegate authority, *they can never delegate responsibility* (Koontz and O' Donnell 1980). Responsibility can be shared. The director of parks and recreation has the total responsibility for everything that occurs within a department. He/she can delegate various tasks to middle or front-line personnel, but he/she is always responsible for their actions. If a subordinate fails or does not perform properly, the manager is still responsible, and will be held accountable. Through the total organizational hierarchy, responsibility is shared, but never delegated. Authority, on the other hand, may come from the top down. Concentrated near the top, it can be delegated in hierarchical organizational structures. In organizations represented by matrices, quality circles, and more free-form structures, authority is more widely distributed at all levels.

Another term often mentioned along with authority and responsibility is accountability. *Accountability is defined as an obligation to report back to one's superior on the carrying out of a given task.* This topic will be covered in the chapter concerned with controlling the leisure service delivery system.

Delegation is a basic and fundamental part of organizing. It is necessary for the delegating authority to accomplish the assigned task, activity, or assignment. The director of parks and recreation employs a superintendent of parks, and very carefully defines the job, outlines goals and objectives and then delegates to the superintendent of parks the authority to carry out the operation of the department. Thus the superintendent is empowered to hire personnel within the framework of the budget, to requisition the necessary supplies and equipment, and to do all else needed to run a division. The superintendent is also held accountable for accomplishing tasks designated by the budget, goals, and objectives.

Similarly, because of the magnitude of the job, the superintendent of parks must divide work into various components and assign them to sections within the division. Other staff members in turn assign tasks, delegate authority, and hold other people responsible. The process continues throughout the organization at each level down to the individual who cuts the grass, lines the ball field, or cleans the restrooms. All of this is made possible because individuals were delegated the authority to carry out their assigned tasks and were held accountable for their performance. In more free-form organizational structures, there are fewer levels or layers. All personnel assume a number of tasks and are expected to respond to varied functions with commensurate authority.

The art of delegation is not simple. Probably as managers move up in the organization, more prove to be ineffective because of their inability to delegate authority. They try to do too much themselves. As a result, subordinates are incapable of making decisions and are thus ineffective. In the delegation of tasks and the corollary authority to perform them, the assignment of duties must be very clear-cut.

The delegation of authority can be either very specific or general. The more specific the delegation, the less imaginative and creative the individual can be in carrying out tasks. This usually occurs at the lower levels of management. At the top level, assignments are relatively general and permit more creativity because people have more experience, education, and training. Quite obviously the delegation of tasks by the superintendent of recreation will be more general and the authority much broader than that of the center director, whose assignments will be more specific and will involve much less authority. Delegation of authority can be made in written form or handled orally. There are advantages and disadvantages of each. These will be discussed in much greater detail in Chapter 11, which is concerned with implementing or directing.

In the functionally organized parks and recreation department, there is necessarily a split of authority in carrying out the overall assignments of the department. In a given case, the recreation division is responsible for programming the softball field, including organizing the teams, providing the equipment and officials, and making sure the teams follow up and play the game. The park division, on the other hand, is responsible for maintaining the files, making sure the lights work, ascertaining that the field is mowed, lined, and watered and seeing that the backstop and other facilities are in good repair. Neither the superintendent of parks nor the superintendent of recreation has the authority or responsibility to attend to all of the factors that will assure a successful softball program.

This arrangement can work if the two superintendents pool their authority and coordinate their activities to assure a smooth operation. Or they can rely on a higher authority when mutual agreement cannot be reached. Another solution would be for the reorganization to permit the recreation division to have the necessary human resources and authority to carry out the total operation of conducting a softball program. This could be accomplished by assigning a maintenance worker to the recreation division to perform the necessary work solely within the recreation division. In many cases, this is the best solution.

When it becomes necessary to constantly pool authority among several managers, some reorganization is obviously necessary. The amount of authority delegated to subordinates should be equal to the task assigned. In other instances, the recovery of delegated authority is necessary.

In smaller agencies, authority is usually centralized to a great extent and retained by the director of a department of parks and recreation. If a growing organization is going to remain effective and efficient, the director needs to decentralize her authority to the various divisions. Decentralization usually occurs as departmentalization takes place. Any organization that continues to centralize its authority is bound to be very slow in arriving at decisions and keeping pace with changing times. As the divisions and sections are formed, the authority for them must be delegated if they are to function properly. *Increased concern for citizens and clients and their desire for more local governmental and business involvement have made this procedure fundamental to effective program delivery.*

Another factor that offsets delegation is the attitude of the manager toward delegation. Obviously, willingness to delegate is dependent upon several factors. Many managers, as they are promoted, are unwilling to let go of their power. For example, the district supervisor who is promoted to superintendent of parks might continue to make the decisions for his replacement regarding the jobs of subordinates. Unwillingness to delegate authority to his replacement can cause many problems. The new district supervisor may become nothing more than a message carrier between the subordinates and the superintendent. As a result, too much time is taken to make minor decisions that could and should be delegated to the new supervisor. Some managers are unwilling to delegate authority for fear that subordinates will make mistakes. No manager should sit by and allow extremely detrimental mistakes to occur repeatedly. However, managers who make too much fuss over mistakes, particularly when they are minor, have their subordinates fearful of making decisions. Managers should not dwell on one or two mistakes, but should acknowledge instead the many good decisions.

A closely related point that affects the delegation of authority is the amount of trust the manager has in her subordinates. The more trust she has, the greater will be her desire to delegate. The astute leisure service manager works at overcoming her weakness in delegation. This is done by defining assignments and delegating authority in accordance with the results she wants and expects. She very carefully selects the right person for the job, maintains good communications, establishes quantifiable and proper controls, and rewards her subordinates when they carry out their tasks in accordance with their delegating authority.

It is important to make sure that the *unity of command* (which means that an employee has only one boss) is followed in delegating authority and that subordinates are held responsible for their work. People who are responsible to more than one manager will find themselves frustrated. Those who have two conflicting assignments will be unable to complete either of them. Unity of command is therefore essential in the delegation of authority.

Whatever the task to be performed, the good manager delegates authority in accordance with it, never more than is necessary. Using the skills of leadership, the manager makes sure the subordinate is responsible for performing the task successfully. Some managers force compliance, others persuade or suggest; but whatever the means, they should use their authority effectively. In most modern organizations, however, the use of coercion is not recommended or even tolerated. The concerns of leadership and leadership techniques will be discussed in greater detail in Chapter 11, which deals with directing the leisure service delivery system.

Line and Staff Relationships

Earlier in the chapter, we discussed the organizational concepts of authority, responsibility, and accountability. These concepts tie the organization together, from the director of the department down to the lowest member of the organization. According to Koontz and O'Donnell (1980), "Authority relationships, whether perpendicular or horizontal, are the factors that make organizations possible, harness departmental activities, insuring coordination to an enterprise"(395). In organizations there are two types of authority: the *line authority* and the *staff authority*. The relationships between line and staff are important and have to be reckoned with. Probably more confusion results from misunderstandings between the two groups than from any other factors in management. Managers must therefore understand the difference between the line and the staff functions.

Line functions and line personnel are directly responsible for accomplishing the objectives and goals of the organization. The staff function refers to those parts of the organization that help the line staff to work more efficiently and effectively in carrying out the primary objectives and goals of the organization. In an authority relationship, the line personnel have the power to provide the service in a leisure service organization. The director, the superintendents of the various divisions, the recreation and park district supervisors, the center director and park manager are all line personnel. They are directly responsible for carrying out the goals and objectives of the organization. Staff personnel consist of the training officer, department safety officer, and various administrative assistants who aid the line operation officers in carrying out their service, but they have no direct authority over other personnel in the organization. They carry out staff assignments that assist the line managers. The authority to manage must rest exclusively with the line officers and their relationship with their subordinates. Failure to understand this distinction can cause much friction and disorganization.

As leisure agencies grow in size and as the line managers become involved in day-to-day operations in carrying out their functions, they must have assistance to take care of detailed work. Therefore, staff personnel are assigned to assist them. Staff personnel are very often highly trained and skilled in given areas. They are hired for their skill and knowledge to help the line personnel function better and more efficiently. As a result of their special skills, they are given exclusive time to devote their efforts and energies in their given area. After they formulate their ideas and prepare their plans for implementation, they present them to the line officers for approval.

Staff personnel who try to convince line officers of the worth of their ideas are more apt to have their efforts rewarded than are those who try to impose their ideas upon line officers. An example might be that of the safety officer who convinces the line officer of the value of having a maintenance worker wear goggles as a protection from blinding sparks. If an employee is incapacitated for a while as a result of an accident, work will slow down. The line officer will recognize that when personnel are laid off, the job will not be done.

Although the need for staff in any large organization has been pointed out, it should also be mentioned that there are certain dangers involved in using staff functions. The first of these is the danger of undermining the line authority. Unity of command is a very important principle: generally one employee should have one supervisor giving directions. With the introduction of the staff functions, the specialist, because of knowledge in a given area, begins to give additional directions and orders that interject a new authority into the organization. If the staff function is not handled carefully, the organization may end up with two individuals directing the same employee, thus causing confusion and creating problems in productivity. As a rule, all direct orders should come from the line supervisor in the organization. The exception to this would be in the case of functional authority, which will be discussed later in this chapter.

If staff personnel cannot convince line personnel of the value of their suggestions or recommendations, the only alternative is to go back to a superior who is a line officer. This line officer can pass the idea down through the chain of command, giving the direct order to the line personnel. This situation might arise if the staff were to recommend that a specific dramatics class be implemented in a given recreation center. If the recommendation is not accepted, the staff person might recommend to his superior the need for a dramatics program at this center in order to have a balanced program. If the superior accepts the staff recommendation, she will in turn pass it down through the line side of the organization, insisting that the center director implement some form of dramatics program. The center director will probably do so only halfheartedly, however, insofar as it came as a direct order. But if the staff person "sells" the center director on the value of the idea, it probably will be implemented wholeheartedly.

Another limitation of the staff function is that although staff personnel are highly trained in their given area, they very often think in a vacuum. They tend not to realize all of the problems involved in the implementation of a program. It is therefore very important that they be made to understand the total problem—all of the factors affecting the operation of a program. That way, they will know how, when, and where to implement programs— where they will work and where they will not work. A good procedure is for the staff personnel to work closely with the line personnel, to involve them in the planning of programs, and to inquire extensively about the operation so that they make recommendations only after being well oriented. Working fairly closely with the line personnel, their suggestions would probably be accepted more readily.

It is important that line personnel keep staff well informed about what is going on in the operation. Staff members are there to assist in line operations. If they are not knowledgeable about what is occurring in the organization, they will not be in a good position to recommend procedures in their specialty. Whenever staff personnel are used, it is their responsibility to develop and maintain a favorable working climate and to foster favorable personnel relationships. This can best be done if staff members take the approach that it is their job to enable the line manager to do an effective job. They should never attempt to assume credit for ideas or to discredit line officers, for obviously this will develop an unfavorable relationship between staff and line personnel. Again, it cannot be stressed too strongly that staff people should convince the line officers of the value of their recommendations rather than try to impose them upon the officers.

Functional Authority

An important factor in organizations, functional authority is given to an individual, generally a staff officer, to take specific action pertaining to matters in which he is the expert. With this functional authority, he assumes authority over the line organization with respect to procedures, purchasing, or public relations. Because of this specialized knowledge and the need for a certain amount of conformity or consistency within the organization, he is given functional authority to exercise influence over the line operation.

Decentralization

According to Allen (1958), "Decentralization refers to the systematic effort to delegate to the lowest level all authority except that which can only be exercised at central points"(163). As the organization grows, it becomes obvious that one manager cannot make all of the decisions. When this happens, the manager must delegate authority to lower-level managers to carry out the goals and objectives of the organization. As the leisure service agency grows to the point that the director can no longer manage the entire department, she must hire a separate superintendent of parks and a superintendent of recreation. In so doing, she is implementing the departmentalization principle.

As a result of this action, it also becomes necessary to form certain service departments. In their formation, delegation of a certain authority to these service sections is needed for them to carry out their work. Several factors should be kept in mind when considering the possibilities of decentralizing authority (Voich and Wren 1968). The first of these is the costliness of the decision. Generally the decisions involving cost are the most important and are made by the manager of the organization, whereas lesser decisions can be passed down or delegated to lower-level and middle-level managers. Another factor that must be considered when decisions are to be delegated is how much they cut across or affect the various divisions under a particular manager. In other words, if a decision will affect both the parks and the recreation division, logically the director should make the decision. However, decisions that affect only one or the other of the operating divisions should be delegated down to the appropriate level.

Another factor to be considered in decentralizing authority is the need for uniformity of policy and procedures. If consistency is desirable among the various operating divisions, then the management at the highest level should retain such decisions or authority. If a division or section must do a great deal of independent decision making to operate, it becomes necessary to decentralize and to delegate authority to it. Failure to delegate or decentralize in this case will stymie that particular operation so that it cannot operate effectively. The manager at a lower level will have to refer constantly to a higher-level manager for decisions. Such efforts would tend to slow down the effectiveness and efficiency of that particular operating section. The greater the decentralization of authority, the more independent a particular section is likely to be.

Very closely associated with the ability of the top-level manager to decentralize and delegate authority is the availability of competent managers. Quite obviously, if lower-level sections or divisions do not have competent managers, the top-level manager will need to make certain decisions and to centralize her authority.

The more competent the manager at any level of the organization, the greater the likelihood that she will decentralize authority.

Associated with the ability to decentralize authority are the control techniques that the manager has at his disposal to evaluate the competency of decisions being made by the lower-level managers. If effective control techniques and evaluation procedures are available to the manager, he can judge whether the lower-level managers are making appropriate decisions; he can determine to what extent he can decentralize his authority. Decentralization has worked well where there have been highly qualified managers. It goes almost without saying that the principle of decentralization is the same as the principle of delegation of authority. When a manager decentralizes, he inevitably loses certain controls. The key to the effectiveness of decentralization is to maintain a proper balance between the force of centralization and decentralization. However, it is becoming increasingly important to bring decision making closer to the participants in order to make leisure service more visible to the people and a vital part of community life.

Boards and Committees

Most local government organizations use advisory or policy-making boards and committees in one form or another. *A committee is nothing more than two or more individuals gathered together for the purpose of effecting group action.* There is no question that the committee is a definite part of an organization. Committees are formed for many different reasons and for various uses. In the leisure service field, the committee sometimes is formed as the governing board. This board has certain authority, usually established by enabling legislation. This authority may call for determining policy, planning, control, or evaluation. The board may hire or need to interact with a chief executive. This person in turn organizes the department, hires the necessary personnel and provides the leadership necessary to implement the policies and recommendations established by the board. Within the staff organization, the chief executive very often uses committees.

Whether the committee is at the level of the board of directors or at the staff level, its primary reason for existence falls into several categories (Koontz and O'Donnell 1980). Group deliberation and judgment are functions of a committee, in keeping with the old adage that two heads are better than one. The committee can jointly ponder a problem or a situation, provide for alternative approaches, and then make decisions. In other instances the committee is asked only to come up with certain recommendations, which are passed up to the executive who appointed the committee. She then makes a decision on the basis of the recommended alternatives.

Often managers rely on a committee to make a decision when they are afraid to take responsibility for it because it may prove unpopular. Although this is an inappropriate reason for using a committee, poor managers often fall back on this tactic. The fear of authority, in terms of placing decision-making power in the hands of a committee, is also an excuse for a manager to divide up authority among several individuals, rather than delegating too much authority to one individual. It provides the manager the final say in many decisions, but it gives subordinates the feeling that they have a certain amount of power in their role on the committee.

The committee also gives various interest groups an opportunity to become involved in the process of making important decisions. Very often in a large organization where several lower-level managers have differences of opinion about a solution to a particular problem, the higher-level manager may delegate authority to a representative committee to find a compromise and to work out a solution. Although this method can sometimes be effective, it is generally the sign of a weak manager. However, the committee can become a tool for dissemination of information and communication.

The committee also becomes a tool for the consolidation of authority. When a decision cannot be resolved by a single manager who does not have enough authority in his work area, it will be referred to a committee for action. As a result, two managers who have to make a decision together can pool their authority and arrive at a solution. Pooling authority is often done when a decision is not significant enough to push it up the chain of command to the director of the organization.

There are many disadvantages in using a committee (Koontz and O'Donnell 1980). Quite obviously several people must come together for group action, which is costly in terms of the number of people involved. All of them are paid while serving on the committee, so the manager should be sure that the committee's purpose is worth the money and resources invested in the committee. Another disadvantage is that very often committees make compromises to the point where the original intent of the decision is lost or severely watered down.

Procedures for Completing Work Assignments

Up to this point, this chapter has covered delegation and decentralization, the relationship between line and staff personnel, responsibility, and accountability. In order to integrate these into a workable management configuration, they will be summarized to explain the process of completing work assignments.

The work must first be defined. This is done in accordance with the plans and goals that the manager has determined in the first step of the management process. If the job is too big to do alone, the manager then delegates certain portions of the work to middle or front-line managers. In bureaucratic organizations, the manager delegates only enough authority for the lower-level manager to carry out that specific section of work. In horizontally structured organizations, each manager has a wider scope of authority to respond to diverse and ever-changing needs or wants of customers or clients.

In addition to delegating authority and work to be performed, the manager must create a sense of responsibility in the employees to get the job done. The manager acts according to the predetermined goals and objectives established in the planning process. Certain timetables, criteria, and other standards are set for accomplishing the work. Accountability is also required so that the manager at the lower level will periodically report back on how the work is proceeding, whether any problems are encountered, and whether deadlines for completing the work can be met. Once the work is done and has been accounted for, the final step is for the manager to measure the results against the predetermined goals and objectives that set the work in motion. At this point, the work process has been completed.

Summary

Many different types of organizational structures are available to today's managers. These range from the traditional hierarchical structure, through more innovative schemes (such as small teams and quality circles) to the inverted "customer as boss" plan.

In most of these different possibilities, questions about certain more or less common elements arise. In looking at organizational structures in terms of departmentalization, line and staff relationships, the service department, and centralization versus decentralization, we have to consider many factors in determining when each of these techniques should be employed. There is a great deal of confusion, misunderstanding and incorrect interchange of each of these four terms. *Departmentalization is the process of dividing an organization into smaller units* when the span of management gets too large for one manager to supervise effectively. In leisure service agencies this is generally handled according to the operating divisions of parks and recreation.

Within the operating divisions there is further division or departmentalization, usually according to geographical areas based on districts. *The service department is created when there is a need for grouping activities for efficiency, effectiveness, or more uniformity of operations throughout the agency.* The service department then services the rest of the operating divisions.

Decentralization can take place in either the service department or in an operating division of the organization by departmentalization. *The purpose of decentralization of sections or decentralization of authority is to delegate work to lower-level managers within the organization.* It becomes evident and logical that no one manager can perform all the work necessary in an organization. The only way to do so is to delegate the work or decentralize it into smaller, lower-level divisions.

Staff and line relationships take place throughout the organization and are not peculiar to any specific section. *Line function or line personnel have direct responsibility for accomplishing the objectives of the enterprise. Staff functions or staff personnel are there to help the line to work more effectively in accomplishing the primary objectives of the enterprise.* For an agency to function effectively, the manager should integrate each of these organizational concepts into the organization through an interactive leadership technique. The more the organization looks to reduce layers of management, the more likely it will be able to facilitate more immediate response to participant/client needs and become more service oriented. As first- and second-level managers become more adept at recognizing the interrelationships of all elements of service delivery and are empowered to work across functions, the greater the likelihood that people's needs will be met.

References

Allen, Louis A. 1958. *Management and organization.* New York: McGraw-Hill.

Koontz, H. and C. O'Donnell. 1980. *Management,* 6th ed. New York: McGraw-Hill.

McFarland, Dalton E. 1958. *Management principles and practices,* 1st ed. New York: MacMillan.

Naisbitt, J. and P. Aburdene. 1985. *Reinventing the corporation.* New York: Warner Books.

Peters, T. 1987. *Thriving on chaos.* New York: Harper & Row.

Peters, T., and N. Austin. 1985. *A passion for excellence.* New York: Warner Books.

Voich, D. Jr., and D.A. Wren. 1968. *Principles of management.* New York: The Ronald Press.

10

MANAGING HUMAN RESOURCES

While the needs of the client or participant are a chief focus in planning, organizing, and delivering services, this approach is effective only if employees are valued in this effort.

The Value of Employees

Naisbitt and Aburdene (1985) point to a trend in business: the move from concern with financial capital to human capital. Inherent in this shift is a basic belief in the value of both employees and customers as it relates to business success and product satisfaction.

Naturally, some bottom-line facts are causing this trend in the labor movement. One has to do with predicted labor shortages. The result may be seen in the elimination of forced retirement, better job mobility for those at lower levels of employment, and improved equal opportunity programs (Naisbitt and Aburdene 1985).

In addition to changes in the structure of industry and government, employees need to overcome a feeling of powerlessness caused by a bureaucratic system (Block 1987). The technique known as empowerment is a way of creating an enjoyable employment experience regardless of organizational layers. Managers are recognizing the value of having employees more willing to think for themselves rather than being burdened by a system over which they feel they have no control.

Empowerment involves using "greatness, courage, and autonomy to prevent maintenance, caution and dependency" (Block

317

1987, 11). Managers can encourage this development by taking time in meetings to deal with issues of morale and motivation and to learn about employees' needs.

A third factor in the trend toward valuing employees is the inverted pyramid concept explained in Chapter 9. If the goal is to recognize the value of front-line employees in serving leisure needs, then their value to the organization is obvious. If there are major impediments to their success in providing quality leisure experiences for clients, then the goals of the enterprise or organization are not met.

In this section the process of managing valuable personnel is covered. Each of the techniques is centered around the basic belief that first-rate managers hire first-rate employees.

Need for Managers

In the field of leisure service, as in any other professional field, the quality of managers and other personnel affects the quality of service or product more so than any other single factor. This is not an unusual situation because a great deal of the managing process involves personnel. It is the manager who plans, sets goals and objectives, organizes the staff, communicates, motivates, and leads. Managers and their personnel deliver the service, promote the program and the budget, and are held responsible for all the functions of making the organization work.

The future of any organization depends upon managers' ability to develop and train personnel from within their organizations to become managers or to secure prospective managers from outside sources. Although the staffing function in many organizations is handled by a centralized personnel department, managers must still do all they can to assist in assuring the selection of the highest quality of personnel in *all* positions, whether at the top level or at the lowest level in the organization.

The employees within an organization are very much aware of the quality of personnel who are being hired. If they see people of inferior ability being hired, their morale and their work will be influenced negatively. The selection of unqualified personnel because of political influence in an organization can seriously hinder its effectiveness. However, if personnel of high quality are hired and if fair and equal employment opportunities prevail within the organization, the staffing function will most likely be successful.

Types and Levels of Positions

The leisure service field has traditionally had three levels of managers. Each level is important and should not be overlooked or minimized. Many factors and relationships are common to all three levels; any differences are only in the scope and responsibility of each respective level. In defining managers earlier, we stated that these are people who handle equipment, manpower, money, material, time, and space on a day-to-day basis.

The first-level or front-line managers usually are responsible for a specific function or facility and from two to ten staff members. These staff members are the recreation leaders, activity instructors, recreation therapists, park maintenance workers, housekeeping staff members, tour guides, program volunteers, and others who provide leisure services.

Middle-level managers are park or recreation supervisors. Many of them are promoted from within the ranks of first-level managers. From an organizational standpoint, they are responsible for geographic areas or special functions such as food services, conferences, fitness programs, park law enforcement, aquatic facilities, and others. They supervise other managers and personnel. They are generally responsible for *broader* areas of work, as well as for larger budgets and more equipment and facilities than are lower-level managers. They generally have greater decision-making authority delegated to them and are governed less by policies, procedures, and other controls.

Middle-level managers must represent first-level managers to those at higher levels in the organization and communicate information between the various organizational levels or elements. Like first-level managers, they have a responsibility for on-the-job training. Middle-level managers should visit their areas regularly and give assistance where it is needed. Their role is vital in the organization; they serve to *link* the agency's goals and objectives with community needs and service requests.

Top-level managers in the leisure service field are the directors of parks and recreation, superintendents of natural resource areas, chief executive officers at leisure enterprises, and others. These managers have the broadest responsibilities and authority. They are responsible for long-range planning, establishing policies, organization structuring and restructuring, coordination, implementation, and many other broad-based managerial functions.

Most leisure service organizations have traditionally adopted a bureaucratic management structure. Now, however, more highly trained professional personnel, a more culturally diverse and demographically changing population, and a rapidly changing society have resulted in the adoption of flatter management structures that can be more responsive and adaptable in providing quality service to clients.

These horizontally structured agencies have fewer levels or layers. As a result, personnel throughout the organization are encouraged and empowered to assume greater responsibility and carry more authority in doing their jobs. Thus each manager, as depicted in Figure 2 of the Overview, Part III, can be more responsive to client desires and more aware of the interrelated elements that affect them during leisure. Because all levels of managers in a flatter organizational structure are more adept at responding to client desires, the organization is more likely to provide quality service.

Qualifications and Job Descriptions

Qualifications and job descriptions are extremely important in securing the right person for a particular job. Job qualifications are established by the agency to indicate the desired educational and personal requirements of the employee for a particular assignment. The job description provides a more detailed explanation of the specific performance expected (Voich and Wren 1968).

It is extremely important that each job be carefully analyzed so that people with the necessary qualifications for the work are hired. Three factors are generally used to determine job qualifications: knowledge, skill, and experience. *Knowledge* is usually associated with education—including self-education—and formal training at institutions of higher learning. Educational requirements may be determined either by establishing a basic level of learning needed to fulfill the job requirements or by giving an examination. The educational requirement may specify that the applicant possess a bachelor's degree or a master's degree in leisure studies. An examination serves to test candidates on the relevant subject matter pertaining to a particular position.

Skill also can be tested by an examination. In the area of sports, candidates may be asked to perform a given skill; they can then be evaluated on their performance. Candidates for leisure service manager may be given a problem-solving exam to determine their skill in a given area. The test might include either an objective or a subjective evaluation.

Experience involves determining from previous employers whether job candidates have been employed for the period of time indicated on the application. A check is also made of the applicants' previous work performance. Past performance ratings, if they are available, are sometimes helpful in appraising applicants' previous work, but these ratings should be only one part of the evaluation process. Letters of reference are also used in many cases. The best way to check an individual's experience is through a phone conversation with previous supervisors. Supervisors tend to be more open and honest in conversation, but reluctant to put negative comments in writing.

As previously indicated, *job descriptions* provide a detailed listing of the work requirements for a given position. The job description usually has four parts. The first is the job title or classification, which gives the classification heading of the job and sometimes a working title. For example, the classification for a position may be supervisor, with a working title such as district supervisor, supervisor of arts and crafts, or park district supervisor.

The second part of a job description is the qualifications; that is, the education or knowledge, skills, and experience required. The third part ordinarily lists examples of duties to be performed, and the fourth provides as much detail about the job as possible to help determine whether applicants for a position are qualified. A job description that is well thought out and carefully researched will serve as a tremendous aid in helping the organization create new jobs and attract, screen, and hire the best possible candidates.

Sources of Personnel

The quality of personnel at all levels will determine an organization's effectiveness, competence, and quality of leisure service offerings made available to the public. Leisure service managers should therefore be aware of and use every resource available to them. Moreover, they should become familiar with state and federal laws that govern the hiring of personnel. These laws identify key steps that must take place to guarantee fairness to all those who apply for employment. In addition to meeting legal requirements, it is important to develop a staff that is representative of the larger society. In some situations, bilingual job announcements may be appropriate.

Personnel may be recruited from within the organization through promotion. Occasionally, however, an organization needs new blood—new ideas and new leadership. A good manager tries to maintain a balance in the organization by hiring the best-qualified persons from within through promotion and from outside through open, competitive exams. In any case, personnel within the organization should be given an equal opportunity to compete for new or promotional jobs. Employees can be motivated if they are encouraged by managers to apply for such jobs, thus realizing growth opportunities within the organization.

Recruiting

Personnel recruitment is often taken too much for granted. When positions are filled from within the organization, the need for extensive recruiting is unnecessary. However, when the manager goes outside the organization to obtain new personnel, a greater degree of recruiting is necessary. Many factors are involved in deciding how extensive the recruiting effort will be.

The number of vacancies is an obvious factor in making this decision. If there are several vacancies, a much larger recruitment program is necessary than if there is only one. Particularly if the vacancy is at the lowest level of management, a great amount of recruiting cannot be justified. Obviously recruitment should be more vigorous for the position of chief executive than for the position of recreation leader.

If a personnel manager knows that several people will retire in the next few years, recruitment efforts may be affected, particularly if promotion from within the agency will be limited.

If the manager has to recruit from outside, the organization will need to be promoted to interested candidates by a representative who attempts to create a good image of the organization. In meetings with college graduates or other prospective employees, the representative conveys the advantages of working for the organization, its benefits, its career opportunities, and its contribution to the community in providing leisure services.

Sending job announcements and promotional material to colleges to be posted on bulletin boards or for displays at conferences is another way to interest prospective candidates. Advertising in professional journals may also attract candidates, although this procedure is impersonal. The more specific the information about salaries, job location, and the like, the more worthwhile this type of advertising will be. Creating a favorable public image serves as an effective recruitment device. By their overall conduct and behavior, representatives can do much to shape the agency's image at conferences and other professional meetings.

Some of the best sources for prospective candidates are national professional organizations, such as the National Recreation and Park Association. Among other things, these organizations can advertise position vacancies in their publications. Several state professional organizations also provide assistance in recruiting.

Personnel may also be recruited at national, regional, and state conferences. "Job marts" that provide opportunities for interviewing job aspirants are available as part of the conference program.

Screening

The next step is screening prospective candidates to see if they meet the minimum qualifications. This initial screening often saves both the out-of-town candidates and the manager undue expense and time if the candidates do not meet the agency's qualifications. There is no reason for a leisure service manager to spend a great deal of time interviewing, only to find that the prospective candidate is not interested in the position or is unqualified. The last phase of recruiting involves the personal interview.

Selecting the Right Person

Selecting the right person for every job is critical because the success or failure of the organization will be determined by the quality of leisure service managers and supervisors. Recruiting and screening prospective employees will be in vain if the final step, selection, is done hastily and improperly.

Many methods are used in selecting candidates. These include testing, interviewing and researching the individual's background. Selection is made in some organizations by the personnel officer, in others by a committee or the manager under whom the person will work. Each procedure has advantages and disadvantages, but whatever the method, the selection of the best candidate for each position is the central objective of the recruitment program.

The final selection should be made by the person under whom the candidate will work. The supervisor will have to work closely with the new employee and he will be responsible for the employee's work. This should be kept foremost in mind when it comes time for the actual selection (Koontz and O'Donnell 1972). Recruitment efforts will be wasted if the manager for whom the prospective candidate will work does not take sufficient time to interview and select the person properly.

Written Examinations

Written examinations have not proven to be very reliable for selecting managers. An examination that might evaluate how familiar candidates are with management principles, function, and techniques can only measure their knowledge of them, not whether they can apply them properly. Often professional competency examinations are combined with intelligence tests in an effort to measure the critical thinking ability of the prospective manager. But these tests may only measure an individual's ability to take a test, not serve as a valid indicator of work capability.

A possible alternative is using a combination of a written exam and an oral one, with less emphasis on the written part and more on the oral part. If written exams are going to be used, they should be reviewed beforehand to determine whether they are current and appropriate for the particular position being tested, and that they contain no cultural biases.

Oral Examinations

Oral examinations are commonly used to evaluate candidates for positions. Generally the examination is administered by two or three top managers who are considered experts in the specific area in which the position is available. They constitute an *evaluating board* that can meet in conjunction with the chief executive or policy board.

The oral examination measures, to a degree, the candidates' ability to interpret, react to, and express themselves in a given situation. It may not be able to measure accurately, however, their overall capability. It does allow the evaluating board an opportunity to see the top three to five job candidates who have survived the preliminary application, testing, and screening procedures.

The oral interview may be improved by developing an interview guide (Jenks and Zevnik 1989) based upon the job description that can suggest appropriate questions.

Assessment Centers

A popular method of selecting personnel (usually at the managerial level) is by means of the assessment center. Through the assessment center, candidates are given a number of exercises that simulate conditions similar to the position for which the person is applying. All candidates participate at the same time and are evaluated by several experienced professionals. The assessment center has either three or four exercises, depending upon the position, the level within the organization, and the requirements of the job. The typical exercises are (1) a group problem-solving exercise, (2) a written exercise, (3) an oral presentation, and (4) a traditional interview.

Group Problem-Solving Exercise

All candidates in the group are presented with a number of realistic problems or situations and asked to study them and determine how they would plan and solve or develop strategies for each situation. Group members are told that they are at a meeting of their peers in a leaderless situation: they are to discuss each problem and come up with a solution or suggested alternatives to deal with each issue. The group then directs itself in a discussion of the issues. Four to six professional evaluators assess the group exercise and evaluate each candidate's skills in the following areas: oral communication, listening skill, impact, sensitivity, adaptability-flexibility, leadership, stress tolerance, initiative-independence-tenacity, analytical ability, decisiveness, organizing and planning, originality-creativity, and judgment.

Written Exercise

Each candidate is given a written assignment with specific instructions and specific issues to address. The candidates are evaluated on how well they write, express themselves, and follow instructions, and on their ability to be creative and to solve problems. Often an "in-basket exercise" that includes a variety of memos, letters, and phone messages is used. The candidates are asked to indicate, in writing, how they would prioritize and deal with each item. Each candidate's written responses are evaluated according to the following factors: sensitivity, adaptability-flexibility, analytical ability, decisiveness, organizing and planning, management control, originality-creativity, judgment, use of delegation, written communication, and technical knowledge.

Oral Presentation

In a simulated situation, each individual candidate is given 15 minutes to prepare a 10-minute presentation to a civic organization or service club on a specific topic. Each candidate then gives a presentation to the evaluators and is evaluated on the following areas: oral communication, impact, sensitivity, adaptability-flexibility, stress tolerance, organizing and planning, originality-creativity, and judgment.

Traditional Interview

Each candidate is interviewed by two or three evaluators and is asked to respond to eight to twelve predetermined questions. Candidates are evaluated on their responses to determine their capabilities and understanding in the following areas: oral communication, listening skill, impact, sensitivity, adaptability-flexibility, stress tolerance, organizing and planning, management control, energy-range of interests, interest-work standards and ambition, and technical knowledge.

Following each exercise, the candidates' scores are recorded and placed on a matrix under the categories Group Exercise, Written Exercise, Oral Presentation, and Interview. Each exercise can be weighted differently, depending on the particular importance of that exercise to the position under consideration. The scores are totaled and an overall score is determined. After discussing the scores and each candidate's strengths and limitations, the evaluators determine which candidates are most qualified. Those with the best scores are then recommended to the hiring authority for further consideration.

Limited Areas of Questioning

Because of the need to protect First Amendment rights and Affirmative Action requirements, many areas of questioning are illegal (see Table 10.1). These include any area that is not relevant to the job or the applicants' ability to perform that job; for example: Are you married? What is your age? Where do you live? Do you have a car? What is your religion or national origin? It is important that interviewers know and understand these areas and questions they cannot ask. It is best to check with the personnel department or agency attorney about such questions.

Performance Ratings of Internal Candidates

If systematic, objective, and properly administered, performance ratings are probably the most valuable measurement of an internal candidate's competence and potential for promotion within an organization. Performance ratings are nontransferable from one agency to another because material in them is considered confidential and is protected by state and federal civil rights laws. Most well-organized departments use some form of evaluation that is administered on an annual or semi-annual basis. One difficulty in using performance ratings as part of the selection process is that unless the same person evaluates all of the candidates, the rating will have little validity. An effort should be made to avoid this difficulty by making certain that the evaluator has an overall understanding of performance rating systems.

The most useful types of performance systems are ones with a numerical score rather than a verbal description of the person being rated. Comparing candidates by using categories such as "satisfactory," "unsatisfactory," "excellent," or "average" is difficult. If performance ratings are objective, well executed, and done periodically, they are the best measurement of a person's abilities. Table 10.2 is an example of an employee achievement plan.

Many times individuals do outstanding work at a lower level in an organization, but when promoted or transferred to a position of more responsibility with additional job pressures, they do not perform as well. Employers should be careful not to promote employees beyond their capabilities. This may seem far fetched, but it does happen and is referred to as the "Peter Principle," which states that managers tend to be promoted to the level of their incompetence (Peter and Hull, 1969).

Table 10.1 Acceptable and Unacceptable Pre-Employment Inquiries

Acceptable Pre-Employment Inquiries	Subject	Unacceptable Pre-Employment Inquiries
"Have you ever worked for this University under a different name?"	Name	Former name of applicant whose name has been changed by court order or otherwise.
Applicant's place of residence. How long applicant has been a resident of this State or City.	Address or Duration of Residence	
"Can you, after employment, submit a birth certificate or other proof of U.S. citizenship or age?"	Birthplace	Birthplace of applicant. Birthplace of applicant's parents, spouse or other relatives. Requirement that applicant submit a birth certificate, naturalization or baptismal record.
"If hired, can you furnish proof of age?" /or/ Statement that hire is subject to verification that applicant's age meets legal requirements.	Age	Questions that tend to identify applicants 40 to 64 years of age.
Statement by employer of regular days, hours or shift to be worked.	Religious	Applicant's religious denomination or affiliation, church, parish, pastor, or religious holidays observed. "Do you attend religious services /or/ a house of worship?" Applicant may not be told, "This is a Catholic/Protestant/Jewish/atheist organization."
	Race or Color	Complexion, color of the skin, or other questions directly or indirectly indicating race or color.
Statement that photograph may be required after employment.	Photograph	Requirement that applicant affix a photograph to his/her application form. Requirement that applicant, at his/her option submit photograph. Requirement of photograph after interview but before hiring.
Statement by employer that if hired, applicant may be required to submit proof of citizenship.	Citizenship	"Are you a United States Citizen?" Whether applicant or applicant's parents or spouse are naturalized or native-born U.S. citizens. Date when applicant or parents or spouse acquired U.S. citizenship. Requirement that applicant produce naturalization papers or first papers. Whether applicant's parents or spouse are citizens of the U.S.

328

Table 10.1 *Continued*

Acceptable Pre-Employment Inquiries	Subject	Unacceptable Pre-Employment Inquiries
Language applicant reads, speaks, or writes fluently.	National Origin or Ancestry	Applicant's nationality, lineage, ancestry, national origin, descent or parentage. Date of arrival in United States or port of entry; how long a resident. Nationality of applicant's parents or spouse; maiden name of applicant's wife or mother. Language commonly used by applicant. "What is your mother tongue?" How applicant acquired skill to read, write or speak a foreign language.
Applicant's academic, vocational, or professional education; schools attended.	Education	Date last attended high school.
Applicant's work experience. Applicant's military experience in armed forces of the United States, in a State militia (U.S.), or in a particular branch of U.S. armed forces.	Experience	Applicant's military experience (general). Type of military discharge.
	Character	"Have you ever been arrested?"
Names of applicant's relatives already employed by the University.	Relatives	Marital status or number of dependents. Name or address of relative, spouse or children of adult applicant. "With whom do you reside?" "Do you live with your parents?"
Organizations, clubs, professional societies, or other associations of which applicant is a member, excluding any names the character of which indicate the race, religious creed, color, national origin, or ancestry of its members.	Organizations	"List all organizations, clubs, societies, and lodges to which you belong."
"By whom were you referred for a position here?"	References	Requirement of submission of religious reference.
"Do you have any physical condition that may limit your ability to perform the job applied for?" Statement by employer that offer may be made contingent on passing a physical examination.	Physical Condition	"Do you have any physical disabilities?" Questions on general medical condition. Inquiries as to receipt of Worker's Compensation.
Notice to the applicant that any misstatements or omissions of material facts in his/her application may be cause for dismissal.	Miscellaneous	Any inquiry that is not job-related or necessary for determining an applicant's eligibility for employment.

Table 10.2 Employee Achievement Plan for the City of Sunnyvale

Name of Employee: __Sally Swift____ Major Program Assigned: Neighborhd. Prog

Classification: _Secretary_____ Department Assigned: Parks & Recreation_____

A. Functional Achievement Goals (Specific duties related to tasks assigned)

1. Provide clerical support for three Recreation Supervisors and Superintendent. Type memos, agendas and general correspondence.
2. Provide clerical support for all of the Coordinators and Leaders—flyers, memos, questionnaires, miscellaneous forms.
3. Answer Recreation phones, provide information, make appropriate referrals, take messages from Park sites daily.
4. Keep formal log of 4 types of payroll distribution requests, hand out paychecks.
5. Process and check time cards weekly.
6. Receive visitors, answer Recreation inquiries.
7. Process reservations.
8. Complete printing requests, forms control.
9. Type and submit forms as required (accident, incident, Worker's Comp., check requests, etc.).
10. Maintain office supplies.
11. Make copies as required.
12. Provide secretarial assistance to the Director in the secretary's absence. Take minutes at Parks & Recreation Commission meetings, when requested.

B. Skill Achievement Goals:

1. Maintain skills as specified in job classification.
2. Keep California Driver's License current (Class ___3___).

C. Standard Achievement Goals:

1. Serve public interest at all times.
2. Comply with safety.
3. Maintain health consistent with job.
4. Be courteous and cooperative.
5. Maintain appearance consistent with position.
6. Be at work on time.
7. Comply with standard operating procedures, administrative policy and the law.
8. Meet work hour norm.

D. Mandatory Goals: (Required training and/or corrective action)

1. Improve tactfulness in relationships with others.
2. Improve leave use record.
3. Reduce typing errors and improve proofreading skill.

E. Optional or Development Goals

F. Plan Acknowledgement

The Achievement Plan described here represents the principal work assignment and goals for the employee named above effective on the date below and until superseded by a new plan.

Employee's Signature _____ Supervisor's Signature _____

Director's Signature _____ Date _____

Distribution: Dept. Office (original); Supervisor; Employee; Personnel File

Efforts should be made to evaluate a candidate's ability with every measurement tool available. An accurate, up-to-date personnel file on all employees can be helpful when it is time to select internal candidates. Any disciplinary action reported or any letters of commendation can sometimes help determine which candidate will be selected. Generally the best measure of a potential candidate is his or her past performance record.

Orientation Program and Placement

The orientation of new employees is very important in starting them off in the right direction. If a position has been vacant for a period of time, an agency tends to want the employee on the job quickly and to be actively involved before becoming familiar with the job and the agency.

One of the best ways to prevent a poor start is by conducting an organized and effective orientation program. Organizations tend to cram too much into too short a period of time. With variations based on agency size and nature, the following are some of the areas that might be presented in an orientation briefing: the department's philosophy, its overall goals and objectives, employee work expectations, and a discussion of employee benefits and professional advancement potential within the organization. Two or three days of field trips should be conducted for the employee. A tour should include visits to the various facilities and programs in operation. The personnel officer should sit down with the new employee and explain the "personal benefits" of the organization. It is also helpful to give the employee a departmental pamphlet that spells out additional details on benefits. The final phase of the orientation program should be spent in an installation similar to the one where the new employee is to be permanently assigned.

During the orientation period new employees have an opportunity to establish rapport with their immediate supervisor. The orientation also gives them an idea of how the job can be accomplished and what work expectations the agency has. It is designed to get the employees off to a good start and to give them confidence. It is also important that they be placed in the right job. A new, inexperienced employee assigned to a brand new facility may easily be overwhelmed by the number of problems and pressures in getting the program off the ground.

An employee new to the community will have no contacts with community leaders, will be unknown to residents, and will therefore be unfamiliar with the needs and interests of the community and its residents. This fact alone could hinder initial service efforts. Generally the most appropriate placement for a new, inexperienced leader is in a stable, well-organized, and well-run facility with an efficient staff so that the employee can start work under fairly normal conditions. The new leader should not be made to feel inhibited about offering new ideas. It is important that the employee's first assignment be a pleasant, satisfying experience. If the new leader gets too heavily involved and tries to make too many changes at once, adjusting to the community may be difficult. Employees need to work with the community in analyzing and fostering social change.

The personality of new managers should be considered in deciding where they will be placed and the staff who will be working for them. Another factor to consider in assigning new managers, whether experienced or inexperienced, is the proper blending of the talents and skills of the employees working in a unit, particularly from a programming point of view. If a whole new area of programming has been previously overlooked, if a particular emphasis needs to be given to the facility, or if a certain need of the community is not being met, the organization should be especially careful in assigning and orienting a new person to the facility. Obviously all of these factors should be considered before the placement process begins.

In addition to the proper placement of managers in the facilities themselves, careful deliberation needs to be given to the placement of district supervisors and other types of managers who will be supervising lower-level managers. The same holds true when assigning middle-level and upper-level managers; their particular strengths in management, skills, personalities, and the like all need to be taken into consideration.

The placement, rotation, and transfer of personnel are matters of concern in an organization. It may be necessary to transfer an individual to make room for a new, inexperienced manager. From time to time it may be necessary to transfer personnel between two, three, or four facilities to strengthen a program, relieve personality conflicts, or eliminate problems arising between the community and the facility manager. Many leisure service managers also tend to rotate personnel periodically to keep managers alert so that they do not become too complacent in their jobs. The rotation of personnel tends to complement the total organization insofar as managers with certain weaknesses can be rotated with managers of reciprocal strengths, thereby improving the overall operation. The rotation itself very often uncovers problem areas that had been overlooked, and generally it keeps the system functioning more smoothly and effectively.

On-the-Job Training

Qualified managers should keep abreast of the latest techniques and information in their profession so that they can perform their jobs satisfactorily. The rapidity and complexity of social change makes on-the-job training a vital part of the staffing process. To a large extent, the size of the organization determines the scope and kind of on-the-job training that it can afford to offer. Larger organizations usually conduct more extensive training programs because of the number of employees available for such training. Also, larger organizations tend to have more entry-level and lower-level managers and other positions that necessitate a training program. Some organizations employ a training officer whose only job is to plan, conduct and evaluate training efforts. Small organizations, on the other hand, have to take advantage of training opportunities provided by local YMCAs, churches, colleges, and other groups. In large metropolitan areas, three or four organizations can sometimes join forces in setting up training programs not economically feasible for any one organization. Whatever the case, an up-to-date agency constantly attempts to keep its employees well informed and properly trained.

Workshops and Conferences

The workshop or conference is probably the most available, on-the-job training method for use by leisure service professionals. Each year national conferences and regional meetings occur. There are also state conferences at which various training sessions and workshops are offered in areas related to leisure service fields. In recent years many workshops and forums have been offered for special programs or maintenance areas. Workshops and conferences of this type give professionals an opportunity to discuss problems, techniques, and procedures with each other so that they may keep up with the latest trends and issues in their field.

In-service Training Program

Probably the most effective of all the job training programs is the continuous, in-service training program, which is more prevalent in larger organizations. These programs are affected by the attitudes of top-level managers who provide time and resources to conduct them. In organizations where these programs exist, usually someone is specifically designated as a training officer to plan for and promote the programs. Ideally, staff members are then rewarded through an incentive plan for participating in a program.

Employee Benefits

As part of the movement toward valuing the human resources that make up an organization, employee benefits packages should be offered to promote willingness and improved job productivity. Often the key reason that a person chooses to work for a particular organization, the benefits package can provide a major source of motivation for employee productivity. These packages are especially valuable to personnel in leisure services because (1) they offer employees the opportunity for quality of life experiences that are also offered to participants and clients and (2) some of the benefits may be fairly easy to implement because the facilities and programs are already available. A leisure service delivery system is ideally suited to offer employee discounts and passes for services, well-designed employee programs, and other creative packages.

Basic Benefits

Fringe benefit packages typically include the basic benefits of insurance, retirement, vacation, health promotion, and sick leave; employee assistance programs; and career development programs.

Because the cost of health insurance is rising, agencies, enterprises, and organizations offer packages that deal not only with treatment, but also with prevention through health promotion in the workplace, employee recreation, and wellness programs. Corporations have offered these services since the late 1800s, but public and nonprofit agencies have been slow to develop similar programs.

Employee Assistance Programs (EAPs)

An EAP provides timely, professional aid for people whose personnel problems might otherwise lead to work impairment, absenteeism, accidents, conflicts in the work setting, or even job termination (Lewis and Lewis 1986). Such programs include counseling and preventive programs.

Career Development Programs

Two major phases of career development are offered—career planning and career management. Employees can gain valuable training and clarify career goals with such a benefit (Lewis and Lewis 1986).

Opportunity for further, formal education for leisure service employees is a key fringe benefit that is related to career development. Many progressive leisure service agencies have an arrangement to pay for additional education of employees, particularly if it is related to their job and will benefit their organization. Employees can enroll in regular college classes in their specific areas of need and interests.

Personnel Problems

Even in the best of leisure service delivery systems, managers encounter personnel problems that cause difficulty. Some basic factors may be at the root of these problems. The next chapter deals with on-the-job, trouble-shooting techniques that may assist in dealing with personnel concerns.

According to Bartolome (1989), "It is natural for people with less power to be extremely cautious about disclosing weaknesses, mistakes and failings"(135). A manager may have a difficult time overcoming the typical lack of trust employees have for those with whom they interact. Certain signs that may indicate trouble in the area of trust are a decline in the flow of information; deterioration of morale; nonverbal signals such as averted eyes, posture, and gestures; and outside signals (Bartolome 1989). It is suggested that

336 Leisure Systems: Critical Concepts and Applications

a manager can resolve certain problems related to trust by keeping communication with subordinates informal, showing support, respect, and fairness with subordinates, and behaving consistently and competently.

Volunteers

It seems appropriate here to say a word about volunteers as service providers. Volunteers are more evident today than ever before in our field. Agencies of all kinds have initiated volunteer programs. We see them in traditional settings such as youth agencies and hospitals and also in places where their involvement is less well known. For example, volunteers work in many state and federal natural resource agencies.

Types of Jobs

Volunteers carry out many different kinds of jobs, often using the core processes discussed in Chapter 7. Frequently they provide activity leadership: they teach swimming, or coach a youth soccer team, or provide bridge instruction. They might work as docents at a park visitor center or as campground hosts. Some carry out maintenance responsibilities. They might volunteer through an organization such as the Lions Club and work on a special project such as a Braille nature trail in a local park. Sometimes they provide clerical assistance or help with transportation. They carry petitions for a park bond drive and help clean up wild fowl caught in oil spills. Serving on advisory committees and agency boards of directors is volunteer service. The range of possibilities is very wide.

Motivations

The range of reasons why people volunteer is also wide. The things we know about motives apply to volunteers as much as to paid staff and participants. Volunteering is behavior. It is subject to the same influences as all behavior. Common motives for volunteering include the needs for achievement, affiliation and belonging. Some people volunteer to be with other people. Others do it out of a sense of altruism, a feeling of helping someone else or contributing to a cause. Being needed is a powerful motivation.

Volunteering can provide satisfactions not found in a regular job and can replace work-type satisfactions lost through retirement. Or it can enable a person to get work experience that might be useful later in seeking paid employment. It can be a major source of meaning in life or a relatively minor commitment made out of a passing sense of duty. An individual might volunteer to satisfy a single motive or there may be many reasons. And of course volunteering can be a leisure experience in itself. Heidrich (1989) suggests that an individual will usually volunteer when there is something that can be personally gained.

Who Volunteers?

No one type of person volunteers. It is not just the middle-aged, middle-class, nonworking woman, not the retired professional with time on his hands, as we often assume. Volunteers are university students, business executives, blue-collar workers, physicians, members of conservation organizations, civil servants, high school teachers, church members—just about anyone.

Volunteers contribute significantly to the leisure service delivery system. They enable agencies to extend services beyond what the staff can provide. Sometimes they bring special talents. Volunteers often infuse enthusiasm and fresh points of view into an agency; they bring new ideas and an eagerness that may be caught by regular staff. They also serve as interpreters of the agency in the community. If they know the agency and feel a part of it, they can be a source of excellent public relations.

Working with volunteers

Volunteers are not free help. An agency cannot merely tack on a "volunteer program" and expect to collect the benefits. To have a successful experience, the staff has to plan for it and identify real jobs, not just busywork, to be done by volunteers. Volunteers have to be recruited and screened to be sure they are appropriate for the agency's needs. Like other staff members, they need to be trained and given good supervision. Sometimes this takes extra tact and sensitivity. They are not paid in the usual sense; they are donating their time. But if they are not doing a good job, corrective actions may be called for. Paid staff members need to be prepared for the involvement of volunteers. To the extent possible, the challenges of the job should be matched with the skills and motives of the volunteer. This is the volunteer's payoff—this and appropriate recognition. Agencies use different methods for providing recognition, such as certificates, badges, news releases, and dinners. Whatever its form, recognition is an important element.

Summary

Staffing is at the heart of effective management. The quality of managers more than any other single factor determines the quality of service that the leisure service agency will deliver. Staffing involves developing good qualifications and job descriptions, recruiting and selecting qualified paid personnel and volunteers, developing an employee benefits package, providing in-service training, and other functions to assure the building and maintenance of the best team possible.

References

Bartolome, F. 1989. Nobody trusts the boss completely—Now what? *Harvard Business Review* 2 (March-April): 135-142.

Block, P. 1987. *The empowered manager.* San Francisco: Jossey-Bass.

Heidrich, K. 1989. The direct approach to motivating volunteers. *Employee Services Management* 32(6): 10-14.

Koontz, H., and C. O'Donnell. 1972. *Management,* 6th ed. New York: McGraw-Hill.

Jenks, J., and B. Zevnik. 1989. ABCs for job interviewing. *Harvard Business Review* 9(July-August): 38-43.

Lewis, J. A., and M. D. Lewis. 1986. *Counseling programs for employees in the workplace.* Monterey, Calif.: Books-Cole Publishing.

Naisbitt, J., and P. Aburdene. 1985. *Reinventing the corporation.* New York: Warner Books.

Peter, L.J., and R. Hull. 1969. *The Peter principle.* New York: Bantam Books.

Voich, D., Jr., and C. A. Wren. 1968. *Principles of management.* New York: Ronald Press.

11

IMPLEMENTING SERVICE

Once basic managerial functions are established in the organization, it is possible to implement the service. Implementation refers to the process of activating the plans and delivering the service to a participant, consumer, or client. All of the parts involved in this service delivery must come together in an organized package that enables a high quality leisure experience. Implementation in this field involves offering an activity program, making a facility available, providing counseling, or engaging in other activities that affect the participant.

Role of Implementing Service

Previous chapters have illustrated how departmental goals and objectives and essential planning processes are established. Organizational concepts to carry out these plans have been explained. The importance of staffing the organization with competent managers has been discussed. This chapter will show how the plans, the organization, and the management team are engaged and activated. This will be done by interpretation of the fourth management process: implementing service. Implementation involves motivation, communication, and leadership.

Work with plans, procedures, principles, and other leisure service matters is relatively simple compared with the complexity of work with the human element of the organization. The implementation process is totally concerned with the people who will enable the organization to function effectively and those who use the service. In various places in the text, we have emphasized the holistic nature of behavior. The individual employee, whether in a managerial position such as that of fitness center recreation supervisor, hospital therapeutic recreation coordinator, or first-level manager such as a center director or park maintenance worker, must be considered as a total human being. When people come to work, their personal ambitions, problems, and frustrations are not left at home. They come to work as total individuals with religious and political interests and concerns about house payments and family problems. The capable manager recognizes these factors and is prepared to deal with them.

Effective managers learn to cope with the problems and frustrations of every individual in the organization and to bring the goals and ambitions of employees into line with the agency's goals and objectives so that they can accomplish their predetermined work. In most organizations the policies and procedures and rules and regulations are developed around human needs. As managers begin to grasp some of these complexities, they become aware of the intricacies of the implementation process, which consists of communicating, motivating, and leading employees and offering quality service to consumers.

Responsiveness to Clients

Martin (1987) states that "quality customer service is the foundation upon which an organization's success and profits are built" (6). In viewing the organization as an inverted pyramid where the client is the "boss," we must recognize that successfully fulfilling client needs is the process of implementing service. In this scenario, managing is not seen as a top-down approach, but as a responsive approach at whatever level exists to satisfy the client. It is then assumed that managerial skill in implementing service rests with all employees. Further, a top manager has a responsibility to ensure that employees are responsive to the constituents who use the service, to be fully aware of front-line concerns related to the client, and "be there" to guide and become informed.

To accomplish this, we need to understand a few key elements in providing client service. Martin (1987) defines four steps in the process of providing service: project positive attitude, identify the needs of clients, provide for their needs, and work to ensure that clients return.

A brief review of what is involved in each step shows the way that a leisure service can be implemented successfully.

Projecting a Positive Attitude

People project either a positive or a negative attitude in a number of ways, and clients will respond in kind to an employee. We communicate a positive attitude through appearance, body language, and voice, each of which can be developed to send a positive message to a client.

Identifying Consumer Needs

In learning what the client or consumer needs, we should consider the timing of the service—being one step ahead of the consumer. We should also be attentive and alert to consumers and provide for their basic needs to feel welcome, important, comfortable, and understood—listening and receiving feedback.

Providing for Needs

Once employees in an organization have a positive attitude and are in tune to the needs of their clientele, they are then in a position to interact dynamically in a service environment. Some of the duties involved in providing client service are to perform back-up duties, send clear messages, say the right thing, and effectively sell the service.

Ensuring Consumer Return

To ensure that consumers return, managers must periodically survey participants on how well the agency is providing quality service and ask how it can do better. Additionally, managers should strive to get feedback from ex-consumers and nonusers. The important point is to know how they see the organization, and this can occur only by seeing it through their eyes.

Facilitating Employee Effectiveness

One important goal to keep in mind about the process of directing is the principle of harmony of objectives (Koontz and O'Donnell, 1980). This principle is concerned with unifying the employees' goals and objectives with those of the agency. The aim is to ensure harmony in all work performed and all assignments done, whether by those at the top level of the organization or at the very lowest level. Employee needs, goals, and aspirations must be in harmony with the overall goals and objectives of the agency.

A participative management approach to the development of goals and objectives is likely to assure that this principle is followed.

Motivation

Much has been written about understanding human needs as a factor in motivating people. Motivation, an important element of the implementing process, is the method by which managers try to stimulate and encourage employees to work in carrying out the mutually developed organizational goals and objectives. Managers may motivate employees by various means and techniques, depending upon such factors as their educational levels and personal needs. Employees can be motivated when they are satisfied, or unmotivated when dissatisfied. Furthermore, if managers give poor direction to employees who report to them, all of the previous efforts involved in the planning, organizing, and selecting of staff can be nullified.

Each component of managing within the leisure service delivery system is important and depends upon the other components. The main emphasis of directing concerns the human factor rather than facilities, money, time, and space. Any manager who wants to deal effectively with motivation must understand the strengths and limitations of staff members, as well as their personal needs. Group needs as well as individual needs sometimes become intermingled and must be dealt with as a whole in undertaking the directing process and moving towards attaining the goals and objectives of the agency. The manager should analyze very carefully what an employee's personal motives are and what should be accomplished when an employee is asked to do some particular work or to change behavior in the interest of the organization. Although no one manager can analyze and understand all the needs of all employees in order to motivate them, the manager does need a broad understanding of some of their basic needs (Hampton, Summer, and Webber 1968, 102-116).

Why are some managers more productive than others? Why does one organization outperform another? The reason is probably not that one manager is making better decisions than another, but rather that individual employees are "turned on" to their work. In some circumstances, employees can be so "turned off" to their job and so unmotivated that they are working far below their capacity.

To increase the productivity in an organization, managers must understand the essence of motivation. Many theories of motivation exist, most of which focus on the fact that individuals, during work or leisure, are striving to meet their personal needs. Anyone who has supervised employees recognizes that individuals' needs vary significantly, sometimes because of their level of maturity, and sometimes because of what is important to them at that particular time. What motivates one employee may have very little effect on another and could even be viewed as demotivating and turning him off. What motivates an employee today may not motivate him tomorrow. Maybe the employee's maturity level has changed or a particular need has been satisfied to the point where he is no longer willing to pursue that action on the job. Employees' needs result in their pursuing a particular goal at a particular time and, if the manager can capture that behavior and direct it in a given way, she can accomplish organizational goals and objectives while the employee is meeting his individual needs.

In an oversimplified way, this is what motivation is all about. The goal of the manager is to accomplish organizational goals and objectives and at the same time give employees an opportunity to meet their own needs. The manager who can accomplish both is the manager who can increase productivity to the greatest extent.

In a well-designed job situation, satisfaction of individual needs and organizational goals are mutually beneficial. If organizational goals alone are seen as important while individual needs are neglected, productivity for both the employee and the organization will be low. Likewise, an organization that meets only individual employee's needs to the detriment of organizational goals will not survive. Although these concepts may seem obvious, how many organizations operate with this philosophy in mind?

Theories of Motivation

Let us examine some popular motivation theories in an attempt to gain insight, as well as to determine what they have in common, and then see what conclusions we can draw for increasing motivation in our organizations.

1. Abraham Maslow (1954) has probably contributed as much to the understanding of motivation as any single individual. We made earlier reference to Maslow in Chapter Five. According to Maslow's theory of human motivation, all individuals have needs based on their level of development and maturity; these needs result in the individual pursuing some particular goal to satisfy those needs; and realizing a goal results in a behavior or an action.

Maslow stated that human behavior is always for a purpose; that whatever an individual does, it is with some purpose in mind, be it conscious or subconscious; and that every behavior has a reason and a logic to it. Our challenge as managers is to try to recognize those needs and behaviors that result in accomplishing work for the organization. Everything an individual does serves a purpose for the individual, whether it is totally understood or not, whether it is appropriate or not.

Maslow probably is best known for his hierarchical classification of needs. It starts with physiological needs—shelter, food, clothing, pay, or what money can buy. These are the most basic needs and are at the bottom of the hierarchy. Moving up, the next set of needs is for security— freedom from hazard, fringe benefits, unions, seniority, job security, and other needs that deal with creating a sense of security for the individual. At the next level are the social or belonging needs—belonging to a group, relationship with one's peers in a work situation, a formal-informal work group. Next come the esteem needs—job title, status symbols, promotion opportunities, recognition, prestige, power. At the top of the pyramid are self-actualization needs—the striving for competence, advancement, creativity, success. All of these needs are important to the individual at different times.

Maslow stated that human wants and needs are insatiable: they cannot be satisfied once and for all. A person who is hungry will look for and ultimately eat food. Once the individual eats, the need is suppressed or diminishes, only to return again. Likewise, a manager cannot compliment people for a job well done and expect that to carry them for the rest of their careers. People continue to seek opportunities for recognition.

2. Another behavioral theorist providing insight into motivation was Chris Argyris (1957). According to Argyris's theory, all individuals are at some level of maturity on a continuum, from that of total immaturity to total maturity. By recognizing each individual's maturity level, a manager is in a position to provide a motivating environment to meet the individual's needs in accord with that level. It was Argyris's point of view that individuals cannot be treated alike. The manager has to (1) understand where an individual worker is in maturity development and (2) provide a work environment that matches the individual's maturity level to release work capacity to the greatest degree possible. According to Argyris, the problem with most organizations is that, when individuals join the work force, they are kept from maturing by management practices common to most organizations. Individuals are given minimal control over their environment and are encouraged to be passive, dependent, and subordinate. They therefore behave immaturely, and this results in poor productivity. Argyris pointed out that the formal organization can actually promote immature behavior with all of its rules, regulations, policies, and procedures that tend to treat people in an immature manner. He also stated that there is a false concept that power and authority should rest in the hands of the few at the top of the organization. In other words, management knows best. As a result, the formal organization does not encourage employees to grow and mature to their full capability. The other side of this coin is seen in Peters and Waterman's excellence criteria, which regard employees as valuable resources to be developed and encouraged throughout the duration of their career paths (Peters and Waterman 1982).

The major impact of Argyris's work in the area of motivation is that of recognizing that every individual is different; that every individual responds differently on the basis of maturity level; and that organizations must find ways to treat people differently, but with fairness and consistency. Argyris indicated that once their physical needs are assured, most workers seek to fulfill the next higher order of needs for security and stability. When these become relatively assured, workers turn toward the highest needs, creativity and self-fulfillment.

The main point to be learned from Argyris's work is that every employee is different and that we should provide a work environment that matches an appropriate maturity level at that particular time. If employees are treated as less mature or more mature than they actually are, they are certain to be less productive.

3. The work of Douglas McGregor (1960) famous for his theory X, theory Y style of management, in many ways parallels the work of Argyris (1957). According to McGregor's theory X, traditional organizations with their centralized decision-making, superior-subordinate pyramid, and external control of work have a negative assumption about human nature and human motivation. Most people prefer to be directed, are not interested in their work, do not want to assume responsibilities, and want safety above all else. Employees are motivated by money, fringe benefits, and the threat of punishment. The theory X supervisor must closely supervise employees and assure the greatest possible amount of control over them because employees are unreliable, irresponsible, and immature, and work is a necessary evil. The theory X approach to motivation implies that employees are incapable of any judgment and self-initiation. Theory X presents a case that only an authoritarian style of leadership will produce any results. Theory X assumes the lowest level of maturity, as it relates to Argyris' continuum of maturity.

At the other extreme, McGregor describes his theory Y management style and motivation. He stated that management needs to have practices based on a more accurate understanding of human nature, that employees are motivated by creating opportunities for social, esteem, and self-actualizing behavior. Work can be, and often is as natural and satisfying as play. After all, both work and play are physical and mental activities. Consequently, there is no inherent difference between work and play, but only in what motivates them. Play is internally controlled. As the individual matures, play turns into two activities, work and recreation. However, work is generally controlled by others—by management and the boss. According to McGregor, our personal motives or needs affect our role and job performance in the organization. As we satisfy our needs, we will more readily cooperate with the organization.

Building on Maslow's theory, McGregor stated that the basic unit of behavior is activity, and that in the work environment the basic behavior results in work, and in work being accomplished in the organization. Individuals are always doing something. Management tries to direct that activity and behavior in order to accomplish organizational goals. The manager must know which motives or needs of the employee are important and will invoke certain behavior or activity that will release work capacity. The underlying philosophy is the conviction that organizations can best be served by providing opportunities for employees to achieve their personal needs while accomplishing organizational goals and objectives.

4. More recently, theory Z created by William Ouchi (1981), concerns the ideal that both theory X and theory Y are correct at certain times. Employees and managers alike should participate in decision making that affects the ultimate outcome—quality leisure experience. Theory Z stresses sharing opinions and reaching consensus among a wide group of employees. Theory J (Japanese style management), however, appears to be in conflict with North American perceptions of management and employee relationships. The Japanese concept of management attempts to place greater emphasis on the overall needs of the organization and long-range goals. Individuals subordinate their identity primarily to the organization. Theory Z is an attempt to blend more traditional North American management (theory X and Y) with Japanese Style management (theory J). Its primary tenet involves consensual decision making as a pretext for contemporary organizations to be most effective while operating from a holistic management perspective (see Figure 11.1).

5. Frederick Herzberg and colleagues (1959) advanced a theory of motivation that is built upon other theories by earlier behavioral scientists, as well as upon experiments he conducted in a work environment. Herzberg's theory, likewise, is based on understanding the needs of individuals and where they are in their development or maturity, which in turn indicates what would really motivate them versus just maintaining a certain level of work. He classified these activities into two groups: activities that are *hygiene* in nature—those needs that when not met will result in job dissatisfaction versus those needs that the individual is striving for— and activities labeled as motivations, which truly provide job satisfaction.

Figure 11.1 Management Theories

Theory X

1. Human beings have inherent dislike of work.
2. People must be coerced, controlled, directed, and threatened with punishment.
3. Human beings prefer to be directed, avoid responsibility, have little ambition, want security above all.

Theory Y

1. Expenditure of physical and mental effort in work is as natural as play or rest.
2. People will exercise self-direction and self-control on services to which they are committed.
3. Commitment to objectives is a function of rewards associated with their achievement—the most significant are satisfaction of ego and self-actualization needs.
4. Average human beings learn not only to accept but to seek responsibility.
5. Under typical conditions of modern industrial life, the intellectual potentialities of the average human being are only partly used.

Theory Z

1. Organizations operate from a base of collective values.
2. Nothing of value occurs as a result of individual effort.
3. Everything that is significant is the product of teamwork.
4. Employees are organized into quality circles (semi-autonomous study groups work on solving job-related quality problems).
5. Employees work for a lifetime. Each person feels a sense of commitment from the organization, and a stake in the enterprise.
6. Work relationships include a wide range of human needs and aspirations.
7. Management has a holistic perspective.

Herzberg indicated that the physical needs, security needs, social needs, and some of the esteem needs fall into the hygiene category. They must be maintained at a certain level, but they in themselves, if they are taken for granted, do not provide for real job satisfaction. Within the hygiene category he placed : the type of supervision, that, even when good, fails to motivate a person, and when poor, affects a person's work negatively. Other hygiene factors are the policies and procedures on the job, the various working conditions relative to the job environment, the interpersonal relationships with fellow employees, peers, and supervisors—the status that the individual has in relation to job security and personal life. When the hygiene factors are maintained at a good level, they improve working conditions and help remove the inhibitors so that employees will do a day's work for a day's pay. They do not assure anything more than that, however. They provide for contentment but no growth and they last only a short period of time. When the hygiene factors are not at an appropriate level, they tend to dehumanize people; people will become unhappy, and work may slow down. When these factors are corrected, work productivity may return to where it was to begin with, but employees may still not be happy.

On the other side of the ledger, Herzberg places the motivators. These are the things that really release work capacity by stimulating the employee to do more than what is expected, thus making the job more exciting, more interesting, and more challenging. People are motivated by what they do. The motivation is in the job itself. Motivation or job satisfaction are found in the opportunity for achievement, recognition, responsibility, and advancement, and in opportunities for personal growth and development. The idea is to create a job that is exciting and to truly enrich the job by loading it vertically, expanding the complexity and completeness of the task so that the worker is constantly learning new things and reaching for new goals and opportunities.

Conversely, loading the job horizontally by merely giving employees more things to do at the same or a lower level is not challenging or motivating to employees. Job rotation fails because they are given jobs that are equally as dull and routine as the jobs just left. Making the work challenging and interesting from the employees' perspective may not be how the employer or company sees the work. Motivators provide for satisfaction from the job experience itself. The opposite of job satisfaction would not be job dissatisfaction, but rather no job satisfaction. The way a job can be made more motivating is to load it vertically and provide opportunities for people to reach for their own higher level.

Ways of Motivating Employees

Management has a choice in how it motivates employees. One choice is to try to make people work, the other is to make people want to work. Motivation is simply a way of getting people to find their own reasons for doing something that their manager wants them to do in the first place. The manager can do so by creating an environment where people want to work and become self-motivated. This is best accomplished by truly understanding the employees and what makes them function and then balancing their personal needs with organizational goals, being mindful that the techniques that work best are mutually beneficial. To assume that the organization can accomplish all that it wants to accomplish without meeting individual needs, will not work and ultimately the employees will revolt. Likewise, an organization that only meets employees' needs will not survive in a free economic system.

From an overall point of view, managers who are successful in motivating employees are those who provide an environment in which appropriate goals are available for employee need satisfaction. The manager can influence the work of an employee by:

1. Recognizing what the needs are
2. Understanding which goals will meet these needs
3. Providing the employees with training to increase their ability to achieve the goals
4. Making goal opportunities available to create expectancy
5. Reinforcing good work with positive feedback

With these understandings managers can significantly influence and increase employees' performance and work capacity.

Failure to understand employees' needs is verified in studies (Gluskinos and Kestelman, 1971) undertaken to determine what supervisors think employees want from their jobs compared with what employees really want. Supervisors were asked to rank from

1 to 10 what employees want from their jobs. Such considerations included:

1. Good working conditions
2. Feeling that they are in on things
3. Tactful discipline
4. Full appreciation for work done
5. Management loyalty to the worker
6. Good wages
7. Promotion and growth opportunities
8. Sympathetic understanding of personal problems
9. Job security
10. Interesting work

More often than not, supervisors ranked good wages, job security and promotion, and growth opportunities as most important to the worker. When workers are asked to rank the same working conditions, studies have indicated they rank: full appreciation for work done, feeling that they are in on things, and sympathetic understanding of personal problems as most important. As this comparison indicates, supervisors and workers see things quite differently.

The task of motivating employees is not simple. It requires constant work, effort, and energy. In summing up how to become most effective and productive, managers should consider the following points:

1. Knowing themselves, their strengths and weaknesses; what they do well and where they need help. This takes constant work and study.
2. Being willing to change their leadership style and behavior and dropping the attitude that they have everything in hand. They should be ready to consider changing themselves and starting the organization in a different direction.
3. Knowing their employees, their needs and what motivates them.
4. Knowing the situation in which they are working, which is constantly changing, and the environment in which they are operating; and being willing to adjust accordingly.

5. Knowing the organizational goals and how they can be tied into helping meet individual employees' needs to be mutually beneficial.

6. Above all else, being sincere in their interest in working with their employees and the public they serve.

The manager should recognize performance problems among the employees. If they are not performing well, the manager should ask these four questions (McGehee 1971):

1. Does the employee really know what to do? Does the individual have the knowledge of what is being asked in order to realistically carry out the assignment?

2. Does the employee know how to do the requested job? Does the individual have the physical, mental and technical skills necessary to do what has been requested? Oftentimes because employees hold a given position, they are assumed to have a certain skill that they may or may not have.

3. Is the employee motivated to do the job? Are there personal conflicts or prejudices that keep this individual from wanting to perform a given assignment? All of these factors can prevent employees from successfully completing an assignment.

4. Finally, is the employee really permitted to do what has been asked? Are there any policies and procedures that prohibit work? Are other employees interfering with accomplishing the assignment, or are there other factors that will slow down the work process?

Communications

Of all the directing processes, communications is probably the most neglected. Although much has been written about communications, it is still misunderstood and poorly practiced in many leisure service organizations. Research to improve communications has been done, but little is really understood about the process. Communication is the transfer and processing of information from one individual to another. Every effort should be made to ensure that the information is understandable to the receiver. In an organization, communication is the method by which all the functions are tied together in order to achieve goals and objectives. Information must flow upward, across, and downward. It is important for all staff members to be informed of what is occurring in an organization. This will not happen without an effective, on-going communication process. Unfortunately this process can encounter many problems.

The first step is one of planning and preparing to communicate in order to motivate and direct employees toward agency goals. Communicators must give some thought to what they intend to say, how to say it, the purpose, and to whom it will be said. For example, the level of the employee with whom one is communicating obviously affects how the communication is to be delivered. The words chosen, whether written or oral and the ability of the person receiving the communication to understand it, are important considerations in the initial phases of the communications process. Sometimes it is even a matter of whether the communication is worth the time, effort, and energy put into it.

Communications fail to bring about their desired results for many reasons. In some instances the sender is at fault; in other instances the receiver has certain shortcomings. In either case the results are generally the same: the misunderstood communique does not produce the desired effect. Instead, time, motion, and energy are wasted.

One of the most common problems is a poorly expressed message (Koontz and O'Donnell 1980). Although the senders generally know what to say, they do not always convey their thoughts to the receivers accurately. Because of poor word choice, words that have a double meaning, poor sentence structure, and grammatical errors, the message is misinterpreted. The outcome is misdirected work and energy.

Especially in larger, more traditional bureaucratic organizations with more than one level in the chain of command, inaccurate transmission or loss of transmission will result in poor or distorted communications. Although the originator of the message may have communicated what was intended, when it was passed down the chain of command, certain words may have unintentionally been changed, left out, or added so that the message was altered. If the communication is transmitted a second time, the same process occurs, further distorting the communique. By the time the message is finally delivered to the person who will implement the directive or do the work, it is so distorted that the receiver may either do just the opposite of what was originally requested or something entirely useless. Of course, organizations that use a team and/or systems management model are more likely to have opportunities for group participation in decision making, thus reducing the loss or inaccurate transmission of communication.

Many other factors result in a loss of the meaning of the original communication. Sometimes lack of attention by the receiver, because of preoccupation or fatigue, distorts the communication. Other times false assumptions by the receiver can result in faulty communications. A distrust or dislike of the person communicating is another reason why a communique might be distorted or changed. Certain prejudices or disagreements with what is being requested by the communicator often result in delay of the communication along the network or in its not being implemented when received. Failure to communicate effectively can become a real problem. All efforts are helpful if the sender gets the receiver's attention first and then has something worthwhile to say.

After completing the planning, organizing and staffing processes, managers direct the implementation of their plans by communicating them to others. Some communication problems can be eliminated by considering whether the communication is delivered as a general or a specific direction. Many factors determine which of the two alternatives should be used. These factors include the given situation, the level of competence of the people to whom the communication is to be directed, the importance of the assignment, and how quickly it has to be completed.

There are disadvantages to oral communications, because once they are given there is no permanent record of what was said. The person who is to carry out the instruction has nothing to review other than what he can remember from the conversation, nor does the manager have anything that she can follow up on in terms of what she specifically requested.

Putting instructions and directions in writing is obviously time consuming because it requires dictation or preparing them in some other way, and then mailing them. They must then be received, read, interpreted, and acted upon. This process takes time and can be very expensive. A simple memo might cost several dollars, whereas a phone conversation might serve the same purpose and be cheaper and faster. On the other hand, written communications may be more carefully thought out, and the sender can review them before they are sent to make certain that the intent of the message is correct. A written communique becomes a permanent record that can be used as a follow-up device. It can be kept in a follow-up folder and checked to see if an assignment was completed, particularly if the message dealt with complicated, long-range projects. Written communications in themselves, however, need not be complicated and complex to be effective. Various printed aids such as the Speedi-Letter or the Redi-Letter can simplify the process of writing. These aids are usually three-page, precarbonized paper forms on which the sender can jot off a quick message. The receiver uses the same form to answer.

Another, more modern form of communicating is through the electronic message, which can be sent via computer. This form of communication is immediate and can give instant feedback to the sender.

Before communications are sent, they should be evaluated for their importance, their type (whether oral or written), their cost, and the follow-up needed. Whatever the type of communication, it should be clear so that the desired compliance can be expected.

Timing is another important factor, but it is often overlooked. From the standpoint of work to be done in response to a communication, employees should be given enough time to allow them to do the job without being unduly pressured. A good time to make a new assignment is right after complimenting an employee on a job well done. The employee will then be likely to undertake the new task with enthusiasm and dedication. If given a new assignment right after being reprimanded, however, the employee will experience additional frustration and will begin the new task with a negative attitude. Whatever the situation, the leisure service manager should take into consideration the factor of timing in the communication process, and thereby the directing process, so as to assure that goals are well planned and thought out and are implemented smoothly.

Communications are tremendously important in determining the degree of success or failure of an organization. They tie together the organization in terms of the planning, organizing, staffing, and other directing processes. Faulty communications can nullify all of the other good efforts. Whenever possible, managerial decisions should be explained and should result in employee feedback. Specifically, the involvement and explanations give the employee who is relaying the communication a better understanding of it. This will assure a better job. On the other hand, the manager need not get approval for the type of communication used. Every communication is important. Some will involve positive, and others negative points of view. All should be well thought out and delivered accurately to gain the desired results.

Leadership

Leadership has been defined by many individuals, and entire books have been devoted to the subject. This section gives an overview of leadership as it relates to the implementation process of management. Leadership is the ability of an individual to motivate, guide, and direct a group of people or an organization toward a desired goal or objective. The effective leader has the capacity and desire to rally individuals to a common purpose. Good, effective managers should be good leaders; however, a leader is not necessarily a manager. As a result, the two terms should not be confused. The manager without leadership ability relies upon authority to command and uses motivation techniques that are mostly negative. Personal leadership occurs when the leader does much of the task, working hand in hand with subordinates. Often this leadership comes to the forefront because subordinates rely upon it. The personal leader does much work that the people could do or could be trained to do.

More recent literature stresses this concept by describing it as MBWA or Management by Wandering Around. First conceived by Peters and Waterman and presented in *In Search of Excellence* (1982), this management style assumes that a manager stays in complete tune with employees by sitting in on sessions of work, walking around a work site, talking to employees, and completing tasks that are necessary at the time.

Supervisory or managerial leaders restrict themselves as much as possible to performing the work that only they can do because of their organizational position. They delegate much of the work to others, particularly the jobs or tasks that others can handle because of their more technical training in a given area. As a result of delegating this work, they are free to supervise and can spend their efforts and energies in leading employees who are responsible to them.

Task versus Relationship Leader Styles

Two differing emphases related to leadership concern task-oriented behaviors and relationship-oriented behaviors. Hersey and Blanchard (1982) developed a "situational leadership" theory. This theory says that leaders change their style, depending upon the maturity of the group or staff. Maturity is a function of the degree to which staff members are capable of performing a task and the degree to which they are willing to do it. The more able and motivated they are, the more mature they are. Of course, individual staff members may differ in their maturity.

With groups or with individual staff members who are relatively immature, leaders should emphasize the task; they should "tell" staff members what to do, when to do it, and how to do it. As employees mature, leaders can shift to an emphasis on both task and relationship behaviors; here leaders tell people what is to be done, but also encourage them and help to strengthen their motivation. Hersey and Blanchard use the term "selling." As maturity increases further, leaders engage in "participating" behavior. They shift away from task behavior somewhat and put more emphasis on relationship behavior. The group knows fairly well what to do and is reasonably motivated; the leader works with the group. With a fully mature group, the leader can "delegate." In this situation, neither task-oriented nor relationship-oriented behavior is required.

The diagram representing the situational leadership theory shows the four types of leadership in Hershey and Blanchard's model: participating (high relationship and low task), selling (high relationship and high task), delegating (low relationship and low task), and telling (high task and low relationship). Presented as a matrix, it plots leadership styles from authoritarian to delegation. A manager who correctly assesses the group and the motivation and communication factors that are called for may map out an appropriate leadership style (Phipps 1987).

Fiedler (1967) developed a "contingency model" of leadership, which also focuses on task and relationship behaviors. He suggested that style depends upon three factors: the power that leaders hold in their positions, their personal relationships with the group, and the degree to which the task is structured. These factors differ in terms of favorableness or unfavorableness. Power, good group relationships, and well-structured tasks put the leader in a highly favorable position. The absence of these is unfavorable. Fiedler suggests that in either highly favorable or highly unfavorable circumstances, the leader should use a task-oriented style. If the circumstances are highly favorable, the leader's relationship with the group is already good. If they are highly unfavorable, the leader does not have much to work with; he or she will have little or no power and poor relationships with the staff and will face a task that is vague. The leader will have the best chance to get something going by focusing on the task. If the situation is neither highly favorable nor highly unfavorable, a relationship-oriented style is best. Here, the leader may be liked, but may have little power or may be working with an unstructured task. Or maybe the task is defined well enough, but the leader is not liked. In any case, a leader who emphasizes relationships is likely to be most effective in overcoming the obstacles in a moderately favorable or unfavorable situation.

Leadership Qualities

Regardless of differences in style, leaders perform three basic functions in the actual process of implementing service. First, they select the right approach. Second, they respond to subordinates' and clients' needs. Third, because of their knowledge and experience, they help subordinates perform their job correctly. They are constantly asking for assistance, in the area of information, supplies, and materials. Occasionally they may even seek advice regarding personal matters not totally related to the job, but ultimately affecting job performance.

Leaders should also be aware of employees' personal needs and recognize that leadership is an influential determinant of motivation (refer to the preceding section on motivation, in which personal needs were stressed). Leaders must be aware of them as a sound basis for a practical motivation system that helps subordinates and employees in seeking satisfaction. If leaders properly assign each employee, they will be more assured of increasing productivity. On the other hand, if an employee is opposed to a task, leaders can expect a work slowdown and possibly complete failure in a given assignment.

Leadership is goal oriented. As a result, it is important for the leader to communicate goals to staff members and in turn, help them develop their own goals that are consistent with those of the organization. The leader makes sure that staff members' goals are quantifiable and attainable so that they will find satisfaction in reaching them easily and often. If goals are too broad and too long range, employees may become frustrated. But when goals are attained as part of the motivation system, employees will be rewarded by a feeling of accomplishment.

Another area that leaders have to be very concerned about is the environment in which employees work. Leaders should do all they can to assure good working conditions in a physical, social, and mental sense. Facilities should be clean and bright, and neither too warm nor too cool. Good mental conditions assure that the employees are not distracted by noise or other employees who interfere with their work. Also to be considered are wages and benefit programs such as sick leave, vacation, and insurance. Sometimes leaders can effect improvements; other times this is not possible. In either case, it should be noted that these social conditions will influence work output.

Specific attention needs to be given to three areas that affect leadership, particularly at the managerial level (Koontz and O'Donnell 1980). The first is empathy. (Refer to Chapter 7 for a discussion of how empathy enhances participant satisfaction and contributes to staff morale). To be effective, a leader has to be aware of the personal problems that affect subordinates. This awareness of employees—who they are, what they are, their capabilities and limitations—is extremely important. Although effective leaders cannot totally comprehend every employee's problems and frustrations, they can take account of personal experience and provide the kind of leadership that will consider their needs. Very often the leisure services director or supervisor who has experienced different levels of responsibility can appreciate the problems and concerns of staff members. Much can be said in favor of leaders who have served at various levels of an organization. Leaders who have empathy are in a much better position to do an effective job than those who do not have this quality.

Objectivity is another factor that affects leadership. Good leaders are objective and fair in their judgments. However, there might be a conflict between objectivity and empathy. To be objective, one must do what is right for the agency in terms of what will benefit the greatest number of people in the community. Although it is not possible to become emotionally involved in all of the problems of staff members, managers must consider them before making a rational, objective decision. Good leaders learn to balance these two factors in the best interest of all concerned. By balancing empathy and objectivity, leaders *create* confidence and understanding in *their* units.

A third characteristic that affects leadership is self-awareness. Good leaders must know their own personal capabilities and limitations, capitalize on their strengths, and minimize their weaknesses. Leaders develop confidence in employees by being honest and sincere and by providing stable, capable leadership. We presented some ideas about self-awareness in Chapter Seven.

Leaders also try to allay the fears and anxieties that employees may have about a particular assignment. It is generally true that people are suspicious of, or at least concerned about, any change in their assignment. They feel that change is a threat to their security, that it may not be good for them, that they may not do well because of it, or that someone may have an advantage over them. People tend to worry about all the bad things that might happen rather than what good might come with the change. Change is inevitable in our fast-moving world, and it is the leader's job to keep pace with change, whether it be technological, environmental, or social. The job is to adjust working conditions in order to accomplish organizational programs.

Leadership deals with three factors: the leaders themselves, the participants or the employees, and the situation. The leaders who design meaningful programs and communicate clear objectives to staff members usually provide the best direction for accomplishing those objectives. The second factor involves those who are led, the staff members or participants. Subordinate personnel put into operation the plans of the leader, and the participants receive guidance, instruction, and directions that increase their ability to have an enjoyable experience. The third factor involves the situation, which consists of all the conditions that affect the leader, the staff members and the participants. They must be given careful consideration because they definitely have an influence on the leader and those being led in accomplishing their job or activity.

It is not important which of the three elements—the leader, those being led or the situation—has to adapt or change to accomplish the goal. Generally all three will have to adjust somewhat. The leader recognizes, however, that often the most difficult factor to change is the situation. Just as we cannot change the weather, so we often cannot change the place in which work must be done and many of the other physical barriers that exist. Because people's prejudices, likes, dislikes, and political and religious beliefs might conflict with the leader's task at hand, it can be very difficult to get those being led to change. Often the factor to manipulate or change is the leader. The leader can change an approach, technique, or attitude more readily than he or she can change the existing situation or those being led. If, by making this adjustment, the leader can efficiently, effectively, and quickly accomplish the task, it should be tried. Although leadership can motivate people, sometimes it simply cannot provide the stimulus.

To be most effective, leaders should also develop their employees' confidence. This is done by the provision of a good orientation, good supervision and a good in-service training program. Employees should receive careful follow-up supervision so that their problems are solved on a day-to-day basis rather than letting them build up. Employees should have a sense of job security, which the supervisor develops by an occasional pat on the back, a compliment for a job well done, financial rewards, and advancement when appropriate.

It should be remembered that managers are as a rule appointed, usually by higher-level managers or a board of directors. Their position is not an elective post. As a result, leaders do not feel dependent upon subordinates, as they might feel if elected. However, employees can do a great deal to help meet deadlines. If they dislike their superior or do not have confidence in him or her, they can do a great deal to slow down work and hinder the leader's own effectiveness.

Leadership, whether it evolves by election or appointment, is learned over a period of time and must be constantly improved. Leadership is the sharing and use of leadership roles among group members that thus allows a more holistic approach in management.

Summary

Many important leadership functions have been stressed in this chapter on implementing service. Managers can improve their effectiveness by learning more about being good leaders. To a large extent, their effectiveness will be determined by how they motivate employees to do their work. Managers should try to know their employees as completely and as well as possible. It is through the work of employees that managers accomplish work. Competent leaders use persuasion instead of force. They consider all aspects of a situation and then deal with it appropriately and honestly. In order to bring about needed change from the standard methods and procedures that are deeply embedded in tradition, managers can sometimes be more effective by working through the informal leaders on the staff who often exercise much power and influence.

It is also known that change does not come about quickly, but requires a period of time for acceptance. Leaders can bring about change more effectively if they plant an idea within a group, allow it to germinate and then observe its development by the group itself. This concept of leadership refers to the importance of the leader's awareness of the feelings and sentiments, likes and dislikes of staff members. Competent leaders concentrate on how they can improve every situation so that it will be in the best interest of the employees as well as the overall organization.

In order to implement service, managers tie together the concepts and processes of motivation, communication, and leadership. Like all of the other managerial functions, they are inseparable. Every manager has a unique personality with certain capabilities. He or she should capitalize on strengths and strive to improve weaknesses where competence is lacking.

References

Argyris, Chris. 1957. *Personality and the organization.* New York: Harper & Row.

Fiedler, Fred E. 1967. *A theory of leadership effectiveness.* New York: McGraw-Hill.

Gluskinos, U. M. and B. J. Kestelman. 1971. Management and labor leaders' perception of worker needs as compared with self-reported needs. *Personnel Psychology.* 24: 242.

Hampton, D.R., Summer, C.E., and R.A. Webber. 1968. *Organizational behavior and the practice of management.* Glenview, Ill.: Scott Foresman.

Hersey, P., and K. Blanchard. 1982. *Management of organizational behavior utilizing human resources,* 4th ed. Englewood Cliffs, N.J.: Prentice Hall.

Herzberg, Fredrick, Bernard Mausner, and Barbara Snyderman. 1959. *The motivation to work.* New York: John Wiley and Sons.

Koontz, H., and C. O'Donnell. 1980 *Management,* 6th ed. New York: McGraw-Hill.

Martin, W. 1987. *Quality client service.* Los Altos, Calif.: Crisp Publication.

Maslow, Abraham. 1954. *Motivation and the personality.* New York: Harper & Row.

McFarland, Dalton E. 1958. *Management principles and practices,* 1st ed. New York: Macmillan.

McGehee, Edward M. 1971. Managing human resources in public agencies. Material presented in seminar, Fort Lauderdale, Florida.

McGregor, Douglas. 1960. *The human side of enterprise.* New York: McGraw-Hill.

Ouchi, William, G. 1981. *How American business can meet the Japanese challenge.* New York: Avon Books.

Peters, T.J., and R.H. Waterman, Jr. 1982. *In search of excellence: Lessons from America's best-run companies.* New York: Warner Books.

Phipps, M. 1987. *A systematic approach to learning leadership.* San Luis Obispo, Calif.: El Corral Publications.

12

EVALUATION—MONITORING AND ADJUSTING

What Is Evaluation?

Perhaps the most important managerial function is that of evaluation. Evaluation involves the process of monitoring and adjusting a leisure service delivery system after using on-going and terminal information gathering. This process is cyclical and should provide a constant source of feedback to promote change. For organizations to succeed, they must establish a customer service action plan. The most important element of the plan is for all personnel to treat customers as if they were lifetime partners (LeBoeuf 1989).

There are two major forms of evaluation—formative or process evaluation and summative or outcome evaluation (Lundegren and Farrell 1985; Theobald 1979). In formative evaluation, we gather data and assess services while they are being offered or while they are in progress. After the service is terminated, we use summative or outcome forms. In-progress evaluation lets us make changes as we go along. Evaluation at the end of a program enables us to decide whether the service met its purpose and whether we should offer it again in the same form, modify it, or drop it.

Before beginning to evaluate a service, we need to ask and answer several questions. What will be the purpose of the evaluation? For whom will the results be intended? Who will use them? What resources for conducting the evaluation are available? What are the constraints? When will it be done? What are the deadlines? Who will conduct it—someone from within the agency or an outsider? For this last question, there are probably advantages to each approach. The insider will know the agency well and have access to much information, but may not be completely objective. The outsider probably will come with no preconceived ideas, but may not really have a grasp of the overall situation.

Several evaluation methods or strategies are available (Lundegren and Farrell 1985; Howe and Carpenter 1985). We can measure a service against some external standard: How does the service match up? Often this method is used with areas and facilities: Do we have enough sanitary facilities at our resident camp to meet standards set by the American Camping Association? The method can be used with activity opportunities: Do we have enough lifeguards assigned to the swimming pools to assure patron safety, and do these individuals meet training standards set by the American Red Cross? We can compare certain dimensions of facilitation with professional criteria: Is the recreation therapist, who works with clients in leisure counseling sessions, registered with a state plan, and does she have an appropriate degree from an accredited university?

Another approach we can use is to assess the degree to which service meets goals and objectives. If we undertook an anti-litter campaign to keep city parks clean, are the parks cleaner now? This approach is related to one in which we try to measure outcomes of our programs in terms of participant satisfaction. How do the individuals who use the services feel about them? Are they satisfied? We might compare costs of a service with known benefits if we are able to quantify benefits and determine true costs.

We can evaluate the entire system for delivering program services. In addition to the degree of goal attainment, we can look at the efficiency of the various steps involved in delivery. Data obtained may be used to make decisions about the overall system.

Professional judgment will be involved in any evaluation effort, but it is also a separate strategy. Here, evaluators use their own experience and training to assess a service. Of course, evaluators must take into account the purposes of the service and the agency philosophy. Within this framework, does the service seem to be effective from the standpoint of the expert?

Sometimes we will use multiple strategies. This approach enables us to take advantage of the strengths of different methods and offset the weaknesses. It permits verification of data through use of different techniques.

The Role of Control

Control as part of the evaluation process is just as important as other management functions. As in any scientific experiment, things that can vary greatly affect the outcome of the experiment. A scientist attempts to control those variables that indeed can be controlled. The same is true when managing a leisure service delivery system. Basic plans, policies, and personnel functions need to be monitored and controlled in order to be as consistent as possible. In this type of environment, evaluation may yield results that will make changes most effective.

Need for Evaluation

In the leisure service field, evaluation has undoubtedly been the weakest and the most disregarded of all of the management functions. For years, practitioners have been saying that the provision of recreation opportunities is concerned with unmeasurable factors that do not lend themselves to objective evaluation. Although there appears to be some truth to this view, the park and recreation profession cannot continue to neglect evaluation and still maintain its dignity and image in the eyes of other professions and legislative bodies. Therefore, planning and evaluating need to be examined very closely and should be considered, for all practical purposes, as inseparable functions of management.

In the chapter concerned with planning, we stated that an organization has difficulty achieving its goals if it does not have a realistic plan of action. We pointed out that good planning procedures set targets to which organization efforts and energies can be directed to obtain the desired goals and objectives. Just like planning, but at the other end of the spectrum, controlling provides organizational feedback about the effectiveness of the implementation of programs and services. Managers, through evaluation, make sure that what is being executed conforms with agency policies and standards.

Also, once the plan is put into action, it is necessary to measure and determine progress. Evaluation measures are used to point out the discrepancies between an agency's plans and its actual accomplishments in order to indicate what is necessary to put the agency back on the correct course. The corrective action may call for one of many different management techniques. It may be minor or major in its consequences. When drastic action appears necessary, it might be necessary to go back and analyze the planning process and very carefully draw up new plans to the point that a practically new service approach emerges. On the other hand, corrective action may necessitate only a minor modification of the plan, goal, or objective to obtain the desired results. In other cases where stronger action is called for, it might result in the reorganization of personnel and divisions, reassignment of people, as well as other necessary changes such as specialized training of personnel, additional staff, improvements in the selection process or even the drastic action of firing employees.

The problem might conceivably stem from the lack of effective leadership and poor direction. In such an instance, improved team effort or better communication might be necessary to put the organization back on course. In just about every case, the close, intimate relationship between the planning and evaluation processes is evident. Probably the most effective kind of evaluation is high quality management.

Effecting Evaluation in the Organization

All organizations should hire and retain top-quality managers because they directly or indirectly affect all other control and evaluation devices. Without the manager, the evaluation function is meaningless. Particularly in the field of leisure service where dealing with people is fundamental, people and programs rather than machinery and products are the style of service. Most evaluation devices involve people and are a measurement of their effectiveness. Such control or evaluation efforts are regarded very negatively or as undesirable by lower-level employees who feel that someone is always looking over their shoulder and trying to catch them making a mistake. This problem has to be dealt with honestly and forthrightly if there is to be a controlled program. A more positive approach would be to prevent things from going wrong by better orientation, supervision, and training. A constant effort should be made to make every employee as effective as possible. The more positive the approach, the easier it is in the long run to make control a helpful tool of management and to make it more acceptable to all employees.

If managers are the key to good evaluation, then they must understand it and believe in its usefulness. In too many instances, managers just pay lip service to evaluation, never using it as a managerial device. Evaluation is a method to prevent plans from going wrong before they get too far off course. It should be forward-looking and probing and should enable managers to predict, at every stage, the possibility of error (Koontz and O'Donnell 1980). It is this type of scrutiny that makes evaluation effective.

Relationship of Evaluation to Goals

As previously mentioned, if evaluation is really going to be effective, good plans in terms of goals, objectives, or standards are necessary. These goals and objectives should be stated in very quantifiable terms. Further, these standards must be understood by all concerned so that they can be implemented. Unless all employees understand exactly what they are to do, their chances of performing up to standard are rather unlikely. This concept was already stressed in the discussion of the planning process.

Very often, as managers get interested in evaluation and try to implement measurement strategies, they realize they will run into difficulties because their goals and objectives are not stated in measurable ways. Often they are too general and open to too much latitude and interpretation. Therefore, before any evaluation can be used, leisure service managers have to state goals and objectives in more exact and measurable terms. For example, if one were to establish the broad objective of strengthening in-service training, it must be presented in precise terms: a six-week first-aid course will be established for new leaders by January 15. This quantifiable objective can then be stated in various standards of attainment; for example: to pass the course, a person must obtain a score of 70 percent. The objective may be broken down further: 40 percent of the test grade will be determined by the students' demonstration of their first-aid ability; and so on for other requirements.

Only in this way can the evaluation really measure the results. The manager can determine whether or not the desired goals were achieved or by how much they were surpassed.

Controls and Corrective Action

In effecting control, the model presented in Figure 12.1 shows the relationship of goal setting to evaluation. The schematic circle 1 indicates the planning process during which the goal is determined and stated in a measurable standard. Circle 2 indicates that the plan is put into action and that the project is implemented to attain the target in circle 4. As action toward the desired target continues, something goes wrong, as indicated by the original goal, and corrective action is instituted to put the agency back on course. Also, a change in the original goal can be made. In any case, some type of corrective action is taken and the project is under way again toward its target. Circle 6 shows the evaluation procedure as a two-way process that functions to ensure that the agency will attain its goals or the alternate goals formulated later. This schematic diagram of the evaluation process, although over-simplified, does indicate that evaluation is a constant process resulting in assessment of stated goals.

Evaluation should be understood by all concerned, from the top manager to the front-line personnel who implement direct service. If employees feel that the controls help them do their job more effectively, they will accept them more readily. To be effective, the controls must measure the effectiveness of the work

Figure 12.1 Model Showing Control Process with Feedback

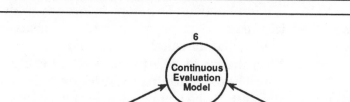

or goals. In the case of a park leader, standards are stated in terms of schedules of work to be done by definite days or deadlines. The control can be a check list that the leader tallies when the work has been completed. The supervisor then notes the check sheet as well as the work to see if the leader has met the standards. If the leader understands that the check sheet helps meet deadlines, it will be valued.

For the control to be helpful, it should point out departures from the standards at the earliest possible point. To find out a week after the fact that a park crew did not meet its deadline is too late. By using the daily check sheet, the leader can tell whether deadlines will be met. Adding help or shifting priorities are corrections that can be made to meet the schedule. Thus the evaluation process should, in a sense, predict the future to determine trends or to alert the manager to problems and allow time for corrections before matters get seriously out of hand. One form of control is the check sheet indicating that a certain job is to be performed on a given day or at a given time. Another form of control also uses a check sheet to indicate the number of work hours it will take to perform a task and provides the park leader with the necessary corrective action if one of the subordinates is ill. In this way, the check list serves as a predictive and corrective instrument because the control itself indicates the corrective action necessary to improve the situation.

Good controls should be objective, and if they are meaningfully determined they will be so (Koontz and O'Donnell 1980). The check list is objective because it represents factual information about the work crew's success in completing the assigned projects according to a given schedule. It eliminates argument or subjective conclusions about the crew's ability to do the job. The check sheet is also economical—another concern of a good control procedure. To spend 99 cents to protect a dollar is foolish. Controls that are very expensive to administer often negate their value. Finally, a control should be flexible in both its method of use and in its corrective action.

In any case, the evaluation process provides a way for managers to see what is going wrong at the earliest possible time, and it helps to eliminate the problems so that the organization will fulfill its work goals. The process should help the manager avoid making similar mistakes in the future.

In many instances, an evaluation program or system has critical times or points at which the manager can check to see if the operations are functioning according to plan. It is a way of measuring a job or program performance along the way. Certain questions need to be explored: Are we still working for our original goal? Is the goal clear in the minds of all concerned?

Very often as agencies undertake a goal, they begin to change their emphasis as the work progresses. Therefore, agencies need to remind themselves constantly of their predetermined goals so that they stay on course. In other cases, as they move toward projected goals, agencies realize that their original goals are not what they really wanted or intended. This realization in itself is important in the control process. Equally important when the manager comes to this conclusion, is altering the goals or targets and also letting all subordinates know about the change. To fail to do so will cause wasted effort and frustration on the part of the work force.

Still other questions need to be asked: Are we meeting our deadlines? Is it important from time to time to stop and see where we are? Are we proceeding on time? Are we ahead or behind schedule?

One of the best ways to control deadlines is to plot out all the activities that must be accomplished to reach a desired goal. Each activity should be given a deadline, and then the manager can determine how much time the total project will take to complete. In Chapter 8 we discussed Program Evaluation Review Techniques (PERT) as a planning process(see Figure 8.1). It can also be a very effective control device (see Figure 12.1). Each circle represents an activity, and each activity is given a deadline. Leisure service managers can see where progress has been made and where it has not.

There are two ways that the manager can change the course of action by the use of controls. One way is to find out what the problem is, where it is, and who is responsible for the problem or unsatisfactory work. At this point, the manager gets the person responsible to go back and correct the work and improve and change habits and practices in the future. Another, more direct method of control is to employ or develop efficient and effective managers. Efficient managers will take precautionary steps and actions *before* plans are ruined. They will see to it that the activity or program never gets off course. Yet even the most skillful manager makes a mistake from time to time, but also takes corrective actions as soon as the error is realized. This is generally done by: (1) *modifying plans*, the method just discussed, and (2) *correcting the problem or deviation*, which can sometimes be done by *reorganizing.* Sometimes difficulties arise when plans are not implemented fast enough because of organizational problems. When this is the case, reorganization may need to be done. Less drastic but sometimes more effective is reassignment of certain personnel. Some of these problems and situations were discussed in Chapter 9.

Another method to correct a problem is by *clarifying duties or assignments.* Often managers take for granted that personnel understand their duties, only to find out that they really do not. Once this is cleared up, some of the problems are eliminated. Additional control devices consist of *hiring additional staff, improving employee selection procedures, requiring additional staff training, and even firing staff members to improve the operation.*

An evaluation program may indicate a need for better directing techniques, that is, stronger or better leadership. In any case, evaluation as a management technique will do much to improve the image of the leisure profession. The recreation and park field has had limited controls and evaluation tools, but in the future even more measurement efforts are going to be necessary so that we can move forward as a recognized and accepted profession.

Evaluation Tools

Personnel

Personnel evaluations have been the most used and most realistic tools in the recreation and park profession to control and evaluate the quality of accomplishments. This approach probably occurred because personnel evaluation systems were adopted from other professions or because governmental civil service systems required them. Personnel evaluation-feedback procedures are used to determine the effectiveness and efficiency of employees. These procedures vary from simple narrative (albeit highly subjective) comments on an employee's work, to detailed, objective evaluation procedures. Employee evaluation is a continual process by which the manager appraises employees' work and offers assistance, direction, or corrective action. More formal evaluations should be done at least semi-annually. Personnel evaluations serve as a guide for additional training, promotion, corrective action, demotion, and salary adjustments. These steps should be constructive and taken as needed, not delayed until an annual or semi-annual evaluation. When the employee performs well, the individual should be told as a reward for a job well done.

Most evaluations deal with general areas or habits of an employee's work: quantity and quality of work, compliance with instructions, thoroughness and neatness, reliability, punctuality, personal relationships with fellow employees and the public, supervisory abilities, personal appearance, health, and other special factors related to specific jobs.

Evaluations are done in two ways. A subjective evaluation is used when the employee is rated by using such phrases as "unsatisfactory," "needs attention," "satisfactory," and "outstanding." Typically these rating devices serve to appraise individuals on aspects of their personality. However, there appears to be no common agreement on what the traits in question mean. Usually there is a place for a paragraph describing the employee's work (see Table 12.1).

The second procedure uses a numerical system of performance standards of the same or similar categories of employees' work. The work is rated on a scale from 1 to 10, with 1 being very poor and 10 being outstanding. The work performance approach provides more objectivity for comparing several employees' work. For the evaluation to be effective, it should be done with meaning and careful thought. In park and recreation systems where it has been tried as a part of promotional procedures, it has been most effective. It has also proved valuable when it has been the basis of giving salary increases. In any system, the evaluation or control is only as effective as the manager makes it. When this approach incorporates employee self-rating procedures, it narrows the discrepancy between the job expectations of the supervisor and the employee.

Facilities

Facility evaluations or controls generally take the form of check sheets used as part of the inspection of facilities or grounds. The check list is stated in terms of the standards that the organization wants to maintain, which are derived from the organizational goals or objectives. The check list is a systematic list of things to be inspected, such as cleanliness of floors, rest rooms, walls, condition of repairs, condition of windows, lighting, and quality of

Table 12.1 Work Performance Report

Name	(Last)	(First)	(Initial)		Period Covered From To

Civil Service Title		Civil Service Staus		If Prob, Date Ends

Department		Division		Unit

Check items ☐+ Strong ☐− Weak ☐√ Satisfactory ☐O Not applicable	Indicate factor rating by "X"			
	Unsatisfactory	Needs Attention	Satisfactory	Outstanding
1. Quantity of Work ☐ Amount of work performed ☐ Completion of work on schedule	Seldom produces enough work or meets deadlines.	Does not always complete an acceptable amount of work.	Consistently completes an acceptable amount of work.	Amount of work produced is consistently outstanding.
2. Quality of Work ☐ Accuracy ☐ Effectiveness ☐ Compliance with instructions ☐ Use of tools & equipment ☐ Neatness of work product	Too poor to retain in job without improvement.	Quality below acceptable standards.	Performs assigned duties in a satisfactory manner.	Performs all duties in an outstanding manner. Exceptional accuracy, skill or effectiveness.
3. Work Habits ☐ Attendance ☐ Observance of working hours ☐ Observance of rules ☐ Safety practices ☐ Personal appearance	Too poor to retain in job without improvement.	Work habits need improvement.	Work habits satisfactory.	Exceptional work habits. Always observes rules and safe practices.
4. Personal Relations ☐ With fellow employees and supervisors ☐ With public	Too poor to retain in job without improvement. Poor supervisory ability.	Personal relations need improvement.	Maintains satisfactory work relations with others.	Exceptionally cooperative with public, co-workers and supervisors.
5. Supervisor Ability ☐ Planning & assigning ☐ Training & instructing ☐ Disciplinary control ☐ Evaluating performance ☐ Delegating ☐ Making decisions ☐ Fairness & impartiality ☐ Unit morale	Work of unit frequently unsatisfactory.	Supervisory ability inadequate in some respects. Work results of unit below par at times.	Obtains good results from subordinates. Controls unit efficiently.	Outstanding ability to get maximum from unit and available resources.

Rater's comments: (attach additional sheets if needed)

RATER'S RECOMMENDATION (for employees under consideration for a merit raise or permanent status) This is to certify that the overall performance of the subject employee is / is not satisfactory. The employee is / is not recommended for a merit raise / permanent status.

This report is based on my observation and knowledge. It represents my best judgment of the employee's performance.
RATER   DATE

I have reviewed this report. It represents the facts to the best of my knowledge. I concur in the recommendation, if any, as to merit raise or permanent status.
REVIEWER   DATE

In signing this report I do not necessarily agree with the conclusions of the rater. I understand that I may write my comments on the reverse side. I have received a copy of this report.   EMPLOYEE'S SIGNATURE   DATE equipment. Other things to be noted are bad odors in rest rooms, messy janitor closets that might be fire hazards, unused equipment not in its proper place, and writing on walls. Check lists are filled out by the inspectors and given to the personnel in charge so that corrections can be made. A follow-up inspection should be made after a reasonable period of time to determine if corrections have in fact been made. Appropriate credit can be given if it is warranted. Such check lists become working standards of performance for custodial personnel and usually bring about high levels of maintenance. Also, a similar check list can be used as a control to assure that work is performed according to a given schedule. Items of work to be performed by given times are specified. Maintenance personnel do the jobs and then check them off, noting the time as well (see Table 12.2).

The objective is very specific and is written in a quantifiable way to determine if it is met or not. The objective is then further broken down into specific tasks that make up the total objective of turf maintenance as well as the unit of measurement, the number of units, the unit costs, the total number of hours to accomplish the task, and the total cost for the task (see Table 12.3).

Each month, budget reports are sent to the managers responsible for evaluating the progress on each objective and each task. These reports along with field visits can help the manager determine, in a very objective manner, whether employees are meeting their goals.

Programs

Program evaluations and controls are probably the weakest in the leisure services because the items being evaluated are not easily measured. The most often used measurement tool for programs has been the attendance count, which gives a corresponding high priority to well-attended activities. The variety of activities at a particular facility has also been used to rate programs. Although these factors are relevant, they provide only a very limited measurement of the total effectiveness of a recreation program. Despite the difficulties, some objectivity can be placed on a program's worth. Theobald (1987) cites several ways that leisure service has been evaluated. The following methods have developed in the field:

Table 12.2 Maintenance Report

Park _____ For Week Beginning _____

I. The following daily maintenance is to be performed and initialed.

	Mon	Tues	Wed	Thur	Fri	Sat	Sun
A. Shelters							
1. Clean equipment room	___	___	___	___	___	___	___
2. Clean tables and benches	___	___	___	___	___	___	___
3. Clean shelter grills	___	___	___	___	___	___	___
4. Clean cement floor	___	___	___	___	___	___	___
5. Replace burned out lights	___	___	___	___	___	___	___
B. Rest rooms (Unlock upon arrival and lock up at 4:00)							
1. Clean lavatories	___	___	___	___	___	___	___
2. Clean urinals and commodes	___	___	___	___	___	___	___
3. Hose out with water	___	___	___	___	___	___	___
4. Replace burned out lights	___	___	___	___	___	___	___
5. Replace toilet paper	___	___	___	___	___	___	___
C. Check tennis nets and posts	___	___	___	___	___	___	___
D. Pick up paper in park	___	___	___	___	___	___	___
E. Clear out grills	___	___	___	___	___	___	___
F. Collect trash and place at pick-up point	___	___	___	___	___	___	___
G. Check all playground equipment	___	___	___	___	___	___	___
H. Check ball fields (Approx. 3:00 PM)							
1. Rake and fill all low areas	___	___	___	___	___	___	___
2. Clean out dugouts	___	___	___	___	___	___	___
3. Line field	___	___	___	___	___	___	___
4. Water if needed	___	___	___	___	___	___	___

II. The following weekly maintenance is to be performed and initialed.
1. Cut all grass. _____
2. Sling all areas not accessible with mower. _____
3. Open all drainage ditches. _____
4. Pull grass around swimming pool and tennis courts. _____
5. Trim hedges. _____

III. List any major work to be performed.
1. _____
2. _____

Date _____

Maintenance Person's Signature

Table 12.3 Parks Maintenance Budget

257 Parks Maintenance
Nappi/Masmori/Jones
Parks & Fac MTC Supv/Park Supv

To provide safe, clean, functional and attractive parks and recreational facilities to meet the passive and active recreational needs of the user.

Fiscal Year	Work Hours	Total Cost	Equivalent Unit Cost
1983-84	77,115	1,876,817	22.72
1984-85	76,313	2,031,700	23.83
1985-86	85,694	2,339,305	25.98
1986-87	87,356	2,483,945	26.87
1987-88	87,356	2,582,784	27.94
1988-89	87,356	3,592,891	
1989-90	87,356	3,806,298	
1990-91	87,356	4,039,317	
1991-92	87,356	4,281,635	
1992-93	87,356	4,539,758	
1993-94	87,356	4,810,818	
1994-95	87,356	5,136,067	
1995-96	87,356	5,444,280	

Note: Increase is reflected in additional maintenance for Shirlay-Lori and Macara Parks. Maintenance cost of $750,000 for the Baylands Park is not reflected in this program, but has been added to the General Fund budget.

1. *Discrepancy evaluation.* Program administrators are asked to what extent programs have met a clearly defined set of objectives.
2. *Professional judgment evaluation.* This is a direct observation approach, using recognized experts.
3. *Socioeconomic evaluation.* This method uses demographic data as bases for comparison.
4. *Evaluation by standards.* This method establishes criteria by which programs are measured.
5. *Decision-oriented model.* Known as the Program Evaluation Procedure (PEP), this model compares the input, processes, and outcomes of recreation programs.

6. *Cost-benefit evaluation.* Projects are evaluated by comparing them with benefits and actual costs.

7. *Importance-performance evaluation.* This method measures participants' thoughts on the importance placed on an activity and the way in which the activity met with their satisfaction.

Theobald cites the need for more and better evaluation tools in the leisure service field. Evaluation programs, people, and processes may serve to thoroughly analyze ways to monitor and adjust.

Probably the reason for objective evaluation is that the program standards in the leisure services have always been articulated in general terms. Even in an area of some objectivity, they are stated too generally. The following is an example: A good program should have a good variety of activities. But how many activities constitute a "variety" of program opportunities? What is a "good" program? Five different activities, ten, twenty, thirty, or how many? Should they include the categories of sports, arts and crafts, drama, or something else? The needs of the community also must be considered. One community might need sports activities; another, arts and crafts. Before an objective evaluation can be implemented, the goals must first be stated in quantifiable terms. This point is stressed in Chapter 8.

Participant Survey

Individual participants may be surveyed at random at various times to determine their satisfaction with the programs. Information about whether the activity or course met their expectations, the quality of instruction, suggestions for improvement as well as other information about specific activities can be asked in an attempt to get feedback for improvement and to see if managers are really meeting their objectives. An example of a participant survey is presented in Table 12.4.

Surveys should also be conducted periodically to receive feedback about community reaction to programs. Such surveys include both users and nonusers. An attempt is made to determine satisfaction with programs, as well as to ask for suggestions about new programs. Information can be gained about why individuals

Table 12.4 Participant Survey

SUNNYVALE PARKS AND RECREATION DEPARTMENT
SPECIAL CLASS EVALUATION FORM

Name of Class _____ Date _____

Instructor _____ Evaluator _____

1. How did you learn about this class?
   Brochure ____ Newspaper ____ Friend ____ Other ____

2. Would you be interested in taking another class in this area? ____

3. What other classes would you be interested in taking through the Recreation Department?

   _____

   _____

4. Did you accomplish what you expected from this class when you first enrolled?
   If no, please comment.

   _____

   _____

   _____

5. Would you encourage your friends to enroll in this class?
   Why or why not?

   _____

   _____

6. Was the instructor willing to help you with special problems? ____

7. Was the instruction clear and understandable? _____

8. Was the instructor organized and well-prepared? _____

9. What improvements might you suggest to facility, class content, organization or instruction?

   _____

   _____

   _____

10. Comment on class size. Too small __ Adequate __ Too Large __

11. Additional comments:

    _____

    _____

    _____

Thank you for your assistance.

are not using programs and facilities.   It may be the cost of activities, poor leadership, poor controls, bad time of day, or many other reasons, all of which can be addressed or corrected. These surveys can be mailed or sent with normal program activity publicity. An example of a typical community survey is presented in Table 12.5.

Careful consideration should be given to preparing surveys, and professional assistance should be sought to assure that they are well done. Ambiguous questions, poorly worded questions, or even the wrong questions will not elicit helpful information and could even be misleading.

In whatever manner feedback is received, it must be used to generate information. Not to use it is poor management and will ultimately discredit the manager. The use of feedback is a wonderful tool to modify programs, put them back on course, make improvements, and reassess planning, all of which facilitate good evaluation and control.

Quality Customer Service

It is increasingly important for employees to be equipped with the knowledge and ability to help participants solve their problems at the point of interaction with the customer. Some questions LeBoeuf (1989) suggests asking employees are:

1. What is your service?
2. What does it do?
3. What are the benefits to the participant?
4. What does it cost?
5. Why is it worth more than it costs?
6. What is the competition and why is our service a better value?

Having answered these questions, employees should ask clients-participants the following questions:

1. What are you trying to accomplish?
2. What do you know about our services?
3. How would you like me to work with you?

Table 12.5 Community Survey

The City of Sunnyvale Parks and Recreation appreciates your response to the following survey. It is part of an on-going effort by the department to provide our participants with meaningful, enjoyable, and convenient leisure opportunities.

Each household responding will receive a coupon good for two complimentary soft drinks, redeemable at the "Hands-on-the-Arts" event. "Hands-on-the-Arts" will be hosted at the Sunnyvale Community Center on June 13th and 14th, 1987.

Please complete the survey and return it along with your mail-in registration form, by March 20, 1987.

The department currently sponsors six major city-wide special events for children and their families:

1) Please check the special event(s) you attended in the last year. Comment for improvement or new ideas.

Event Comment

Spring Eggstravaganza _____
(March-April)

Sport-a-rama (May)   _____

Fourth of July Celebration _____
(July)

Baylands Run (August) _____

Haunted House & Halloween _____
Fun House (October)

Holiday Package (December) _____

2) What new ideas do you have for city-wide special events:
_____
_____
_____

3) Which times would adults in your household prefer to attend fitness classes or activities?

6-7:30am _____   7:30-9 am _____   Noon-1pm _____

5:30-7 pm _____   7-9pm _____   Other (please specify) _____

4) In the past 12 months have you or a member of your household participated in a Recreation (Cultural Arts) tour or excursion? Yes _____ No _____

If Yes, how many tours?

1-2 _____   3-5 _____   5 or more _____

If No, reason: New to the area _____ Didn't know about _____ Too busy _____

                Program schedule not convenient _____   No prior interest _____

5) In the past 12 months have you or a member of your household attended an exhibition at the Sunnyvale Creative Art Center Gallery? Yes _____ No _____
If Yes, how many times?   1-2 _____   3-5 _____   5 or more _____

If No, reason: New to the area _____   No prior interest _____

                     Too busy _____   Didn't know about _____

382

Table 12.5 *Continued*

6) In the past 12 months have you or a member of your household attended a performance at the Sunnyvale Performing Arts Center? Yes _____ No _____

If **Yes,** what type of performance did you attend?

Musical _____   Comedy _____   Drama _____   Dance _____

Childrens' Theatre _____   Music _____

If **No,** reason: New to the area _____   No prior interest _____

Too busy _____   Didn't know about _____

7) The last time you or a member of your household participated in a department program, how did you handle your registration?

Mail-in Registration _____   **Walk-in Registration** _____

If by **Walk-in Registration,** why? Prefer walk-in to mail-in registration _____

Missed mail-in deadline _____

Wanted to pay with cash _____

Other (please specify) _____

8) Did you know that the Sunnyvale Parks and Recreation Department offers a full spectrum of programs and services for adults ages 50 years and older at the Multi-Purpose Senior Center? Yes_____ No _____

9) Did you know that Sunnyvale Parks and Recreation Department offers programs and services for adults with disabillities? Yes_____ No _____

10) Indicate number of individuals in your household under the appropriate age bracket.

Age 0-5	6-12	13-19	20-29	30-39	40-49	50-59	60-69	70-79	80+
_____	_____	_____	_____	_____	_____	_____	_____	_____	____

11) For which of the following activities would members of your household be interested in registering? (Check as many as are appropriate)

_____ Summer Teen Basketball League
_____ Year Round Adult Lap Swim
_____ Youth Fitness/Aerobics Classes
_____ Summer Adult Basketball League
_____ Weight Lifting and Exercise
_____ Adult Soccer League Running or Jogging
_____ Tai Chi Classes
_____ Family Swim Time
_____ Adult Gymnastics
_____ Adult Aerobics
_____ Bicycling Tours
_____ Sr. Citizen Swim Time
_____ Bicycling Races
_____ Windsurfing Lessons
_____ Youth Golf Camp
_____ Adult Water Exercise Class
_____ Other (Please specify)

4. How soon do you need this service?

5. How can we be of greatest help to you?

It is critical that employees listen for total meaning. Leisure managers can then begin to respond with quality client/participant service by matching the agency's solutions with the clients' needs. Managers can respond most effectively to their clientele by rewarding them with kindness, empathy, and solutions to their leisure problems:

1. Deal with the client's feeling.

2. Solve the problems that brought the client to you in the first place.

3. When clients are upset, angry, or unhappy, they are giving you information. Concentrate on listening for information that will help you solve the problem.

4. Listen with empathy.

5. Take action to solve the client's problems.

Evaluating to Achieve Customer Satisfaction

Once service goals are established, they must be measured. Each employee should write an answer to the following question: "What results do I (we) produce and how do they benefit the client-participant?" By answering this question, employees are then free to think about their jobs in terms of the participant. Next, middle-level managers should sit down with each group of staff members and decide what results they are to attain by a certain date.

The following guidelines are helpful for establishing goals and performance measures related to customer or participant satisfaction.

1. Employee goals should contribute to the organization's ultimate goal of serving participants.

2. State the goal in terms of results that you as a manager want to achieve (e.g., reducing the number of participant complaints by 30 percent, increasing the number of complimentary letters received per month by 10 percent; increas-

ing the amount of dollars coming from repeat customers by 20 percent).

3. Goals should be brief and simple, and should be written down to measure clarity and commitment.

4. Let employees set their own goals whenever you can. It increases motivation and commitment.

5. Challenging but attainable goals lead to the best performance.

Managers must reward employees for providing quality participant service. Ways to reward great service include opportunities for advancement, time off, recognition, increase in pay, prizes, and more freedom.

Quality participant-client service must be a continuing, top priority for the entire organization. Managers at all levels must become personally involved in listening to and helping both employees and participants (see Figure 12.2).

Summary

Leisure managers can easily see from this chapter that the five functions of management—planning, organizing, staffing,

Figure 12.2 Quality Participant Service Management Cycle

implementing, and evaluating—are inseparable. The evaluation function ties together the other four functions and gives them additional meaning. Evaluation is particularly important because it lets managers know whether they are on the right course in attaining their goals. If they are off course, the evaluating function helps to get them back on target. Finally, it tells them if they arrived where they wanted to be. It measures accomplishments.

References

Howe, C.Z., and G. M. Carpenter. 1985. *Programming leisure experiences.* Englewood Cliffs, NJ: Prentice Hall.

Koontz, H., and C. O'Donnell. 1980. *Principles of management,* 5th ed. New York: McGraw-Hill.

LeBoeuf, M. 1989. *How to win customers and keep them for life.* New York: Berkeley Books.

Lundegren, H., and P. Farrell. 1985. *Evaluation for leisure service managers: A dynamic approach.* Philadelphia: Saunders College Publishing.

McFarland, Dalton E. 1968. *Management principles and practices,* 1st ed. New York: MacMillan.

Theobald, W. 1979. *Evaluation of recreation and park programs.* New York: John Wiley & Sons.

Theobald, W. 1987. Historical antecedents of evaluation in leisure program and services. *Journal of Park and Recreation Administration* 4(5):1-9.

CONCLUSION

We hope that the preceding twelve chapters have provided the reader with a sound foundation to understand the dynamics of the leisure service field and the society in which it exists. The conceptual framework presented in this text contends that for recreation and park agencies— whether public, private nonprofit or commercial organizations—to most effectively serve the leisure and human needs of people, they must incorporate a systems perspective in the delivery of leisure services. Systems are integrated wholes whose properties cannot be reduced to those of smaller units. Living systems are not confined to individual organisms and their parts. The same aspects of wholeness are exhibited by social systems such as a family or a community organization.

The systems approach provides a helpful philosophical and operational method for conceptualizing relationships. It is a basis for formulating action-oriented approaches for enhancing the quality of life within a community. At the core of the overall societal system is the individual organism. The human being is embedded with a number of ecological and social subsystems within a community. Each element of the community influences other elements. The interrelationships of various agencies and people of the community subsystems will have some effect, directly or indirectly, on other members of the community.

Recreation and leisure service organizations are part of an arena of continual social interaction. The organization and provision of recreation and leisure services do not take place in a vacuum. Public, private nonprofit, and commercial leisure service organizations are all linked in some form to the larger community system.

The leisure service delivery system (LSDS) is a product of the society. It is influenced by current social conditions, and in turn it exerts an influence upon society. The LSDS reflects historical events as well as developments related to the field, and predictions and visions about the future that have relevance for the field.

People exhibit behavior when they engage in leisure. It is primarily intrinsically motivated; that is, we engage in leisure because of the enjoyment that comes directly from the experience, rather than because of some other secondary motivation. We engage in leisure because we anticipate enjoyment, spiritual transcendence, satisfaction, excitement, adventure, and human contact.

The leisure service profession is made up of agencies and organizations that exist to provide opportunities for people to engage in leisure behavior. The main goal of these agencies is to provide certain kinds of places and personnel to enable people to experience leisure. The places may be parks, zoos, spas, art studios, libraries, or concert halls. The personnel may be leaders, instructors, environmental naturalists, maintenance workers, therapists, or resort administrators.

Leisure service agencies use their resources of places and personnel, as well as legislation and finances, to deliver leisure services. The system of leisure services at the community level is comprised of four interdependent and interrelated elements: the social environment, physical resources, leisure service organizations, and the recipients—people. Each element influences the other. When one element changes, it is likely to have an impact on one or more of the others. In the recreation and park field, personnel and places are elements an agency can deploy to provide leisure services.

All leisure service personnel who work to plan, organize, encourage, facilitate, and manage leisure opportunities are most effective when they comprehend the totality of interactive human, social, and physical environments, and the organizational relationships that exist within a community. Leisure service providers—leaders, therapists, sports specialists, day care directors, executives—must recognize the interrelated nature of the field if they are to maximize their effectiveness as professionals.

Leisure service managers of the 1990s must become aware of how society affects what they do, whatever their specialty or position in an organization. This LSDS approach encourages professional recreators to realize that they cannot operate in a vacuum. The LSDS approach suggests that service providers need to grasp the significance of leisure, its importance to individual enrichment and community life. The LSDS approach encourages leisure service professionals to see the ecological relationships between the public they serve and the kinds of processes they use, and to understand that they work with others' behaviors and that their professional techniques must respond to clients' needs and interests in appropriate ways.

Leisure opportunities provide the context for individuals to participate in a myriad of satisfying and growth-enhancing experiences. These experiences contribute to individual well-being, facilitate social bonding for groups, and result in improving the habitability and quality of community life. The interdependent ingredients of the delivery system—the physical environment (topography, transportation, housing, environmental impact), the social environment (cultural, ethnic, education and health factors), leisure service organizations (staff behavior, goals and objectives, programs), and human concerns (individual motivation, needs, experience, self-concept, competencies)—must be acted upon in an integrated, interactive manner to bring about the most meaningful participation. The delivery of leisure services occurs through effective, holistic organizational management and a service-oriented structure. Management of leisure services using this client-oriented approach involves a recognition of how each element or subsystem operates in a dynamic manner within the community system and the corresponding impact that each decision and action has upon all other environments.

A New Age paradigm or constellation of values, beliefs, knowledge, and behavior is emerging. It emphasizes the interconnectedness and interdependence of all phenomena. The fundamental premises of the evolving New Age paradigm are that recreation and leisure experiences do not exist in isolation from the rest of a person's life. The goal of all forms of management processes is linked to promoting individual life enrichment, human development, and enhancement of communitywide needs. This conceptual, service-oriented systems management perspective—holistic, ecological, and interactionist service delivery model—blends well with the human organism's natural tendency to integrate mind, body, and spirit and the community system's desire for moral commitment, association, and participation of its members.

In a healthy community system, the various elements strive for a balance between self-assertion and integration. Leisure service agencies ideally provide a full range of opportunities. They extend from one end of the service delivery continuum of agency-organized and agency-conducted services to individually encouraged and guided participation, to self-directed expressions that may lead to leisure independence at the other end. For an organism to be healthy, it has to preserve its individual autonomy, but at the same time it has to be able to integrate itself harmoniously into larger systems. Whereas other subsystems of family, neighborhood and work traditionally provided a symbolic connection of the individual to community life, leisure has emerged as a form of human association that provides a holistic mind-body-spirit expression of self for individuals. Leisure has also emerged as a means in which shared interests, representative of one's lifestyle, provide a more appealing and relevant connection with others.

The role of the recreation, park, and leisure profession in the last decade of the twentieth century appears to require a new direction. All forms of organizational sponsorship will be challenged to develop a more flexible and client-oriented comprehensive delivery system to respond more capably to the dynamic, ever-changing context of community life and diverse needs and life circumstances of people.

With the increased use of technology in North American society and the segmenting and fractionalizing of traditional forms of human association (workplace, family, and neighborhood), each individual has been set free to find happiness and to secure both self and group identity within the community. From the perspective of a New Age paradigm, living systems are made up of human beings, social systems, and ecosystems. Each system is self-organizing and interconnected with the others. Recognizing these interrelationships enables organizations and individuals to see the impact of individual and group decisions on other persons and structures. The mechanistic model and the traditional leisure service concepts and processes gained independent identification. However, they have had no particular connection with other nondirect service professional roles and responsibilities or societal issues that affect leisure choices and behavior. These issues include the environmental movement; women's, disabled, and racial-ethnic group rights movements; and antinuclear war and peace movements, to name a few.

The New Age approach, which accommodates the holistic, ecological leisure service delivery system concept, seeks to discover linkages and interrelationships. The New Age paradigm, and indeed the concepts discussed in this book, call for a reconstruction of the philosophical foundation, professional knowledge base, and management and service delivery framework for much of the recreation, park, and leisure profession. The linear, competitive, rational and quantitative characteristics and values of the mechanistic paradigm, still largely representative of many leisure service agencies, require a 180-degree turnaround in thinking and approach to professional practice. Leisure, as with other elements of our existence, has meaning to the extent that we perceive our experience as emanating from within our own being and in connection with the rest of the community, societal, and global systems.

Hierarchical, paternalistic, and bureaucratic bases for the leisure service organizational structures, combined with a structure unconnected to other professions and societal subsystems, invariably result in the diminishing of the relevance and meaning of the leisure experience. The effective leisure service leader or manager who operates under a systems and more free-form organizational structure recognizes that it is the individual participant who imparts meaning to his or her life, rather than primarily adapting to environmental structures. This provides the basis for all human service providers to better facilitate opportunities for individual self-expression and the connection of people to others in the community.

It is our belief that managers will be most successful in providing relevant services and meeting the leisure needs of participants by understanding the dynamics of systems and their influences on the delivery of leisure services. Leisure service professionals need to understand the full extent to which each managerial function must operate in a coordinated and integrated manner within the context of a systems framework if they are to respond effectively to individual clientele or community needs.

Our challenge in initially developing the leisure service delivery system concept and writing the *Leisure Service Delivery System* book in 1973 was to attempt to resolve the confusion that had stymied the recreation, park, and leisure field and had kept it from being more effective in responding to the human condition.

We believe that the ideas set forth in that book contributed some insight and provided an initial framework to enable emerging leisure professionals to function more effectively on the job. We hope that readers of this book, *Leisure Systems*, will gain still more insight into the dynamics of leisure service delivery and will become even more proficient as service providers. We are at a stage in the development of our profession where our knowledge of the leisure phenomenon, human behavior, and organization and management of leisure service agencies requires new thinking in order to mesh with new perceptions, values, and knowledge that are being discovered about how human beings interact and grow. We believe that the leisure experience is central to human growth and that leisure service agencies can assist each individual to fulfill a variety of human needs and, in the process, contribute to a stronger sense of community.

INDEX